Food for Life

SECOND EDITION

AUTHOR
Jane Witte
Instructor, Ontario Institute for Studies in Education, University of Toronto,
University of Western Ontario, Brock University, Queen's University

FEATURE WRITERS
Healthy Living and *Career Profiles*
Patrice Baker
Elora Public School, Upper Grand District School Board

Literacy in Your Life and *Food for Thought*
Shirley Choo
Former Literacy Resource Teacher, North Vancouver School District

Recipes
Tess Pappas
Freelance Recipe Tester

Historical Perspectives
Gloria Troyer
Freelance Writer, Broadcaster, Author

Thinking Critically, Safety Check, and Web Connections
Jane Witte

 **McGraw-Hill Ryerson**

Toronto   Montréal   Boston   Burr Ridge, IL   Dubuque, IA   Madison, WI   New York   San Francisco
St. Louis   Bangkok   Bogotá   Caracas   Kuala Lumpur   Lisbon   London   Madrid   Mexico City   Milan
New Delhi   Santiago   Seoul   Singapore   Sydney   Taipei

McGraw-Hill Ryerson
Food for Life, Second Edition

ISBN 978-0-07-073997-0
ISBN 0-07-073997-8

http://www.mcgrawhill.ca

1 2 3 4 5 6 7 8 9 10 TCP 9 0 1 2 3 4 5 6 7 8

Printed and bound in Canada

PUBLISHER: Patty Pappas
DEVELOPMENTAL EDITORS: Jocelyn Wilson, Ellen Munro
MANAGER, EDITORIAL SERVICES: Crystal Shortt
SUPERVISING EDITOR: Shannon Martin
COPY EDITOR: Karen Rolfe
PERMISSIONS EDITOR: Maria DeCambra
EDITORIAL ASSISTANT: Michelle Malda
MANAGER, PRODUCTION SERVICES: Yolanda Pigden
PRODUCTION CO-ORDINATOR: Jennifer Wilke
COVER AND INTERIOR DESIGN: Valid Design & Layout/Dave Murphy
ELECTRONIC PAGE MAKE-UP: Valid Design & Layout/Valerie Bateman
COVER IMAGE: T. Ozonas, Fruit and Vegetable Stand, Masterfile Corporation

I would like to thank my family, Sheldon, Zach, and Mallory, for their continued support of my work; Jocelyn Wilson for her unending patience and dedication to this project; and Patty Pappas for seeing my potential as an author.

—Jane Witte

ACKNOWLEDGEMENTS

Reviewers and consultants of *Food for Life, Second Edition*

The author and editors of *Food for Life, Second Edition*, thank the reviewers and consultants listed below for their thoughtful comments and suggestions. Their input has been invaluable in ensuring that this textbook meets the needs of the teachers and students involved in food and nutrition courses.

General Reviewers

Judy Chan
Eric Hamber Secondary School
Vancouver, British Columbia

Susan Ehman
Mount Royal Collegiate
Saskatoon, Saskatchewan

Andy Ormiston
Lord Selkirk Secondary Comprehensive School
Selkirk, Manitoba

Christine Smith
Retired from Bowness High School
Calgary, Alberta

Agriculture Reviewer

Liz Gomes
Bachelor of Science in Agriculture, Master of Science, University of Guelph

Catholic Reviewer

Caroline Zacharko
Holy Trinity High School
Edmonton, Alberta

First Nations Reviewer

Irene Oakes
Nekaneet First Nation Centre for School Based Experiences
Faculty of Education, University of Saskatchewan, Saskatoon, Saskatchewan

Franco-Manitoban Reviewer

Claire Normandeau
Collège Louis-Riel
Winnipeg, Manitoba

Food and Kitchen Safety Reviewers

Mary Gale Smith
University of British Columbia,
Faculty of Education, Department
of Curriculum Studies
Vancouver, British Columbia

Mary Leah de Zwart
Queen Elizabeth Secondary School
Surrey, British Columbia

Consultants

Jenny Garrels
Elphinstone Secondary School
Gibsons, British Columbia

Jennifer Johnson
École Panorama Ridge Secondary School
Surrey, British Columbia

Marline Poon
Crossing Park School
Calgary, Alberta

Mary Gale Smith
University of British Columbia,
Faculty of Education, Department
of Curriculum Studies
Vancouver, British Columbia

Contents

A Tour of Your Textbook

Welcome to *Food for Life, Second Edition*. This textbook will fulfill the requirements of the food and nutrition course in your province, as well as provide additional information on topics such as wellness, living with special considerations, body image, and lifestyle choices. It will also examine food and kitchen safety in the food and nutrition classroom, at home, and in commercial establishments. It will teach you what you need to know to become wise consumers, and all about meal planning and preparation. Many healthy recipes are available for you to try out throughout the text, including such things as snacks, salads, desserts, and main courses from a variety of cultures. Career profiles will introduce you to a wide range of people and professions in food and nutrition in Canada. Finally, you will discover how agriculture has changed in recent years to provide food for Canadians in an environmentally friendly and safe way that will be sustainable in the years to come.

Unit Opener

- A **photograph** suggests what the chapters in the unit will be about.
- A **Unifying Concepts** list outlines the general topics included in your province's curriculum that will be studied throughout the unit.
- A **list of chapters** provides a glimpse of what to expect in the unit.
- An **Overview** outlines the topics that will be explored in the unit.

Connecting to the Community for the Unit

- After each unit opener, **a list of activity choices for each chapter** is provided that will help you find out more about an aspect of your community and how it relates directly to you.
- Each chapter offers **a choice of two activities**, from which you will choose one to complete.
- **Putting It All Together** outlines the steps for putting together the chapter activities to create a Connecting to the Community project for the unit.
- **Assessment** provides you and your teacher with a rubric that you can use to assess the Connecting to the Community project for the unit.

Chapter Opener

- A **Key Concepts** list outlines the topics from your province's curriculum that will be explored in the chapter.
- The **Key Terms** are the important words that will be introduced in the chapter.
- A **general statement** tells you what you will be learning about in the chapter.
- A **scenario** at the beginning of each chapter includes students who are taking a food and nutrition course and how they are applying some aspects of it to their lives.
- A **photograph** illustrates the content of the scenario and aspects of the chapter content.

Connecting to the Community, Chapter Summary, and Activities

- At the end of each chapter, the **Connecting to the Community activities for the chapter** are outlined. Ways that you can present the information you will gather about the community are presented.
- The **chapter summary** provides a list of topics that were looked at in the chapter.
- A choice of **activities** enables you to analyze, evaluate, remember, understand, and apply the information you have learned in the chapter as well as create something new from this information.

This textbook was designed and written to make *food and nutrition* understandable, interesting, and appealing to today's students.

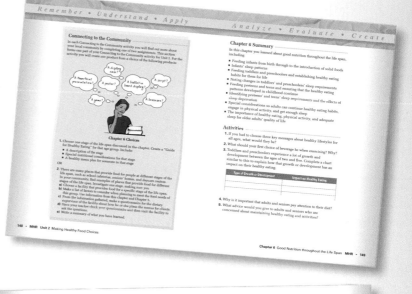

Literacy in Your Life

Magazine and news articles related to food and literacy are included in this two-page feature. Instructions on how to read the articles will guide you through them, and questions following the articles will explore what you have understood about them.

Healthy Living

Current informational items related to food, nutrition, health, safety, and other topics are explored in most chapters.

Thinking Critically

Newsworthy topics related to food, health, lifestyle, and other issues appear in most chapters. Questions following the text encourage you to think about both sides of an issue and come to a conclusion about the issue yourself.

Thinking Critically | Bottled Water

It is hard to go anywhere these days without seeing someone drinking a bottle of water. People seem to understand that water is essential for a healthy body. However, some questions do arise:

- Is bottled water better than tap water?
- How is the increase in the use of bottles affecting the environment?
- Should water, a life essential, be an expensive commodity?

Better Than Tap Water?
Manufacturers and importers of water are required to meet health and safety standards. These are the same standards that municipalities have to meet with regard to our water supplies. If you are concerned about mineral deposits or other substances that can change the taste of your tap water, you can filter the water before drinking it.

The Environmental Impact
Have you ever thought about where all the bottles go after people have finished drinking the water?

It is quite common to see empty water bottles littering parks and streets. It is estimated that over 80 percent of water bottles are not recycled. Also, recycling water bottles uses energy, which negatively affects the environment.

An Expensive Commodity?
How much did you pay for your last bottle of water? Bottles of water usually cost more than a dollar. When gas prices rose in 2006 to over a dollar a litre and then went over that price, consumers were outraged. Yet people are willing to pay more for a bottle of water half that size. Many social justice groups have grave concerns regarding the selling of water. They want access to good-quality drinking water for everyone, regardless of income.

Activity

1. Based on what you have read about bottled water, write a two-page article for your school newspaper discussing your position on the use of bottled water.

Historical Perspectives

Articles about the history of foods, health issues, domestic items, body image, and other topics that arise within the chapter are explored more fully. This full-page feature appears in every chapter and includes photographs.

Career Profiles

Profiles of people in food and nutrition science related occupations will appear in most chapters. These will provide you with a glimpse at some careers in these fields.

HISTORICAL PERSPECTIVES
Harvest Festivals

Communities all across Canada stage harvest festivals. These include fall fairs, parties, and community suppers to mark the harvest of crops, to remember their pioneer heritage, and to appreciate nature's bounty. Autumn harvest festivals are a time of cheerful celebration: the crops have survived natural disasters and food is plentiful.

Festivals began in antiquity as religious and ritual observances of the seasons and often included sacred community meals or feasts. Our European ancestors held celebrations of thankfulness for a good harvest. Some First Nations peoples held two thanksgiving celebrations—one in the spring, when the sap ran in the maple trees, to give thanks for the deliverance from the winter, and one in the fall, at harvest time. Today "Harvest Festival" or "Thanksgiving" is the most observed harvest ritual in Canada.

The very first Canadian Thanksgiving celebration took place in 1578 in what is now Newfoundland. Martin Frobisher, a British explorer and navigator, held a ceremony to give thanks for surviving the long journey across the Atlantic. Other settlers who arrived later continued to hold ceremonies to give thanks. These are thought to have influenced the Canadian Thanksgiving we celebrate today.

For a few hundred years, Thanksgiving was celebrated in either late October or early November. The first official Thanksgiving Day in Canada, after Confederation, was observed on April 15, 1872. It had nothing to do with a harvest festival; it celebrated the recovery of the Prince of Wales from a serious illness. In 1908, the holiday was fixed on a Monday in October, but the date later fluctuated between October and November.

Thanksgiving became an official holiday in 1957, when Parliament announced the day would be "a day of general thanksgiving to almighty God for the bountiful harvest with which Canada has been blessed."

FIGURE 3-6 Many communities across Canada have harvest festivals. In Waterford, Ontario, citizens hold a Pumpkin Fest.

Career Profile | Jennifer Eld, Counsellor for Eating Disorders

The Calgary Counselling Centre is a non-profit organization that began an eating disorders program in 1995. This program has offered specialized counselling to thousands of clients suffering from bulimia, anorexia, and binge eating.

Jennifer Eld is one of 60 full-time staff members who provide counselling for clients, including those diagnosed with eating disorders. Her own interest in eating disorders stems from her personal body-image struggles as a teenager. This led her to Mount Royal College where she obtained a diploma in Social Work. She then went to the University of Calgary for a Bachelor of General Studies and a Bachelor of Social Work.

Jennifer now works with clients suffering from eating disorders as well as people who excessively use diet pills, laxatives, exercise, and restrictive diets to reduce their weight. She sees bulimic behaviour most often, and usually works with female clients between the ages of 18 and 40.

During a typical day, Jennifer will work individually with up to four clients. For each client, she explores the person's history to try to find the root cause of the eating disorder. This is the most difficult part of her job, since the development of an eating disorder may be the result of many psychological and physical factors. Jennifer then works with the client to determine how much change he or she can manage. She also teaches clients skills such as healthy emotional expression, coping strategies, and building self-esteem. For each client, Jennifer keeps updated files, including plans, progress, and setbacks. She is also involved in a number of special projects, such as the development and delivery process of the "Towards Healthy Eating Group," a group in which counsellors enrol interested clients, offered at the Calgary Counselling Centre. The clients are people struggling with anorexia, bulimia, or an eating disorder not otherwise specified.

When working with teenagers, Jennifer strongly believes they need to hear the right message about healthy eating. Teens need to be very aware of the impact of the media on our society. Images of beauty, success, happiness, and love are communicated through the media by means of advertising and entertainment. It is vital that people remain critical of the media's goals and recognize their substantial impact on people in society. Unrealistic expectations are set by the media, and people who believe these expectations but cannot reach them are at risk of developing poor self-esteem. An even greater problem results if friends, family, or peers have these unrealistic expectations as well. Unrealistic expectations can lead to long-term damage, often well into adulthood.

It is extremely important for young people who are struggling with body image, an eating disorder, and/or low self-esteem to reach out for support. Early intervention can help make recovery successful. Jennifer suggests that people seeking help contact their physician or local hospital to be referred to an appropriate professional.

"Unrealistic expectations are set by the media, and people who believe in these expectations but cannot reach them are at risk of developing poor self-esteem."

Chapter 8 Body Image and Lifestyle Choices MHR • 199

Recipes

Relevant, healthy recipes from many cultures appear in most chapters. These recipes have been tested and you can prepare them during your food and nutrition classes to learn food preparation and cooking techniques first-hand.

Easy Tomato Basil Bruschetta

Ingredients

6 slices light rye bread
2 tbsp (25 mL) extra-virgin olive oil, divided
18 cherry or grape tomatoes, coarsely chopped
5 leaves fresh basil, chopped
2 large roasted red bell peppers (from a jar), drained and coarsely chopped
1 clove garlic, minced
2 tbsp (25 mL) freshly grated parmesan cheese
1 tsp (5 mL) hot pepper sauce (optional)
½ tsp (2mL) black ground pepper
½ tsp (2 mL) salt
¼ cup (50 mL) feta cheese, crumbled (optional)

Preparation

- Arrange bread on baking sheet. Brush lightly with 1 tbsp (15 mL) of the olive oil. Toast under preheated broiler for 3 minutes or until light brown.

- In a medium bowl, toss cherry tomatoes, basil, red peppers, garlic, parmesan, the remaining olive oil, hot pepper sauce (if using), pepper, and salt. Distribute evenly on top of bread. Sprinkle with feta cheese (if using).

- Broil until heated through, about 5 minutes. Cut each slice of bread in half diagonally.

Servings: 6

Reading Labels for Fat Content
Reading labels to find out the type and percentage of fat in a food is important to your overall health. Understanding fat type and content helps you make wise choices. Nutrition Facts tables in Canada must now list amounts and percentages of fat, saturated fats, and trans fats. Both saturated fats and trans fats increase the risk of heart disease, so look for lower numbers. Remember to look at serving sizes as well and compare them to the actual amount that you would normally eat.

◄ Safety Check

This brief margin feature provides safety tips relevant to the chapter content.

Food for Thought ►

Interesting tidbits of information about topics that arise in the chapter appear periodically in the margins of the text.

There are an estimated 650 000 hazardous chemical products in existence and as many as 1000 new ones are produced every year. Only 2 to 3 percent of them have been tested for the threat they may pose to humans and animals. There is mounting evidence that many of these chemicals can alter sexual and neurological development, impair reproduction, cause cancer, and harm the immune system.

To find out more about chemical hazards, go to this Web site and follow the links.

www.mhrfoodforlife.ca

◄ Web connection

One or more Web sites related to the content are provided in each chapter. You can use these Web sites to find out more about a topic or to do further research on various topics.

Influences on Food Choices and Food Patterns

Overview

Most Canadians are able to obtain enough food to keep themselves healthy. In fact, most of our food habits and food patterns (our usual patterns of eating) are influenced by many factors other than hunger. In this unit you will look at a number of different factors that influence

- Why we eat what we eat
- When we eat
- How we eat it

Connecting to your community is an important part of being a good citizen. Everyone has a responsibility to one another. Both the Connecting to the Community activity at the beginning of each unit and the Connecting to the Community activity at the end of each chapter are designed to help you find out more about your own community.

Throughout the text you will be asked to consider your community and how it connects to you. A variety of activities will be presented and you will be offered choices as to how you want to present the information you have learned about your community. The choices for Unit 1 are as follows:

- Chapter 1: Understanding Personal Food Choices
  - Choice 1: One-page article on how food insecurity is addressed in your community. OR
  - Choice 2: A list of foods that fit within "The 160-km Diet" in your community, using the four food groups from *Eating Well with Canada's Food Guide* as an organizer.
- Chapter 2: Influences on Food Patterns and Customs
  - Choice 1: A one-page summary titled "Food Patterns and Customs in Our Community." OR
  - Choice 2: A script for a talk show with "experts" explaining the influences on what people eat in the community.
- Chapter 3: Food Traditions and Etiquette
  - Choice 1: An illustrated summary of a special occasion a culture in your community celebrates. OR
  - Choice 2: A skit that showcases a culture in your community and the role food plays in it.

Putting It All Together

At the end of Unit 1, you should have completed *three pieces of work* — one for each chapter. Follow these steps to complete your product.

- Read over and edit your work from the chapters.
- Ask a peer or a parent/guardian to edit your work as well.
- Write an introduction to your product that pulls all the pieces together. Edit this as well.
- Type or write a good copy, as required.
- Find pictures to enhance your pieces of writing.
- Decide on a title for your product.
- Design how the product will be set up. Draw a rough copy on blank paper before you put the product together.
- Put the product together.

Assessment

The following rubric will be used to assess the work you do on the Connecting to the Community for Unit 1.

Criteria	1	2	3	4
Shows knowledge of the different factors that affect why people eat	Shows limited knowledge of the different factors that affect why people eat	Shows some knowledge of the different factors that affect why people eat	Shows considerable knowledge of the different factors that affect why people eat	Shows a high degree of knowledge of the different factors that affect why people eat
Conducted research into the different factors related to why and what people eat	Conducted research into the different factors related to why and what people eat with limited effectiveness	Conducted research into the different factors related to why and what people eat with some effectiveness	Conducted research into the different factors related to why and what people eat with considerable effectiveness	Conducted research into the different factors related to why and what people eat with a high degree of effectiveness
Use of critical and creative thinking process	Limited use of critical and creative thinking process	Some use of critical and creative thinking process	Considerable use of critical and creative thinking process	Uses critical and creative thinking process with a high degree of skill
Communicates for different audiences and purposes	Communicates for different audiences and purposes with limited or no effectiveness	Communicates for different audiences and purposes with some effectiveness	Communicates for different audiences and purposes with considerable effectiveness	Communicates for different audiences and purposes with a high degree of effectiveness

one

Understanding Personal Food Choices

I n this chapter you will explore some of the factors that influence your food choices. Which factors affect the food choices of Jemma and Jamal during a typical morning?

Jemma wakes up early since she likes to shower and have plenty of time to get ready for school. She makes herself a fruit and yogurt smoothie to sip while she gets dressed. She knows that her body needs to have a good start in the morning to keep up her strength for hockey. She is playing very well this year and hopes to get a scholarship.

Jamal sleeps in until the last second, rushes through his shower, throws on some clothes, and runs downstairs. He sees that his mom has left out some breakfast foods in the kitchen. Jamal is experiencing a growth spurt and is always hungry. His mom tries to help him fill up before he leaves for school.

At school, Jemma and Jamal smell the aroma of freshly baked carrot muffins coming from the cafeteria. Jemma rushes off to a student council meeting while Jamal heads to the cafeteria with his friends.

Key Concepts

Influences on personal food choices

- To meet physical needs
- To satisfy hunger
- To satisfy the senses
- To meet psychological needs
- To meet social needs

Key Terms

comfort foods
food insecurity
food secure
food stylist
hunger
nutrients
nutrition
psychological needs

WHY YOU EAT

Have you ever stopped to think about all the different reasons why you eat what you eat during a day? Most people eat for a wide variety of reasons. Check the following list. Which of these reasons remind you of your own eating habits?

- The food was prepared for you.
- The food looked and smelled good.
- You saw a food advertisement and had to have that food.
- You were bored.
- You were sad.

The Early Canadian Diet

The English word *diet* originated in 1566 and meant "to take one's meals or to feed on." Dietitians use the word *diet* to mean all of the food a person eats on a regular basis. Sometimes people alter their eating habits for various reasons, including weight loss, disease prevention, food allergies, or improvement of mental and physical health. Others adopt special diets because of their religious or personal beliefs regarding some foods, as in the case of vegetarians, who do not eat meat.

The first pioneers' and early homesteaders' diet consisted of what they could gather. They ate fruit, nuts, plants, and wild berries. Meat consisted of whatever they could catch, including squirrels, moose, deer, and even bears. They ate fresh fish from the rivers. First Nations people taught them many things, such as how to tap trees and make maple syrup. Pioneers' diet became more varied after they established farms and grew crops, made preserves, and raised animals. In time, general stores provided canned foods, fruits, and imported spices that enhanced their diet.

Access to a greater variety of food does not mean a diet is necessarily healthy and nutritious. To ensure Canadians did not suffer from nutritional deficiencies, and to improve their health, Canada's first food guide, called *Canada's Official Food Rules*, was introduced to the public in 1942. The earliest food guides were developed by the Canadian Council on Nutrition, 1938-1969. Appointed by the federal government, this group consisted of medical experts, scientists, and welfare workers. In 1938 the Council developed the first Dietary Standard for Canada. The Dietary Standard described "the amounts of essential nutrients considered adequate to meet the needs of practically all healthy persons." A daily eating plan helped people of all ages choose their food and maintain a nutritious diet that contributed to maintaining good health.

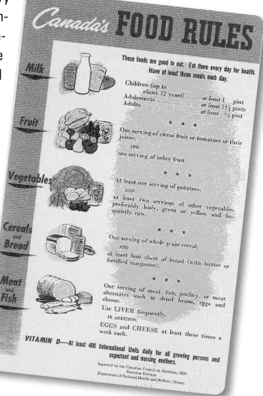

FIGURE 1-1 Canada's food guide was revised in 1949 to reflect recommendations made by provincial nutritionists and further understanding of nutrient requirements. How was this version different from the current guide, as described in Chapter 5?

- You were nervous.
- You were out with friends and everyone else was eating.
- It was meal time.
- It was something to do while watching TV.
- You needed the food to keep your energy level up.
- You needed the food to stay healthy.

These are only a few of the many reasons why people eat. In Canada, most people have enough food. According to Health Reports by Statistics Canada, about 15 percent of Canadians reported **food insecurity**—not having access to enough food to eat—in the 2000-2001 Canadian Community Health Survey. This survey found that most of the reasons people eat have little to do with their physical need for food.

Let's explore in more detail some of these reasons.

Physical Needs

Human bodies need a particular type of fuel to do the work that keeps them alive and maintain their bodily systems. To achieve optimum health, your body requires **nutrients**. Your body uses nutrients, which are the chemicals found in foods, to carry out its functions. **Nutrition** is the study of nutrients and how the body uses them. If you do not provide your body with the nutrients it needs, you are at risk for health problems now and in the future. What aspects of good nutrition and health maintenance do you expect this course to teach you?

Good nutrition also allows the body to function at its best. With good nutrition you look better and have the energy to be alert and active. Athletes know whenever they haven't taken in enough nutrients because they run out of energy. Most of us recognize when we've run out of energy. Have you ever felt really low on energy just before a meal? Our bodies act like cars running out of gas—they cannot perform.

Lack of nutrients can also cause you to be tired. Many students who skip breakfast find themselves nodding off during morning classes. Being tired and irritable from lack of nutrition also affects your attitude toward life.

Good nutrition keeps your body healthy and is an important reason why people eat.

FIGURE 1-2 A basketball player knows how important it is to keep the body well fueled. Why is being aware of what you eat so important to an athlete?

Healthy Living

Hunger in Rural Canada

It is difficult to believe that many people living in the food-producing areas of our country do not get enough to eat. **Rural Canada**, containing most of the country's prime agricultural land, is the last place where we would expect to find hungry people.

Hunger in rural Canada has a number of causes. People in rural areas have fewer options for employment because fewer jobs are available, and most jobs in rural areas are lower paying than an equivalent job in a big city. The **rural economy** is often affected by **uncontrollable factors,** such as drought or flooding. When such things occur, farming communities do not produce as much food, and the farms do not prosper.

People in rural areas do not have access to many **social services** since these are often located in cities, and rural areas do not usually have public transportation to help people get to nearby cities. Consequently, grocery shopping is often done at smaller, more expensive shops. These shops have to pay the higher costs of shipping food **greater distances** and therefore must charge their customers more for their food. Typically, prices for meat, fruit, and fresh vegetable increase the most, while snack foods such as chips and candy cost the same as they do in more urban centres. This makes it even more difficult for low-income families to purchase nutritious food. Many rural Canadians must rely on other **support systems** to provide their dietary needs.

FIGURE 1-3 Why do you think it would be more difficult for low-income families to obtain nutritious food in rural areas?

The **Canadian Association of Food Banks (CAFB)** conducts a national research program called HungerCount and distributes food to food banks all across the country. They rely on help from transportation companies, which often transport food to remote areas at cost. CAFB also relies on donations from large corporations, small businesses, and community groups to help fund the purchase and transportation of food to rural food banks.

As of March 2006, there were **638 food banks** in Canada and they supplied approximately **800 000 people** with emergency food supplies. The number of food banks located in rural communities has increased from 270 per 64 000 people a month in 2004 to 325 per 65 000 people a month in 2006. This shows a significant increase in need.

Hunger

When was the last time you felt truly hungry? Teens and young children experience **hunger** more than adults do because their growing bodies need food more than adults do.

Hunger is the physical sensation that tells your brain it is time to eat. People who really listen to their bodies recognize the sensation of hunger. When they feel hungry, they eat until they feel full. Being able to recognize the feelings of both hunger and fullness helps people to eat in a healthy way.

If people do not recognize the feeling of fullness, then they will overeat, and there is growing concern in Canada about obesity, especially in children. There is also concern for those who do not recognize hunger and do not provide their bodies with enough fuel to maintain their health. Children, especially, need proper nutrition to develop to their full potential.

As a nation, Canada is **food secure**. This means that Canada has enough food to feed all Canadians. However, some people in Canada do not have access to enough food and so experience food insecurity. This means they do not have a stable source of food. There are many reasons for food insecurity. Some people do not have enough income to pay for basic living expenses. Once they have paid for their housing, they have very little money left for food. Others, who are ill, permanently disabled, or temporarily disabled due to an accident, are not able to provide food for themselves and their families.

As mentioned earlier, food insecurity is not just an urban issue; it affects people all across Canada. Often, in rural Canada, access is the biggest barrier to food security. Many programs attempt to address food insecurity. Read the following Thinking Critically feature to learn more.

FIGURE 1-4 Some people are unable to recognize the sensations of hunger or fullness. This may cause them to be extremely thin or obese.

Operation Sharing Closes Its Food Bank in Woodstock

In September 2006 **Operation Sharing** in Woodstock, Ontario, closed its food bank—not because there were no longer any people who needed support, but because the community found a better way to support them. **"Food for Friends"** is a program that provides access to food with dignity for the individuals and families who need assistance.

Traditionally, a food bank is used by individuals or families who need emergency food for only a few days until they are able to achieve a consistent food supply themselves. When food is required, the individual goes to the food bank and asks for food. The person is assessed and information is recorded regarding his or her situation. The individual is then given a food supply based on what is available on the shelves at that time. This depends on the non-perishable foods that the general public has donated. For some people who need food, these items may not fit their dietary or religious restrictions.

Food for Friends is a program that allows individuals and families to obtain food from grocery stores. The person applies to the food card program in the same way that he or she would apply to a food bank. Once the application is completed, the person may receive the card(s) to shop for the food they need at that specific time.

The **food cards** are issued in amounts of $10 or $25. They look like debit cards so they will not attract attention from other shoppers. The cards cannot be cashed in. If the grocery bill is under the amount on the card, no money is refunded to the patron. If the grocery bill is higher than the cards, the patron is responsible for the outstanding balance.

Anything purchased with the food cards must be a non-taxable food item. This ensures that no unhealthy items will be purchased. Perishable items, such as bread, eggs, milk, and produce, which are not available through traditional food banks, can be purchased. As well, individuals and families can meet their cultural, religious, and health food needs by choosing foods that are suitable to their situation.

The cards are issued on a limited basis. If Operation Sharing finds that an individual or family is becoming dependent on the cards, the organization offers counselling to the patrons. This ensures that patrons who use the food cards will find a way to provide themselves with a secure source of food.

Food for Friends is entirely **supported by the community** of Woodstock. Operation Sharing estimates that if the entire population of Woodstock (about 34 000 people) donated a quarter each time they went grocery shopping, a total of nearly $400 000 a year could be collected. This would eradicate hunger in the community.

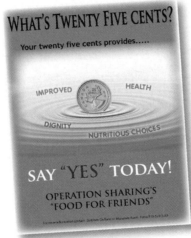

WHAT'S TWENTY FIVE CENTS?

Your twenty five cents provides.....

IMPROVED   HEALTH

DIGNITY   NUTRITIOUS CHOICES

SAY "YES" TODAY!

OPERATION SHARING'S "FOOD FOR FRIENDS"

FIGURE 1-5 An Operation Sharing Card enables people in Woodstock, ON, who need community assistance with food to purchase it at major grocery stores.

Questions

1. Compare the advantages and disadvantages of food banks and Food for Friends as emergency food suppliers.

2. If Food for Friends were operating in your community, how much money, based on the population, could they potentially collect a year if each family donated 25 cents when they shopped once a week? If the donations in Woodstock represent one-quarter of its population, how much do you think your community could collect?

The Senses

Have you ever walked by a food stand or a bakery and seen something that looked so good that you had to stop and buy it? Has the smell of dinner cooking ever made you hungry and drawn you to the kitchen before it is time to eat? Both of these reactions are caused by your senses. Your senses play a major role in what you eat. If your senses are attracted to a food, you find the food appealing. Sometimes your senses can trick you, and you may actually like something your senses do not, such as when something that doesn't look appealing is actually very tasty.

Your Sensory Organs	
	You see the food and then decide if it looks appetizing or not. Food that is displayed attractively looks more appetizing.
	You judge a food by its smell. Many people are drawn to food by its aroma. Many people are especially alert to the smell of their favourite foods, such as bread baking. Sometimes your sense of smell can warn you away from foods. For example, many people recognize the smell of milk that has gone sour.
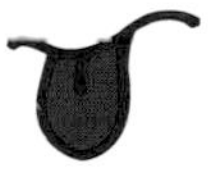	Your taste buds are small sensors that tell you about the flavour of foods. People crave certain flavours. A sweet tooth is actually a sweet tongue. People's tongues can also pick up bad flavours and warn you not to swallow food that is tainted or rotting.
	Some foods have a sound that is familiar and enticing, such as popcorn popping.
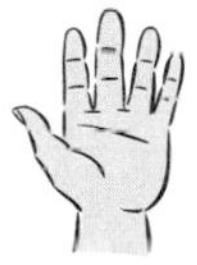	Some foods feel right to the touch. People know by touch or texture the difference between a fresh, crisp apple and a soft, stale one.

Have you ever gone to the food cupboard immediately after seeing an ad on TV because the ad made you crave something? Food advertisers arrange food to look appealing and delicious. A person who prepares food for advertisements, commercials, menus, and media events is called a **food stylist**. A food stylist creates and presents the food you see in a commercial to entice you and to make you want it. Often the foods are so "staged" they are no longer edible.

Taste buds develop over time. Children grow up learning to like the flavours of the foods they have

FIGURE 1-6 Food stylists use artificial means to make food look even better than it does in real life. Do you think food enhancement creates false hope for consumers when they go grocery shopping? Why or why not?

FIGURE 1-7 Imagine what you look like when you try something new. Is your expression similar to this baby's?

been fed by their families and caregivers. Often their favourite foods are those from their family's culture. As you grow older, you are exposed to foods from outside your family and your tastes become more varied. Adults often eat foods that they would never have tried as children. What food have you been introduced to by a friend recently that you do not eat at home?

Taste is a learned sense. Sometimes, when you try a new food for the first time, you do not really like it; but the more you try it, the more you grow to like it. If you have ever watched a baby's reaction to a new food, you have witnessed his or her sense of taste developing first hand.

Psychological Needs

Have you ever experienced food in the following ways?

- As a reward
- As a punishment
- To comfort you
- To show affection for you
- To make you feel secure
- To exert power over you
- To provide pleasure

You have probably experienced most of these. When food gains a psychological meaning, it becomes something more than a means to obtain the necessary nutrients for good health.

Psychological needs are those that have to do with your mind and your emotions. Your food habits are learned, and the psychological reasons why you eat are varied. Infants and children learn their basic food habits from the way in which they are fed and the reasons why food is given to them.

Many children are rewarded or punished with food. People who were rewarded for good behaviour as children with a cookie or a chocolate bar will often reward themselves as adults in the same way. Children who experience food as a punishment and are denied certain foods for poor behaviour may have an unhealthy relationship with food later in life. They may deny themselves food when they feel they are bad or overeat foods they were denied as children. People need to consider carefully the use of food as a reward or punishment for children.

Many people have foods that make them feel better. For some, a bowl of hot soup on a cold day is comforting. Others find a traditional dish that was cooked in their family home—like curry or bannock—

Chunky Chicken Soup

Ingredients

1 tbsp (15 mL) vegetable oil
3 lb (1.5 kg) chicken pieces, skin removed
12 cloves garlic, halved lengthwise
1 each leek and large onion, chopped (or 2 onions)
1 sweet green pepper, chopped
1 can (28 oz/796 mL) tomatoes, mashed
1-½ tsp (7 mL) salt
1 tsp (5 mL) dried thyme
½ tsp (2 mL) pepper
6 potatoes (1-1/2 lb/750 g), peeled and quartered
4 cups (1 L) coarsely chopped savoy cabbage (or 2 cups [500 mL] halved green beans)

Preparation

- In Dutch oven, heat oil over medium heat; brown chicken in two batches, about 8 minutes per batch. Transfer chicken to plate; drain off fat from pan.

- Add garlic, leek, and onion; cook over medium heat until golden, about 8 minutes. Return chicken to pan along with green pepper, tomatoes, salt, thyme, pepper, and 4 cups (1 L) water; bring to boil. Reduce heat; cover and simmer for 15 minutes.

- Add potatoes; cook for 15 minutes. Add cabbage; cook until tender, about 10 minutes. Skim off fat. (Make-ahead then let cool for 30 minutes. Refrigerate until cold. Transfer to airtight container and refrigerate for up to 2 days.)

Servings: 6 to 8

Web connection

To find more recipes, go to this Web site and follow the links.

www.mhrfoodforlife.ca

FIGURE 1-8 Many people eat soup as a comfort food when they are ill. Why do you think soup makes them feel better?

to be comforting. Still others will reach for ice cream or chocolate in difficult times. These foods are called **comfort foods**. What are your comfort foods? Are they foods that were given to comfort you as a child?

Food can also be used as a source of power. Young children will often refuse to eat in order to get their way. Other times they will clean their plates to get their dessert. Teens will express their independence by refusing to eat the food that has been prepared for them and eating something else.

Much research has been done on the psychology of food. Researchers spend a great deal of time trying to figure out the psychological reasons behind people's food choices. Marketers use this information to sell people food. Health professionals use this information to help people make better food choices.

Literacy in Your Life

Before Reading

Think about what you know about this topic.

1. In the chart, read the bold headings in the column "Personality Types." Think about what each of their eating habits might be like.

2. What words do you think describe the kind of person you are? Do you think the foods you eat reflect the kind of person you are?

During Reading

1. Do you identify with an eating personality or recognize the types of eating personalities in others?

2. Do you agree that everyone fits into these personality types? Why or why not?

Language Extension

Psychological, psychologically, and psychologist come from the word *psychology*, which means "the science of the human mind." It comes from the Greek word *psyche*, which means "spirit, soul, mind."

What's Your Eating Personality?

Personality Types	What They Eat	Psychological Reasons for Eating	Advice
The Earth Child Has four distinct personalities: ■ Gentle soul ■ Passionate and emotional artistic type, strong-minded in opinions and politics, which are often green ■ Rigid herbivore. Views types of foods as good or bad ■ Eats food to stay alive, not for pleasure	■ Fresh, wholesome foods ■ Garlic and fresh herbs in everything	■ Eats within a scientific, medical, and nutritional framework ■ Eats within a moralistic framework	■ Learn to get all the nutrients the body needs ■ Vegetarians can have low levels of iron, zinc, vitamin B12, and protein
The Wolf ■ Male, aggressive, volatile, macho ■ Possibly a workaholic ■ In touch with undeveloped physical desires	■ Red meat	■ Meat was rare and difficult to come by in hunter-gatherer societies, so eating meat means being strong and macho, powerful and dominant over nature	■ Adult carnivores eat more than the recommended 175-250 g of meat a day and are no longer lean and hungry predators ■ Today he is a middle-aged, apple-shaped male with a high-stress job, sedentary lifestyle, and at increased risk for various diseases ■ Needs a healthier lifestyle and a more balanced plate—one-third meat or alternatives, two-thirds grains, and fresh fruits and vegetables
The Muncher ■ Eats anything, all the time ■ Bored, distracted, eats without thinking ■ Rushed, overwhelmed by life, addicted to convenience	■ Whatever is quick and handy—has snacks in cupboard, candy in desk drawer	■ Fat and salt were hard to come by in hunter-gatherer societies so people have deep cravings for both, which are now readily available in snack foods	■ Needs more balance and structure in his/her eating habits (and maybe in his/her life) ■ Needs more fruits and vegetables

Personality Types	What They Eat	Psychological Reasons for Eating	Advice
The Comfort Seeker ■ Some may feel overwhelmed by change or stress	■ Prefers feel-good foods over more adventurous fare—puddings, buttery mashed potatoes, peanut butter sandwiches, macaroni and cheese	■ Craves familiarity and security that comfort foods evoke ■ Thinks eating will make him/her feel better if busy or overtired	■ If food is his/her sole source of comfort, seek other emotional outlets, such as calling a friend or going for a walk
The Socializer ■ The unifying force among family and friends ■ Brings people together with food and hospitality ■ Dislikes aggressiveness or upsets ■ Busy	■ Easy one-dish meals ■ Nibbles while cooking ■ Finishes food on children's plates rather than eating a meal ■ Eats comfort foods when she/he has time	■ Sharing is sometimes more important than the actual food ■ Keeps food memories/ traditions alive	■ So busy taking care of others that she/he doesn't sit down to a relaxed meal her/himself ■ Is probably overweight and improperly nourished
The Pleasure Seeker ■ Outgoing, adventurous, passionate, risk-taker ■ Confident, creative, doesn't need a recipe ■ Comfortable in kitchen	■ Sets table with wide assortment of colours, textures, and tastes ■ Shops by the season ■ Eats a wide variety of foods	■ Food is a sensual experience ■ Always open to new taste sensations, eager to explore and experiment ■ A rebel—may resist modern foods	■ Eat a balanced diet that adds spice to life
The Referee ■ Uptight and obsessive ■ Lives life in an orderly, organized manner ■ A technical genius ■ Has no tolerance for life's curveballs	■ Eats only foods that are good for his/her health ■ Knows the exact number of nutrients, calories, and fat grams in every morsel of food	■ Eats within a scientific, medical, and nutritional framework that is good for his/her health but involves no pleasure ■ Might have difficulty dealing with emotions, letting go, and experiencing the moment	■ Try stepping outside the rules to experience food just for pleasure
The Routine Follower ■ Old-fashioned and rigid ■ Wants everything in its place ■ Doesn't want to experiment or try new foods ■ Reacts to stress by eating "safe," or familiar, foods	■ Roast beef, boiled potatoes, corn—traditional foods ■ Likes to eat the same meals at given times throughout the week	■ Tends to be slightly more anxious in other areas of life as well ■ May be a risk-taker in other areas of life and strives for safety when eating	■ For young people, introduce a variety of novel foods ■ For adults, try one new vegetable every day
The Maple Leaf Forever ■ Patriotic ■ A traditionalist ■ Has a regional outlook	■ Early Canadian fare— pancakes, oatmeal, back bacon, poached salmon, fiddle heads ■ Seasonal, local ingredients		■ Choices are healthy because they are varied, fresh, and seasonal ■ Balance high calorie choices with low-fat milk and side salads ■ Could add some ethnic foods for a cross-cultural experience

After Reading

1. What are some examples of your favourite foods? Why are they your favourite foods?

2. Do you think it is possible to change from one food personality type to another, or to change the foods you eat and how you eat? Why or why not?

Parents and teachers try to help children understand their food choices. As students in this course, you will begin to learn how to pay attention to the psychological reasons for why you make certain food choices.

Social Needs

When you go out with your friends, do you have something to eat? When family gets together, are there specific foods involved? Do you associate certain foods with your cultural celebrations? Most people enjoy special foods and beverages at particular social events. These help meet some of the individual's social needs.

Often when you get together to enjoy food and beverages with your friends, the actual food is not as important as the social aspect and the friendship. Usually when friends come to visit, they are offered food or beverages by the host. What types of food and beverages do you offer your friends when they come over?

Most family gatherings centre around food. When was the last time that you met with your extended family that food was not involved? Many families have special foods that have been served for generations and are considered family favourites or specialties. Does your family have a specialty?

Celebrating special occasions often involves food. Birthdays have cakes, weddings have special meals, and every religious celebration has its own food. You will learn more about the role food plays in special occasions in Chapters 2 and 3.

Other social events include specific foods. What foods and/or beverages do you associate with the following events?

FIGURE 1-9 Meals served at weddings are a significant part of the celebration. Here an Uygur family waits for guests to arrive. Why do you think the meal is so important?

- Going to a movie
- Attending a concert
- Playing a baseball game
- Watching a hockey game
- Going to a horseback-riding competition
- Going on a picnic
- Going camping
- Talking with friends
- Attending a place of worship

You can probably list foods that people commonly eat at such events. Did your classmates list the same foods?

Lesley Stowe, Caterer and Food Entrepreneur

Lesley Stowe began her journey into the food industry after tasting incredible food creations in Italy and France. She trained as a chef at La Varenne École de Cuisine in Paris, and then returned to her hometown of Vancouver and started a cooking school in the Wise Owl Kitchen Shop. This led to her catering business, Lesley Stowe Fine Foods in 1985. Her focus was to use natural ingredients of the finest quality to make delicious, nutritious food. As well as catering, she specialized in creating desserts for many restaurants in the Vancouver area.

Leslie realized that Vancouver had quite a limited selection of specialty items, so she launched the unique and extremely successful Lesley Stowe Fine Foods Shop in 1990. She was able to devote time and effort to tracking down and supplying Vancouver shoppers with rare cheeses, oils, and coffees. She also sold her own fresh appetizers, soups, salads, main dishes, and desserts, and provided tastings as well as classes at the shop. She extended her cooking classes to offer courses in Calgary and even Italy.

Lesley has recently become famous for her Raincoast Crisps. These crackers are available in several varieties, such as spicy sundried tomato, rosemary raisin, cranberry hazelnut, and fig and olive. Leslie makes them from scratch in small batches with the best ingredients and sells them to gourmet stores internationally. This enterprise has become so successful that she has decided to close the gourmet store in Vancouver, and is starting a gourmet food mail order business. Individuals or retail locations will soon be able to order dips, pizza dough, and other specialty items, as well as Raincoast Crisps.

If asked about the most important considerations when buying food ingredients, Lesley returns to the same ideas. She stresses that "recipes can be very simple, as long as the ingredients are of the highest quality possible and have the fewest preservatives." In an interview by Catherine Jheon from "Food for Thought," Lesley stated that "the use of local and seasonal ingredients needs to be encouraged by everyone interested in good food."

Lesley has collaborated with others to create several *Girls Who Dish!* cookbooks. They are full of unique dishes fit for any connoisseur, but the recipes are written in easy steps and have received critical acclaim. Her own cookbook, *The Lesley Stowe Fine Foods Cookbook,* was recently published and has been praised by many. Her new cookbook is full of exciting recipes, including her famous Death by Chocolate dessert, which she originally created for Bishop's restaurant. Finally, the original recipe is in print for anyone to try.

"The use of local and seasonal ingredients needs to be encouraged by everyone interested in good food."

FIGURE 1-10 Raincoast Crisps are just one example of Lesley Stowe's fine food products that have become popular.

LIFESTYLE AND FOOD CHOICES

Have you ever bought some fast food because you only had time to "grab a quick bite?" When was the last time you ate something because you did not have a choice, or because it was the best of some bad choices?

Most people try to make healthy food choices. Sometimes people's lifestyles cause them to make choices they might not make otherwise. For example, many teens have part-time jobs. These jobs may prevent teens from eating meals with their families. Often teens take a meal to work or buy something to eat there. The first job for many is actually in the fast-food industry, so often they end up eating more fast food than they did before they got the job.

Always being busy can also have an impact on your food choices. According to *Profiling Canadian Families III*, from the Vanier Institute of the Family, 75 percent of couples with children under the age of 18 have two working parents or guardians. Some parents work different shifts and so both cannot be at home for meals with the family. In other families, parents commute to work and come home in the early evening. In this case, children often have a snack after school to tide them over until their parents or guardians come home. Many teens prepare the evening meal for their families. Single-parent families face challenges eating together as well. According to a Statistics Canada report in 2004, approximately 16 percent of families were single-parent families. In these families, if the parent is working, the children end up helping out more with food preparation and cleanup.

Many children are involved in out-of-school activities as well. Scheduling meals around these activities can be a challenge even for families with a stay-at-home parent, and it can be an even greater challenge for single and working parents. Families with more than one child involved in activities can struggle to fit in meal times. Feeding children is often squeezed in between or on the way to some activity.

People's busy lives have led to the growth of the fast-food industry, the development of drive-through restaurants, and cup holders in vehicles. What would you

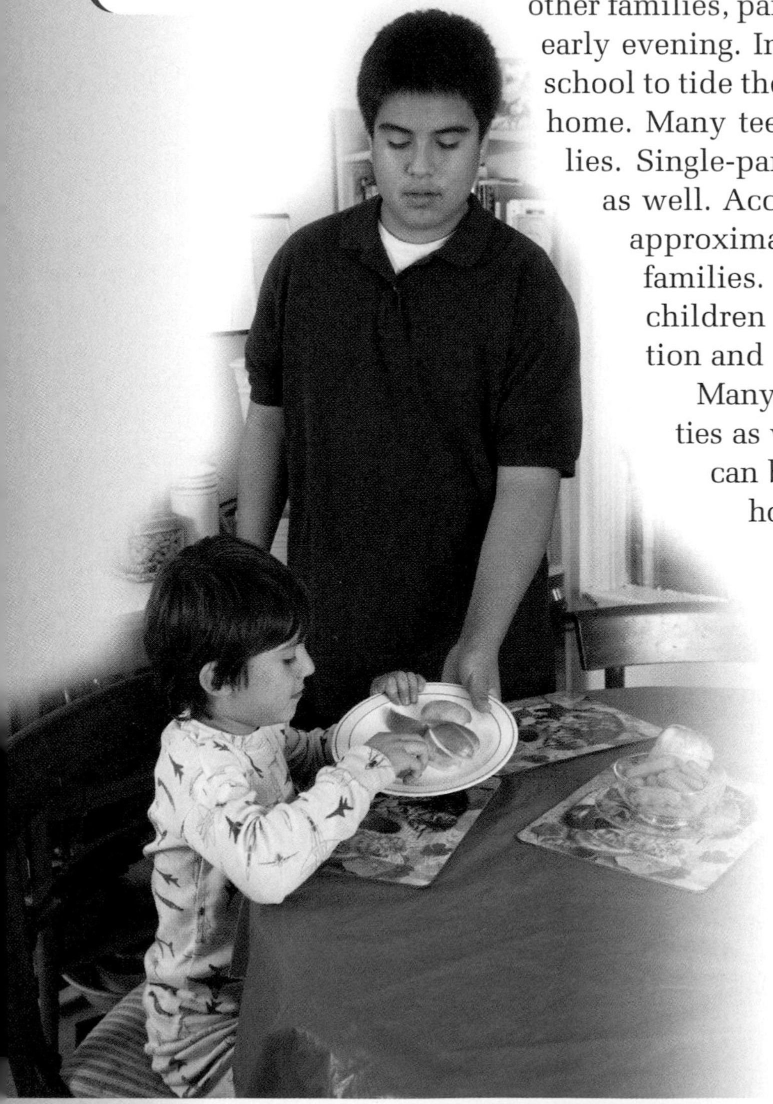

FIGURE 1-11 When parents and guardians work, often teens care for younger siblings as well as prepare the evening meal.

do if vehicles were not equipped with cup holders so that people can eat on the run? What if there were no drive-through restaurants?

A person's lifestyle has a major impact on her or his food habits. How has your lifestyle influenced your parents' eating habits and how have your parents' lifestyle affected yours?

MAKING HEALTHY CHOICES

You must be wondering how you can make healthy food choices when there are so many factors at work. The answer is simple:

- Learn about the foods that will help you maintain your health.
- Think about why you make the food choices you do.
- Find healthy food choices by learning to read and understand nutrition labels.

This course is a good first step in making healthy food choices for your current and future health.

FIGURE 1-12 Have you ever been surprised by what you read on a nutrition label for one of your favourite foods?

Connecting to the Community

In each Connecting to the Community activity you will find out more about your local community by completing one of two assignments. This section forms one part of your Connecting to the Community for Unit 1. For the activity you will create one product from a choice of the following products.

A display case?

A script?

A PowerPoint presentation?

A poster?

A bulletin board display?

A game?

A brochure?

Chapter 1 Choices

1. Contact local agencies to find out how food insecurity is addressed in your community. Answer the following questions in the form of a one-page article for your Connecting to the Community product.

   ■ Who provides the service?
   ■ What types of services are available? (For example, food bank, soup kitchen, community garden)
   ■ Where do people have to go to get access to food?
   ■ Is transportation provided?
   ■ How many people in your community are affected by food insecurity?
   ■ What are the causes?
   ■ How can teenagers become involved and make a difference in their community when it comes to food insecurity?

OR

2. "The 100 Mile Diet" encourages buying locally-produced food because buying foods produced within 100 miles (160 km) reduces the impact of transportation on the environment. Purchasing food this way also helps increase the freshness of foods, since they do not have to be harvested so early. Using the food groups from *Eating Well with Canada's Food Guide* as an organizer, list foods that are produced within 160 km of your community.

A n a l y z e • E v a l u a t e • C r e a t e

Chapter 1 Summary

In this chapter, you looked at some of the factors that influence people's food choices. These included:

- Physiological reasons, such as nutrients to help you maintain a healthy body, prevent fatigue and disease, and keep a positive attitude
- Reasons for food security and insecurity in Canada
- How parents and guardians use food to influence children's behaviour and the psychological impact this has on children as adults
- Reasons why some foods comfort people
- The role food plays in social events
- Factors that affect people's lifestyle today and how this influences their eating habits

Activities

1. Your friend, an athlete, does not believe that the food she eats has an impact on her health and performance. Explain the concept of nutrition and nutrients to your friend.

2. What is food insecurity? Give three reasons why people might experience food insecurity.

3. What are the dangers of using food as a reward or punishment?

4. Think of three social occasions that you have attended that involved food, and use your memory of them to complete a chart similar to the one below.

Occasion	Foods and Beverages Consumed	Special Significance

Write a half-page summary of the social role of food in these events.

5. List the different psychological ways in which people experience food. Write a three to five minute script that portrays at least four of them.

6. Take a good look at the impact your lifestyle has on your food choices. Develop an action plan to help you incorporate more healthy foods into your diet. Share your plan with your parent or guardian. Have him or her comment on the plan. Follow the plan for a week. Share the plan, the additional comments from your parent or guardian, and the results with your teacher in a one-page report.

CHAPTER 2

Influences on Food Patterns and Customs

Key Concepts

Influences on food patterns and customs, including

- Geography and climate
- Historical influences
- Religion
- Culture
- Family arrangements

Key Terms

climate
culture
food customs
food habits
food patterns
food processing
geography
hydroponics
subsistence agriculture

In this chapter you will explore factors that influence food patterns and customs that go beyond personal choices.

After school, Takis stops at the market on the way to soccer practice. He loves fresh fruits when they are in season. He thinks they taste better when they are grown locally, not shipped in from other countries. He learned in his geography class that, historically, before advances in transportation and safe storage of foods, consumers could get only locally grown foods.

On the way, Takis and his friend Raza talk about their favourite foods. Raza's parents immigrated to Canada from Pakistan and they use a lot of curry spices in their food. Raza loves spicy foods because he grew up with them. His favourite food is his mother's "company" curry. She makes it only when all their relatives come over for a special celebration. Raza knows a special event is approaching when he sees the chicken marinating in yoghurt in the fridge.

Takis has a harder time deciding on his favourite food. His mom's background is German and her special dishes include

custard pies and bean and cucumber salad. She uses a lot of cream and milk in her cooking. Takis's dad's background is Greek and the foods he cooks are very different from his wife's. Takis's dad cooks with lots of fresh ingredients, especially tomatoes, green peppers, and garlic. When his dad prepares a special meal, he usually makes dolmades—vine leaves stuffed with a rice-and-ground-meat mixture—or stifado—lamb stew with onions. Takis loves both dishes.

FOOD PATTERNS AND CUSTOMS

In Chapter 1 you learned about personal influences on your food choices. In this chapter you will explore other factors that influence both your **food patterns** and your **food customs.** Food patterns are a reliable sample of traits, acts, tendencies, or other observable characteristics related to food that is eaten by a person or group. For example, in some cultures turkey is the preferred meat at Christmas, while in others it is fish. Food customs are all the uses, practices, or conventions that regulate **food habits**. Food habits are the ways people, as individuals, eat and cook foods on a regular basis.

Try to remember the foods and beverages that you have consumed in the past two days. Do they fit into any of the following categories?

- Fruit or vegetable that is locally grown and in season
- Fruit or vegetable that stores well over the winter
- Food that was frozen and thawed before it was eaten
- Meat from an animal that is raised locally
- Food that was imported to Canada and not grown locally
- Food that used new technology to produce it
- Food that was cooked in a microwave oven
- A convenience food
- Food that was eaten for religious or philosophical reasons
- Food that was not eaten because of your values or beliefs
- Food that is significant to your culture
- Food that was cooked by you because your parent(s) or caregiver(s) was not at home
- Food that was cooked by a stay-at-home parent
- Food that was cooked by a member of your extended family
- Food that was advertised on television

How many did you identify? Probably quite a few. Many factors come into play in people's food patterns and customs—your philosophy or religious beliefs, your culture, the availability of foods, who has fed you. All these factors determine what you eat. Let's take a closer look at some of them.

GEOGRAPHY AND CLIMATE

A dictionary definition of **geography** is "a science that deals with the description, distribution, and interaction of the diverse physical, biological, and cultural features of the earth's surface." Looking at food patterns and customs like a geographer, you can make some interesting discoveries.

Web connection

To find out more about food customs around the world, go to this Web site and follow the links.

www.mhrfoodforlife.ca

In the past, before countries could transport foods over long distances, people had to eat the foods that were available to them locally. What was available depended on the geographic features of the area. Those features include:

- Landforms—flat, rolling hills, or mountains
- Soil quality—sandy, rich, loamy, or rocky
- Water—freshwater, salt water, abundance or lack of water

The type of land and the water near or around it affected the natural availability of plants and animals for food.

Land that is mountainous with rocky soil may have a freshwater stream. In this type of area you naturally find freshwater fish; animals that could adapt to mountain climbing, such as goats, sheep, and bears; and plants such as berries.

Meadows with good soil might have a freshwater river, lake, or stream nearby. The food available would be freshwater fish, grazing animals such as deer and buffalo, and many different plants, since the soil would be good for growing.

Land near an ocean can have either rocky or sandy soil, and can be either flat or mountainous. Salt water fish would be readily available, as well as a variety of plants and animals, depending on other geographic factors. Think about the geographic features in your area. What types of foods do you think are not available there naturally?

Food for Thought

Cranberries are British Columbia's largest berry crop. The province produces 17 million kilograms of cranberries, valued at $25 million, each year. These berries are grown by 50 family farm operations on a total of 1150 hectares.

FIGURE 2-1 The geographic features of an area influenced the foods that were naturally available to people who lived there. What type of foods would be naturally available in a mountainous region?

Around 3000 BCE an agricultural revolution occurred, during which people developed agricultural skills and began growing crops and raising animals. The types of crops grown and animals raised were also affected by geography. Mountains are not the best places to grow crops such as wheat, but the plains of southern Alberta and Saskatchewan are ideal for grain crops. In mountain valleys, silt and mineral runoff from the mountains create a rich soil in which fruit trees flourish, such as in the Okanogan Valley in British Columbia. In northern parts of Alberta, the soil is not as good for growing crops as it is in the south, but it is perfect for grazing animals and provides pasture for cows and horses. People all over the world have adapted to geography in order to produce food.

FIGURE 2-2 The types of food grown or animals raised depends on geographic features such as soil quality. What type of land would not support the grazing of animals?

In the past, people rarely travelled great distances because of natural barriers to travel, such as mountains, deserts, oceans, or lakes. These barriers also made it difficult to trade with or transport foods to or from other groups of people. Now that technology is available to transport foods from all over the world, geography no longer plays the major role in food supply that it once did. Canada trades food with many different countries around the world.

FIGURE 2-3 When you go to a grocery store and read the labels on foods, especially on produce during the winter months, what do you discover about where these foods were grown?

Climate is the average pattern or condition of the weather at a place over a period of years. It also has a major influence on food. Different crops can be grown in different climates. World climate classifications include

- Tropical
- Subtropical
- Arid
- Semi-arid
- Mediterranean
- Temperate
- Oceanic
- Continental
- Alpine
- Subarctic
- Polar
- Antarctic

Web connection

To find out more about climate zones, go to this Web site and follow the links.

www.mhrfoodforlife.ca

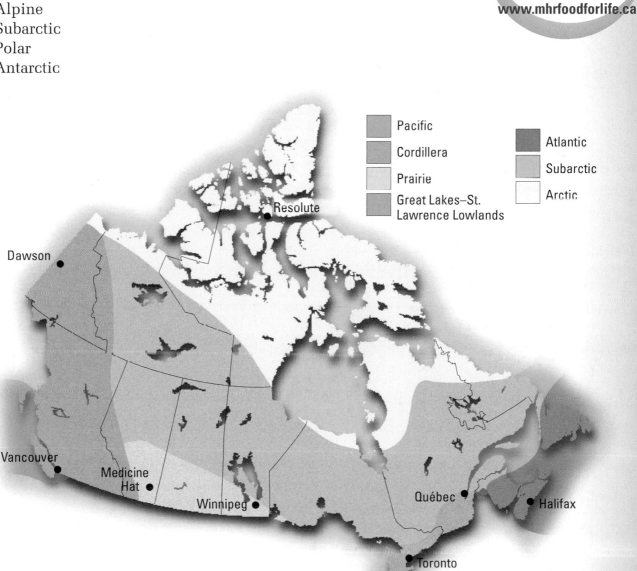

Pacific
Cordillera
Prairie
Great Lakes–St. Lawrence Lowlands
Atlantic
Subarctic
Arctic

Resolute
Dawson
Vancouver
Medicine Hat
Winnipeg
Québec
Halifax
Toronto

FIGURE 2-4 Which zone do you live in? How does the climate affect what can and cannot grow there?

About **half a million years ago**—The discovery of fire

About **3000–2700 BCE** Agricultural Age

1400–1600 Migration, travel, and trade

1750–1850 Industrialization

1800–1850 Urbanization

1800 on—Modern food processing

1870 on—Science and technology

The length of the seasons in each climate zone depends on latitude, longitude, and proximity to water. The largest climate zone in Canada is Subarctic—with short cool summers and long cold winters, and very little precipitation. The climate in the Canadian Arctic is influenced by its high northern latitude, which brings very dry and frigid conditions all year long.

Southern Canada is temperate and therefore has four distinct seasons. The Great Lakes have a moderating influence on the climate in southern Ontario, where the winters are short and mild and the summers are hot and humid. The Prairie Provinces are subject to climatic extremes—hot dry summers and cold winters. Even though both coasts of Canada are affected by large oceans, the effects are felt differently in each area. On the West Coast the winter is very mild and rain is more common than snow. In Atlantic Canada, the winds also affect the climate, causing humid summers and very cold winters.

The Canadian climate limits our growing season to spring, summer, and early fall. It also means that farm animals must be sheltered to protect them from cold harsh winters. Increasing demand for fresh fruits and vegetables during the winter months has led to increased importation of these foods into Canada from all over the world. Growth in the production of greenhouse vegetables also helps meet Canadian demands for fresh produce year round.

HISTORY

Progress and development have had a major impact on food. If you look back at history, you can see changes in food patterns resulting from changes in technology or practice. Consider the following examples:

- *Fire.* The discovery of fire allowed people to eat cooked foods. This increased the consumption of meat and fish worldwide. People also developed a taste for cooked fruits and vegetables. Baking, and all the baked goods people enjoy, would not be possible had people not discovered how to cook.
- *Agriculture.* Once people stopped the nomadic lifestyle of following food, they began to cultivate crops and raise animals. This not only changed the types of foods they ate, but also provided them with a more stable food supply. Early farmers grew enough food for only themselves and their families. This is called **subsistence agriculture** and still goes on in many developing countries.

FIGURE 2-5 In early times, farmers provided food for only themselves and their families. Who provides food for us now?

- *Migration, travel, and trade.* Early European explorers discovered new cuisines, spices, and customs. They brought back some of these and introduced them to their home country.
- *Industrialization.* The Industrial Revolution in Europe changed the way people thought about doing things. People moved from small cottage industries to large-scale factories. This change also had an impact on all aspects of food production and distribution—from agriculture to **food processing** to shopping for food.
- *Urbanization.* When people moved to cities in large numbers, the face of agriculture changed drastically. No longer were there many farmers on small farms producing food for only themselves and their families. People living in cities could not feed themselves the way rural people could. If you live in a city, you do not expect your neighbours to have cows in their backyard or on their balconies. Agriculture had to change to feed cities. Farms grew larger, and food was transported into cities and sold at markets and grocery stores.

Web connection

To find out more about the history of food, go to this Web site and follow the links.

www.mhrfoodforlife.ca

FIGURE 2-6 Urbanization means that farmers must produce enough food to feed the people living in cities. How have farmers adapted to this demand?

The Refrigerator

The refrigerator is Canada's most used household appliance. At present, 99.7 percent of Canadians own a refrigerator (Statistics Canada, 2005). The refrigerator changed people's pattern of living and the way they shopped and ate. It affected households socially too, since people no longer had to buy their food every day. The mass production of modern refrigerators did not begin until after 1945.

Through engineering and technology, refrigerators gradually became more reliable and inexpensive. In the 1940s, freezer compartments were added. Between 1950 and 1960, extra features were built in, such as automatic defrosters and icemakers. During the 1970s, refrigerators became more energy efficient.

Refrigerators changed everything. People no longer depended on the delivery of ice for cooling food. Daily chores changed, since people did not have to shop each day. Milk delivery disappeared in many areas since there was no longer a need for fresh milk to be delivered door to door. Many butcher shops closed because people stopped shopping daily for fresh meats. Curing meat became a year-round activity and no longer a seasonal event. Refrigeration improved meat quality and meant that food was safer and lasted longer.

As cities grew, so did consumer demand for fresh foods, especially vegetables and fruits. Produce that wasn't available fresh became readily available if frozen. Groceries of all kinds were available just about anywhere in the country year-round. Expanded markets and the widespread distribution of produce resulted in healthier diets. People ate better because they had healthier choices—meat, milk, eggs, cheese, produce, and fish—all year around. Since they no longer had to worry about spoilage, families began to shop weekly, buying an entire week's food supply in one trip.

Today, people can buy almost anything they want at their local supermarket, thanks in part, to refrigerators.

FIGURE 2.7 The modern refrigerator began with the invention of the icebox (left) and evolved to include a freezer that defrosted itself and an automatic ice-cube maker (right). How did the invention of the refrigerator change people's food-buying patterns?

- *Modern food processing.* This involves the methods used to transform raw ingredients into food for consumption by humans or animals; for example, tomatoes are changed into ketchup, meat into hot dogs, soy beans into tofu. Begun in the 1800s with the canning of fruits and vegetables, food processing has since become more mechanized with the development of technology. Technology has increased production and allowed for the safe handling of food through the use of sterile conditions during processing. New technologies allow foods to be refrigerated and frozen. Can you imagine living without a refrigerator in your home? Other processing technologies have given products a longer shelf life so that people can store food until needed.

- *Science and technology.* Advances in both science and technology have changed not only what foods are produced but also how foods are processed. Development of hardier crops has allowed Western Canada to become a world-class producer of wheat.

  Greenhouse technology has allowed people to produce fresh vegetables in winter months for Canadian and foreign markets. Increased understanding of **hydroponics**—the growing of plants in water-based solutions with added chemicals and nutrients—has led to the development of a whole new way of producing food. Lettuce, tomatoes, peppers, and other crops are grown year round in greenhouses using hydroponics.

- *Improved knowledge of nutrition, wellness, and health.* Increased research and understanding of health have led to different eating patterns and customs. Research has shown direct links between nutrition, wellness, and overall health. People now know that their food habits have a direct impact on their health. Some food patterns increase the risk of developing diseases such as heart disease and diabetes, while other food patterns reduce the risk.

Many people are starting to pay more attention to the impact their food choices have on their health now and for the future. This awareness has resulted, among other things, in fast-food restaurants changing their menus to include healthier choices and nutritional information.

FIGURE 2-8 People's desire to make better nutrition part of their lives is changing the way fast-food restaurants do business. Have you noticed any healthy choices on the fast-food menus you've seen lately? Are they really healthy?

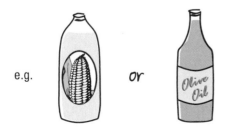
Most people have heard of at least one scare related to Canadian food and health, usually through the media or Internet. The fact is not all information on the Internet is accurate. Keep in mind the principles of good nutrition when reading food-related e-mail or accessing food and nutrition Web sites.

Here are a few examples of *misinformation* related to health.

The experts are always changing their minds about what healthy eating really is.
Sometimes nutrition experts get different results from their studies—one says caffeine is bad for you; another says it is OK. However, the main messages—eat in moderation; eat a variety of foods from all four food groups; reduce fat, salt, and sugar; and eat more vegetables—have remained the same for some time.

Healthier foods are always far more expensive than other foods.
Although some healthy ingredients can be more expensive, often you need to use them only in very small amounts. For example, olive oil is more expensive than other vegetable oils but only small amounts are usually needed. Sometimes choosing the healthier alternative can actually save you money.

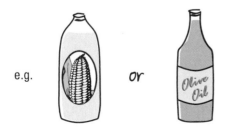

If the label says "low fat" or "reduced fat," then the product is always a healthy choice.
To claim that a product has "reduced fat," the amount of fat must be at least 25 percent lower than the standard product. However, these types of

foods tend to be high in fat and energy in the first place, so the "reduced-fat" version can still have high amounts of both.

If you want to have a healthier option, it's best to choose a vegetarian dish.
Some vegetarian dishes contain a great deal of fat, especially if they are made with lots of cheese, oil, pastry, or creamy sauces, or if they have been fried. Consequently, they are not necessarily a healthier option.

Red meat is always very high in fat and poultry is always low in fat.
Removing visible fat can make a big difference to the fat content of meat. In fact, lean red meat is quite low in fat at 4–8 grams per 100 grams.

Most of the salt in your diet is added at the table.
Only 10 to 15 percent of the sodium you eat comes from the salt you add when cooking food or at the table. Seventy-five percent of the salt in your diet comes from processed foods. Reading the sodium content on processed food labels will improve your consumer awareness (and your health).

Activity

1. Think of a health claim you have heard about food and nutrition. Go to a reliable source for information, such as your local health authority, Health Canada, or the Dietitians of Canada Web sites. Research the health claim and write a half-page article on the validity of the claim.

RELIGION, BELIEFS, AND VALUES

Food plays an important role in many religious ceremonies. In ancient times, people believed in many different gods and tried to please their gods through various ceremonies, offerings and rituals. Food was central on these occasions.

Many societies and cultures developed special ceremonies that involve food. These ceremonies were overseen by the leaders of the group and eventually passed on to the next generation. In many societies, these ceremonies became part of a religion. Consequently, in most religions today, food plays an important role in certain ceremonies. Many religions also give special significance to seasonal food tasks—planting and renewal in the spring, harvesting and celebrating the harvest in the fall. Can you think of any others? What foods are associated with them?

Many people in Asian countries will eat any animal as long as "its back is to the sky" or it walks on four legs. Both Jews and Muslims are prohibited from eating pork or pork products because of the ancient belief that pigs were unclean animals. Many Buddhists and Hindus are vegetarians because they believe there is spiritual equality among all living creatures; therefore, they will not eat the flesh of animals.

FIGURE 2-9 Food plays an important role in the ceremonies of many of the world's religions. What ceremonies have you attended that involved food?

The following table provides some information about the special significance of food for six of the world's religions. Remember that this is generalized. Often different communities and sects of religious groups practise their religions differently.

Significant Foods of Six Religions

	Judaism	Buddhism	Christianity	Islam	Hinduism	First Nations
General Information	Jews can be Reform, Conservative, or Orthodox, based on the degree of adherence to the Jewish laws. "Kashrut" refers to the laws pertaining to food in the Jewish religion.	The dietary rules of Buddhism, which is more a life philosophy than a religious doctrine, depend on which branch of Buddhism is practised and in what country.	Various faiths, including Roman Catholic, Orthodox, and Protestant, have their own different practices.	Regulations surrounding food are called "halal."	"Food is God (Brahman)" is a common Hindu saying. Food is thought to be an actual part of Brahman, rather than simply a Brahman symbol.	The earth is the mother of all life. Plants and animals have spirits and must be respected and cared for.
Food Restrictions and Regulations	"Kosher" means that a food is permitted or "clean." Anything considered "unclean" (such as pork and shellfish) is strictly forbidden.	In his lives on Earth, the Buddha cycled through various animal forms before he took on the form of a human being. This is why most Buddhists are vegetarian.	Catholics fast and avoid meat on certain days. All Christians celebrate Easter and Christmas with special foods.	Prohibited foods, such as those containing pork and alcohol, are called "haram." It is thought that the Creator turns a deaf ear to a Muslim who eats haram foods.	People who practise the Hindu religion don't eat meat. They also avoid foods whose manufacture may have caused pain to animals.	Thanks must be given when taking the spirit of a plant or animal.
Significant Foods and Rituals	Passover commemorates the birth of the Jewish nation. The foods eaten help to tell the story of the Exodus. For example, bitter herbs recall the suffering of the Israelites under Egyptian rule.	Buddhist monks and nuns are not allowed to cultivate, store, or cook their own food. Instead, they must rely on "alms," donations from the community of believers.	Bread and wine symbolize the body and blood of Christ.	The month of Ramadan requires mandatory fasting during sunlight hours.	Fasting depends on the person's caste (social standing) and the occasion. For example, rules regarding fasting depend on whether the day has religious or personal significance.	When the moon is full in June or July, the people of the prairies celebrate the Sundance. Dancers fast during the time of the Sundance.

CULTURE

Culture is defined as the shared customs, traditions, and beliefs of a large group of people, such as a nation, a race, or a religious group. Culture also has an impact on food patterns and customs. These customs are part of what helps the group maintain its identity.

Food plays an important role in many cultures. Every culture has traditional ways of preparing, serving, and eating foods. Most of these traditions have to do with the history of the culture as well as the geography of the area where the culture originated. Some cultures developed in a time of strict social groupings. Consequently, the wealthy or more important social classes ate the better foods, while the lower social groups ate the less desirable foods. European nobility, for example, frowned on fresh fruits and vegetables, and consequently often developed scurvy. In southeastern Asia, the climate is hot and moist, which is ideal for growing rice, so rice became a staple food there. For the First Nations peoples who inhabited the Pacific Coast of Canada, food was plentiful. Access to abundant fish and seafood made them important to their diet. Salmon was—and still is—a staple.

Another factor that influenced food culture was the availability of certain resources. In some cultures, such as in China and India, fuel for cooking was often scarce. Food was cut into small pieces so it would cook quickly. Other cultures had plenty of fuel and developed cooking techniques that required more time and fuel, such as simmering and roasting.

Cultural celebrations usually have special foods associated with them. What you think of as "traditional" foods served at a wedding are likely very different from the "traditional" foods served at weddings in other cultures. Often the food at weddings and other important cultural and religious occasions are very specifically defined.

As discussed earlier, some cultural groups have strict dietary rules as well. Often those rules have to do with religion, but sometimes they simply reflect the culture of the group. Most cultures have etiquette—the appropriate conduct in social or official gatherings, including eating together. If you are not a part of the culture, you may not fully understand the etiquette required in certain situations. Etiquette will be examined more closely in Chapter 3.

In Canada, we are introduced to the foods of a wide variety of cultures. You will take a closer look at culture and food in Chapter 16.

To find out more about the food habits of different cultures, go to this Web site and follow the links.
www.mhrfoodforlife.ca

FIGURE 2-10 Some cultures had access to firewood as a source of fuel for cooking. These groups would make a pot of stew and let it simmer for a day or even two. Can you imagine how your food patterns and lifestyle might change if you could not cook for long periods of time?

Connecting to the Community

In each Connecting to the Community activity you will find out more about your local community by completing one of two assignments. This section forms one part of your Connecting to the Community activity for Unit 1. For the activity you will create one product from a choice of the following products.

Chapter 2 Choices

1. For this chapter, consider the following factors and how they influence the food patterns and customs of the people in your community:

   - Geography
   - History—Refer to at least two of the periods on the timeline on p. 30
   - Religion—Discuss at least two of the religious groups in your community
   - Culture—Discuss at least two of the cultural groups in your community

   Complete a one-page summary and title it "Food Patterns and Customs in Our Community."

OR

2. Complete a 10-minute script for a talk show explaining the influences on what people eat in your community. Bring "experts" on the talk show to discuss their area.

   Consider the following factors and how they influence the food patterns and customs of the people in your community:

   - Geography
   - History—Refer to at least two of the periods on the timeline on p. 30
   - Religion—Discuss at least two of the religious groups in your community
   - Culture—Discuss at least two of the cultural groups in your community

Chapter 2 Summary

In this chapter you learned about some of the factors that influence food patterns and customs.

- Geography and climate affect the types of foods available in different areas of the world and in Canada.
- Factors such as landforms, soil quality, and availability of water determine which plants are grown and which animals are raised.
- Historical changes—from the discovery of fire, to industrialization and urbanization, to increased knowledge and understanding of nutrition, wellness, and health—have had an impact on food patterns and customs.
- Religion and philosophy influence food patterns. Some religions forbid certain foods; others encourage fasting; many have specific foods for special ceremonies and occasions.
- Culture also determines the foods that people eat on a regular basis, the foods they consume for special occasions and ceremonies, and the etiquette surrounding the way they eat the foods.

Activities

1. Using the key terms at the beginning of the chapter, create a word search puzzle that you and your classmates could use to help you study for a test. Be sure that you include answers with the definitions.

2. Consider the land forms, soil type, and availability of water in the area in which you live. How would these factors have influenced the types of foods naturally available in the area before foods could be grown or imported? Find a traditional recipe from your area that includes some of these foods.

3. Research one of the religions listed in this chapter. Find out how and what foods play a role in
   a) Celebrations
   b) Ceremonies
   c) Food taboos or restrictions
   d) Food traditions
   e) Fasting or other food patterns prescribed by the religion

   Create an electronic presentation or bulletin board to display what you have learned about food and the religion you chose.

three

CHAPTER 3

Food Traditions and Etiquette

Key Concepts

- Food symbolism
- Food for special occasions
- Food etiquette
  - in the classroom
  - in the home
  - on special occasions
  - differences between cultures

Key Terms

etiquette
food symbolism
status foods

In this chapter we discuss food traditions, food symbolism, etiquette, and the effects they have on what and how we eat.

Jade and her friends are having lunch in the school cafeteria. Jade is very excited about the Chinese New Year celebrations that her family will be attending on the weekend. She is taking her friend Lisa. Tonight, Lisa is coming over to get lessons in Chinese etiquette. Since this is a traditional celebration, Lisa wants to understand the table manners and other etiquette she will need to use in order to show respect.

The girls discuss food symbolism and the significance that some foods have in their families and cultures. Jade explains the meaning of some of the foods that will be served at Chinese New Year—bamboo shoots and dumplings for wealth, eggs for fertility, fish served whole for prosperity, noodles for long life, and tangerines for luck. Lisa explains how bread and wine become the body and blood of Jesus Christ according to the Communion ceremonies at her Catholic church. Jessica talks about how scalloped potatoes and ham has become her traditional birthday dinner. Sarah laughs. She is Jewish and ham is never served in her home.

The girls also discuss how their manners are different here in the cafeteria from what they are in other places, such as at home or at a fancy restaurant. Jade says that her manners are at their worst in fast-food places.

SYMBOLIC FOODS

Read through the following list of foods. Do any of them have a special meaning for you?

- Hard-boiled eggs dyed red
- Birthday cake
- Long noodles
- Whole fish
- Peking duck
- *Latkes*
- *Besan barfee*
- *Gullac*
- Buffalo
- Yellow rice
- Wedding cake
- The three sisters: corn, beans, and squash
- Lychee
- Salmon
- Red sherbet gelatin
- Milk and cookies

If any of these foods has a special meaning to you, then you have some understanding of **food symbolism**. Food symbolism means giving a food a particular meaning in a particular context. Perhaps you knew that the hard-boiled egg is a Chinese symbol of fertility, and you may even have seen them being handed to guests at a "red egg and ginger party" to celebrate the birth of a child. Red eggs are symbolic in other cultures as well, including Greek and Ukrainian. Why do you think that is?

If you are Muslim, yellow rice served on festive occasions may symbolize sunshine to you. Perhaps you also eat red sherbet gelatin to celebrate *Mirac Kandili*, the night on which Muhammad ascended to the seventh Heaven, according to Islam.

You may have heard the story of the three sisters—corn, beans, and squash—and understand that in some First Nations cultures they are considered gifts from the Creator to sustain life. You may see the buffalo as a symbol of self-sacrifice, as do the

FIGURE 3-1 The buffalo once sustained First Nations peoples of the plains in Canada. For that reason, the buffalo became a symbol of self-sacrifice. Do you know which province includes a buffalo on its flag? Which other provinces have food symbols on their flags? What does this say about the role of these foods in the history of the provinces?

Plains Peoples, who see it as the animal who gave its whole self for their survival. Salmon may have a different meaning for you if you are from the West Coast of Canada, or northern Japan, or the East Coast of England.

The foods that people eat have many symbolic meanings that come from a variety of sources.

Web connection
To learn more about the meaning of food, or food symbolism, go to this Web site and follow the links.

www.mhrfoodforlife.ca

Status Foods

Some foods have a certain status, or prestige, associated with them. **Status foods** are usually expensive and often difficult to obtain. When people serve them to guests or order them at a restaurant, they feel special. Some foods gain status because they are hard to find, either because they are difficult to produce or because supplies are deliberately kept low. Specialty chocolate is a good example.

Think about some of the foods that celebrities are reported to eat—caviar, eggs from rare birds, exotic fish and game animals. Do you ever wonder whether celebrities really like these foods, or just eat them because it gives them social status?

Sometimes foods gain status because the nature of the processing needed to prepare them makes them expensive. However, too much of these foods can lead to poor nutrition since, generally, the more processed a food is, the lower its nutritional value. Packaged and frozen foods, for example, often contain more salt than homemade versions of the same foods. Historically, white flour, which required more processing, was for the rich, while the lower classes ate more coarsely ground whole grains. Today, white bread is more readily available and often cheaper than whole-grain breads although whole-grain breads are now known to be more nutritious. The status of white flour has changed with our knowledge of nutrition.

FIGURE 3-2 Some celebrities eat status foods. Have you ever tried an exotic food and been disappointed? What was it? Why were you disappointed?

Literacy in Your Life

Before Reading

1. Look around. Do you see symbols on clothing, appliances, or food packages? A symbol on its own does not mean anything, but over time has come to mean something special. Foods eaten on special occasions are also symbols of important cultural or religious traditions that have developed over time.

2. Read the title of the article reproduced here. What do you think the symbols in a Chinese New Year feast might be? How many can you list in your notebook?

During Reading

Think about what you are reading. Think about the foods and what they symbolize, as well as the joy of having family together.

1. When you see a word that is not in English, pronounce it the way it looks. Note that these words are in *italics*. The titles of books and the names of magazines and newspapers are also in italics.

2. The journalist who wrote this article wants you to know about modern, Western Chinese traditions at New Year. She does this by describing the worlds of Karen Soon and Rosemary Gong. Why would a journalist use this technique?

FIGURE 3-3 Why do you think the head of the duck is offered with the meat when Peking Duck is served?

The New Year: A Feast of Symbols

Twenty-five-year-old Karen Ann Soon admits that, growing up, she disliked some parts of Chinese New Year's dinner. "When I was younger, it really grossed me out how they had the [duck] heads on the plate," she told the *Georgia Straight*. Her father explained that serving the bird intact shows that it's whole and not "broken," which the Chinese consider bad. Soon also thinks her family explained the symbolism behind certain dishes—like long noodles signify long life—but she's fuzzy on the details. "They probably told me, but when you're younger you don't really care."

Soon, a fifth-generation Chinese Canadian, says that Chinese New Year is the only Chinese holiday her family celebrates. Her father is of Chinese descent and her mother is Polish-Swedish. All her aunts and uncles married non-Chinese spouses. Yet every year her family gathers for a New Year feast. Although Soon may not fully understand the tradition and symbolism behind the meal, it's still a meaningful get-together.

That's true for a lot of Chinese people in North America, says third-generation Chinese American Rosemary Gong, who was raised in California. "I grew up doing all the [Chinese] celebrations," she told the *Straight* by phone from her San Francisco office. "I just practised them because that's what my family did." However, she said, she didn't fully comprehend why they did certain things, like cleaning the house from top to bottom in preparation for the New Year. (It symbolizes a new beginning and sweeping out old misfortune.) "The single most important obligation for a Chinese family is Chinese New Year dinner," Gong says, emphasizing that everyone is expected to attend.

Traditional New Year's foods served at the meal are loaded with symbolism. Whole foods indicate everything is complete. Long, leafy greens like Chinese broccoli are said to bring parents long lives. Bird's-nest soup indicates youthfulness. In her book, Gong says, "A 'monks' vegetarian dish, called *jai choy*, is the most significant New Year's dish because every one of its ingredients promises to deliver good fortune, prosperity, and longevity. Dried oysters denote good business; *fat choy* (sea moss that looks like long, black hair) means prosperity; Chinese black mushrooms fulfill wishes from east to west." Even the number of courses is significant; eight is fortuitous because in Chinese "eight" sounds like "to grow."

Vancouverite Soon says that her grandmother used to cook the meal when she was younger but now they go out to a restaurant. The family orders different dishes from year to year, depending on who is in charge. "If she [Soon's grandmother] is ordering the food, she gets the traditional dishes, but if my father's ordering, he just gets dishes that everybody likes." Gong tells the *Straight* that Chinese New Year helps perpetuate the culture even as it evolves. "It's part of our identity in carrying this on."

Soon doesn't speak Chinese, and neither do her aunts, uncles, and father. "The only Chinese he knows is how to order Chinese food," she says. Perhaps that says something about the centrality of food to culture.

FIGURE 3-4 Why is the dish *jai choy* the most significant Chinese New Year dish?

After Reading

Reflect and think about what you read. Try one of these activities.

1. Both Karen Soon and Rosemary Gong talk about the loss of most of their cultural traditions, yet food traditions remain with them. Why do you think immigrants hold on to food traditions even as they adapt to other aspects of another culture?

2. Make a list of the special foods that symbolize the New Year to you. Compare these to the foods enjoyed by your grandparents or others of your cultural heritage. Why do you think things have or have not changed over the generations?

Language Extension

1. *Symbolism, symbolize,* and *symbolic* come from the word *symbol,* which means "something that stands for something else." It comes from the Latin root *symbolum,* which means a "token or mark."

2. *Signifies* and *significant* comes from the word *signify,* which means "to have meaning or importance." It comes from the Latin root *signum,* which means "sign."

Do you see any similarities and differences in the meanings of these two families of words?

Food for Thought

In the Hindu religion, when a loved one dies, the immediate family grieves for a period of 11 to 13 days. The family must limit their diet during this period. They are prohibited from consuming salt, meat, and certain vegetables. Family and friends bring gifts of food, especially fruit.

Comfort Foods

Comfort foods make people feel good. Comfort foods usually express feelings such as love, affection, friendship, hospitality, and sympathy. Some examples of comfort foods include,

- Preparing a favourite meal for someone's birthday
- Offering to share your pizza with a friend at lunch
- Preparing a special snack when your friends come over to watch a movie
- Inviting someone who is new in the neighbourhood to dinner
- Making homemade soup for someone who is not feeling well
- Taking food to the home of a friend who has lost a loved one

Cultural Differences

Culture has an impact on what certain foods symbolize. Often, foods that were key to the survival of the early people of a culture have a strong symbolic significance. Because of the role the buffalo had in the survival of many First Nations peoples, it became a symbol of the whole society. Every part of the buffalo was used to support life. The skin was used for clothing and protection, the bones were used for utensils and other tools, and the meat was eaten. The buffalo was said to sustain life. West Coast First Nations peoples depended on the salmon for life. Consequently, salmon took on a special significance in their cultures. Asian and European cultures also had symbolic foods that were special because they had been necessary for their early survival. A good example of this is the significance of bread around the world.

FIGURE 3-5 Bread is symbolic of many things, which vary from culture to culture. Does bread have a special meaning for you?

Often called "the staff of life," bread has played a crucial and often symbolic role in the diets of many cultures. Wheat and other bread grains often represent the rebirth of life in the spring. Because of this, bread was associated symbolically with female deities and fertility. Bread is also an essential part of many harvest festivals. Throughout history, for many cultures, bread and bread grains carry symbolic significance. For example:

- In ancient Egypt, wheat kernels were placed in graves to ensure the survival of the dead in the afterlife.
- Bread and cereal grains were associated with agricultural or fertility goddesses—Isis in Egypt, Demeter in Greece, and Ceres in Rome.
- In Christianity, bread is the symbol of eternal life in the body of Jesus Christ.
- *Matzo* is the unleavened bread that Jews eat during Passover to celebrate the Exodus from Egypt.

- Hittites believed that leavened bread helped ward off epidemics, provided it was placed in a special barrel.
- In the Middle Ages, Belgians believed that bread kneaded on Christmas Eve protected them from lightning.
- In many cultures, bread and salt are given to newlyweds as symbols of health and prosperity.
- When a daughter is born in Sweden, people prepare a flat, round bread with a hole in it. They eat the bread on the day the daughter gets married.
- *Kulich* (Russian Easter bread) is a domed, cylindrical loaf that is decorated with religious symbols of Easter, surrounded with dyed eggs, topped with a beeswax candle, and taken to church to be blessed.

FOOD FOR SPECIAL OCCASIONS AND CELEBRATIONS

Food plays an important role in many other celebrations and special occasions.

Think about the foods you eat

- At a wedding
- During cultural or religious observances, such as Ramadan, Kwanzaa, Hanukkah, Christmas, Tet (Vietnamese New Year), or St-Jean-Baptiste Day
- To celebrate a birth, confirmation, or anniversary
- At a birthday party

Did you find any similarities among the foods involved? Do you think your friends had the same foods in mind as you did? No matter what religion or culture you belong to, food has always played a significant role on special occasions. The difference is in the foods that are eaten.

New Year's Day, January 1

Starting the New Year with the right food is thought to bring good luck for the coming year. Some of the special foods served around the world on New Year's Day are

- Greece: A special sweet pastry baked with a coin inside it
- Scotland: Haggis (sheep's stomach stuffed with oatmeal and offal), gingerbread biscuits, and scones
- Spain: Twelve grapes, meant to be put into the mouth one at a time at each chime of the clock at midnight
- Japan: Up to 20 dishes are cooked and prepared a week ahead. Each food represents a New Year's wish. For example, seaweed asks for happiness in the year ahead.

Food for Thought

Many cultures eat something that symbolizes luck at New Year's. Often the shape or colour of the food resembles money, which is why cabbage or greens are so common in many traditions. Green is the colour of some money, but it also symbolizes hope, growth, and prosperity.

Harvest Festivals

Communities all across Canada stage harvest festivals. These include fall fairs, parties, and community suppers to mark the harvest of crops, to remember their pioneer heritage, and to appreciate nature's bounty. Autumn harvest festivals are a time of cheerful celebration: the crops have survived natural disasters and food is plentiful.

Festivals began in antiquity as religious and ritual observances of the seasons and often included sacred community meals or feasts. Our European ancestors held celebrations of thankfulness for a good harvest. Some First Nations peoples held two thanksgiving celebrations—one in the spring, when the sap ran in the maple trees, to give thanks for the deliverance from the winter, and one in the fall, at harvest time. Today "Harvest Festival" or "Thanksgiving" is the most observed harvest ritual in Canada.

The very first Canadian Thanksgiving celebration took place in 1578 in what is now Newfoundland. Martin Frobisher, a British explorer and navigator, held a ceremony to give thanks for surviving the long journey across the Atlantic. Other settlers who arrived later continued to hold ceremonies to give thanks. These are thought to have influenced the Canadian Thanksgiving we celebrate today.

For a few hundred years, Thanksgiving was celebrated in either late October or early November. The first official Thanksgiving Day in Canada, after Confederation, was observed on April 15, 1872. It had nothing to do with a harvest festival; it celebrated the recovery of the Prince of Wales from a serious illness. In 1908, the holiday was fixed on a Monday in October, but the date later fluctuated between October and November.

Thanksgiving became an official holiday in 1957, when Parliament announced the day would be "a day of general thanksgiving to almighty God for the bountiful harvest with which Canada has been blessed."

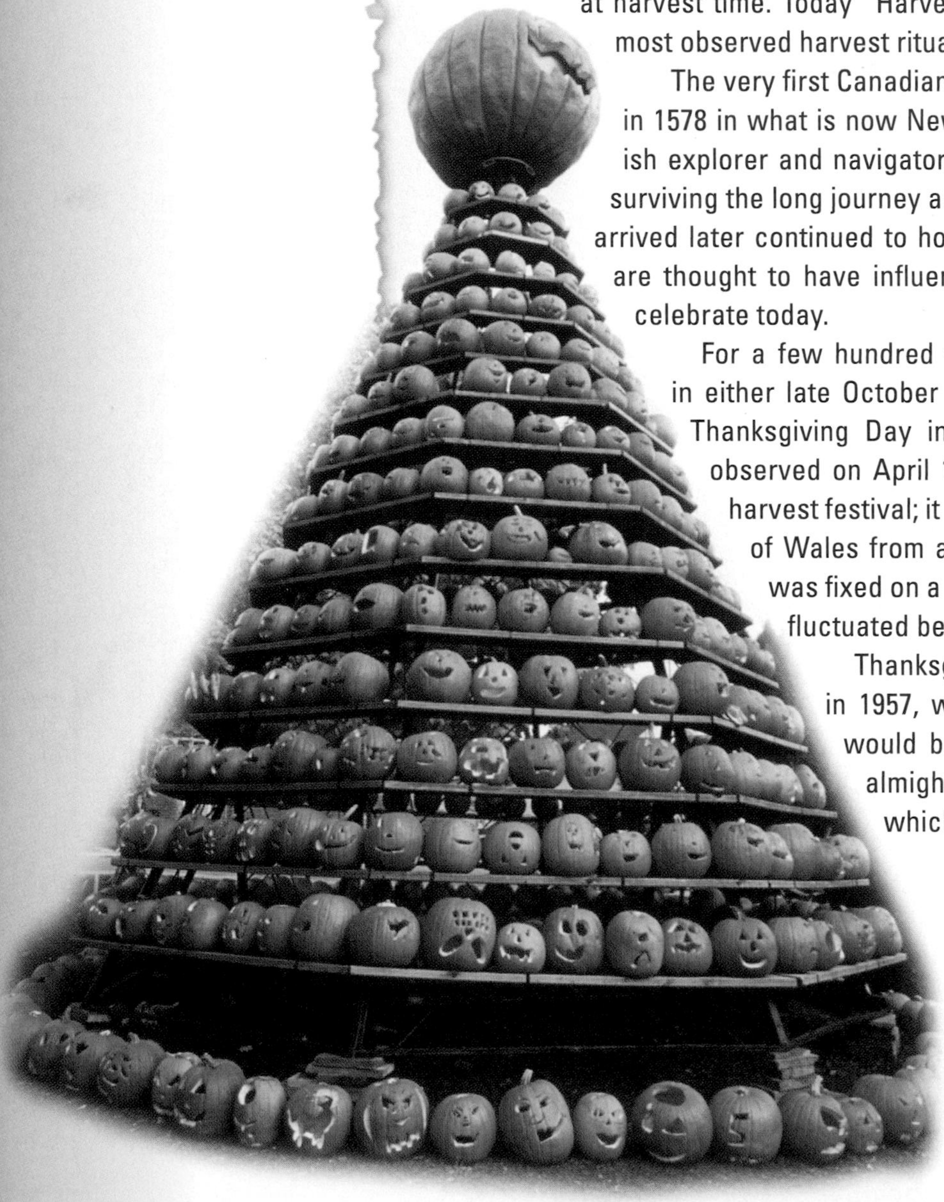

FIGURE 3-6 Many communities across Canada have harvest festivals. In Waterford, Ontario, citizens hold a Pumpkin Fest.

Lunar New Year

In many Asian countries, the New Year does not start on January 1, but with the first full moon in the first lunar month. Traditional Asian New Year's foods include

- China: Fish, chestnuts, and fried foods
- Korea: Dumpling soup
- Vietnam: Meat-filled rice cakes and shark fin soup
- Japan: Buckwheat noodles (*soba*) and sweetened rice wine

Web connection

To learn more about food and celebrations, go to this Web site and follow the links.

www.mhrfoodforlife.ca

Chinese New Year Sticky Rice

Ingredients

2 cups (500 mL) glutinous rice
½ cup (125 mL) long grain rice
¼ cup (50 mL) soy sauce
3 tbsp (50 mL) oyster sauce
1 tbsp (15 mL) Chinese cooking wine
2 tsp (10 mL) sesame oil
1 tsp (5 mL) vegetable oil
1 cup (250 mL) fresh oyster mushrooms, chopped
1 lb (450 g) lean pork loin, cut in ¼-inch (0.5 cm) dice
1 can (10 oz/284 mL) water chestnuts, drained, rinsed, and finely chopped
6 green onions, thinly sliced diagonally
1 clove garlic, minced

Preparation

- In a large saucepan, bring 3 ½ cups (875 mL) water to boil. Stir in glutinous rice and long-grain rice. Cover and reduce heat to low; simmer until tender and liquid is absorbed, about 20 minutes. Remove from heat and fluff with fork.

- Meanwhile, in a small bowl, stir together soy sauce, oyster sauce, cooking wine, and sesame oil and set aside.

- In a large non-stick skillet heat vegetable oil over medium-high heat; add mushrooms, pork, water chestnuts, green onions, garlic and soy sauce mixture. Cook, stirring often, until pork is no longer pink inside; about 5 minutes. Add to rice; stir well.

Servings: 8–10

Weddings

Foods served at weddings vary greatly among cultures. Even within the same culture, a wide variety of food is prepared.

- China: Roast suckling pig, fish, pigeon, chicken, lobster, and a bun stuffed with lotus seeds are commonly served. It is especially important to offer both lobster and chicken: the lobster represents the dragon and the chicken the phoenix, so including both on the menu is thought to harmonize the newly-joined families.

- Indonesia: Food served depends on the region and religion but may include spicy rice dishes like *nasi goreng*, dim sum, sushi, or even Western recipes like beef Wellington.

- Italy: Food is a very important part of an Italian wedding. Bow-tie shaped twists of fried dough sprinkled with sugar represent good luck. A roast suckling pig or roast lamb is often the main dish, accompanied by pastas and fruits. The traditional Italian wedding cake is made from biscuits.

- Korea: Noodles are served because they represent longevity.

- Norway: The traditional wedding cake is made from bread topped with cream, cheese, and syrup.

- Britain: It is said that the honeymoon originated at a time when the father of the bride gave the groom a moon's (month's) worth of mead (a wine made from honey) before the bride and groom left after the ceremony.

FIGURE 3-7 When you think of a wedding, do you imagine something like this? Every culture celebrates a wedding in different ways. Which foods are served when your culture celebrates a wedding?

Genève McNally, Wedding and Event Planner

Genève has acquired many skills on her journey to becoming a well-known wedding planner. She held a variety of jobs in the restaurant and hotel business before and while attending Vancouver Community College, where she received her Hospitality Diploma in 1999. She went on to become the catering coordinator at Brock House Restaurant, a popular wedding venue. After six years of experience, clients and staff encouraged her to start her own wedding planning company. With the help of her colleague and new business partner, Sarah Shore, DreamGroup Productions Inc. became a reality.

DreamGroup Productions began its career with 15 weddings the first year in business, and 27 in the second year. Since then, the partners have organized many fabulous occasions, approximately 40 events each year. While most of these events are weddings, DreamGroup also creates corporate parties, birthday parties, and a wide variety of theme parties for all occasions.

To be a successful event planner requires a number of skills. Event planners must be patient, well organized, energetic, and able to attend to all details, no matter how small. Genève explains that these qualities are very important to making each special event perfect. Couples who choose wedding planners recognize that the expertise and connections that a wedding planner has will help to make their day as special as possible.

Genève describes her work environment as "non-stop hectic." Talking on the phone or e-mailing vendors, clients, and potential clients takes about 60 percent of her time, while meetings with clients and travelling take another 30 percent. The final 10 percent is the part everyone sees—the event itself. Wedding planners work with couples through a long series of tasks—deciding on a budget, location, and menus; setting up schedules and appointments; communicating with many different vendors; and coordinating musicians and decorators.

When planning wedding meals, Genève prefers to work with caterers whom she knows and has worked with in the past so that she can confidently include foods that the couple, and their culture, enjoy. If something especially exotic is required, she is happy to work with caterers of her clients' choosing.

The most interesting and elegant wedding meal that Genève had the pleasure of organizing was for a reception attended by 180 people on Granville Island. Each course of the meal was presented "cocktail style" and servers delivered each course to the mingling guests as they talked and celebrated, surrounded by white orchids and candlelight. Seafood chowder, curried prawns, boeuf bourguignon, sushi, oysters, and chocolate fondue were just a few of the delicacies offered to the crowd.

"Event planners must be patient, well organized, energetic, and able to attend to all details, no matter how small."

Birthdays

Birthdays are usually special occasions. In many families, special foods are associated with a birthday dinner. Birthday parties began in medieval Europe. People believed that by coming together to celebrate a birthday, they would ward off the evil spirits that people were supposed to be susceptible to on their birthdays. In many countries, traditional foods are served on birthdays. For example,

- Australia: Birthdays are often celebrated by sharing a decorated birthday cake with lit candles, which the person celebrating the birthday blows out while making a wish.
- England: A cake may be baked containing symbolic objects that foretell the future. If your piece of cake has a coin in it, for example, it is believed you will be wealthy one day.
- Ghana: A child's birthday breakfast is a fried patty made from mashed sweet potato and eggs. Traditional birthday party fare includes a dish made from fried plantain (a kind of banana).
- Korea: For a first birthday, the child is dressed and seated in front of a range of objects including fruit, rice, calligraphy brushes, and money. Whichever item the child picks up predicts his or her future; for example, picking up rice indicates material wealth. After this ceremony, the guests eat rice cakes.
- Western Russia: The birthday boy or girl is given a fruit pie instead of a cake.
- Mexico: A papier-mâché container (called a *piñata*) in the shape of an animal is filled with lollipops and other treats. The blindfolded child hits the *piñata* with a stick until it breaks open. Everyone shares the treats.

FIGURE 3-8 The *piñata* is a Mexican birthday tradition. Have you ever seen one at a Canadian birthday party?

ETIQUETTE

According to the *Gage Canadian Dictionary*, **etiquette** is the "conventional rules for conduct or behaviour in polite society." In general, etiquette refers to the manners that people are expected to use in social situations. It is a way for societies to ensure order and respect during social occasions. Good etiquette at meals shows respect for the people who are providing the food and for the other guests present. In this chapter, we will look at etiquette and manners related to meals and the consumption of food at home, in the food and nutrition classroom, as a guest in someone's home, and in situations involving various cultures.

In the Food and Nutrition Classroom

When you are eating in the food and nutrition classroom, your teacher will probably ask you to set a formal table and use proper table manners. These will be the general rules of etiquette in Canadian culture. Below is an outline of the etiquette that would be expected of you.

- Place the napkin on your lap.
- Wait until everyone is served before you begin eating.
- Pick up only serving dishes that are within reach, so you do not have to stretch in front of someone else. If you cannot reach a serving dish, ask someone to pass it to you.
- Do not talk with your mouth full.
- If you are having trouble getting food onto your fork, use your knife or a piece of bread to push it on.
- Cut food into bite-size pieces before eating.
- Do not use your own eating utensils to serve yourself or others.
- Sit up straight.
- Do not put your elbows on the table.
- If you cough or sneeze, cover your mouth and nose, and turn to one side. If you cannot stop, leave the table.
- Do not apply makeup or fix your hair at the table.
- Remove your hat while eating.
- It is impolite to bring any electronic devices, such as mobile phones, laptops, or music players, to the table. If you are carrying a cellphone, turn it off.

FIGURE 3-9 Your teacher may require you to follow basic Canadian etiquette while eating in the food and nutrition classroom. Is this the same etiquette that you use at home? In the school cafeteria? At a fast-food restaurant? Are there cultural differences between these basic rules and your family's etiquette?

At Home

The etiquette practised in Canadian homes at mealtimes varies and is influenced by many factors. When families sit down to a special meal, they often follow more formal etiquette. Some families have what they call "company" etiquette as well as everyday etiquette. This means that parents may be stricter about manners when guests are present than at a family meal. Sometimes family meals are not served at the table and some of the basic etiquette rules do not apply. For example, if people serve themselves at the stove, then they do not need to worry about passing serving dishes around the table.

Basic etiquette is also influenced by culture. Different cultures have different rules for what should and should not occur at mealtimes. They also have different rules for how to show appreciation to the host.

When Visiting a Friend

Web connection

To learn more about etiquette, go to this Web site and follow the links.

www.mhrfoodforlife.ca

When eating at a friend's house, try to pay attention to the etiquette of your host. This could mean following the lead of your friend or his or her parents or guardians. In general, you should use your company manners to start with and then see what etiquette is observed by your host. If your cultural background and your friend's background are different, then you may want to ask for some pointers ahead of time. Good manners show respect for your host, and you would not want to insult your friend or his or her family.

Cultural Variations

Etiquette develops throughout the history of a culture. For example, before societies became more civilized, mealtimes could be very dangerous, as many diners carried knives. Some etiquette arose to protect diners from each other. In earlier European cultures, knives were kept on the table. When diners were finished, they lay their knives on the plate to show that they were done. Keeping knives visible allowed for the safety of the other diners. In Japan, food was cut into small pieces before cooking and diners used chopsticks to eat. This kept knives away from the table all together.

In Western cultures, meals usually take place around a table and each person has his or her own place. Moving into someone else's place at the table is considered bad manners. Each person's place is defined by the table setting. Serving dishes are passed around the table and each person puts a share on his or her plate. It would be inappropriate for everyone to reach into the centre of the table and help themselves to the food. Other cultures have a common serving area in the centre of the dining place. In some Asian cultures, for example, foods are cooked in the centre of the dining area and dished out to the people sitting around it.

Below are some examples of etiquette around the world.

- In China, cleaning your plate is considered rude. The hosts might think that they did not provide you with enough food.
- In Austria, when making a toast, look into the other person's eyes to acknowledge his or her presence.
- In France, asking for a condiment such as ketchup is considered an insult to the chef.
- In India and Sri Lanka, food is eaten with the fingers and only with the right hand. It is not polite to eat with the left hand.
- Inuit and South Sea Islanders burp to show appreciation after a good meal.
- In Poland, superstition says that flipping over a fish on the plate will cause a fisher's boat to capsize.
- In a Spanish *tapas* bar, it is impolite to put toothpicks, olive pits, napkins, or other garbage back on the bar; use the floor, since someone will sweep up regularly.
- In Japan, slurping your noodles loudly shows appreciation for a good meal.

Etiquette is different in every culture, so remember, it is better to ask and be polite than not to ask and be considered rude.

FIGURE 3-10 Do you know how to behave politely in different cultures? How does this culture's etiquette differ from yours?

Connecting to the Community

In each Connecting to the Community activity you will find out more about your local community by completing one of two assignments. This section forms one part of your Connecting to the Community for Unit 1. For the activity, choose and create one of the following products.

Chapter 3 Choices

1. For this chapter, consider the various cultures in your school and community. Choose one and research a special occasion that this culture celebrates with special foods. For that special occasion, find

   - The name and origin of the celebration
   - The typical menu
   - The special significance of three different foods or dishes served

   Using pictures and words, summarize the occasion you have chosen.

OR

2. In this chapter we discussed etiquette and how it can vary in different situations. Describe the dining etiquette that is suitable

   - During lunch at school
   - In your home
   - In a fast-food restaurant
   - At a friend's house
   - For a special occasion

Chapter 3 Summary

In this chapter you learned about some of the symbolic ways in which people use food.

You saw that

- Food can be used to show status or emotion.
- Food symbols are specific to a culture and can have religious significance.
- A simple food such as bread can have many symbolic meanings.
- Food has an important role in many celebrations.
- The same occasion can have different foods associated with it, depending on where the occasion is being celebrated.
- Etiquette and good manners show respect for your host and the other people around you.
- Many rules of etiquette vary from culture to culture.

Activities

1. Define food symbolism. Make a list of foods that have symbolic meaning in your life. Compare your list with that of a friend. What are the similarities? What are the differences?

2. Define status foods. Make a list of foods that have status in some societies. Explain how two of these foods are status foods.

3. Food often symbolizes people's feelings. For each of the following, give an example of an occasion and a food that could symbolize
   - Affection for a family member
   - Friendship
   - Hospitality
   - Comfort
   - Sympathy

4. In your own words, explain how the etiquette expected of you in the food and nutrition classroom is similar to or different from when you are eating lunch at school.

5. What manners are expected in your home? How similar are they to the basic etiquette described in this chapter? How are they different? To what can you attribute these differences?

Making Healthy Food Choices

UNIFYING CONCEPTS

- To understand the importance of nutrition to your overall health
- To identify and understand the functions and sources of nutrients
- To identify and compare the components of a nutritionally-balanced diet
- To understand and use *Eating Well with Canada's Food Guide*
- To analyze personal eating practices
- To create nutritious meals throughout your life span
- To understand special dietary needs
- To have a healthy body image
- To understand healthy eating patterns

Overview

This unit focuses on making food choices that will contribute to your overall health now and in the future. You will learn about nutrition, nutrients, and how the body digests and uses food. Understanding *Eating Well with Canada's Food Guide* will help you make food choices that will fulfill your nutritional needs. You will also discover how to make wise food choices, which may change at different stages of your life. You will look at special food needs of particular groups as well. The unit ends with a look at body image and healthy lifestyle choices.

Connecting to your community is an important part of being a good citizen. Everyone has a responsibility to each other. Both the Connecting to the Community at the beginning of each unit and the Connecting to the Community activity at the end of each chapter are designed to help you find out more about your own community.

Throughout the text you will be asked to consider your community and how it connects to you. A variety of activities will be presented and you will be offered choices as to how you want to present the information you have learned about your community. Your choices for Connecting to the Community for Unit 2 are:

- Chapter 4: How the Body Uses Food
    - Choice 1: A story that will teach young children about nutrients.
    - Choice 2: An informative presentation for an adult audience that will provide them with basic information about the nutrients the body needs.
- Chapter 5: A Guide to Healthy Food Choices
    - Choice 1: A product to inform adults about *Eating Well with Canada's Food Guide.*
    - Choice 2: A week-long menu that would provide the nutrient needs of a family of four according to *Eating Well with Canada's Food Guide,* as well as healthy activities for the family.
- Chapter 6: Good Nutrition throughout the Life Span
    - Choice 1: Create a "Guide for Healthy Eating" for one age group that represents part of the life span.
    - Choice 2: Investigate an example of a place or service that provides food for different stages of the life span.
- Chapter 7: Living with Special Considerations
    - Choice 1: Develop a script for a health talk show based on information about two of the issues discussed in the chapter.
    - Choice 2: Create an awareness campaign to help people to understand one of the issues discussed in the chapter.
- Chapter 8: Body Image and Lifestyle Choices
    - Choice 1: Find and organize information about agencies and non-profit organizations that offer support for people with eating disorders.
    - Choice 2: Develop an awareness campaign to help people understand the influence the media have on body image.

Putting It All Together

At the end of Unit 2, you will have completed *five pieces of work*—one for each chapter. Follow these steps to complete your product.

- Read over and edit your work from the chapters.
- Ask a peer or a parent/guardian to edit your work as well.
- Write an introduction to your product that pulls all the pieces together. Edit this as well.
- Type or write a good copy, as required.
- Find pictures to enhance your pieces of writing.
- Decide on a title for your product.
- Design how the product will be set up. Draw a rough copy on blank paper before you put the product together.
- Put the product together.

Assessment

The following rubric will be used to assess the work you do on Connecting to the Community for Unit 2.

Criteria	1	2	3	4
Shows knowledge of nutrition and the importance of it to the health of members of the community.	Shows limited knowledge of nutrition and the importance of it to the health of members of the community.	Shows some knowledge of nutrition and the importance of it to the health of members of the community.	Shows considerable knowledge of nutrition and the importance of it to the health of members of the community	Shows a high degree of knowledge of nutrition and the importance of it to the health of members of the community
Conducted research on the different factors related to healthy food and lifestyle choices for members of the community.	Conducted research on the different factors related to healthy food and lifestyle choices for members of the community with limited effectiveness.	Conducted research on the different factors related to healthy food and lifestyle choices for members of the community with some effectiveness.	Conducted research on the different factors related to healthy food and lifestyle choices for members of the community with considerable effectiveness.	Conducted research on the different factors related to healthy food and lifestyle choices for members of the community with a high degree of effectiveness.
Uses critical and creative thinking processes.	Limited use of critical and creative thinking processes.	Some use of critical and creative thinking processes.	Considerable use of critical and creative thinking processes.	Uses critical and creative thinking processes with a high degree of skill.

CHAPTER 4

How the Body Uses Food

I n this chapter you will look at how the human body uses the food that you eat. You will develop an understanding of nutrition and the nutrients that the human body requires.

Sunita is really looking forward to the new unit in her food and nutrition class. The class will be talking about food, nutrition, and nutrients. Sunita hears a lot of things about nutrition and knows that much of what she hears is not true.

Sunita is also concerned because some of her friends listen to everything and often change their eating habits. She is sure that it is not healthy to follow every trend without knowing the facts. She wants to be able to speak knowledgeably about this with her friends so they will stop changing their eating patterns for the wrong reasons. Her parents have always encouraged healthy eating and don't believe in following every fad that comes along.

Some of what Sunita hears sounds crazy, but some of it sounds like it could be true. She knows she needs a better understanding of nutrition and nutrients to be able to make wise choices for herself, and to help her friends make wise choices as well. She wants to be able to tell what a good fat is and what a bad fat is. How can she tell what is true about carbs? Is red meat bad or good for you?

As discussed in Chapter 1, nutrition is the study of how the body uses the nutrients you provide for it. In this chapter you will take a closer look at nutrition and its impact on your health. You will look at different nutrients and the roles they play in providing your body with the balance of nutrients it needs. Too much or too little of a nutrient can have a negative effect on your health.

NUTRIENTS

In the study of nutrition, nutrients have been classified into six major groupings:

- *Carbohydrates*—The main source of energy
- *Fibre*—A carbohydrate that does not provide energy, consisting of non-digestible plant material
- *Proteins*—Used to build, maintain, and repair body tissues. Proteins also provide the body with energy.
- *Fats*—A concentrated energy source that is used to transport other nutrients

- *Vitamins*—Chemical compounds that help regulate the body's processes and help other nutrients do their jobs
- *Minerals*—Elements that help the body function properly. Minerals also become part of the body's tissues (e.g., the mineral calcium helps build bones).

All six groups of key nutrients above play important roles in your overall health. Not having enough of any one group can cause health problems. Water is also essential to life since it makes up most of your body weight.

FIGURE 4-1 The best way to provide your body with essential nutrients is by eating a wide variety of foods. Do you eat a variety of foods?

Dietary Reference Intakes

Dietary Reference Intakes (DRIs) are comprehensive nutrient values that can be used to assess and plan diets for healthy populations. DRIs are based on the current knowledge of nutrition and nutrient needs. Health Canada and other health providers use DRIs to help guide Canadians toward good nutrition and health.

DRIs were used in the development of the 2007 version of *Eating Well with Canada's Food Guide*. They are established by Canadian and American scientists through a review process overseen by the U.S. National Academies, which is an independent, non-governmental body.

The Function of Nutrients

Let's look at each nutrient group in more detail.

Carbohydrates

Carbohydrates are the main source and the most easily digested source of energy. They are often referred to simply as starches and sugars. The main source of carbohydrates is plants. To get enough carbohydrates, you should eat a variety of the following foods:

- Vegetables
- Fruits
- Grain products
- Legumes

All of these provide your body with carbohydrates.

When you do not eat enough carbohydrates, your body will use other stored nutrients as a source of energy. When this happens, your body may be missing the nutritional value of the energy-producing nutrient. For example, if a person cuts carbohydrates out of his or her diet, the body may use protein as a source of energy, denying itself the other function of protein—to build, repair, and maintain cells. It is very important that you consume enough nutrients so that each can do its job.

Carbohydrates come in two categories based on their composition: simple and complex.

Simple Carbohydrates

Simple carbohydrates are also called sugars. These carbohydrates are quickly broken down into a usable form by the body. Sugars are a natural part of foods. Sugars that occur naturally in fruits are called *fructose*. Those that occur naturally in grains are called *maltose*. Those that occur naturally in milk are called *lactose*. Most foods that contain these naturally-occurring sugars also provide the body with other essential nutrients.

Web connection

To learn more about Dietary Reference Intakes go to this Web site and follow the links.
www.mhrfoodforlife.ca

Food for Thought

Many foods are sweetened by a processed mixture of fructose and glucose that is cheaper than sugar. Thirty years ago, it didn't exist, but today the average American consumes 42 pounds (19 kilograms) of this mixture a year. *High fructose corn syrup* is found in cereals, crackers, yoghurt, breads, ice cream, ketchup, and other convenience foods. This sweetener does not trigger a sense of fullness when eaten; instead, it increases the desire for more food.

FIGURE 4-2 Do you eat a lot of empty-calorie foods?

Other sugars, which are called refined sugars, are extracted from plants and used to sweeten foods. These sugars are called *sucrose*. Sucrose comes mainly from sugar cane or sugar beets. Refined sugars are also found in corn syrup, maple syrup, honey, molasses, and brown sugar. Unlike the naturally-occurring sugars, refined sugars do not add any other nutrients to the body. **Calories**, or the energy you get from food, are refined sugars' only food value. Eating foods that are high in refined sugars is referred to as eating **empty calories,** because all you get is the calories without any added nutrients. Consuming large amounts of these foods can lead to weight gain and health issues related to being overweight. Another risk is that you could fill up on foods that do not contain the nutrients your body needs and become undernourished. These high-calorie foods do not provide a steady source of energy; rather, they cause a rapid rise in your energy level that leads to sugar "highs" and "lows."

Complex Carbohydrates

Complex carbohydrates are made up of large molecules of simple carbohydrates joined together. Due to the nature of their composition, they take longer to break down in the body. They are good for your health because they take longer to digest and provide you with a steady blood sugar level. This, in turn, provides you with a steady source of energy. A steady source of energy allows you to perform your daily activities without feeling tired. Complex carbohydrates are broken down into two subcategories: starches and fibre.

Starches

Starches can be found in

- Legumes, such as peas and lentils
- Some vegetables, such as potatoes and corn
- Grains in the form of rice, pasta, and bread products

As with naturally-occurring sugars, starches bring other nutrients with them, providing good food value. Many athletes will consume pasta before a sporting event because it is said to "stick with you." The complex carbohydrates in pasta break down slowly and provide athletes with a steady energy source.

Fibre

Dietary fibre is the only form of carbohydrate that does not provide the body with energy. Fibre consists of non-digestible plant material. Fibre comes from plant sources, such as

- Vegetables
- Fruit
- Grain products
- Legumes

There are two kinds of dietary fibre, soluble and insoluble. Most sources of fibre contain both.

A high-fibre diet can ward off many digestive ills, including chronic constipation, irritable bowel syndrome, and colon cancer.

Soluble Fibre

Soluble fibre will dissolve in water. This type of fibre increases the thickness of the stomach contents and has been shown to reduce levels of cholesterol in the blood. Soluble fibre is found in vegetables, fruits, legumes, and oat products.

Insoluble Fibre

Insoluble fibre will not dissolve in water. Instead, it absorbs water like a sponge. Since it has this capacity, it becomes bulk in the digestive system. This bulk helps to move food through the large intestine, promoting regular bowel movements. Insoluble fibre has been shown to lower the risk of colon cancer. It is found mainly in fruits, vegetables, and whole grains.

Many people do not consume enough fibre. Finding good sources of fibre for your diet now can lead to improved health later in life. Avoid heavily processed foods, since the fibre is usually lost during processing. Look for whole grains, and eat raw vegetables and fruits.

FIGURE 4-3 Eating whole grains is one way to increase the fibre in your diet. Do you choose whole-grain products when possible?

Proteins

Proteins are the nutrients that help the body grow, maintain, and repair cells and tissues. Proteins are used to make hormones, enzymes, and antibodies. About one-fifth of your body's total weight is made up of proteins. Your skin, muscles, hair, eyes, and bones are all made of protein.

Proteins also play an important role in regulating the body's processes and help fight diseases because they are part of the immune system.

When people do not consume enough carbohydrates and fats, and their fat reserves get used up, the proteins they consume will be used by the body for energy. When this happens, the proteins are not used for building and repairing cells. This is why it is important to have a balanced diet, so that the body does not have to use proteins for energy.

You can find proteins in many foods. Animal sources of proteins include

FIGURE 4-4 People do not need to be bodybuilders to develop healthy muscles. Proteins help build muscle. Do you consume enough protein to maintain healthy muscle development?

- Meat
- Poultry
- Fish
- Seafood
- Eggs
- Milk products

Plant sources of proteins include

- Legumes
- Peanuts and other nuts
- Vegetables
- Grain products

High-protein diets produce rapid weight loss by stimulating the loss of fluids from the body. Some researchers believe that high-protein diets do more harm than good. In some cases, proteins can increase the risk of ill health. For instance, a high-protein diet can worsen the symptoms of liver and kidney disease.

Most Canadians consume enough proteins in their diet. In fact, most people eat too much. When people eat too many proteins, the excess is broken down and stored in their bodies as fat.

Proteins are made of chains of chemical building blocks called **amino acids.** These chemicals are arranged and linked together in many different ways. There are also many different amino acids. Nine have been identified as essential amino acids because they must come from the food that you eat. If you do not eat enough essential amino acids then your body can make them, if necessary.

During the digestive process, proteins are broken down into amino acids, which are then stored in the body. When your body needs to build or repair tissues, it uses as many stored amino acids as it needs.

A person with a protein deficiency does not have enough stored amino acids to do the job.

There are two types of proteins: complete and incomplete. Complete proteins supply all nine essential amino acids. Complete proteins come from meat, poultry, fish, seafood, eggs, milk products, and soy products. Plants, with the exception of soy, supply incomplete proteins—meaning they do not give us all nine essential amino acids. However, if you know how to combine plant proteins effectively, you can get all the essential amino acids that you need. It is very important that you understand proteins if you decide to eat a vegetarian diet that excludes all animal proteins. Vegetarians need to know how to combine foods so that they can maintain a healthy body.

The majority of Canadians get most of their proteins from animal sources, which tend to have a higher fat content than do plants. However, leaner cuts of meat are now available since producers and animal science researchers continue to study breeding and animal nutrition. Since people tend to eat too much fat, health professionals now recommend that Canadians also look to plant sources to meet more of their protein needs.

FIGURE 4-5 Vegetarians must be careful to get enough protein in their diets. Why are they especially at risk for protein deficiencies?

Fats

The body needs some fat to be healthy. Functions of fat include

- Provides heat and energy for the body
- Promotes healthy skin and normal cell growth
- Supports the functioning of the kidneys and eyes
- Carries fat-soluble vitamins A, D, E, and K in the body
- Acts as a cushion around vital organs such as the heart and liver
- Helps form the protective coverings around nerves
- Moves through the digestive system slowly and helps you feel full longer

Eating too much fat is not good for your health. It can increase the risk of illnesses, such as heart disease and cancer. Eating too much fat can also lead to being overweight or obese. Health issues related to obesity include joint problems, increased risk of diabetes, and heart disease.

Eating too much of the wrong types of fat should be avoided, but cutting fat out of your diet completely deprives your body of the benefits

Web connection

To learn more about good eating habits, go to this Web site and follow the links.

www.mhrfoodforlife.ca

of fat. To get the benefit of fat without the health risks, remember to

- Limit your fat intake.
- Eat more complex carbohydrates.
- Choose low-fat foods.
- Know which foods contain high amounts of fat, for example, butter, margarine, oils, cream, sour cream, salad dressing, fried foods, some baked goods, and chocolate.
- Be careful not to eat too many foods that have moderate amounts of fat, such as some cuts of meat, nuts and seeds, nut butters, egg yolks, whole milk, and some cheeses.
- Read the labels on food products to see how much and what type of fat you are getting in one serving.

FIGURE 4-6 Fat has many important functions in your diet. What are the risks of eating too much fat?

Fats come from either animal or plant sources. Fats from animal sources are usually solid at room temperature. Animal sources of fat include milk, cheese, eggs, butter, meat, and fish. Fat from plant sources include the plants themselves as well as products made from plants, such as nut butters, nut oils, and margarine. Plant-source fats are usually liquid at room temperature.

Cholesterol

Cholesterol is not a fat. It is a fat-like substance that is present in all body cells and is needed for many essential body processes. It helps in the digestion of fat and the production of vitamin D. Adults manufacture all the cholesterol they need, so they do not need cholesterol in their diets. Infants and children do not produce enough cholesterol, so they need some cholesterol in their diets.

Cholesterol circulates in the bloodstream in chemical groupings called **lipoproteins.** There are two major kinds of lipoproteins:

- *Low-density lipoproteins (LDL)* take cholesterol from the liver, to wherever it is needed in the body. If there is too much LDL cholesterol in the body, then the excess amounts can build up on the walls of the arteries. This buildup of LDL cholesterol can increase the risk of heart attack or stroke because it reduces blood flow. LDL cholesterol is often called "bad" cholesterol for this reason.
- *High-density lipoproteins (HDL)* pick up excess cholesterol and return it to the liver, where it does not harm the body. HDL cholesterol is often called "good" cholesterol.

Safety Check

Reading Labels for Fat Content

Reading labels to find out the type and percentage of fat in a food is important to your overall health. Understanding fat type and content helps you make wise choices. Nutrition Facts tables in Canada must now list amounts and percentages of fat, saturated fats, and trans fats. Both saturated fats and trans fats increase the risk of heart disease, so look for lower numbers. Remember to look at serving sizes as well and compare them to the actual amount that you would normally eat.

Testing can determine the total amount of cholesterol in your bloodstream, as well as the amounts of LDL and HDL cholesterol. There are increased health risks if total cholesterol and LDL levels are too high and if the HDL level is too low. As people age, they should be careful about their cholesterol levels. Monitoring cholesterol levels often becomes a routine part of medical checkups for older adults.

To reduce the amount of cholesterol you eat, limit your intake of foods that are high in cholesterol. Animals manufacture cholesterol in the same way as people do, so foods from animal sources contain cholesterol. Meat, poultry, fish and other seafood, as well as eggs all contain cholesterol. Following the suggestions in *Eating Well with Canada's Food Guide* for the amounts of Meat and Alternatives to eat will help you maintain healthy levels of cholesterol. For more information on *Eating Well with Canada's Food Guide*, see Chapter 5: A Guide to Healthy Food Choices.

Types of Fat

Fats in food are made up of four types of fatty acids. Two types are unsaturated. These are the "good" fats. The other two types of fats are saturated and trans fat, which are the "bad" fats. The good fats help you maintain a protective level of HDL cholesterol and reduce your level of LDL cholesterol. The bad fats increase the amount of LDL cholesterol in your bloodstream.

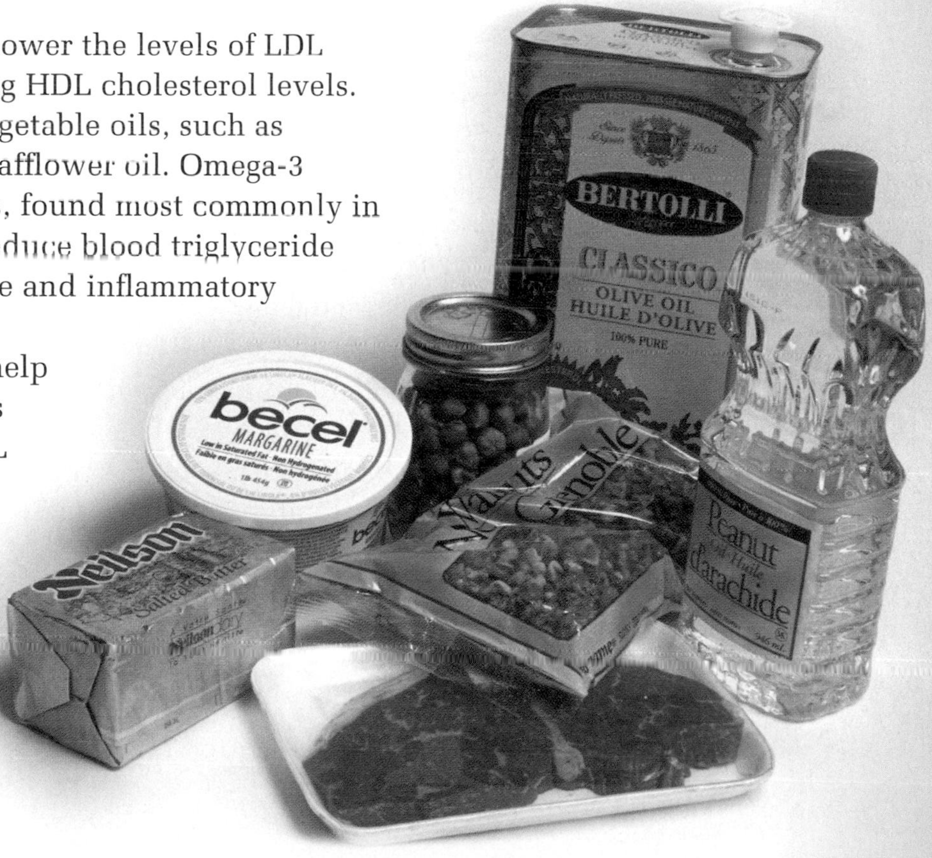

FIGURE 4-7 Some foods that seem healthy may not be. Can you identify which foods in this photograph contain healthy or unhealthy fats?

- *Polyunsaturated fats* help lower the levels of LDL cholesterol while increasing HDL cholesterol levels. They are found in many vegetable oils, such as corn oil, soybean oil, and safflower oil. Omega-3 polyunsaturated fatty acids, found most commonly in fish, have been shown to reduce blood triglyceride levels and improve immune and inflammatory disorders.
- *Monounsaturated fats* also help lower LDL cholesterol levels and raise the amount of HDL cholesterol in the blood. Sources include olive oil, olives, avocados, peanuts, peanut oil, and canola oil.
- *Saturated fats* raise levels of LDL cholesterol in the blood. Foods high in

Web connection

To find out more about making healthy fat choices go to this Web site and follow the links.

www.mhrfoodforlife.ca

saturated fat should be eaten in small amounts. Animal sources of saturated fats include fatty meats and high-fat milk products, such as cheese. These are the main sources of saturated fats in the Canadian diet. There are plant sources of saturated fat as well, such as palm kernel, coconut oils, and manufactured hydrogenated vegetable oils. These are commonly used in processed and packaged foods.

■ *Trans fats* are produced when vegetable oils are partially hydrogenated. Trans fats are the most unhealthy type of fat because they not only increase bad cholesterol (LDL), but also reduce good cholesterol (HDL).

Making Healthy Fat Choices

The following tips will help you make healthy fat choices:

■ *Limit the total amount of fat you eat.*
  – Choose foods with less fat.
  – Use only a small amount of fat in food preparation.
  – Limit spreads, dressings, rich sauces, gravies, high-fat desserts, and snack foods.

■ *Avoid trans fat.*
  – Buy food with zero trans fat or the lowest amount of trans fat per serving.
  – Limit commercially-baked goods, crackers, cookies, snack foods, and deep-fried fast food, which is usually cooked or prepared with trans fats.
  – Read labels for trans fat content.

■ *Reduce saturated fat.*
  – Limit shortening, butter, hard or hydrogenated margarine, and high-fat sauces.
  – Choose lean cuts of meat and limit processed meats.
  – Choose lower-fat milk products.

■ *Choose monounsaturated fat.*
  – Use olive oil, canola oil, or peanut oil when cooking and baking.
  – Choose salad dressings and soft, non-hydrogenated margarines.
  – Snack on small handfuls of nuts.

■ *Increase omega-3 fatty acids.*
  – Eat two fish meals a week.
  – Sprinkle flaxseed, wheat germ, walnuts, or pumpkin seeds on cereal or yoghurt.
  – Choose food fortified with omega-3 fatty acids.

FIGURE 4-8 Omega-3 eggs are produced by hens that are fed a diet of omega-3-rich grains, such as flaxseeds. Omega-3 fatty acids help the body increase HDL cholesterol. What other foods contain omega-3?

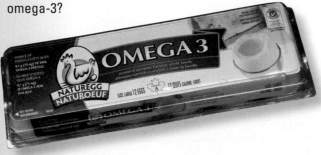

Vitamins

Vitamins help keep your body's tissues healthy and your body's systems working properly. Vitamins assist carbohydrates, fats, and proteins in the work they do in the body. Some vitamins have **antioxidant** properties, which mean that they protect cells and the immune system from harmful chemicals in the air, certain foods, and tobacco smoke. Other vitamins have been shown to help protect the body from heart disease and cancer. Research into the functions of vitamins is ongoing. The more people learn, the better they will be able to improve their health by eating foods that are high in vitamins.

Types of Vitamins

Research has identified 13 different vitamins. Only one vitamin, vitamin D, is produced by the body. The rest are found in the foods you eat. There are two main types of vitamins:

- *Water-soluble vitamins* dissolve in water and will pass easily into the bloodstream in the process of digestion. Water-soluble vitamins include vitamin C and the eight B vitamins. Water-soluble vitamins are not stored by the body and must be consumed on a regular basis.
- *Fat-soluble vitamins* are absorbed and transported by fat in the body. They include vitamins A, D, E, and K. Fat-soluble vitamins are stored by the body in fat, so that when your body needs these vitamins, it draws them from stored fat.

The charts on pages 75–76 list the functions and food sources of these nutrients.

FIGURE 4-9 What important vitamins come from fruits and vegetables? Why is variety important when choosing fruits and vegetables?

Vitamins

Early nutritional scientists and researchers did not understand the importance of eating a well-balanced diet. For many years they believed that people got diseases like scurvy, rickets, pellagra, and beriberi from unknown infections, toxins, or food poisoning. It wasn't until the late 1800s that scientists discovered "deficiency diseases." Research studies proved that it wasn't always what people ate that made them sick; it was what they didn't eat.

In the early part of the 20th century, the pioneers of nutritional research believed that certain foods contained an "accessory food factor" that prevented or cured deficiency diseases. They thought that the accessory food factors belonged to a group of organic nitrogen-containing compounds called "amines." The researchers named their discovery "vitamines." Research later confirmed that the compounds were not amines, so they dropped the final "e," creating the word "vitamins." Vitamins are chemicals found in foods.

It wasn't until the 1930s that chemists were able to separate vitamins from food, creating "natural" supplements. At the same time, large pharmaceutical companies found a way to produce "synthetic vitamins." The boom for large-scale production of consistent and measured doses led to the commercialization of the vitamin pill that is popular today.

Studies about how vitamins work in people's bodies, how they are stored and used, and how and why they prevent diseases continues even today. Canadian medical doctors Wilfred E. Shute and Evan V. Shute proved that vitamins could be used as medicine in cardiology. By introducing megadoses of vitamin E for patients suffering from various heart diseases, they were able to reverse and prevent cardiovascular disease in over 30 000 patients from 1940 to 1970. The Shute brothers were Canadian pioneers in orthomolecular medicine, curing a disease via nutritional therapy.

Researchers later found that vitamins may cause illness when taken in megadoses, producing toxins when the body cannot quickly use up fat-soluble vitamins. Doctors today continue to learn new facts about vitamins and their use in preventing and curing diseases.

FIGURE 4-10 Before the discovery and understanding of vitamins, people suffered from vitamin-deficiency diseases. The girl on the right suffered from rickets, caused by a lack of vitamin D.

Getting Your Vitamins

Vitamins can be found in a wide variety of foods. Some vitamins have a limited number of sources, while others are found in many foods. Follow these simple rules to ensure that you are getting enough vitamins in your diet:

- Eat a variety of vegetables and fruits every day.
- Drink milk fortified with vitamin D.
- Eat whole-grain or enriched-grain products.

Water-Soluble Vitamins

Vitamin/Functions	Food Sources
Thiamin (Vitamin B₁)	
- Helps turn carbohydrates into energy - Needed for muscle coordination and a healthy nervous system	- Enriched and whole-grain breads and cereals - Legumes - Lean pork - Liver
Riboflavin (Vitamin B₂)	
- Helps your body release energy from carbohydrates, fats, and proteins	- Enriched breads and cereals - Milk products - Green leafy vegetables - Eggs - Meat, poultry, fish
Niacin (Vitamin B₃)	
- Helps your body release energy from carbohydrates, fats, and proteins - Needed for a healthy nervous system	- Meat, poultry, fish - Enriched and whole-grain breads and cereals - Legumes
Vitamin B₆	
- Helps your body use carbohydrates and proteins - Needed for a healthy nervous system - Helps your body make non-essential amino acids, which then build body cells	- Poultry, fish, pork - Legumes - Nuts - Whole grains - Some fruits and vegetables - Liver and kidneys
Folate (Folacin, Folic Acid)	
- Works with vitamin B₁₂ to help build red blood cells and form genetic material - Helps prevent birth defects - Helps your body use proteins - May help prevent heart disease	- Green leafy vegetables - Legumes - Fruits - Enriched and whole-grain breads
Vitamin B₁₂	
- Helps your body use carbohydrates, fats, and proteins - Works with folate to help build red blood cells and form genetic material - Needed for a healthy nervous system	- Found naturally in animal products, such as meat, poultry, fish, shellfish, eggs, and milk products - Some fortified foods - Some nutritional yeasts

Water-Soluble Vitamins (continued)

Pantothenic Acid	
■ Helps your body release energy from carbohydrates, fats, and proteins ■ Helps your body produce cholesterol ■ Needed for a healthy nervous system ■ Promotes normal growth and development	■ Meat, poultry, fish ■ Eggs ■ Legumes ■ Whole-grain breads and cereals ■ Milk ■ Some fruits and vegetables
Biotin	
■ Helps your body use carbohydrates	■ Green leafy vegetables ■ Whole-grain breads and cereals ■ Liver ■ Egg yolks
Vitamin C (Ascorbic Acid)	
■ Helps maintain healthy capillaries, bones, skin, and teeth ■ Helps your body heal wounds and resist infections ■ Aids in absorption of iron ■ Helps form collagen, which gives structure to bones, cartilage, muscle, and blood vessels ■ Works as an antioxidant	■ Fruits—orange, grapefruit, tangerine, cantaloupe, guava, kiwi, mango, papaya, strawberries ■ Vegetables—bell peppers, broccoli, cabbage, kale, plantains, potatoes, tomatoes

Fat-Soluble Vitamins

Vitamin/Functions	Food Sources
Vitamin A	
■ Helps protect you from infections ■ Helps form and maintain healthy skin, hair, mucous membranes, bones, and teeth ■ Helps you see normally at night ■ Works as an antioxidant	■ Milk products ■ Liver ■ Egg yolks ■ Foods high in beta carotene
Vitamin D	
■ Helps your body use calcium and phosphorus ■ Helps your body build strong and healthy bones and teeth	■ Fortified milk products ■ Egg yolks ■ Higher fat fish—salmon and mackerel ■ Fortified breakfast cereals and margarine
Vitamin E	
■ Works as an antioxidant	■ Nuts and seeds ■ Green leafy vegetables ■ Wheat germ ■ Vegetable oils
Vitamin K	
■ Necessary for blood to clot normally	■ Green leafy vegetables ■ Vegetables and fruits ■ Milk products ■ Egg yolks ■ Wheat bran and wheat germ

Healthy Living
Vitamin Supplements

Do you take a multivitamin every day? Many people do, for a variety of reasons.

Our bodies require a relatively steady supply of over 50 different nutrients. The best way to get these nutrients is by following *Eating Well with Canada's Food Guide* and by ensuring that you eat a wide variety of foods from all categories. However, some people should discuss taking vitamin supplements with their health-care providers. These people include

- **Vegans (who eat only food from plant sources).** Vegans often have difficulty obtaining vitamin B_{12}, vitamin D, iron, zinc, and calcium because these nutrients are usually found only in animal products. Vegans may need to take a vitamin supplement on a regular basis.

- **Women of child-bearing age.** Folic acid is a supplement recommended by Health Canada for women who may become pregnant. It affects the spine and brain development of a fetus very early in a pregnancy, often before the woman knows she is pregnant.

- **Pregnant women.** Health Canada and *Eating Well with Canada's Food Guide* now recommend that pregnant women take a daily multivitamin containing folic acid and iron.

- **Seniors.** Adults over age 50 should take calcium and vitamin D supplements to maintain strong bones. Health Canada now recommends this supplement in *Eating Well with Canada's Food Guide*.

- **Endurance Athletes.** These athletes may need additional iron in the form of a supplement because of their very high oxygen needs. They should discuss this with their physician.

- **People with food allergies.** Those who suffer from milk allergies may need calcium and vitamin D supplements if they do not get these nutrients from other dietary sources.

- **People with identified deficiencies.** People who are diagnosed with conditions such as anemia will need to take a physician-recommended dose of iron.

FIGURE 4-11 Do people in your house take any of these vitamin supplements? Why? Why not?

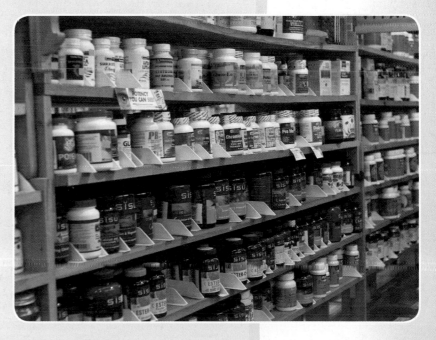

Minerals

Minerals play an important role in your overall health. They are part of your body, like the calcium in your teeth and bones. Other minerals are used to make substances that your body needs for optimal health.

Minerals are divided into three main groups:

- *Major minerals*, which you need in relatively large amounts, such as calcium, phosphorus, and magnesium.
- *Electrolytes*, major minerals that work together to maintain your body's fluid balance, such as potassium, sodium, and chloride.
- *Trace minerals*, which you need in small amounts but that are as important as other nutrients. Examples are iron, copper, zinc, iodine, and selenium.

Getting Your Minerals

Getting enough minerals in your diet will help keep you healthy. Getting too little or too much of certain minerals can cause health problems. Iodine, for example, can cause thyroid problems if you eat too much or too little. Eating a wide variety of foods ensures that your diet is rich in minerals. Two minerals that are especially important for teens are calcium and iron.

Calcium

Calcium helps build strong bones and teeth. If you do not take in enough calcium, your bones will become weak and brittle. Older adults who do not consume enough calcium during their lifetime may develop a disease called **osteoporosis**. Osteoporosis is a condition in which the bones become too porous, making them weak and fragile. People with this condition may break bones very easily and have stooped posture. Women are at greater risk for this disease than men. Building strong and healthy bones during the early years of your life has quality-of-health and quality-of-life benefits in your later years.

FIGURE 4-12 Why is exercise important for healthy bones?

To build healthy bones

- Eat calcium-rich foods, such as milk, legumes, and dark-green leafy vegetables.
- Follow guidelines for healthy eating.
- Play a sport or exercise regularly.
- Avoid tobacco products, alcohol, and excess caffeine.

Iron

Your body needs iron to build hemoglobin, the substance in your red blood cells that carries oxygen to all parts of your body. If you do not get enough iron, your body cannot get enough oxygen to its cells. **Iron deficiency anemia** is the condition that results when a person does not get enough iron. People who have anemia are often tired, weak, short of breath, and pale.

To ensure that your body has enough iron, eat

- Lean red meat
- Legumes
- Dried fruits
- Grain products
- Dark-green leafy vegetables
- Foods rich in vitamin C to help your body absorb iron.

Major Minerals

Mineral/Functions	Food Sources
Calcium	
<ul><li>Helps build bones and maintain bone strength</li><li>Helps prevent osteoporosis</li><li>Helps regulate blood clotting, nerve activity, and other body processes</li><li>Needed for muscle contraction, including the heart</li></ul>	<ul><li>Milk products</li><li>Canned fish with edible bones (e.g., sardines, salmon)</li><li>Legumes</li><li>Dark-green leafy vegetables—broccoli, spinach, and turnip greens</li><li>Tofu made with calcium sulfate</li><li>Calcium-fortified orange juice and soy milk</li></ul>
Phosphorus	
<ul><li>Works with calcium to build strong bones and teeth</li><li>Helps release energy from carbohydrates, fats, and proteins</li><li>Helps build body cells and tissues</li></ul>	<ul><li>Meat, poultry, fish (e.g., salmon)</li><li>Eggs</li><li>Legumes</li><li>Milk products</li><li>Grain products</li></ul>
Magnesium	
<ul><li>Helps build bones and make proteins</li><li>Helps nerves and muscles work normally</li></ul>	<ul><li>Whole-grain products</li><li>Green vegetables</li><li>Legumes</li><li>Nuts and seeds</li></ul>

Trace Minerals

Mineral/Functions	Food Sources
Iron	
■ Helps carry oxygen in the blood ■ Helps cells use oxygen	■ Meat, fish, shellfish ■ Egg yolks ■ Dark-green leafy vegetables ■ Legumes ■ Enriched or whole-grain products ■ Dried fruits
Iodine	
■ Responsible for your body's use of energy	■ Saltwater fish ■ Iodized salt
Copper	
■ Helps iron make red blood cells ■ Helps keep your bones, blood vessels, and nerves healthy ■ Helps your heart work properly	■ Whole-grain products ■ Seafood ■ Organ meats (e.g., liver, kidneys) ■ Legumes ■ Nuts and seeds
Zinc	
■ Helps your body make proteins, heal wounds, and form blood ■ Helps in growth and maintenance of all tissues ■ Helps your body use carbohydrates, fats, and proteins ■ Affects the sense of taste and smell ■ Helps your body use vitamin A	■ Meat, liver, poultry, fish, shellfish ■ Milk products ■ Legumes, peanuts ■ Whole-grain breads and cereals ■ Eggs ■ Miso (fermented soybean paste)
Selenium	
■ Helps your heart work properly ■ Works as an antioxidant	■ Whole-grain breads and cereals ■ Vegetables (amount varies with content in soil) ■ Meat, organ meats, fish, shellfish
Fluoride	
■ Helps strengthen teeth and prevent cavities	■ In many communities, small amounts are added to the water supply to help improve dental health

Electrolytes

Mineral/Functions	Food Sources
Sodium	
■ Helps maintain the fluid balance in your body ■ Helps with muscle and nerve action ■ Helps regulate blood pressure	■ Table salt ■ Processed foods
Chloride	
■ Helps maintain the fluid balance in your body ■ Helps transmit nerve signals	■ Table salt
Potassium	
■ Helps maintain the fluid balance in your body ■ Helps maintain a regular heartbeat ■ Helps with muscle and nerve action ■ Helps maintain normal blood pressure	■ Fruits—bananas and oranges ■ Vegetables ■ Meat, poultry, and fish ■ Legumes ■ Milk products

Phytochemicals

Phytochemicals are disease-fighting nutrients that come from plants. It is estimated that all plants have between 50 and 100 different phytochemicals. Research is showing that phytochemicals may play a role in fighting diseases such as cancer.

Beta carotene is one of the best known phytochemicals. It is the substance that gives fruits and vegetables their yellow, orange, and dark-green colours. The body uses beta carotene to produce vitamin A. Beta carotene is believed to help prevent some forms of cancer.

Web connection

To learn more about nutrition, go to this Web site and follow the links.

www.mhrfoodforlife.ca

FIGURE 4-13 Scientists are discovering that many phytochemicals reduce disease. How can eating carrots protect your health?

Phytochemicals

Phytochemical	Food Source	Potential Health Benefits
Beta carotene	▪ Yellow and orange vegetables and fruits ▪ Dark-green vegetables	▪ May play role in slowing the progression of cancer
Allyl sulfides	▪ Onions, garlic, leeks, chives, shallots	▪ May play role in cancer prevention ▪ May play role in lowering blood pressure and cholesterol
Indoles	▪ Cabbage, broccoli, kale, cauliflower	▪ May play role in cancer prevention
Saponins	▪ Soybeans, legumes ▪ Most vegetables	▪ May prevent cancer cells from multiplying
Lutein	▪ Kale, spinach, collards, mustard greens, romaine lettuce	▪ May protect against blindness
Phytosterol	▪ Soybeans and some soy products ▪ Nuts ▪ Whole-grain products ▪ Many vegetable oils	▪ May play role in cancer prevention ▪ May lower cholesterol

Loreen Wales, Dietitian

"As a teenager I remember thinking that I was invincible. No one could tell me anything I did not already know. … Over the past 10 years I have heard far too many regrets from people about how they chose to live their lives and wish they could do it over again, but unfortunately we only get one chance. Healthy eating and exercise habits are important."

Throughout high school, Loreen enjoyed chemistry, math, and biology but she also knew she wanted to work with people. This led her to an interest in health care and a discussion with a dietitian. Loreen found that dietitians need a strong background in nutrition and food as well as excellent interpersonal skills. They are licensed professionals and play a major role in health care. She decided this was the career path for her.

Loreen attended the University of Alberta. She has a Bachelor of Science degree with a major in Food and Nutrition as well as a Bachelor of Arts degree in Psychology. She also completed an internship at the Royal University Hospital in Saskatoon in 1997. Loreen worked for nine years with people with kidney disease.

Revive Nutrition began in 2006 when Loreen and two colleagues created their vision of a nutrition consulting company. The goal of Revive Nutrition is to empower people to live a well-balanced lifestyle. For part of her day, Loreen is responsible for the many administrative tasks involved in running a business— accounting, coordinating meetings, marketing, and networking. The rest of her time is spent with clients. For this part of the job, she believes compassion and curiosity are the most important qualities to keep her motivated and to best help her clients.

People who go to Revive Nutrition Consulting are there for support, information, and encouragement. They may have been diagnosed with diabetes, heart disease, anemia, or a variety of other illnesses. People come for assistance with lifestyle choices such as vegetarianism or weight management. Women who are pregnant may also ask for assistance and advice.

Loreen and the other dietitians at Revive work with clients to create a lifestyle plan. This plan incorporates the client's health concerns, activity level, desire to change poor habits, and medical information. Once a plan is established, the dietitian works with the client to support and motivate him or her to make long-lasting, healthy lifestyle changes.

Water

Water is essential for human survival. People can live only a few days without it. Your body is between 50 and 60 percent water and your blood is about 80 percent water.

Water is critical to many of the chemical reactions that occur in your body. It also allows your body to regulate its temperature through perspiration. When your body is too hot, it perspires, which cools the body and allows it to get rid of waste products.

Your body uses 2 to 3 litres of water every day. In order to replace this water, you need to drink about 2 litres of water each day. When you exercise, or on hot days when you sweat more than usual, you should drink even more water.

You can get water from other sources, such as

- Milk
- Juice
- Soup
- Fresh vegetables, such as lettuce
- Fresh fruits, such as watermelon

FIGURE 4-14 Why is drinking water good for your health? Has the popularity of drinking bottled water had any effect on your environment?

It is hard to go anywhere these days without seeing someone drinking a bottle of water. People seem to understand that water is essential for a healthy body. However, some questions do arise:

- Is bottled water better than tap water?
- How is the increase in the use of bottles affecting the environment?
- Should water, a life essential, be an expensive commodity?

Better Than Tap Water?

Manufacturers and importers of water are required to meet health and safety standards. These are the same standards that municipalities have to meet with regard to our water supplies. If you are concerned about mineral deposits or other substances that can change the taste of your tap water, you can filter the water before drinking it.

The Environmental Impact

Have you ever thought about where all the bottles go after people have finished drinking the water?

It is quite common to see empty water bottles littering parks and streets. It is estimated that over 80 percent of water bottles are not recycled. Also, recycling water bottles uses energy, which negatively affects the environment.

An Expensive Commodity?

How much did you pay for your last bottle of water? Bottles of water usually cost more than a dollar. When gas prices rose in 2006 to over a dollar a litre and then went over that price, consumers were outraged. Yet people are willing to pay more for a bottle of water half that size. Many social justice groups have grave concerns regarding the selling of water. They want access to good-quality drinking water for everyone, regardless of income.

Activity

1. Based on what you have read about bottled water, write a two-page article for your school newspaper discussing your position on the use of bottled water.

HOW YOUR BODY USES THE FOOD YOU EAT

Digestion

Digestion is the process of breaking down the food that you eat into nutrients that your body can use. Your digestive system begins in your mouth and extends throughout your entire body. As food passes through the digestive system, many things happen.

Mouth

Even before you put food in your mouth, your digestive system begins to work. Looking at or smelling food can stimulate the production of saliva in your mouth. Saliva is a digestive fluid that begins the breakdown of food. Food is also broken down in your mouth as your teeth chew and grind it into tiny pieces. Chewing mixes the food with saliva and makes it easier to swallow and digest.

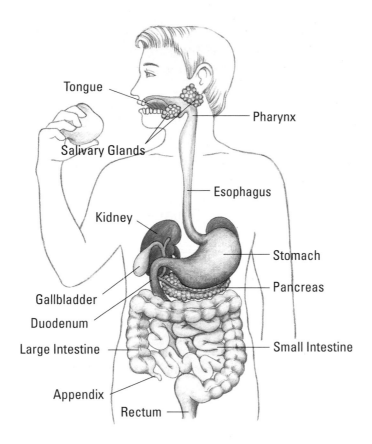

Tongue

Pharynx

Salivary Glands

Esophagus

Kidney

Stomach

Pancreas

Gallbladder

Duodenum

Large Intestine

Small Intestine

Appendix

Rectum

FIGURE 4-15 Did you know that your digestive system starts to work even before you put food in your mouth?

Esophagus

Once you swallow a piece of food, it goes into the esophagus, which is a long tube that connects the mouth to the stomach. A series of wave-like motions is created by the expansion and contraction of the muscles of the esophagus. This process, called **peristalsis**, moves food down to the stomach. Peristalsis goes on throughout the digestive tract, moving food along as it is digested.

Stomach

The stomach, a muscular pouch, is the widest part of the digestive system. It can hold about 1 litre of food at a time. The walls of the stomach make gastric juices, which are a combination of acid and enzymes. These break down the food into nutrients. The stomach churns the food into a thick liquid called chyme.

Have you ever noticed that eating some foods keeps you feeling full longer? That is because different foods take longer to break down than others. Carbohydrates take the shortest amount of time, then protein, and finally fats.

The Small Intestine

The broken-down food, or chyme, is released from the stomach into the small intestine. Looking at the diagram, you can see that the small intestine is the first of two long tubes in the digestive system. It gets its name from its size, since it is the smaller of the two intestines. Three different digestive juices are involved in digesting chyme in the small intestine.

- Bile is a substance that helps the body digest and absorb fats. Bile is produced in the liver and is stored in the gallbladder until needed.
- Pancreatic juice contains enzymes that help break down carbohydrates, proteins, and fats. It is produced in the pancreas.
- Intestinal juice is produced in the small intestine and works with bile and pancreatic juice to break down food.

The final breakdown of food results in

- Carbohydrates being turned back into simple sugar, called glucose, which is the body's basic food supply
- Fats turning into fatty acids
- Proteins turning into amino acids

Vitamins and minerals do not need to be broken down. They can be used by the body in the same form as they exist in food.

Once the food has been broken down into these nutrients, digestion is complete and your body is ready to use them.

The liver produces bile, which is delivered to the gallbladder for storage until it is released to assist in the digestion of fats. The liver produces 0.72 litres of bile every 24 hours!

HOW YOUR BODY USES NUTRIENTS

To use nutrients, the body has to absorb them in order to take them where they will be used or stored for later use.

Absorption of Nutrients

Most absorption takes place in the small intestine. The lining of the small intestine has a series of folds that are lined with billions of tiny finger-like projections called villi. They increase the surface area of the small intestine so that more food can be absorbed.

Processing and Storing of Nutrients

Once the villi absorb the nutrients, they are carried to the liver through the portal vein, a large blood vessel. The liver turns the nutrients into a form that the body can use. Nutrients that are not needed immediately can

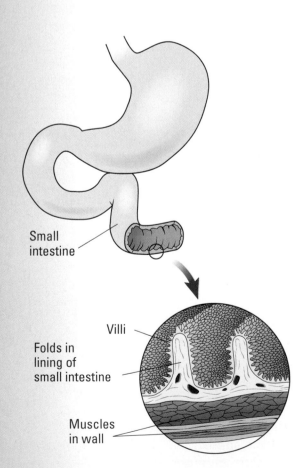

Small intestine

Villi

Folds in lining of small intestine

Muscles in wall

FIGURE 4-16 Your body contains billions of villi that transport nutrients to the bloodstream to be used by your body. What happens to nutrients that are not needed right away?

be stored for later use. Glucose is converted by the liver into glycogen, the form in which glucose is stored. If there is more glucose than can be stored as glycogen, then the glucose is turned into fat. Excess fatty acids and amino acids are also turned into fat. These fats are then deposited throughout the body as an energy reserve.

Minerals are stored in a variety of ways. Iron, for example, is stored in the liver and bone marrow, while calcium is stored in bones and teeth. Fat-soluble vitamins are stored mainly in the liver, although some can be stored in body fat.

Nutrients that cannot be stored for a long period of time are removed from the body with other wastes. Water-soluble vitamins are not stored by the body. If you eat too much of a vitamin source, the body uses what it needs and then the kidneys remove the rest. Have you ever heard of someone who takes megadoses of vitamin C to fight a cold? The body will actually use only what it needs and the excess vitamin C will be removed in the urine. Unusable calcium and excess iron are removed from the body with other wastes through the large intestine in feces. Fibre that cannot be digested helps push other wastes through the large intestine for removal.

Using Nutrients

The bloodstream carries nutrients throughout the body to the individual cells, where they are used for specialized purposes. Glucose is combined with water to give you energy. This process is called oxidation. The result of this combination is the energy and heat needed to power your cells. Your body needs energy for two reasons:

- To maintain its basic functions, such as breathing, digesting food, and creating new cells. Even when you are resting or sleeping, your body is still working. The minimum amount of energy it takes to maintain life processes is called the **basal metabolism**. In general, most people use about two-thirds of the calories they consume for basal metabolism. Your basal metabolic rate, or BMR, is the amount of energy needed to maintain your basal metabolism. This amount depends on different factors, such as age, body size, and body composition (ratio of lean to fat tissue).
- Physical activity is the other reason your body needs energy. The more active you are, the more energy you need.

Amino acids are carried in the bloodstream; they are the building blocks of the body. When your body needs to build or repair tissue, amino acids are called into action. Vitamins, also carried in the bloodstream, play an important role in conjunction with enzymes. Together, they support the metabolic activities that occur to keep your body healthy and renewed by building and repairing cells.

Connecting to the Community

In each Connecting to the Community activity you will look to your local community to complete one of two assignments.

This section will form one part of your Connecting to the Community for Unit 2. The activity will involve creating a choice of products, including

Chapter 4 Choices

1. In this chapter you learned about the main nutrients and what they do for the body. Write a story for young children that can be read aloud to teach them about nutrients. Make sure that you include the following information in your story

- The main nutrients—carbohydrates, fibre, proteins, fats, vitamins, minerals, and water
- The function of each nutrient
- Good sources of each nutrient

Make sure that your story includes graphics and a simple storyline for schoolchildren from preschool to Grade 3.

OR

2. Create an informative presentation for an adult audience that would provide them with basic information about the nutrients the body needs. Make sure your presentation includes

- The main nutrients—carbohydrates, fibre, proteins, fats, vitamins, minerals, and water
- The function of each nutrient
- Good sources of each nutrient

Chapter 4 Summary

In this chapter you learned about nutrition and how the human body uses nutrients to function and maintain health. This included

- The nutrients the body needs to function—carbohydrates, fibre, proteins, fats, vitamins, minerals—and water.
- The function of nutrients and good food sources for them.
- The digestive process and how the body uses food.

Activities

1. You were introduced to many new terms in this chapter. Use the words from the Key Terms list at the beginning of the chapter and create a Word Search puzzle with definitions to use as a study guide.

2. Name the main nutrients and their functions. List one source for each nutrient.

3. What are DRIs? What are two uses for them?

4. What is the difference between a complete and an incomplete protein? Give an example of each.

5. What happens to excess fat-soluble vitamins? What happens to excess water-soluble vitamins? Give three examples of each type of vitamin.

6. Water is often overlooked as a nutrient. Explain why it is essential to people's overall health.

7. Define phytochemicals and the role they play in the body.

8. Two diseases, osteoporosis and iron deficiency anemia, are caused by insufficient amounts of necessary nutrients. These are called deficiency diseases. Research another deficiency disease. Create an awareness poster that includes the following:
   - Name and definition of the disease
   - Symptoms of the disease
   - Food sources of the missing nutrient

9. Plan a snack for you and your friends to eat after school that will provide you with a variety of nutrients. Find a recipe and try the snack at home. Write a one-page report on your activity.

10. Choose one of the nutrients studied in this chapter. Do further research on the nutrient. Create an ad for the nutrient that will sell its benefits to consumers. Be sure to consider
    - Functions and benefits
    - What happens if you have too little or too much of it
    - Sources of the nutrient

A Guide to Healthy Food Choices

I n this chapter you will learn about *Eating Well with Canada's Food Guide* and how you can use it to help you make healthy food choices.

When Kaya met Alex for lunch, Alex told her that they are learning about Eating Well with Canada's Food Guide *in the food and nutrition class. Kaya shares the story of her cousin Ben. While he was growing up he "ate like a kid." He enjoyed fast food and after-school snacks like chips and soft drinks. When Ben reached Grade 11, he was 198 cm (6 ft. 5 in.) tall and overweight.*

During the summer between grades 11 and 12, Ben watched his uncle Scott and his friends compete in a triathlon. Ben was inspired by his uncle's friend Joe, who finished the race even though he was suffering from throat cancer. That August, Ben changed his eating and exercise habits. He began to follow Eating Well with Canada's Food Guide *to improve his eating habits and overall health. He wanted to participate in a triathlon to raise funds for cancer research to help his uncle's friend.*

Key Concepts

- How *Eating Well with Canada's Food Guide* was developed
- Recommended servings
- Key nutrients and the four food groups
- Fats and oils
- Variety
- Beverages and water
- Different ages and stages of development
- Physical activity
- Sample menus
- *Eating Well with Canada's Food Guide: First Nations, Inuit, and Métis*
- Developing your own food guide

Key Terms

bran
endosperm
food guide
germ
nutrient dense

By the time the triathlon came, Ben had lost over 32 kg (70 lbs.). He convinced two of his friends to enter with him, and together they finished the race and raised funds to support cancer research. Joe's team of 233 athletes raised over $455 000. Kaya is very proud of Ben and shares the story of his success every chance she gets.

WHAT IS A FOOD GUIDE?

Have you ever used one of these?

- A road map
- A travel guide
- Game instructions
- A tour guide

All provide you with directions about how to do something. A road map shows you how to get somewhere. When you look at the map, there may be a number of routes you can take. Someone might suggest a specific route, but it is not the only route you have to choose from. When you look up the word *guide* in the *Gage Canadian Dictionary*, you will find the definition "a person who or thing that shows the way, leads, conducts, or directs."

Eating Well with Canada's Food Guide is a guide to help Canadians make food choices that will lead them to healthier lives. Like the routes on a road map, it is not the only way to make healthy choices. In fact, many **food guides** have been developed. Other countries have their own food guides. For example, the United States produced the *Food Pyramid*, which varies slightly from the food rainbow concept used in *Eating Well with Canada's Food Guide*.

FIGURE 5-1 Have you ever looked at a road map and noticed that sometimes there are several ways to get to the same place? How do you decide which route to choose?

The History of Canada's Food Guides

Canada's food guides began as a simple list of food rules in 1942. It was designed to help Canadians provide their families with nutritious and healthy meals while living on rations during World War II. Prevention of disease through proper nutrition was the goal. Throughout its history, the appearance and message of Canada's food guides have changed, but the basic goal of promoting the health of Canadians through good food choices has not.

FIGURE 5-2–5-4
How have these food guides changed over the years? Has the purpose changed?

How and Why Food Guides Are Developed

Food guides are basic education tools designed to help people follow a healthy diet. Food guides are not designed to be followed precisely but to help people learn how to make healthy food choices.

In the design of *Eating Well with Canada's Food Guide*, Health Canada used

- Sophisticated dietary analysis
- National nutrition goals
- Data from food-consumption surveys
- Current information about food supply and production in Canada
- The science of nutrient requirements to create a practical pattern of food choices
- Variety and flexibility in the choices given
- A wide variety of stakeholders to ensure that the guide meets the needs of the diverse population of Canada

An Eating Pattern

Eating Well with Canada's Food Guide is set up as an eating pattern. It tells you the types and amounts of food that you need to eat each day. It divides food into four categories that are based on nutrient groups. Following the eating pattern helps people to

- Get enough vitamins, minerals, and other important nutrients
- Reduce the risk of obesity, Type 2 diabetes, heart disease, certain types of cancer, and osteoporosis
- Achieve overall health and vitality

When developing the eating pattern, Health Canada considered the following scientific evidence:

- Nutrient needs and the eating patterns that fulfilled them
- Evidence that certain foods reduced the risk of chronic diseases
- Meeting nutrient standards and Dietary Reference Intakes (DRIs) for good health and prevention of chronic diseases, while avoiding too much of any one nutrient

Web connection

To learn more about *Eating Well with Canada's Food Guide*, go to this Web site and follow the links.

www.mhrfoodforlife.ca

EATING WELL WITH CANADA'S FOOD GUIDE

The rainbow concept was designed to show foods that Canadians typically eat in each food group. Not all Canadians will eat all the foods listed, and you may not know what some of the foods are. Each arc of the rainbow represents one of the four food groups. The length of each coloured arc symbolizes the proportion of foods from that group that you should eat. In order, from longest to shortest, these are:

- Vegetables and Fruit
- Grain Products
- Milk and Alternatives
- Meat and Alternatives

Why Four Food Groups?

Canada's food guides have been divided into food groups since the very beginning. The number and name of the groups has changed as scientists have learned more about nutrition. The four food groups represented in the 2007 version represent foods that most Canadians recognize. These are grouped by

- How people traditionally use the foods (e.g., legumes, beans and lentils are traditionally used as a meat substitute)
- How the foods have traditionally been classified
- The agricultural base from which they originate

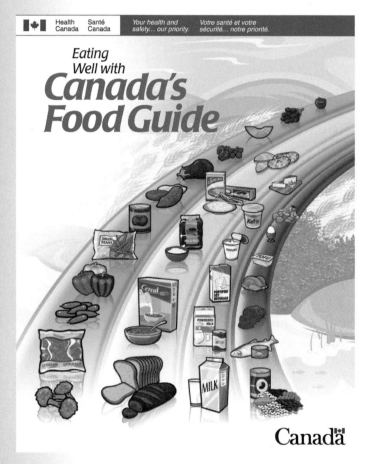

FIGURE 5-5 Look at *Eating Well with Canada's Food Guide* and consider the following questions:

- Which group has the most examples? Why?
- Which group has the fewest examples? Why?
- In each group, do you see foods that you normally eat?
- In each group, are there foods that you do not recognize?

The table below shows how each of the four food groups contributes a certain combination of nutrients to a healthy eating pattern.

Some Important Nutrients in the Food Groups

Key Nutrient	Vegetables and Fruit	Grain Products	Milk and Alternatives	Meat and Alternatives	Vegetables and Fruit, Grain Products, Milk and Alternatives, Meat and Alternatives
Protein			✓	✓	✓
Fat			✓	✓	✓
Carbohydrate	✓	✓	✓		✓
Fibre	✓	✓			✓
Thiamin		✓			✓
Riboflavin		✓	✓	✓	✓
Niacin		✓		✓	✓
Folate	✓	✓		✓	✓
Vitamin B_6	✓			✓	✓
Vitamin B_{12}			✓	✓	✓
Vitamin C	✓				✓
Vitamin A	✓		✓		✓
Vitamin D			✓		✓
Calcium			✓		✓
Iron		✓			✓
Zinc		✓	✓	✓	✓
Magnesium	✓	✓	✓	✓	✓
Potassium	✓	✓	✓	✓	✓

As you can see from the chart above, each food group provides you with a different set of nutrients. When all food groups are combined, as in the last column, you get all your essential nutrients. That is why eating a variety of foods from all food groups is important. You need to make sure that your choices within the food groups are good choices. Some foods are more **nutrient dense** than others. Nutrient-dense foods have a high nutrient content and a lower energy content (calories). In general, the extra calories come from sugars and fats. By eating nutrient-dense foods, you get essential nutrients without added calories.

Examples of Nutrient-Dense and Less Nutrient-Dense Foods

Food Group	Nutrient Dense	Less Nutrient Dense
Vegetables and Fruit	Sweet potato	French fries
Grain Products	Whole-grain bread	Muffin
Milk and Alternatives	1% white milk	2% chocolate milk
Meat	Lean grilled fish	Battered and deep-fried fish sticks

Eating Well with Canada's Food Guide makes some general suggestions for people to follow to attain optimum health:

- Eat the recommended amount and type of food each day.
- Eat at least one dark-green and one orange vegetable each day.
- Choose vegetables and fruit prepared with little or no added fat, sugar, or salt.
- Have vegetables and fruit more often than juice.
- Make at least half your grain products whole grain each day.
- Choose grain products that are lower in fat, sugar, and salt.
- Drink skim, 1%, or 2% milk each day.
- Select lower-fat milk alternatives.
- Have meat alternatives such as beans, lentils, and tofu often.
- Eat at least two servings of fish each week.
- Select lean meat and alternatives prepared with little or no added fat or salt.
- Include a small amount of unsaturated fat each day.
- Satisfy your thirst with water.
- Limit foods and beverages high in calories, fat, sugar, and salt.
- Be active every day.

Recommended Servings by Food Group

In the following chart, notice that the number of servings is determined by

- Food group
- Age
- Gender

Scientific research shows that people's nutrient needs change as they age. Young children need a smaller amount of food than older children and adults. At certain ages in a person's life, gender also influences nutrient needs. The recommended amounts are the average amounts that people should eat. Some people who are at a healthy weight may find they need to consume more choices because they have a higher activity level. These people should consider the balance in the eating pattern established by *Eating Well with Canada's Food Guide*.

Eating Well with Canada's Food Guide's Recommended Number of Servings per Day

	Children			Teens		Adults			
Age in Years	2–3	4–8	9–13	14–18		19–50		51+	
Gender	Girls and Boys			Females	Males	Females	Males	Females	Males
Vegetables and Fruit	4	5	6	7	8	7–8	8–10	7	7
Grain Products	3	4	6	6	7	6–7	8	6	7
Milk and Alternatives	2	2	3–4	3–4	3–4	2	2	3	3
Meat and Alternatives	1	1	1–2	2	3	2	3	2	3

Serving sizes vary by type of food in each food group. These will be examined in detail below.

THE FOUR FOOD GROUPS

All four food groups are important. No one group provides you with all your nutrient needs. You cannot replace one group with another. *Eating Well with Canada's Food Guide* reminds you to eat a variety of foods within each group and from all groups. Let's look at each food group individually.

Vegetables and Fruit

Vegetables and fruit contain important nutrients, such as vitamins, minerals, and fibre. Generally, they are low in fat and calories. When you consume a diet that is rich in vegetables and fruit, you help to reduce the risk of cardiovascular disease and some types of cancer.

Vegetables and fruit provide you with many important nutrients, including

- Carbohydrates
- Vitamins A, C, and some B vitamins, such as folate
- Potassium
- Magnesium

These nutrients work with other nutrients to provide your body with overall health benefits.

You should eat more vegetables and fruit than foods from the other food groups. You can eat them in a variety of forms—fresh, juice, frozen, canned, or dried. Be sure to eat all colours of vegetables and fruits as well—yellow, orange, dark green, and red.

Sometimes the way in which the vegetables and fruit are prepared adds fat or calories. Frying potatoes adds fat and calories, and sprinkling sugar on berries adds calories. Keep in mind how you prepare the foods as well as what the foods contain.

Web connection

To learn more about attaining or maintaining good health through food and nutrition, go to this Web site and follow the links.
www.mhrfoodforlife.ca

Some suggestions for preparing vegetables and fruit include

- Steam or microwave vegetables.
- Toss chopped vegetables with small amounts of olive oil and roast in the oven.
- Serve both vegetables and fruit raw.
- Use fresh herbs, spices, flavoured vinegar, and lemon juice instead of salt.
- Avoid fruits in heavy syrup.
- Choose unsweetened frozen fruit.
- Look for fruit juice content in beverages.

Reading labels is important when purchasing or choosing prepared foods since some products with vegetable or fruit in their name are composed mainly of fat or sugar. Read labels carefully on foods such as

- Fruit candies, such as rolled-fruit snacks and gummies
- Vegetable chips
- Jams or spreads
- Ketchup and other condiments
- Fruit or vegetable drinks, cocktails, "ades," or punches

Make Your Servings Count

To get the best nutrient value from your vegetable and fruit servings, remember these important tips.

✓ TIPS FOR CONSUMERS ...

Choose vegetables and fruit prepared with little or no added fat, sugar, or salt.

You can do it wherever you are—at home, at school, at work, or when eating out!

✓ Steam or microwave vegetables with sliced ginger or garlic.

✓ Toss chopped vegetables with a small amount of olive oil and roast in the oven.

✓ Make a main dish of lots of vegetables with a little bit of oil in a stir-fry or a ratatouille.

✓ Serve a platter of raw green peppers, celery sticks, and broccoli with dips containing low-fat yoghurt or low-fat sour cream.

✓ Use fresh or dried herbs, spices, flavoured vinegars, or lemon juice instead of salt to enhance the flavour of vegetables.

✓ At the cafeteria, pick an apple, orange, or fruit salad rather than a piece of pie or pastry.

✓ Ask for salad dressing on the side and use only a small amount.

✓ Avoid choosing fruit products with "sugar" or "syrup" near the beginning of the ingredient list. These foods usually contain more calories per serving than unsweetened varieties.

✓ Look for lower-sodium canned vegetables.

✓ When eating out, use the pepper shaker instead of the salt shaker.

✓ Substitute healthier options such as a baked potato or salad with dressing on the side for french fries and poutine.

John Bishop, Restaurateur, Chef, and Author

John Bishop has been often described as Vancouver's "Green Giant." Originally from Wales, John discovered his love of food as a child, making omelettes for his siblings instead of doing his homework. He disliked school until he enrolled at the Llandudno Hotel and Catering College. After graduation, John worked in a variety of restaurants in England and Ireland, as well as on the cruise ship *Queen Mary*.

John came to Vancouver, BC, in 1973 and worked in an Irish pub. There he met and married Theresa Krause. They began their life together on a 4.8 hectare

"Fresh local food tastes the best."

(12 acre) farm near Fort Langley, BC. In 1975, John went to work at Il Giardino for famous chef Umberto Menghi. The restaurant, which was a huge success, was featured in over 100 episodes of *The Elegant Appetite* cooking show. These good times didn't last, however. Ten years later, after a disagreement with a staff member, John quit. With the financial help of a good friend, John then established Bishop's Restaurant.

John began his restaurant with a new approach. Instead of importing ingredients and relying on tried and true recipes, he realized that using local produce and game would make Bishop's Restaurant unique. John no longer telephoned international sources for the delivery of food for his restaurant. Instead, he met regularly with Gary and Naty King, local organic farmers from Surrey. They worked with John on an ongoing basis to provide ingredients for his seasonal menus. Soon, all of John's ingredients were from local sources. The ingredients were picked when ripe, and different ingredients were available at different times.

John's methods not only made his restaurant unique and highly successful but also changed the attitude of many restaurateurs in British Columbia. Dozens of chefs who had worked for him moved on to open their own restaurants, using the same principles—that fresh, local food tastes the best. The demand for high-quality local produce has dramatically increased the farming economy of the Okanagan Valley, Vancouver Island, and the Fraser Valley.

Meanwhile, John continues with his own restaurant and has written four cookbooks. His latest, co-authored with chef Dennis Green, contains 100 of John's award-winning recipes. His cookbooks also pay tribute to local, sustainable food and the farmers who grow it.

At home, John collects art and antique silver, especially food-service items. He cooks for his family in their renovated kitchen. His wife Theresa, daughter Gemma, and son David have all spent time at Bishop's Restaurant, helping when needed.

What Is a Serving of Vegetables and Fruit?

Dark-green and Orange Vegetables

 Asparagus
(125 mL, ½ cup, 6 spears)

 Mustard greens
(250 mL, 1 cup raw)

 Beans, green
(125 mL, ½ cup)

Okra
(125 mL, ½ cup)

 Bok choy/Chinese cabbage (Choi sum)
(125 mL, ½ cup cooked)

 Peas
(125 mL, ½ cup)

Broccoli
(125 mL, ½ cup)

Pepper, sweet, green
(125 mL, ½ cup, ½ medium)

Brussels sprouts
(125 mL, ½ cup, 4 sprouts)

Pumpkin
(125 mL, ½ cup)

 Carrots
(125 mL, ½ cup, 1 large)

Seaweed
(125 mL, ½ cup)

Chard
(125 mL, ½ cup raw)

Snow peas
(125 mL, ½ cup)

Dandelion greens
(250 mL, 1 cup raw)

Spinach
(250 mL, 1 cup raw)

 Endive
(250 mL, 1 cup)

 Squash
(125 mL, ½ cup)

Fiddleheads
(125 mL, ½ cup)

 Sweet potato
(125 mL, ½ cup)

Kale/collards
(250 mL, 1 cup raw)

Yam
(125 mL, ½ cup)

 Leeks
(125 mL, ½ cup, ½ leek)

 Zucchini
(125 mL, ½ cup)

 Lettuce, romaine
(250 mL, 1 cup raw)

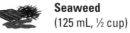 **Mesclun mix**
(250 mL, 1 cup raw)

FIGURE 5-6 Look at these servings. Can you tell how many serving equivalents you had yesterday?

More Vegetables and Fruit

Some orange-coloured fruit can be substituted for an orange vegetable. See the fruit marked with an asterisk (*).

Apple
(1 medium)

Apricot, fresh*
(3 fruits)

Avocado
(½ fruit)

Bamboo shoots
(125 mL, ½ cup)

Banana
(1 medium)

Beans, yellow
(125 mL, ½ cup)

Beets
(125 mL, ½ cup)

Berries
(125 mL, ½ cup)

Bitter melon
(125 mL, ½ cup, ½ pod)

Cabbage
(125 mL, ½ cup)

Canteloupe*
(125 mL, ½ cup)

Cauliflower
(125 mL, ½ cup, 4 flowerets)

Celery
(1 medium stalk)

Chayote
(125 mL, ½ cup)

Cherries
(20)

Corn
(1 ear, 125 mL, ½ cup)

Cucumber
(125 mL, ½ cup)

Dried fruit
(60 mL, ¼ cup)

Eggplant
(125 mL, ½ cup)

Fig, fresh
(2 medium)

Fruit juice
(125 mL, ½ cup)

Grapefruit
(½ fruit)

Grapes
(20)

Guava
(125 mL, ½ cup, 1 fruit)

Honeydew melon
(125 mL, ½ cup)

Kiwi
(1 large fruit)

Kohlrabi
(125 mL, ½ cup)

Lettuce (e.g., iceberg or butterhead)
(250 mL, 1 cup raw)

Lychee
(10)

Mango*
(125 mL, ½ cup, ½ fruit)

Mixed vegetables
(125 mL, ½ cup)

Mushrooms
(125 mL, ½ cup)

Nectarine*
(1 fruit)

Orange
(1 medium)

Papaya*
(½ fruit)

Peach*
(1 medium)

Pear
(1 medium)

Peppers, bell
(125 mL, ½ cup, ½ medium)

Pineapple
(125 mL, ½ cup, 1 slice)

Plantain
(125 mL, ½ cup)

Plum
(1 fruit)

Potato
(125 mL, ½ cup, ½ medium)

Radishes
(125 mL, ½ cup)

Rhubarb
(125 mL, ½ cup)

Tomato
(125 mL, ½ cup)

Tomato sauce
(125 mL, ½ cup)

Turnip
(125 mL, ½ cup)

Vegetable juice
(125 mL, ½ cup)

Watermelon
(125 mL, ½ cup)

Before Reading

1. Read the title of the article. What kind of diets can you name? For example, there are vegetarian or dairy-free diets. Can you think of others?

2. The following article is about Brendan Brazier, a triathlete who eats only fruits, vegetables, and grains. He does not eat any animal products such as meat, dairy products, eggs, or honey. He is a vegan.

During Reading

1. There are two main themes in this article. The first is the life of Brendan Brazier; the second is his book, in which he describes an approach to nutritional health. As you read, think about what Brendan Brazier says about the connection between stress and the foods we eat.

FIGURE 5-7 Brendan Brazier created the Thrive Diet to improve his performance as a triathlete by reducing nutritional stress. In the process, he became a vegan. What may have been the cause of his "nutritional stress"?

Thriving on a Vegan Diet

By Michelle Magnan, Canwest New Services

"Even if you have just one (vegan) meal or one snack a day, the benefits will be felt ... It's certainly not about cutting everything out that you like or want to eat."

Put down the doughnut. Step away from the hamburger. Sure, they're bad for you, but they're also making you tense. It may sound strange, but it's true. Your food is stressing you out.

Brendan Brazier, a Vancouver-based professional Ironman triathlete and author of *The Thrive Diet*, explains in his new book that "stress is anything that causes strain." He says nutritional stress, which is "created by food because of its unhealthy properties," accounts for 40 percent of the average North American total stress load. "That's significant because it has the same effect on the body as any other stress," says Brazier, a long and lean 32-year-old. "The body doesn't know the difference. When you eat foods that are refined, processed, and really hard to digest, that's ultimately more stress and work for your body."

Brazier believes that eating whole, natural, and high-alkaline foods, such as vegetables, fruits, and grains, reduces nutritional stress. He outlines his vegan way of eating in *The Thrive Diet*. "The main premise of the book has to do with reducing stress through better nutrition, because stress is a root cause of so many problems, whether they be mild ones like sleep irritation and gaining weight easily, or bigger ones like depression and digestive problems."

With loads of tasty-looking recipes and a 12-week meal plan, Brazier's book is a veggie lover's dream. But what about us meat-lovers? "It's not all or nothing," he says. "Even if you have just one (vegan) meal or one snack a day, the benefits will be felt ... It's certainly not about cutting everything out that you like or want to eat."

The promises of adhering to the Thrive Diet sound fantastic—better sleep quality, less joint inflammation, improved mental clarity, and stronger bones, to name a few. While reduced body fat is another result, weight loss is not the diet's focus. "[The book is] for optimizing health, and when your health is optimal, then you'll be closer to your ideal body weight," says Brazier.

Optimizing performance was Brazier's ultimate goal when he started experimenting with different diets as an aspiring 15-year-old athlete. In search of the best plan, he experimented with high-carb, low-carb, high-protein, and low-protein diets. Then he tried a plant-based diet. The results were not good. "I felt tired, I was hungry, and I wasn't recovering well at all," he says.

Eventually, Brazier realized he wasn't getting enough essential nutrients, like iron, calcium, and omega-3 fatty acids. He started to blend his own nutrient-rich smoothies, and saw an improvement in how his body recovered from intense physical training. Through years of experimentation and concocting his own foods, he formed what has become The Thrive Diet.

This time, the results have been good. Brazier competed as a professional Ironman for six years, from 1998 to 2004. He perfected his smoothies and homemade energy bars, turning them into an award-nominated product line called Vega that is sold in most health stores across Canada. Last year, he won his second Canadian 50-kilometre Ultra Marathon championship.

While Brazier is an athlete and even provides sports-specific recipes, he says the diet is for anyone looking to get healthy. "If you reduce stress through better nutrition, you can think more clearly and you can get more done," he says. "A lot of white-collar workers are really interested in that aspect of it. Some people may never go 100 percent vegan and that's fine. It's all about progression, not perfection."

> **Language Extension**
>
> *Vegan* and *vegetarian* come from the word *vegetable*, which means "a plant with edible parts." It comes from the root *vegere,* which means "lively."

After Reading

1. Do you think Brendan Brazier is promoting a book about his personal lifestyle and diet to make money, or is he mainly interested in good health?

2. In groups of four, discuss whether a vegan diet is good for everyone. Take a partner to form two teams. One team takes the "yes" position and thinks of as many reasons as possible to support veganism. The other team takes the opposing point of view. List your ideas on a web. Share your discussion with the class.

Grain Products

Grain products are on the second arc of the rainbow. Grain products, particularly whole-grain products, are a good source of fibre and are typically low in fat. Foods that are rich in fibre can help you feel full and satisfied for a long period of time. A diet that is rich in whole grains helps to reduce the risk of cardiovascular disease.

The grain products group provides you with

- Carbohydrates
- B vitamins—thiamin, riboflavin, niacin, and folate
- Iron
- Zinc
- Magnesium
- Fibre

Food for Thought

Most portions of food served in restaurants are at least two times and sometimes as much as eight times greater than standard recommended serving sizes in *Eating Well with Canada's Food Guide.*

These nutrients combine with other nutrients to make you healthy.

There are many choices in the grain products group. They include cereals, pasta, rice, and products made from grain flours.

Remember that a serving is not defined as what you are served but as the suggested size and weight. Often when people eat grain products in a restaurant, they get more than a serving. Think of the last time you had a bowl of pasta in a restaurant. Was it more than a serving?

What Is a Serving of Grain Products?

FIGURE 5-8 Look at these servings. Can you tell how many serving equivalents you had yesterday?

Whole Grain

Bagel, whole grain (½ bagel, 45 g)	**Couscous, whole wheat** (125 mL, ½ cup cooked)	**Popcorn, plain** (500 mL, 2 cups)
Barley (125 mL, ½ cup cooked)	**Crackers, rye** (30 g)	**Quinoa** (125 mL, ½ cup cooked)
Bread, pumpernickel or rye (1 slice, 35 g)	**Crackers, whole wheat** (30 g)	**Rice, brown** (125 mL, ½ cup cooked)
Bread, whole grain (1 slice, 35 g)	**English muffin, whole-grain** (½ muffin, 35 g)	**Rice, wild** (125 mL, ½ cup cooked)
Bulgur (125 mL, ½ cup cooked)	**Muffin, whole-grain** (½ muffin, 35 g)	**Roll, whole wheat** (1 roll, 35 g)
Cereal, cold, whole grain (30 g)	**Pasta/noodles, whole-grain** (125 mL, ½ cup cooked)	**Tortilla, whole wheat** (½ piece, 35 g)
Cereal, hot, whole grain, e.g.,oatmeal (150 g, 175 mL, ¾ cup cooked)	**Pita, whole-grain** (35 g, ½ pita)	**Waffle, whole wheat** (1 small, 35 g)

Berry-Blast Four-Grain Muffins

Ingredients

1 ½ cups (375 mL) whole wheat flour
1 ¼ cups (300 mL) (or 50 mL large-flake oats)
¼ cup (50 mL) cornmeal
¼ cup (50 mL) natural bran
1 tsp (5 mL) each baking powder, baking soda, salt, and cinnamon
⅔ cup (150 mL) brown sugar
2 eggs
1 ½ cups (375 mL) buttermilk
¼ cup (50 mL) vegetable oil
1 tsp (5 mL) vanilla
1 ½ cups (375 mL) fresh or frozen blueberries

Preparation

- Preheat oven to 375°F (190°C).

- Lightly oil or spray 12-cup muffin tin. Measure flour, oats, cornmeal, natural bran, baking powder, baking soda, salt, cinnamon, and brown sugar.

- In a small bowl, whisk eggs with buttermilk, oil, and vanilla. Pour over flour mixture. Stir just until moistened. Add berries and stir until evenly distributed. Do not overmix. Spoon mixture into muffin cups.

- Bake in centre of preheated oven for 20 to 25 minutes, or until golden and tops are firm to the touch. Let cool in pan on rack for 5 minutes. Transfer to rack. Let cool.

Servings: 12

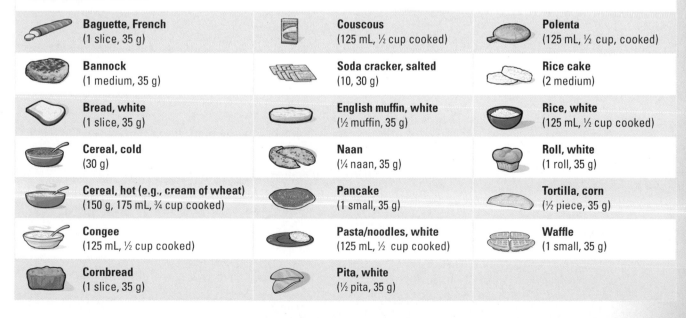

Non-Whole-Grain

	Baguette, French (1 slice, 35 g)		**Couscous** (125 mL, ½ cup cooked)		**Polenta** (125 mL, ½ cup, cooked)
	Bannock (1 medium, 35 g)		**Soda cracker, salted** (10, 30 g)		**Rice cake** (2 medium)
	Bread, white (1 slice, 35 g)		**English muffin, white** (½ muffin, 35 g)		**Rice, white** (125 mL, ½ cup cooked)
	Cereal, cold (30 g)		**Naan** (¼ naan, 35 g)		**Roll, white** (1 roll, 35 g)
	Cereal, hot (e.g., cream of wheat) (150 g, 175 mL, ¾ cup cooked)		**Pancake** (1 small, 35 g)		**Tortilla, corn** (½ piece, 35 g)
	Congee (125 mL, ½ cup cooked)		**Pasta/noodles, white** (125 mL, ½ cup cooked)		**Waffle** (1 small, 35 g)
	Cornbread (1 slice, 35 g)		**Pita, white** (½ pita, 35 g)		

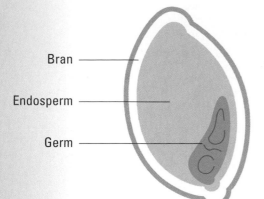

Bran

Endosperm

Germ

FIGURE 5-9 Did you know that each part of the grain gives you different nutrients?

Making Your Servings Count

People need to consider whole grains when they make grain product choices. Whole grains contain all three edible layers of the grain seed or kernel. Each layer provides a unique combination of nutrients.

- **Bran** provides fibre, B vitamins, minerals, phytochemicals, and some protein.
- **Endosperm** consists mainly of carbohydrate and some protein.
- **Germ** contains B vitamins, unsaturated fats, vitamin E, minerals, and phytochemicals.

When whole grains are refined into white flour, the bran and the germ are removed. As you can see in the illustration, that is where the majority of the nutrients come from and these nutrients are lost in the processing. This means that white flour is less nutrient dense than whole wheat flour. Enriched white flour has some of the vitamins and minerals restored, but it is not as nutrient-dense as whole grain.

✔ TIPS FOR CONSUMERS …

Make at least half of your grain products whole-grain each day …

You can do it wherever you are—at home, at school, at work, or when eating out!

✓ Start your day with a bowl of oatmeal, whole-grain cereal, or whole wheat toast.

✓ Try whole grains used in different cultures, such as bulgur, pot barley, quinoa, and wild rice.

✓ Substitute brown rice in recipes that call for white rice, and use whole wheat pasta instead of regular pasta.

✓ Bake with whole wheat flour. In most recipes, you can substitute half of the white flour with whole wheat flour.

✓ Pick a cereal that is made with whole grains or bran, or one that is at least a "high source" of fibre.

✓ Look at the ingredient list rather than the colour of the food when you choose whole-grain foods. Some brown bread, for example, is simply white bread coloured with molasses. The first ingredient should be a whole grain, such as whole-grain wheat.

✓ Order pizza made with a whole wheat or whole-grain crust.

Milk and Alternatives

The Milk and Alternatives group is the third arc of the rainbow. This group provides essential nutrients including

- Calcium
- Vitamin A
- Vitamin D
- Vitamin B$_{12}$
- Riboflavin
- Zinc
- Magnesium
- Potassium
- Protein
- Fat

These nutrients combine to help build strong bones and teeth. They help reduce the risk of osteoporosis. Included in this group are milk, fortified soy beverages, canned milk, powdered milk, cheese, and yoghurt.

Some types of yoghurt contain probiotics, the opposite of antibiotics. Probiotics are live bacteria that promote good health, but they must be eaten every day to be effective, because the bacteria do not stay in our intestines.

What Is a Serving of Milk and Alternatives?

Milk

	Milk, skim, 1%, 2% (250 mL, 1 cup)		**Milk, lactose reduced** (250 mL, 1 cup)
	Milk, chocolate (250 mL, 1 cup)		**Milk, powdered** (25 g, 75 mL, ⅓ cup)
	Milk, evaporated, canned (125 mL, ½ cup undiluted)		**Milk, powdered** (250 mL, 1 cup reconstituted)
	Milk, goat's, enriched (250 mL, 1 cup)		**Milk, whole** (250 mL, 1 cup)

Alternatives

	Kefir (175 g, 175 mL, ¾ cup)		**Buttermilk** (250 mL, 1 cup)
	Paneer (50 g, 1 ½ oz)		**Cheese, block** (e.g., cheddar, mozzarella, Swiss, feta (50 g, 1 ½ oz)
	Pudding/custard (made with milk) (125 mL, ½ cup)		**Cheese, cottage or quark** (250 mL, 1 cup)
	Yoghurt (plain and flavoured) (175 g, 175 mL, ¾ cup)		**Cheese, goat's milk** (50 g, 1 ½ oz)
	Yoghurt drinks (200 mL)		**Fortified soy beverage** (250 mL, 1 cup)

FIGURE 5-10 Look at these servings. Can you tell how many serving equivalents you had yesterday?

Some foods from this group have high fat content. For this reason, you are encouraged to choose lower-fat options. Canada's milk is fortified with vitamin D and some soy beverages that are labelled "fortified" also contain vitamin D. This is because, in Canada, people do not get enough exposure to the sun, and thus often lack naturally occurring vitamin D. It is important that you consume adequate amounts of vitamin D to build and maintain strong, healthy teeth and bones.

Making Your Servings Count

When you eat milk and alternatives, start by following these easy tips from *Eating Well with Canada's Food Guide.*

✓ TIPS FOR CONSUMERS …

Drink skim, 1%, or 2% milk each day…

You can do it wherever you are—at home, at school, at work, or when eating out!

✓ Use low-fat milk when preparing scrambled eggs, hot cereal, casseroles, and soups.

✓ Create smoothies by blending low-fat milk or a fortified soy beverage with a combination of fresh or frozen fruit.

✓ Have a glass of low-fat milk rather than soft drinks or fruit drinks.

✓ Pack milk to drink with your lunch in a reusable container with an ice pack.

✓ Use low-fat evaporated milk instead of cream or coffee whitener in coffee or tea.

✓ Mix chocolate milk with low-fat white milk to get less sugar in a serving.

✓ Drink lactose-reduced milk or fortified soy beverages if you have been diagnosed with lactose intolerance or lactose maldigestion.

✓ Make low-fat milk or fortified soy beverage a permanent item on your grocery list.

✓ Try a latte made with low-fat milk.

✓ Mix fruit and whole-grain cereal with lower-fat yoghurt or kefir for a nutritious breakfast or snack.

✓ Use low-fat evaporated milk instead of cream in soups.

✓ Serve lower-fat vanilla or fruit-flavoured yoghurt.

✓ Round out your lunch by including a cup of low-fat milk or yoghurt.

✓ Try a lower-fat version of your favourite cheese. Replace half the cheese in a recipe with lower-fat cheese.

✓ Use varieties of hard, aged cheese such as old cheddar or parmesan. They can add a lot of flavour to dishes even when used sparingly.

✓ Serve lower-fat plain yoghurt with canned or fresh fruit and a sprinkle of cinnamon.

Meat and Alternatives

The final arc of the rainbow is Meat and Alternatives. This group supplies important nutrients such as

- Iron
- Zinc
- Magnesium
- B vitamins—thiamin, riboflavin, niacin, vitamin B_6, and vitamin B_{12}
- Protein
- Fat

This group includes the following foods: meat, poultry, fish, seafood, eggs, and meat alternatives including legumes (chickpeas, kidney beans, and lentils), nuts and seeds, and tofu.

Too much saturated fat is a concern in the Canadian diet, so Health Canada recommends that you limit your servings of meats and instead use alternatives more often. Saturated fats pose a risk to your health as a cause of cardiovascular disease. Eating fish has been shown to reduce the risk of cardiovascular disease so consuming more fish is also recommended.

Vegetarians also need to eat foods from the Meat and Alternatives group. Their choices will include a wide variety of the alternatives.

FIGURE 5-11 Look at these servings of meat and alternatives. Can you tell how many serving equivalents you had yesterday?

What Is a Serving of Meat and Alternatives?

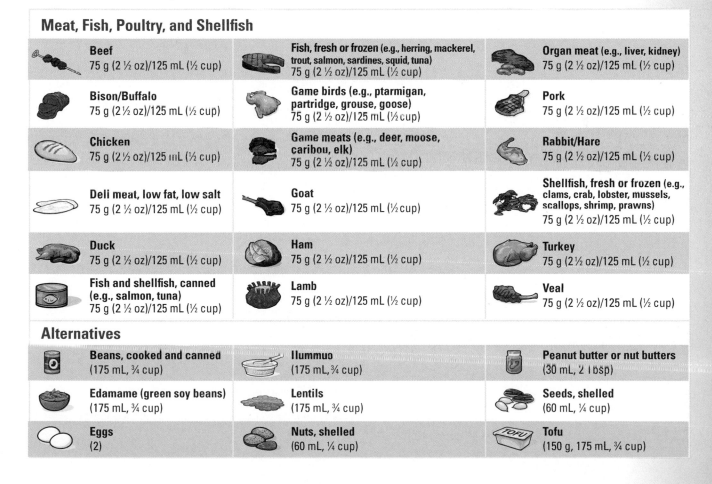

Meat, Fish, Poultry, and Shellfish

Beef 75 g (2 ½ oz)/125 mL (½ cup)	**Fish, fresh or frozen** (e.g., herring, mackerel, trout, salmon, sardines, squid, tuna) 75 g (2 ½ oz)/125 mL (½ cup)	**Organ meat** (e.g., liver, kidney) 75 g (2 ½ oz)/125 mL (½ cup)
Bison/Buffalo 75 g (2 ½ oz)/125 mL (½ cup)	**Game birds** (e.g., ptarmigan, partridge, grouse, goose) 75 g (2 ½ oz)/125 mL (½ cup)	**Pork** 75 g (2 ½ oz)/125 mL (½ cup)
Chicken 75 g (2 ½ oz)/125 mL (½ cup)	**Game meats** (e.g., deer, moose, caribou, elk) 75 g (2 ½ oz)/125 mL (½ cup)	**Rabbit/Hare** 75 g (2 ½ oz)/125 mL (½ cup)
Deli meat, low fat, low salt 75 g (2 ½ oz)/125 mL (½ cup)	**Goat** 75 g (2 ½ oz)/125 mL (½ cup)	**Shellfish, fresh or frozen** (e.g., clams, crab, lobster, mussels, scallops, shrimp, prawns) 75 g (2 ½ oz)/125 mL (½ cup)
Duck 75 g (2 ½ oz)/125 mL (½ cup)	**Ham** 75 g (2 ½ oz)/125 mL (½ cup)	**Turkey** 75 g (2 ½ oz)/125 mL (½ cup)
Fish and shellfish, canned (e.g., salmon, tuna) 75 g (2 ½ oz)/125 mL (½ cup)	**Lamb** 75 g (2 ½ oz)/125 mL (½ cup)	**Veal** 75 g (2 ½ oz)/125 mL (½ cup)

Alternatives

Beans, cooked and canned (175 mL, ¾ cup)	**Hummus** (175 mL, ¾ cup)	**Peanut butter or nut butters** (30 mL, 2 Tbsp)
Edamame (green soy beans) (175 mL, ¾ cup)	**Lentils** (175 mL, ¾ cup)	**Seeds, shelled** (60 mL, ¼ cup)
Eggs (2)	**Nuts, shelled** (60 mL, ¼ cup)	**Tofu** (150 g, 175 mL, ¾ cup)

Making Your Servings Count

Even small amounts of fish contain omega-3 oils and will lower blood pressure and prevent artery plaque, two precursors of artery blockages that cause heart attacks.

✔ TIPS FOR CONSUMERS …

Have meat alternatives such as beans, lentils, and tofu often …

You can do it wherever you are—at home, at school, at work, or when eating out!

✓ Each week, plan a couple of meals using dried or canned beans or lentils.

✓ Add tofu, peas, beans, or lentils to soups, stews, and casseroles.

✓ Top a salad with beans, hard-cooked egg, or nuts or seeds.

✓ For lunch at work or school, try bean salad, lentil and rice pilaf, or a bowl of vegetarian chili or tofu stir-fry.

✓ Make your own trail mix by combining your favourite cereal with a handful of unsalted nuts or sunflower seeds.

✓ Add nuts to your vegetable stir-fry.

✓ Buy different types of beans and lentils. Have you tried navy beans or red lentils?

✓ When eating out, try different soybean-based foods such as tempeh.

Eat at least two servings of fish each week …

✓ Wrap a fish fillet with vegetables and herbs in parchment paper or aluminum foil and bake in the oven.

✓ Pack a tuna or salmon salad sandwich for lunch at school or work.

✓ Buy fresh or frozen fish such as cod, haddock, salmon, or sole that has not been breaded, battered, or deep-fried.

✓ Use leftover fish or canned fish to make mini patties and serve with a low fat dip.

✓ When dining out, order the catch of the day. Choose fish seasoned with herbs and lemon rather than a rich sauce.

Select lean meat and alternatives prepared with little or no added fat or salt …

✓ Tenderize lean cuts of meat by using a marinade or a slow-cooking method such as stewing or braising.

✓ Remove skin from poultry before cooking or buy skinless pieces.

✓ Choose lean cuts of meat such as "round" or "loin." If the cut of meat is not lean, trim off as much visible fat as possible. Drain and discard fat from cooked ground meat.

✓ Use herbs and fresh salsas instead of salt to season and flavour fish, meats, and poultry. Try rosemary with chicken or fresh mango salsa with pork.

✓ Make sandwiches with lower-fat, unprocessed meats such as roast beef, pork, lamb, turkey, or chicken.

✓ Limit higher-sodium deli and luncheon meats such as corned beef, bacon, ham, hot dogs, pepperoni, salami, and smoked meat.

✓ Try lean wild or game meats such as bison, caribou, deer, elk, and moose.

International scientists conducted a study in 10 countries over five years with 500 000 people who ate beef, lamb, pork, veal, and processed meat varieties (ham, bacon). Those who ate red meat twice a day increased their risk of bowel cancer by 35 percent over those who ate one portion a week. (*The Guardian*, June 15, 2005)

OTHER CONSIDERATIONS IN *EATING WELL WITH CANADA'S FOOD GUIDE*

The 2007 food guide, *Eating Well with Canada's Food Guide,* provides Canadians with information on more than just the four food groups. The scientists at Health Canada believed it was important to discuss other dietary considerations.

Oils and Fats

The body needs a certain amount of oil and fat to help it absorb the fat-soluble vitamins A, D, E, and K. Oils and fats provide the body with calories and essential fats. You need to pay attention to the type as well as the total amount of fat you eat. In Chapter 4: How the Body Uses Food, you read about the different types of fat. Try to keep the amount of saturated fat in your diet low. Consuming more unsaturated fats will improve your health.

Health Canada recommends that you include 30-45 mL (2–3 tbsp.) of unsaturated fat each day. This includes oil used for cooking, salad dressings, margarine, and mayonnaise. Health Canada also recommends that your other food choices be low in fat.

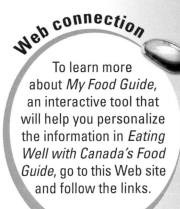

Web connection

To learn more about *My Food Guide*, an interactive tool that will help you personalize the information in *Eating Well with Canada's Food Guide*, go to this Web site and follow the links.

www.mhrfoodforlife.ca

✓ TIPS FOR REDUCING FAT

✓ Use vegetable oils such as canola, olive, and soybean.

✓ Choose soft margarines that are low in saturated and trans fats. Limit butter, hard margarine, lard, and shortening.

✓ Read nutrition labels and look for lower amounts of saturated and trans fats.

✓ Replace or substitute unsaturated fats or oils for saturated fats.

✓ Use only a small amount of oil or low-fat cooking spray to sauté or stir-fry foods.

✓ Avoid deep-fried foods.

Fish Oil

Fishing communities in Canada have used fish oil for centuries. It was used as a fuel in lamps, as a softener for leather, and in animal feed. First Nations peoples have been eating Pacific wild salmon for thousands of years as well as using it in ceremonies and cultural events. In Canada, fish oil is derived from two sources—the livers of white fish such as cod and the flesh of the fatty Pacific salmon.

Fishers rubbed cod liver oil on their aching joints as early as the 1700s. The oil was not absorbed by their skin quickly, though, so they began to drink it to get faster results. In its original form, cod liver oil is very thick, like corn syrup, and has an awful smell and taste. Some fishers would mask the flavour by putting raw fish livers between slices of bread to make it easier to eat. They believed that cod liver oil helped fight a cold when at sea.

By the mid-19th century, the use of steam processing improved the quality, flavour, and colour of cod liver oil. By the early 20th century, scientific research proved that cod liver oil could cure illnesses linked to malnutrition. It was used to treat rheumatic diseases as well as rickets, a deficiency disease caused by a lack of vitamin D.

FIGURE 5-12 People have known about the health benefits of cod liver oil for hundreds of years. Ask your parents and grandparents if they remember being given it when they were children.

Cod liver oil was mass produced to conform to pharmaceutical standards by the 1930s. It became available to the public in the form of capsules in 1936. During World War II, the Canadian Ministry of Food's Welfare Food Scheme distributed the oil free to pregnant and nursing mothers as well as to children up to five years of age.

By the 1970s scientists discovered that Pacific wild salmon contained omega-3, a polyunsaturated, "good" fat. Sockeye salmon has the most omega-3. Eating salmon or taking a salmon-oil supplement benefits the heart significantly. Salmon oil has higher essential fatty-acid content than cod liver oil, but cod liver oil has vitamin D, which is important during the winter months when Canadians are not exposed to as much sunshine. You can ensure that you become a healthy adult by eating salmon or by taking salmon-oil supplements.

Beverages

The first recommendation for beverage consumption is to satisfy your thirst with water. You learned in Chapter 4: How the Body Uses Food that water is essential to life, and that you need to consume enough water to maintain your health. Drinking water satisfies thirst without adding calories to your diet.

Soft drinks, sports drinks, energy drinks, coffee, and tea can add calories to your diet. Many of these drinks also contain caffeine or sodium. Excess caffeine and sodium can cause health problems. Read the label to find the amount of sugar, fat, sodium, or caffeine a drink contains.

✓ TIPS FOR BEVERAGE CONSUMPTION

✓ Drink more water in hot weather.

✓ Increase water consumption when active.

✓ Limit the amount of beverages you consume that are high in calories and low in nutrients. These include fruit-flavoured drinks, soft drinks, sports and energy drinks, and sweetened hot or cold beverages.

✓ Drink low-fat milk and/or water with meals.

FIGURE 5-13 Why has water become such a popular refreshment?

Food for Thought

The Harvard School of Public Health conducted a study in 2000 of 460 high school girls who drank soft drinks on a regular basis. The researchers found that (1) the girls were three times as likely to break arms and legs because the acid in soft drinks promoted loss of calcium resulting in weakened bones, and (2) the soft drinks replaced some milk consumption, so less calcium was available to strengthen bones.

Healthy Living

Soft Drinks

What bottle do you reach for when you are thirsty? A sports drink? A juice? A slushy? An iced coffee or tea? Milk? If you are like many teenagers, you'll grab a soft drink. In fact, according to Agriculture and Agrifood Canada, soft drinks are the most popular beverage, averaging 117 litres (35 gallons) a year per Canadian. In Canada, there are more than 200 flavours and 25 brands of soft drinks to choose from.

Health officials are worried about the increase in soft drink consumption. Soft drinks have serious side effects. For example, the amount of **sugar** consumed in one 355 mL (12 ounce) can of soft drink ranges from 40 to 75 grams (1.4 to 2.6 ounces). According to many health authorities, this is about the amount of total added sugar a person should consume in one day, not in one drink. According to a study reported in *Pediatrics* in March 2006, drinking one soft drink a day could mean a weight gain of as much as nearly 0.5 kilogram (1 pound) a month.

Health officials are also concerned about the type of sweeteners used in soft drinks. Since the early 1980s, manufacturers have used a sweetener called **high fructose corn syrup (HFCS)**. It is very inexpensive, has a long shelf life, is available in large quantities, mixes very easily with water, and tastes much sweeter than traditional cane sugar. However, the body treats HFCS differently than cane sugar. Although small quantities of fructose are easily handled by the body, high fructose corn syrup is believed to increase the risk of developing diabetes. Also, studies have shown that unlike cane sugar, HFCS does not create the chemicals that tell the brain that a person is full.

Nearly all purchased sweetened drinks available use HFCS. Many popular sports drinks have more calories than soft drinks and **extra salt** as well. Energy drinks have HFCS and large amounts of **caffeine**, and a medium-sized iced coffee can have as many as 300 **calories**, 40 grams (1.4 ounces) of which are sugar. Fruit drinks almost always have HFCS as their second ingredient after water, so even if they are made with some real fruit juice, they are not a healthy alternative.

A further concern for health officials is that by drinking soft drinks, teenagers are consuming fewer servings of **milk** and not getting enough calcium. Only one in five teenage girls meets the calcium requirement for her age group according to a University of Saskatchewan study. Reduced calcium intake during adolescence can cause lifelong bone strength problems. Studies show that girls who drink soft drinks instead of milk have a higher rate of bone fractures than those who consume three to four servings of milk per day.

Check out any vending machines in your school to find out what kinds of drinks are in them. Many schools and school boards have banned HFCS-sweetened drinks in their vending machines. What does your school do?

FIGURE 5-14 Many vending machines contain a variety of drinks to choose from, but even drinks that seem healthy may be loaded with sugar and/or salt. What kinds of health risks might these drinks contribute to over time?

ADVICE FOR DIFFERENT AGES AND STAGES

You have already read about how recommended serving sizes take into consideration both age and gender. Health Canada provides further advice for three other groups: children, women of child-bearing age, and men and women over the age of 50.

Children

Following *Eating Well with Canada's Food Guide* helps children grow and thrive by providing their bodies with the optimal nutrition. Remember that young children have smaller appetites, but still need calories to fuel growth and development. To help them get all the foods they need, follow these simple guidelines:

- Serve small, nutritious meals and snacks each day.
- Do not restrict nutritious foods because of their fat content.
- Offer a variety of foods from each of the four food groups.
- Be a good role model by eating nutritious foods yourself.

Women of Child-bearing Age

Women of child-bearing age need to take good care of their bodies and pay attention to their nutrient needs. It is best for both the mother and the developing child if the mother goes into pregnancy following a nutritious eating plan. Most health care professionals will recommend a multivitamin that contains both folic acid and iron. Pregnant and breastfeeding women need more calories and should be careful to include an extra two to three servings from *Eating Well with Canada's Food Guide* each day. Variety in food guide servings should be the goal, in order to provide all essential nutrients.

FIGURE 5-15 Eating healthy snacks yourself encourages young children to do the same.

Men and Women over 50

As people age, their need for vitamin D increases. Health Canada recommends a daily vitamin D supplement to meet this need. Older adults should be sure they are getting enough calcium in their diet to maintain bone health and prevent osteoporosis and fractures. As well, older adults should pay increasing attention to their consumption of fats and salt, since these can cause serious health problems with increased age.

LIVING A HEALTHY, ACTIVE LIFESTYLE

Health Canada recommends that all Canadians live an active lifestyle. Ideally, adults should try to get between 30 and 60 minutes of moderate activity every day. This includes exercises such as walking briskly, running, climbing stairs, and riding a bicycle. Children and youth need to be active at least 90 minutes a day.

FIGURE 5-16 What benefits does staying active throughout your lifetime offer in your later years?

TIPS FOR INCREASING ACTIVITY

✓ Start slowly and build up to a longer period of time.

✓ Take the stairs instead of an escalator or elevator whenever you can.

✓ Go for a brisk walk at lunch or after dinner.

✓ Walk part of the way to school, inline skate, or bicycle if you can.

✓ Play sports, such as soccer, baseball, or pick-up hockey, with friends.

✓ Take up a new sport.

✓ Increasing your physical activity and eating well can benefit you and your family. Encourage your parents and your siblings to join you.

Limiting food and beverages that are high in fat, sugar, or salt is also a good idea. These include

- Cakes and pastries
- Chocolate and candy
- Cookies and granola bars
- Doughnuts and muffins
- French fries
- Potato chips, nacho chips, and other salty snacks
- Fruit-flavoured drinks
- Soft drinks
- Sports and energy drinks
- Sweetened hot or cold drinks

The benefits of eating well and being active include

- Having better overall health
- Feeling and looking better
- Maintaining a healthy body weight
- Having more energy
- Lowering your risk of diseases
- Building stronger muscles and bones

Web connection

To learn more about healthy eating and active living in Western Canada, go to this Web site and follow the links.

www.mhrfoodforlife.ca

MENUS BASED ON *EATING WELL WITH CANADA'S FOOD GUIDE*

You may be wondering how you could create a menu that follows *Eating Well with Canada's Food Guide*. Later in the text, menu planning will be examined in greater detail, but for now, here are some age- and gender-specific menus that show you how to plan a menu that meets the requirements of Canada's food guide.

FIGURE 5-17 Sample One-Day Menu for Olivia, a Three-Year-Old Girl

Recommended Daily Food Guide Servings

	Vegetables and Fruit	Grain Products	Milk and Alternatives	Meat and Alternatives
Girl 2–3 years	4	3	2	1

Number of Food Guide Servings

Menu	Vegetables and Fruit	Grain Products	Milk and Alternatives	Meat and Alternatives	Added Oils and Fats
Breakfast ■ ½ bowl of whole-grain cereal (15 g) ■ 125 mL (½ cup) of 2% milk		½	½		
Snack ■ 60 mL (¼ cup) carrot sticks and broccoli florets with salad dressing ■ Water	½				✓
Lunch ■ ½ salmon sandwich on whole wheat bread (made with 30 g or 1 oz of canned salmon and mayonnaise) ■ 60 mL (¼ cup) red pepper strips and cucumber slices ■ 125 mL (½ cup) milk ■ 1 peach	½ 1	1	½	½	✓
Snack ■ Oat rings cereal (15 g) ■ 125 mL (½ cup) milk		½	½		
Dinner ■ 125 mL (½ cup) spaghetti with tomato and meat sauce (about 40 g or 1 ½ oz of meat) ■ 125 mL (½ cup) milk ■ 125 mL (½ cup) applesauce	½ 1	1	½	½	✓
Snack ■ ½ banana	½				
Total Food Guide Servings for the Day	4	3	2	1	Limited

FIGURE 5-18 Sample One-Day Menu for Malcolm, a 12-Year-Old Boy

Recommended Daily Food Guide Servings

	Vegetables and Fruit	Grain Products	Milk and Alternatives	Meat and Alternatives
Boy 9–13 years	6	6	3–4	1–2

Number of Food Guide Servings

Menu	Vegetables and Fruit	Grain Products	Milk and Alternatives	Meat and Alternatives	Added Oils and Fats
Breakfast ■ 1 small slice of leftover cheese pizza on whole wheat crust ■ 250 mL (1 cup) milk ■ 125 mL (½ cup) orange juice	 1	1 ½	½ 1		
Snack ■ 1 whole-grain granola bar ■ Water		1			
Lunch ■ Roast beef sandwich with 75 g (2 ½ oz) beef and mayonnaise on 2 slices of whole-grain bread ■ 250 mL (1 cup) milk ■ 1 nectarine	 1	 2	 1	1	✓
Snack ■ 125 mL (½ cup) cantaloupe cubes with low-fat fruit yoghurt dip ■ Water	1		½		
Dinner ■ Chicken stir-fry with 75 g (2 ½ oz) chicken and 250 mL (1 cup) broccoli and red peppers cooked in canola oil ■ 175 mL (¾ cup) whole wheat noodles ■ 250 mL (1 cup) milk	 2	 1 ½	 1	1	✓
Snack ■ 125 mL (½ cup) blueberries	1				
Total Food Guide Servings for the Day	6	6	4	2	Limited

FIGURE 5-19 Sample One-Day Menu for Emily, a 16-Year-Old Female

Recommended Daily Food Guide Servings

	Vegetables and Fruit	Grain Products	Milk and Alternatives	Meat and Alternatives
Female 14–18 years	7	6	3–4	2

Number of Food Guide Servings

Menu	Vegetables and Fruit	Grain Products	Milk and Alternatives	Meat and Alternatives	Added Oils and Fats
Breakfast ■ 1 whole wheat tortilla with 15 mL (1 Tbsp) peanut butter or cream cheese ■ 1 banana ■ 250 mL (1 cup) skim milk	 1 	2 	 1	½ 	
Snack ■ 1 apple ■ Water	1				
Lunch ■ Tuna salad sandwich (30 g or 1 oz of tuna and mayonnaise) on 2 slices of rye bread ■ 125 mL (½ cup) orange juice ■ 125 mL (½ cup) baby carrots with dip	 1 1	 2 		½ 	✓ ✓
Dinner ■ 500 mL (2 cups) spinach salad with 125 mL (½ cup) strawberries and kiwi and 60 mL (¼ cup) almonds ■ Salad dressing ■ 1 whole wheat bagel ■ 50 g (1 ½ oz) cheese ■ 250 mL (1 cup) skim milk	2 1 	 2 	 1 1	 1 	 ✓
Total Food Guide Servings for the Day	7	6	3	2	Limited

Do these sample menus appeal to you? What could you change in the menus that would still meet the required number of servings?

EATING WELL WITH CANADA'S FOOD GUIDE: FIRST NATIONS, INUIT, AND MÉTIS

In 2007, Health Canada released its first national food guide that reflects the values, traditions, and food choices of First Nations, Inuit, and Métis peoples. The food guide includes their traditional foods in each of the four food groups. It also includes foods that can be purchased in many of the remote communities in which they live. Affordability of foods in northern and remote communities was also a consideration in the choices of foods that represent the four food groups.

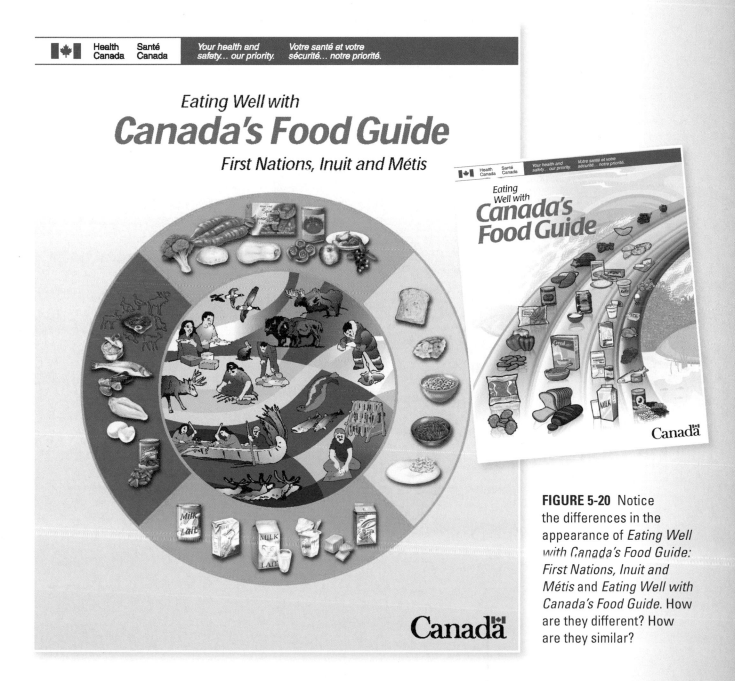

FIGURE 5-20 Notice the differences in the appearance of *Eating Well with Canada's Food Guide: First Nations, Inuit and Métis* and *Eating Well with Canada's Food Guide*. How are they different? How are they similar?

The food guide was developed as a tool to help individuals in First Nations, Inuit, and Métis communities make food choices from traditional foods and foods that are available to them. A guide that reflects the foods that these groups eat will help them to make healthier eating choices.

There are a few differences between *Eating Well with Canada's Food Guide: First Nations, Inuit and Métis* and *Eating Well with Canada's Food Guide*. The First Nations, Inuit, and Métis version is circular in shape, not rainbow-shaped. On the outside of the circle, food choices from each of the four food groups are represented, while on the inside, the ways in which First Nations, Inuit, and Métis peoples access their food are shown.

Recommended Servings and Choices

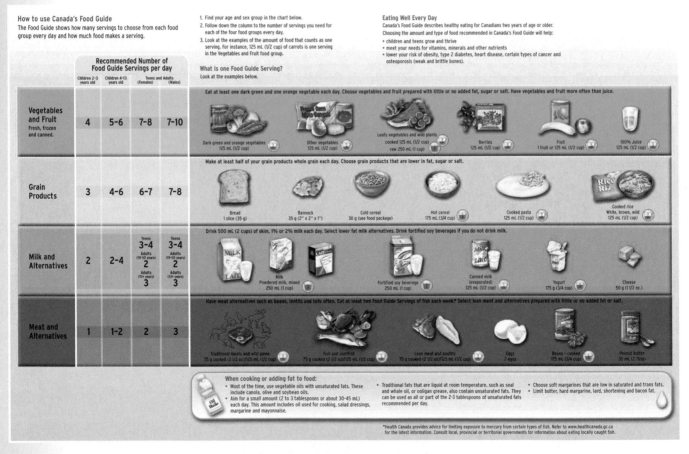

FIGURE 5-21 How do the serving choices and foods represented in this guide compare to those in *Eating Well with Canada's Food Guide*

Eating Well with Canada's Food Guide: First Nations, Inuit, and Métis
has a different approach to choices. Notice that teens and adults are
grouped together. The same colours represent the food groups in this
guide as in *Eating Well with Canada's Food Guide*. Choices also represent traditional First Nations, Inuit, and Métis foods. For example:

- Vegetables and Fruit: Berries and wild plants
- Grain Products: Bannock and wild rice
- Milk and Alternatives: Canned and powdered milk. The back
  cover of *Eating Well with Canada's Food Guide: First Nations,
  Inuit and Métis* notes that many First Nations, Inuit, and Métis
  peoples do not consume milk products, so traditional foods such
  as fish with bone, shellfish, and nuts are listed as sources of
  calcium.
- Meat and Alternatives: Deer, elk, moose, seal, and other wild
  game

Eating Well with Canada's Food Guide: First Nations, Inuit and Métis
is Health Canada's first attempt to provide a guide tailored to the needs
of First Nations, Inuit, and Métis peoples. It looks and is different from
Eating Well with Canada's Food Guide and can work as the one tool to
improve eating habits and the overall health of these Canadians.

You have looked at the historic variations in Canada's food guide
and seen how the guide changed. Do you think that *Eating Well with
Canada's Food Guide: First Nations, Inuit and Métis* could be adapted
over time to better suit the needs of these groups of Canadians?

FIGURE 5-22 How are the
food and nutrition needs
of First Nations, Inuit, and
Métis families different
from those of other
Canadians?

Connecting to the Community

In each Connecting to the Community activity you will find out more about your local community by completing one of two assignments. This section forms one part of your Connecting to the Community for Unit 2. For this activity you will create one product from a choice of the following products.

Chapter 5 Choices

1. Create a product to inform adults about *Eating Well with Canada's Food Guide.* Your presentation should include

   - The four food groups
   - Examples of foods from each group
   - Recommended servings, taking age and gender into consideration
   - The size of a serving
   - Other considerations
   - Active living suggestions
   - Sample meal plans

OR

2. Plan a menu for a week to meet the nutrient needs of a family of four according to *Eating Well with Canada's Food Guide.* Include the following information:

   - Age and gender of each family member
   - Recommended servings per food group for each family member
   - A list of the family's favourite foods and which food group(s) they belong to

Chapter 5 Summary

In this chapter you learned about healthy food choices. You also

- Learned about *Eating Well with Canada's Food Guide*
- Looked briefly at the history of Canada's food guides
- Studied the food groups and how they were determined
- Examined the recommended number of servings and choices within each food group
- Looked at samples of serving sizes
- Considered the use of fats and oils, specialized food needs of different age groups, and the necessity of exercise in a healthy lifestyle
- Reviewed *Eating Well with Canada's Food Guide: First Nations, Inuit, and Métis*

Activities

1. When was the first food guide introduced in Canada? What was it called? Why was it introduced? How has the purpose changed? How has it remained constant?

2. What is a DRI and why is it important?

3. Why is eating a variety of foods important?

4. Why do you need fats and oils in your diet? Why should Canadians pay attention to the amount and type of fats they consume?

5. What are nutrient dense foods? From each of the food groups, give an example of a food that is nutrient-dense and one that is not.

6. Plan a menu for a day that would provide the nutrient needs of your family according to *Eating Well with Canada's Food Guide*. Include the following information:
   - Age and gender of each family member
   - Recommended servings per food group for each family member
   - A list of your family's favourite foods and which food group(s) they belong to
   - Menu suggestions for
     - Breakfast
     - Lunch
     - Dinner
     - Two or more snacks

CHAPTER 6

Good Nutrition throughout the Life Span

Key Concepts

Nutritional considerations for

- Infants
- Toddlers
- Teens
- Adults
- Older adults

Key Terms

antibodies
baby formula
bond
breastfeeding clinics
express milk
immune system
peer pressure
sedentary

In this chapter you will learn about different nutrient considerations for people in different stages of the life cycle.

Michael can't help thinking about the things he notices now that he is taking the food and nutrition course at school. This past weekend his family had a big barbecue. In class, they just finished a lesson on the different food needs people have at different stages of their lives. At the barbecue, he saw this in action. His uncle Andre loves ribs, but now that he is getting older, the really spicy ones don't agree with his digestive system so he has to eat the mild ones. Michael laughs to himself as he remembers his uncle warning his cousin Shemar that his time will come.

Michael also noticed that his older cousin, Tamika, cut food for her toddler Cory into small, manageable pieces. She also made sure that Cory could not reach the hot serving plates and burn himself. Michael's younger cousin, Yasmina, complained

because she loves corn on the cob, but now that she has braces, she has to cut the corn off the cob before she can eat it. She grumbles that it just doesn't taste the same. Michael is amazed at how often he can connect what he is learning at school to his life and his family.

In Chapter 5 you examined *Eating Well with Canada's Food Guide.* We saw that the food guide recommendations take into consideration the age and gender of the person consuming the food. In this chapter, different age groups and their special nutrient needs will be looked at more closely.

CARING FOR INFANTS

Breastfeeding and Bottle-feeding

Most people know that infants cannot eat the same food as adults, but do you know what type of food infants should eat at each stage of development? Do you know when to add cereal to their diet? Solid foods? What type of milk they need when they first go off breast milk or formula? Knowing the answers to these and other questions will help caregivers ensure that an infant's development is supported by healthy eating.

The Canadian Pediatrics Society recommends breastfeeding for all babies. Breast milk has the right amount and quality of nutrients to suit a baby's first food needs. It is easiest on the digestive system, so there's less chance of constipation or diarrhea. Breast milk also contains **antibodies**, proteins that help fight off harmful bacteria. Antibodies help the baby develop his or her **immune system**, which helps the body fight off bacteria, viruses, and other harmful substances. Babies who are exclusively breastfed should get a daily supplement of vitamin D, since it is not in breast milk. Vitamin D supplements for infants are available as drops.

Some mothers and babies find breastfeeding difficult because the baby has difficulty latching on to the breast, or other problems. **Breastfeeding clinics** are available to help new mothers learn to breastfeed their babies. Support is available from the moment the baby is born, and specialists visit new mothers and babies in their homes, or help them in breastfeeding centres.

When a mother cannot or chooses not to breastfeed, she uses **baby formula**, a specially formulated liquid designed to meet the nutritional needs of infants. Baby formula should also be fortified with iron to meet the baby's nutritional needs. Parents should consult their health-care professional when deciding which type of formula to use. Sometimes parents may need to try different brands of formula, since not all babies digest formula the same way. Babies who seem colicky (a digestive problem) may just be reacting to something in the formula.

FIGURE 6-1 Breast milk has special properties that formula cannot duplicate. If possible, new mothers should try to breastfeed. Do you think people's attitude toward breastfeeding has changed in the past few years? Why or why not?

Babies who are bottle-fed should be given formula for the first nine to 12 months. After this time, they can drink regular milk.

Bottle-feeding does not mean the baby is limited to formula. Many breastfeeding mothers **express milk** by using a special pump to extract milk from the breast so it can be stored for later use. This milk can be put in a bottle and fed to the infant by someone other than the mother. Many fathers like to take an active role in caring for their infant children. When fathers bottle-feed their child, they have an opportunity to **bond**, becoming emotionally attached to him or her. Do you know how you were fed as an infant? Did someone other than your mother feed you?

Introducing Solid Foods

At about six months of age, babies begin to need more calories and nutrients than breast milk or formula can provide. This is the time to introduce solid foods into the baby's diet.

How do you know when to introduce solid foods? Signs that a baby is ready for solid foods include

FIGURE 6-2 When babies are bottle-fed, fathers can become involved in the feeding process. Why is it important for fathers to be actively involved in caring for their infants?

- The baby seems hungry earlier than usual.
- The baby can sit up without support and has good control of his or her neck muscles.
- The baby holds food in his or her mouth without pushing it out on the tongue right away.
- The baby shows interest in food when others are eating. The infant opens his or her mouth when he or she sees food coming.
- The baby can let you know he or she doesn't want food by leaning back or turning his or her head away.

FIGURE 6-3 At what age did you start to eat solid foods? Do you know what your first food was?

What Do You Feed a Baby?

Food for Thought

Giving babies milk separately from meals promotes better absorption of iron.

As you learned in Unit 1, taste buds develop as people age. This is why it is important to introduce foods one at a time to babies. You also need to wait between three and five days before introducing another new food. That way, if the baby has a reaction to a food, you'll know which food it was. Often, a baby's experience with his or her first solid foods gives rise to funny stories that parents like to tell later. Since the sensation of solid food takes time to get used to, many babies make some very funny faces. Ask your parents or guardians if you or your siblings made faces when introduced to solid foods. They may even have some pictures that commemorate the occasion!

The order in which foods are introduced to a baby is influenced by cultural and family traditions. While many parents introduce a single-grain cereal to their babies as their first food, the type of cereal grain—rice or barley, for example—may vary. Other foods that babies are introduced to also depend on the types of foods their families eat.

Any food offered to babies should be plain, with no added sugar or salt. If you are preparing foods for a baby at home, make sure the foods are not overly spiced, since babies have sensitive digestive systems. Commercially-prepared baby food is fine, but read the nutrition labels to ensure that sugar and salt are not included.

When and What Foods to Introduce to Baby	
	■ At 6–9 months, offer a baby 30–60 mL (2–4 tbsp) of iron-fortified infant cereal twice a day. Then try other grain products, such as small pieces of dry toast or unsalted crackers. ■ At 9–12 months, offer the baby other plain cereals, whole-grain bread, rice, and diced pasta.
	■ At 6–9 months, offer a baby puréed, cooked yellow, green, or orange vegetables. ■ At 9–12 months, progress to soft, mashed, cooked vegetables.
	■ At 6–9 months, offer puréed cooked fruits, and very ripe mashed fruits (such as bananas). ■ At 9–12 months, try soft fresh fruits, peeled, seeded, and diced, or canned fruit packed in water or juice (not syrup).
	■ At 6–9 months, offer puréed cooked meat, fish, chicken, tofu, mashed beans, or egg yolk. ■ At 9–12 months, mince or dice these foods.
	■ At 9 months, offer foods like whole yoghurt (3.25% or higher), cottage cheese, or grated hard cheese. ■ At 9–12 months old, offer whole cow's milk (3.25%). After 12 months of age, the baby should not have more than 720 mL (24 oz) of milk products per day. Too much milk can lead to iron-deficiency anemia.

Infant Sleep Patterns

Most infants will sleep between 16 and 20 hours a day for the first six months of their lives. Their bodies need sleep to continue the growth and development that occurs in the first year. For most babies, this time is divided equally between day and night. Most infants will wake up every three or four hours because they are hungry. At around three months of age, most babies begin to sleep for longer periods during the night and shorter ones during the day. Between six and 12 months of age, babies tend to nap for three hours during the day and sleep for 10 or 11 hours during the night.

TODDLERS

Once babies become toddlers, they begin to feed themselves. Often, this can be a very messy experience for the whole family! As toddlers explore their food, they learn about it through their senses. Touching foods and sometimes putting it in places where adults would not is part of how toddlers learn to feed themselves.

Between the ages of two and five, children are often referred to as preschoolers. This is a time when young children experience a lot of growth in terms of their

- Large motor skills—learning to walk, run, and be physically active
- Fine motor skills—learning how to feed themselves, handle utensils, and drink from cups, glasses, and other containers
- Size
- Social development
- Language development

FIGURE 6-4 This toddler is having a good time learning about food. Do you have a similar picture of yourself when you were young?

All of these changes have an impact on feeding toddlers. As their fine motor skills develop, toddlers can feed themselves more easily and will make less of a mess when they do. When they are experiencing a growth spurt, toddlers will be hungry more often and require more frequent small meals and snacks. When they begin to mature socially, they will begin to notice foods that their friends eat and want to eat the same foods. The development of language means that a toddler might also make it clear that he or she does not like a certain food.

FIGURE 6-5 What were your favourite foods when you were little? Do you still like some of the same foods?

Guidelines for Feeding Toddlers

Here are some guidelines on how to feed toddlers healthy foods:

- Get them started feeding themselves by offering soft finger foods, such as bananas and dry cereals, since these allow for more success and less mess than foods that require a spoon.
- Encourage independence. Children need time to practise their skills. Success helps children feel good about themselves.
- Ignore awkwardness or messiness during feeding. It is part of the learning process. Cleanup may be made easier by putting some newspapers under the child's chair. Some people put a special mat around the child's highchair.
- Encourage a child who eats very quickly to slow down by talking between spoonfuls. It also helps if adults eat slowly, use a calm voice, create a relaxed setting, put small amounts of food on the table, or use gentle reminders to chew the food.
- Allow a child to take some responsibility for choosing what to eat and then respect the choice. For example, let the child choose between two vegetables on the table. Once the child has made a choice, express pleasure that the child is eating a vegetable.
- Try to understand that when a child dumps and drops food over the side of a high chair, this is normal behaviour at this stage of development. Once the child has learned the skill of dumping and spilling, it becomes a game. This behaviour should not be rewarded by continually picking up the food; instead, after the third time, take away the food. Often, this behaviour is simply a sign that the child is full.
- Encourage a child who dislikes vegetables to eat them by calling them something more descriptive and fun. For example, if the child is interested in colours, have the child eat the "green

Children should not be on low-fat diets. Thirty to 50 percent of an infant's calories and more than 30 percent of a toddler's calories should be from fat. Fat keeps a child's temperature consistent, helps digest vitamins, helps develop and cushion internal organs, is needed for brain growth, and assists in general growth and development.

balls" (peas) and "orange circles" (carrots) from a bowl of mixed vegetables. If the child is interested in numbers, count the number of peas or carrots in a spoonful before giving it to the child.

- Encourage toddlers to pick food from the serving plate so they can determine how much and what they want to eat. This also helps reduce everyone's frustration during the "no" stage.
- Encourage toddlers to eat a variety of finger foods and foods requiring a spoon. This helps toddlers learn how to use utensils, and having finger foods makes it easier for them to eat something.
- Avoid talking constantly about eating and watching expectantly while the child eats.

Adult Influence

Adults and other caregivers should model healthy eating for young children. Children learn by watching and imitating others. If adults refuse to eat certain foods, often children will refuse that food as well. Do you have the same food preferences and dislikes as your parents? Have you ever tried something that is not served at home and been surprised that you like it?

Adults also should be careful of the significance they attach to foods. Sometimes adults refuse to let children try certain foods or eat a lot of certain foods, such as sweets. When food is forbidden, it often becomes more desirable. It is best that adults model good eating habits to young children and show them balanced eating patterns. Eating some sweets is fine; eating too many is not.

Storing Supplements
Keep nutritional supplements, especially vitamins marketed to children, in a safe place. Young children often confuse supplements with candy and enjoy the flavour. Children can be harmed by large doses of supplements. Make sure they are stored out of reach and out of the sight of children.

FIGURE 6-6 Why is it important to model good eating habits for children?

Healthy Eating for Life

Developing healthy eating habits in young children is very important. Habits developed in childhood stay with people through adulthood. Poor eating habits can lead to poor health in childhood and later in life. Increased health risks due to poor eating patterns include

- Obesity, which can cause psychological problems, including low self-esteem
- Breathing disorders due to the strain obesity puts on the respiratory system
- Bone and joint disorders caused by poor calcium intake and, if a person is obese, too much weight on bones and joints
- Type 2 diabetes, which develops in people who have risk factors and poor eating habits, including the consumption of excess sweets, and obesity
- High cholesterol, which can result from a diet that is high in fat and cholesterol and can lead to stroke and heart problems later in life.

According to the British Columbia Ministry of Health, these preventable, chronic diseases are among the most important health issues of the 21st century. In British Columbia, as in other provinces, the Ministries of Health and Education are making efforts to improve children's health by encouraging them to develop healthy eating and physical activity habits during their youth. When British Columbia hosts the 2010 Olympics, the province's goal is to be the healthiest population to host the games. To do this, the provincial government developed a series of programs grouped together around the Act-Now BC Web site. Is your province promoting healthy eating and physical activity? If so, how?

Active Living

You may have noticed that many of the health conditions listed earlier were related to both unhealthy eating habits and a lack of physical activity. Being physically active is another important part of life-long health. As we saw in Chapter 5: A Guide to Healthy Food Choices, Health Canada has added information on healthy activity to the food guide.

Families who are active together discover many health benefits. The long-term health of both parents and children is affected positively by physical activity. Children will develop good life-long habits and continue to enjoy these activities, and parents will bene-

Food for Thought

According to Statistics Canada, in 2007, two out of every three adults in Canada are considered overweight.

Web connection

To learn more about healthy living, tips on eating, physical activity, and healthy environments, go to this Web site and follow the links.

www.mhrfoodforlife.ca

fit from improved fitness. It is never too late to become active. Time spent together being active as a family can create many good memories and times of sharing. Do you participate in any activities with your family?

Some family-friendly activities include

- Hiking
- Walking
- Bicycling
- Skiing
- Swimming
- Skating
- Canoeing
- Tobogganing

FIGURE 6-7 Children need to develop healthy activity routines in the same way that they need to develop healthy eating habits. Are there any activities that you do now that you began doing as a child?

Sleep Requirements

Like infants, toddlers need more sleep than older children and adults. Between the ages of one and three, children may or may not take a nap on a regular basis. They should sleep between 10 and 13 hours a day. The sleep needs of 3-to-5-year-olds are a little less, and most no longer need to take naps. However, they are still developing and experiencing rapid growth, so sleep is important to their overall health.

PRETEENS AND TEENS

Maintaining Healthy Eating Habits

The preteen and teen years are also a time of rapid growth and change in the body. Ideally, healthy eating habits developed in childhood are carried through these years. Providing developing and growing bodies with the proper nutrition is essential for both current and future health.

The preteen and teen years are also a time when young people start making more of their own food choices. Many teens help out with grocery shopping and preparing meals, and by doing so they begin making important decisions for their families.

Healthy eating means starting the day with a healthy breakfast. Eating breakfast will help you not only perform better all day long, but also maintain a healthy weight. If you skip breakfast, you lower your metabolism and your body burns calories more slowly. You will also tend to fill up on less healthy foods later in the day. The end result? You are hungry, have low energy, and start to gain weight.

Food for Thought

In January 2007, the Health Science Center at the University of Colorado released findings that said that students who eat healthy breakfasts do better academically and have fewer behaviour problems. What they eat is also important. A breakfast that has whole grains, fibre, protein, calcium, fruit, and is low in sugar will boost memory and concentration.

FIGURE 6-8 Do teens eat fast food because they like it or because they feel pressured to fit in with their peer group?

Food for Thought

Teen magazine reported that 35 percent of girls between the ages of 6 and 12 have been on at least one diet and that 50–70 percent of them are normal weight, yet the girls believe they are overweight.

Outside Influences

During the preteen and teen years, parents' influence on their children's food choices decreases and other factors begin to have a greater influence. These include

- *Peers.* Teens spend a lot of time with their friends, and food is often a part of the social fabric of their relationship. Teens will go out for food with friends. Often parents are surprised to find their teens now eating foods that they used to refuse, because their friends enjoy them.

- *Money.* As teens begin to earn their own money, they often have the resources to make food choices that their parents would not make for them.

- *The media.* The media has a bigger influence on preteens and teens than it does on younger children. Preteens and teens will often purchase foods that they find appealing because of advertising. With their own money from part-time work, teens can afford to act on the influence of the media.

- *Peer pressure.* This can be very different from the influence of friends. **Peer pressure** is the feeling that you have to do what your peers are doing. Too many preteens and teens feel pressured to change their eating habits to fit in with their peers. Unhealthy eating habits can result.

- *Body image.* Many teens feel the same peer pressure to attain a certain body image. Even though they know that the image is not natural, they will still change their eating patterns to try to fit in. This will be explored more fully in Chapter 8: Body Image and Lifestyle Choices.

- *Hunger.* During the teen and preteen years, teens experience a lot of growth and development and, just like growing toddlers, feel hungry more often. Satisfying hunger with healthy foods is essential during this time.

FIGURE 6-9 Breakfast is an important start to the day. What are the problems with skipping breakfast? What breakfast foods are healthy, quick and easy to prepare?

Thinking Critically | Energy Drinks—The Whole Story

What Are Energy Drinks?

Energy drinks are beverages such as Red Bull®, Venom®, and Adrenaline Rush®. They contain large doses of caffeine and other legal stimulants such as ephedrine and ginseng. Energy drinks may contain as much as 80 mg of caffeine, the equivalent of a cup of coffee. There are 23 mg of caffeine in a cola, significantly less than in an energy drink. These drinks are marketed to people under 30, and especially to high school and college or university students.

Are There Short-Term Dangers to Drinking Energy Drinks?

Individual responses to caffeine vary, and energy drinks should be used carefully. Their stimulating properties can boost the heart rate and blood pressure (sometimes to the point of palpitations), dehydrate the body, and, like other stimulants, prevent sleep.

You should not consume energy drinks while exercising, since the combination of fluid loss from sweating and the diuretic quality of the caffeine can leave you severely dehydrated.

Energy drinks are not necessarily bad for you, but they shouldn't be seen as "natural alternatives" either. Some of the claims they make—such as "improved performance and concentration"—can be misleading. If you think of them as highly caffeinated drinks, you'll have a more accurate

FIGURE 6-10 Do you think energy drinks are good or bad for you?

picture of what they are and how they affect you. You wouldn't use a cola or coffee as a sports drink, so why would you use an energy drink?

Questions

1. What are the dangers of energy drinks?

2. Which has more caffeine, a cola drink or an energy drink?

3. If your friend were a performance athlete, what would you tell him or her about using energy drinks as sports drinks?

- *Activity levels*. The more active you are, the more food you will need. Teens who are more **sedentary**—less active—do not need the same amount of food as active teens. When teens change their level of activity, they need to be sure that they are consuming what their body needs to support their new activity level.

Web connection

To learn more about food and nutrition, behaviour, and development from childhood to the teenage years, go to this Web site and follow the links.

www.mhrfoodforlife.ca

The following 15 Ways to Feel Good Inside were taken from the Act-Now BC Web site and provide some excellent guidelines to help teens eat healthier.

15 Ways to Feel Good Inside

Want to feel great? Then think about what goes into your body. Fast food can bog you down. Eat well and you'll be stronger, and have better concentration and more stamina. Your hair, skin, teeth, and nails will show the results—and you'll feel better mentally and physically.

Here are a few simple tips for better food and beverage choices:

1. *Get the day off to a good start.* Before school, build a breakfast around healthy foods like fruit, low-sugar cereals, hot oatmeal, rice, whole-grain breads, bagels, English muffins, smoothies, and yoghurt.

FIGURE 6-11 Why do you think some restaurants serve such large portions?

2. *Say NO to supersizing.* Have you noticed portions seem bigger today than they were when you were a child? It's not your imagination. But few of us need all that food—and none of us needs all the extra calories, fat, and sugar that come with large, jumbo, or supersize meals.

3. *Keep it interesting.* Food doesn't have to be boring. Try something different like wraps and rice cakes, tortillas, crisp breads and chapatis, naan and corn cakes, as alternatives to bread.

4. *Be lean with meat.* Choose lean meats, fish, and skinless chicken in place of sausages and processed meats.

5. *Not mad about meat?* How about trying some of the protein-power alternatives like lentils, tofu, eggs, cheese, chickpeas, baked beans, and kidney beans?

6. *Choose low-fat milk products.* Make low-fat milks, yoghurts, and cheeses your choice. Or consider the non-dairy alternatives, such as calcium-fortified soy milk. Salmon with bones, almonds, baked beans, and broccoli are also good sources of calcium.

7. *Get out of food ruts.* Avoid ordering the same foods at lunch from the school store or cafeteria or eating only your favourite foods.

8. *Think twice about takeout.* There are lots of healthy take-out options to choose from. Try sushi, pita wraps, baked potatoes, souvlaki, kebabs, vegetable or seafood pizzas, tabbouleh, falafels, steamed rice with vegetables, rotisserie chicken, or grilled fish. Healthy desserts include fruit salad or a fruit smoothie.

9. *Listen to your stomach.* Eat until you've had enough, not until you're full. Your stomach will let you know the difference. (And eating more slowly will give your stomach time to send the "full" message to your brain before you overload!)

10. *Avoid comfort eating.* Notice if you're eating simply because you're bored, sad, or lonely. These can lead to bad eating habits later in life.

11. *Feed your growth spurts.* There's a good reason why you may feel hungry all the time. It's probably a growth spurt, so keep up your vitamins, minerals, and calories with healthy, fresh food.

12. *Go for healthy snacks.* Snacks between meals are okay but keep them healthy. Grab a piece of fruit, a cob of corn, a tub of low-fat yoghurt, tuna salad, nuts and dried fruit, a sandwich, or lower-fat cheese.

13. *Hydrate with water.* Drink water as your first option before reaching for juices, soft drinks, or energy drinks.

14. *Stay focused.* Improving your eating habits for a day or even a week isn't too hard. The trick is keeping it up. It helps to involve family and friends in your plans to eat healthy—especially the people preparing your meals.

15. *Go easy on supplements.* With the right variety of foods, you won't need vitamin supplements or bodybuilding powders.

The Need for Sleep

Teens and preteens often think that their bodies don't require sleep, but they do. Children between the ages of 10 and 12 still need about nine hours of sleep a day. Teens need between eight and nine hours, and most teens do not get enough sleep. This causes inattentiveness, decreased short-term memory, delayed response time, and inconsistent performance. Many teens stay up later and sleep in on weekends. This inconsistency does not help them perform well. Going to bed around the same time every night and getting up about the same time every morning is better for their overall health.

ADULTS

Reaching adulthood does not mean that healthy eating stops. It is essential to continue healthy eating and activity patterns even then. Recent studies in British Columbia show that the rates of overweight and obese adults are increasing, while at the same time, adults are not getting enough servings every day from each of the four food groups in *Eating Well with Canada's Food Guide*. Almost 80 percent of adults do not eat enough fruits and vegetables, and most adults do

Sleep and the Circadian Rhythm

As far back as the 4th century BCE, Alexander the Great of Greece observed that the leaves of certain plants opened in the day and closed at night. Earth's own natural biological clock was called "the circadian rhythm" (*circadian* is a Latin word meaning "around a day"). Circadian rhythms are regular changes in mental and physical characteristics that occur in the course of a day.

Long ago, people slept when the sun set and got up when the sun rose, following their own biological clocks. With the invention of electric lighting in the mid-1800s, people's natural sleep patterns began to change. Extending daylight artificially into the night reduced sleep from nine hours to seven hours a night. As time went on and more countries became industrialized, the amount of sleep began to vary from one night to the next. This created problems with people's natural circadian rhythms.

Doctors and scientists believe the disruption of people's natural internal clocks causes health-related problems. The circadian rhythm is controlled by brain cells located in the hypothalamus part of the brain. This system is slow to respond to change. When travellers pass from one time zone to another, they suffer from disrupted circadian rhythms and experience an uncomfortable feeling known as "jet lag."

By not following their own natural clocks and not sleeping when it is dark outside, people are preventing their circadian rhythms from establishing a pattern. Scientific studies have shown that people who work night shifts are more susceptible to health problems. Disrupting your circadian rhythm creates a perpetual state similar to jet lag.

Until the 1950s most people thought that sleep was an inactive, dormant part of their lives. Scientists Gustav Kramer and Klaus Hoffmann proved scientifically the existence of a biological clock.

FIGURE 6-12 People who work night shifts pay the price by having sleep and health disorders. Why do you think this is the case?

Because of research, it is now known that sleep plays a huge role in brain development. If you do not get enough sleep, the part of the brain that controls language, memory, planning, and sense of time is severely affected. People's sleep patterns have an effect on their physical and mental health in many ways. Scientists and doctors are still working to understand all the ways people's sleep habits influence their health and lives.

not consume enough milk products for bone health. It is not that adults do not have enough to eat; it is that they do not eat the right foods. Eating the wrong foods contributes to the high rates of obesity. Healthy levels of physical activity are also important for adults. Being a couch potato or an armchair athlete has negative consequences now and later in life.

ActNow BC has also developed guidelines for adults to help them improve their eating habits. Read the list below and share it with an adult you care about.

FIGURE 6-13 How do the adults in your life practise healthy eating and remain active?

10 Ways to Turn over a New Leaf

Everyone needs a variety of healthy foods every day. Eating well can give you more energy, help you sleep better, and make it easier to concentrate. And those are just the short-term benefits.

Do you think your eating habits could use some improvement? Here are a few simple ways that ActNow BC has developed to boost nutrition without radically changing your lifestyle.

1. *Enjoy food.* Sometimes we eat without thinking about it. Take time to taste and enjoy your food—with other people if possible, and without distractions like television.
2. *Keep your bones strong.* Choose low-fat milks, yoghurts, cheeses, or other sources of calcium and vitamin D.
3. *Snack healthy.* Replace cookies, cakes, chocolate, energy bars, chips, and pastries with vegetables and low-fat dips, rice crackers, fruit, low-fat milk products, cherry tomatoes, dried fruit, and nuts.
4. *Downsize your order.* Some food outlets offer to "supersize" your meal, providing extra calories, fat, and sugar. Say no. No one needs all that extra food.
5. *Go slow.* Sit, and eat slowly. You'll not only enjoy your meals more, you'll make your digestive system much happier. Avoid eating on the run, at your desk, or in a stressful environment.
6. *Shop healthy.* Fill your shopping cart with mostly fruits, vegetables, legumes (such as dried peas, beans, and lentils), and whole-grain cereals.

FIGURE 6-14 Can you identify the things this person is doing to ensure she gets the maximum benefit from her food?

FIGURE 6-15 What benefits does eating fruit for dessert provide that eating a baked good doesn't?

Healthy Living

Make Dessert a Treat

Like many developed nations, Canadians are battling obesity. According to Statistics Canada, over one-quarter of Canadian children and nearly two-thirds of all adults are overweight. There is no single cause. Reduced activity; the availability of inexpensive, tasty snack foods; increased advertising; portion size; and restaurant meals all contribute to a situation in which people take in more calories than they burn off. This leads to weight gain. It doesn't happen overnight but, rather, over a length of time when poor food and activity choices become habitual.

Dessert is one habit that can seriously contribute to weight gain. Here are five ways to help you change your mind about dessert.

1. **A taste for something sweet can be satisfied in a healthy way with fruit.** Fruit is very low in fat and provides vitamins and fibre to your diet. Many exotic fruits are available that can help make any dessert seem very special. Pomegranate, passion fruit, star fruit, dragon fruit, and yellow kiwi are new to many people and can make dessert look as terrific as it tastes. For a really interesting treat, skewer fruit such as mango, pineapple, and peaches, and broil or grill them until they caramelize.

2. **Switch from high-fat ice cream and frozen yoghurt to low-fat varieties.** They taste good and help you meet your calcium requirements. Avoid added items like caramel, chocolate chips, or cookie crumbs, which add fat and sugar and disguise the flavour of the ice cream or yoghurt. Sorbet has even less fat but check that the amount of sugar in the product is low in the particular brand you choose.

3. If you are cooking dessert, **many recipes can be altered by lowering the amount of sugar used.** Often you can use half the amount called for. Also, you can usually substitute some of the fat (oil, butter, or margarine) with puréed apple or pumpkin. If a recipe calls for nuts, chop them smaller and use half the amount. Some people, especially if they are diabetic, substitute sugar with Splenda® or stevia, both low-calorie sweeteners that can be used in cooking.

4. **Portion size is a huge contributing factor to overeating.** If you are in a restaurant, split dessert at least two ways, and three or four if possible. At home, use a small plate and take a small amount. When visiting family or friends, request a half-sized portion of dessert and eat it slowly, savouring every bite.

5. If you are in the habit of having dessert after every dinner, make a change by choosing other fun activities to do on certain nights of the week. **You can still look forward to dessert, but make it a special treat.**

7. *Take shortcuts.* Frozen, dried, or canned fruits and vegetables are great for convenience. Pre-cut vegetables are perfect for stir-frying, steaming, roasting, or baking.

8. *Change your focus.* Make vegetables, rather than meat or potatoes, the dominant food on your plate.

9. *Have a plan.* Decide on the level of your "healthy" commitment. Work out realistic goals and write them down. Check your progress regularly and make changes where you think you need them.

10. *Stay on course.* Be prepared for setbacks and look at barriers to your healthy eating plans as they occur. Notice why and when you're slipping and try to get back on track as soon as possible.

Web connection

To learn how to change your food habits or to find answers to your nutrition questions, go to this Web site and follow the links.

www.mhrfoodforlife.ca

Adults Need Sleep, Too

Many adults do not get enough sleep. Even though adults lead busy work and family lives, they still need to find time to get between seven and nine hours of sleep a night. Not getting enough sleep causes many of the same problems as it does for teens, such as inattentiveness, decreased short-term memory, delayed response time, and inconsistent performance. Another issue with adults is that when they are sleep deprived, they can fall asleep in the wrong places. Falling asleep at your desk at work is embarrassing, but falling asleep at the wheel of a vehicle can be deadly.

SENIORS

Healthy eating is very important for older adults. As people age, their appetite decreases, their nutrition needs change, and sometimes their sense of taste changes. Seniors need fewer calories but just as many nutrients and—in some cases—even more than younger adults. Seniors need to pay attention to their diet to ensure that they are getting enough of the right nutrients. For example, people over 50 need more calcium, vitamin D, and vitamin B_6 than younger adults. Health Canada now recommends a nutritional supplement of vitamin D for anyone over the age of 50, since it is missing in the diets of many older Canadians. Seniors need to pay close attention to their bone health, because their bones become more brittle as they age.

FIGURE 6-16 Why is it important for seniors to practise healthy eating?

Gordon Becker, Cook in a Care Facility

Gordon Becker has worked for Capital-Care Lynnwood, a long-term nursing facility for adults with complex physical and mental illnesses, for 25 years. He began his food industry work as a dishwasher, then a cook, and then a dining room chef, at The Edmonton Inn and at No. 700 Wing, an air force club in Edmonton. Gordon attended the Northern Alberta Institute of Technology, taking the two-year Commercial Cooking program. He also completed courses in Food Service Nutrition and Management, Principles in Food Purchasing, and Food Safety.

Gordon is now the Support Services Supervisor at Lynnwood in Edmonton. Lynnwood provides three meals a day to the residents, so often Gordon is up at 5:30 a.m. to begin breakfast and lunch preparations. Some days he has the second shift, beginning at 9:00 a.m. On this shift, he assists the morning cook with breakfast and lunch and prepares the main dish for supper. On the 10:00 a.m. shift, he helps prepare supper and then dessert for the next day. There is no downtime in a busy place like Lynnwood.

Meal planning in a residential care facility requires a great deal of attention. The Lynnwood manager and dietitian both have important input, as do the residents and their families. Some residents require food to be very soft or even puréed. Different health concerns must also be addressed, such as diabetes or heart problems. Ethnic preferences and vegetarian choices also must be considered, as well as providing two or three choices at each meal to accommodate likes and dislikes. Meal plans must also take into account the requirements of *Eating Well with Canada's Food Guide* and government legislation for residential meals. The cooking staff changes the menu in the spring and fall, taking into consideration seasonal food preferences and availability.

Gordon particularly enjoys preparing nutritious meals that are appealing to the eye. He has received high praise for his beef stew, chicken cacciatore, veal parmesan, and roast beef. A winter dinner item that is very popular is Caribbean mango chicken, and in summer, he often makes a salmon filet. Gordon's favourite part of his job is spending time with the residents and seeing that the meals he prepares make a difference in their daily lives.

If you are interested in being a cook, Gordon has some wise advice: "The most important quality you need is dedication to your work. Always look for ways to improve your skills and knowledge by taking courses and learning from others."

"The most important quality you need is dedication to your work."

Getting the Most from What You Eat

The following suggestions will help seniors maximize the health benefits of the foods they eat.

Web connection

To learn more about health issues related to aging and seniors, go to this Web site and follow the links.

www.mhrfoodforlife.ca

- *Grains.* Many seniors reduce their activity so their need for grain products is also reduced. Extra servings from this category can lead to weight gain so seniors should aim for the lower number. Whole grains and enriched grain products are the best choices to supply needed energy and fibre.
- *Vegetables and fruit.* Seniors should choose more vegetables and fruit of all colours. The brighter the colour the more nutrients these foods contain. Seniors do not need the extra calories that come from fatty or sugary sauces on these foods.
- *Milk and alternatives.* People over age 50 need extra calcium and vitamin D for bone health. Calcium may also help control weight and blood pressure. Most seniors don't get enough calcium in their diets.

   If a senior needs to gain weight, they should use higher-fat milk; otherwise, choose lower-fat milk products and other calcium-rich foods. They can add skim milk powder to sauces, soups, and other cooked dishes, have a salmon sandwich, a salad with added nuts such as almonds, puddings, and casseroles made with skim milk.
- *Meat and alternatives.* Keeping in mind lowers levels of activity, seniors should choose leaner meats, poultry, and fish as well as dried peas, beans, and lentils.

Food for Thought

Eating fish once or twice a week, particularly types rich in omega-3s, reduces the risk of death from heart disease by one-third, according to research by scientists at the Harvard School of Public Health.

Fat in the Diet

Seniors need some fat in their diet to provide energy and essential nutrients, such as vitamins A, D, E, and K, and to maintain body cells. Owing to lower activity levels, seniors should be careful about how much and what types of fat they eat. Moderation and lower fat choices should be the goal. Seniors should try to

- Moderate fat intake but not eliminate it completely. Monounsaturated fats decrease the risk of developing heart disease and cancers.
- Eat a variety of foods in moderation, and limit higher-fat foods such as doughnuts, commercial muffins, and other bakery items.
- Eat more vegetables and fruits, which are naturally low in fat, and flavour them with a dash of lemon juice and herbs instead of butter or margarine.

Orange-glazed Pumpkin Cake

Ingredients

2 ¼ cups (550 mL) all-purpose flour
1 ½ tsp (7 mL) baking powder
¾ tsp (4 mL) baking soda
1 tsp (5 mL) cinnamon
½ tsp (2 mL) each ginger, nutmeg, allspice, and salt
½ cup (125 mL) butter, room temperature
1 cup (250 mL) brown sugar
¼ cup (50 mL) orange juice
2 eggs
1 tsp (5 mL) vanilla
1 cup (250 mL) canned pumpkin purée (not pie filling)
½ cup (125 mL) chopped candied or crystallized ginger

Glaze
1 ¼ cups (300 mL) sifted icing sugar
2 tsp (10 mL) finely grated orange zest
2 tbsp (30 mL) orange juice

Preparation

- Preheat oven to 350°F (180°C).
- Lightly oil or spray a 9 × 13 inch (3 L) baking pan.
- In medium bowl, stir flour with baking powder, baking soda, cinnamon, ginger, nutmeg, allspice, and salt. Set aside.
- In large bowl, using an electric mixer, beat butter with brown sugar until creamy. Beat in juice, eggs, vanilla, and pumpkin until blended. Gradually stir in flour mixture, mixing just until smooth, about 2 minutes. Stir in candied ginger.
- Scrape batter into pan and smooth surface. Bake in centre of oven for 30–35 minutes, or until sides of cake pull away from pan and a cake tester inserted in centre of cake comes out clean.
- Meanwhile, for glaze, stir icing sugar with zest in small bowl. Gradually stir in juice until glaze is of spreading consistency. While cake is warm, spoon glaze down centre of cake and gently spread to cover. Cool, cut into squares, and serve.

Servings: 18

Active Living

As for everyone, activity is important for seniors. Finding ways to be active helps improve a senior's overall health. Seniors should consult a health-care professional before beginning a new exercise routine.

The *Canadian Physical Activity Guide for Older Adults* advises that there are three types of activities seniors can incorporate into a balanced physical activity program:

- *Endurance*—to increase heart rate, breathing rate, and body temperature, and in the process strengthen heart and lungs and help them function more efficiently.
- *Flexibility*—to help keep muscles relaxed and joints mobile.
- *Strength and balance*—to have adequate muscular strength to allow the body to meet the demands of daily living and protect joints and muscles from injury.

Getting a Good Night's Sleep

Seniors still need the same seven to nine hours of sleep that younger adults require. However, they may find that uninterrupted sleep is difficult. Medical problems, such as bowel or kidney disease, may interrupt the sleep of older adults. Pain and discomfort may cause problems getting to sleep and may wake a senior during the night. Trying to find a way to get a good night's sleep is important for a senior's overall health.

HEALTHY EATING FOR LIFE

As you can see, healthy eating and activity are important for your health throughout your life. Maybe you will be like Michael and be able to see how people at different stages of their lives stay healthy in your extended family.

FIGURE 6-17 Why is healthy eating and activity important at all stages of life?

Connecting to the Community

In each Connecting to the Community activity you will find out more about your local community by completing one of two assignments. This section forms one part of your Connecting to the Community activity for Unit 2. For the activity you will create one product from a choice of the following products:

Chapter 6 Choices

1. Choose one stage of the life span discussed in the chapter. Create a "Guide for Healthy Eating" for that age group. Include:
   - A description of the stage
   - Special nutritional considerations for that stage
   - A healthy menu plan for someone in that stage

OR

2. There are many places that provide food for people at different stages of the life span, such as school cafeterias, seniors' homes, and daycare centres. In your community, find examples of places that provide food for different stages of the life span. Investigate one stage, making sure you
   a) Choose a facility that provides food for a specific stage of the life span.
   b) Make a list of factors to consider when planning to meet the food needs of this group. Use information from this chapter and Chapter 5.
   c) From the information gathered, make a questionnaire for the dietary supervisor of the facility about how he or she plans the menus for clients.
   d) Have your teacher check your questionnaire and then visit the facility to ask the questions.
   e) Write a summary of what you have learned.

Chapter 6 Summary

In this chapter you learned about good nutrition throughout the life span, including

- Feeding infants from birth through to the introduction of solid foods
- Infants' sleep patterns
- Feeding toddlers and preschoolers and establishing healthy eating habits for them for life
- Noting changes in toddlers' and preschoolers' sleep requirements
- Feeding preteens and teens and ensuring that the healthy eating patterns developed in childhood continue
- Identifying preteens' and teens' sleep requirements and the effects of sleep deprivation
- Special considerations so adults can continue healthy eating habits, engage in physical activity, and get enough sleep
- The importance of healthy eating, physical activity, and adequate sleep for older adults' quality of life

Activities

1. If you had to choose three key messages about healthy lifestyles for all ages, what would they be?

2. What should your first choice of beverage be when exercising? Why?

3. Toddlers and preschoolers experience a lot of growth and development between the ages of two and five. Complete a chart similar to this to explain how that growth or development has an impact on their healthy eating.

Type of Growth or Development	Impact on Healthy Eating

4. Why is it important that adults and seniors pay attention to their diet?

5. What advice would you give to adults and seniors who are concerned about maintaining healthy eating and activities?

CHAPTER 7

Key Concepts

Nutritional considerations for people who

- Are pregnant and lactating
- Are athletes
- Are vegetarians
- Have special physical or psychological needs
- Have diseases or illnesses, including
  - cardiovascular disease
  - diabetes
  - osteoporosis
  - inflammatory bowel disease
  - food allergies
  - food intolerances

Key Terms

food allergy
food intolerance
food sensitivity
glycogen
histamine
immunoglobulin E (IgE)
lactose intolerance
lacto-ovo vegetarian
lacto-vegetarian
ovo-vegetarian
pesco-vegetarian
phytates
risk factor
vegan

Living with Special Considerations

In this chapter you will explore some of the food and nutritional needs of people who have special requirements. A person could have special nutritional needs for various reasons, such as having food allergies, being pregnant and lactating, competing in a demanding sport, or living with an illness.

Seventeen-year-old Catrina is a competitive skier. She loves the feeling of flying down the slopes. She competes in giant slalom and downhill skiing. During the off-season, Catrina works out two to three hours a day doing yoga, lifting weights, sprinting, running, and performing different stop-start exercises on her bicycle to strengthen her legs. Catrina trains at the gym at Canada Olympic Park most of the time or uses the gym at Southern Alberta Institute of Technology in Calgary, Alberta.

During the skiing season, Catrina competes at various mountain sites around Alberta and British Columbia. She takes her sport quite seriously and tries very hard to eat well. She balances her diet with lots of protein and complex carbohydrates. She knows that to be competitive, she must provide her body

with good quality food. Luckily, she does not have a sweet tooth and does not crave the empty calories that foods like candy and chocolate would give her.

Chapter 6: Good Nutrition throughout the Life Span, looked at the food needs of people at different stages of the life cycle. In this chapter you will examine the food needs of people who require special considerations. These special considerations can be specific to a stage of the life cycle, such as pregnancy, or they can be long-term considerations such food allergies or living with diabetes. People who experience these conditions know that they have an impact on their food intake and their nutritional needs.

PREGNANT AND LACTATING WOMEN

The nutritional intake of pregnant and lactating (breastfeeding) women has an impact on the health of both the mother and child. Women who are of child-bearing age and are considering becoming pregnant need to pay particular attention to their diet. Women usually do not know they are pregnant until after they have missed at least one menstrual cycle, which means that they have been feeding a developing fetus for a few weeks without knowing it. That is why it is important to establish healthy eating habits before pregnancy.

Following the recommendations of *Eating Well with Canada's Food Guide* is a good place to start learning healthy eating habits. In addition to the information found in the food guide, consider the following tips adapted from the Alberta Ministry of Health.

Web connection

To find out more about healthy pregnancies, take a quiz. Go to this Web site and follow the links.

www.mhrfoodforlife.ca

FIGURE 7-1 Pregnant women get a lot of advice. What is a good source of advice about nutrition for pregnant women?

✓ TIPS FOR PREGNANT WOMEN

General

✓ Choose a variety of different foods from each of the four food groups each day.

✓ Emphasize high-quality foods that are rich in the nutrients pregnant women need:
  – whole-grain products
  – vegetables and fruit
  – lower-fat milk products
  – lean meats
  – lower-fat meat alternatives

✓ Limit foods that are less nutritious and higher in fat, salt, sugar, or caffeine.

✓ Drink plenty of water. Pregnant women need more water than non-pregnant women.

✓ No amount of alcohol can be considered safe for pregnant women to drink. Babies whose mothers consumed alcohol during pregnancy are at risk for alcohol-related disorders called fetal alcohol syndrome disorders (FASDs).

✓ Pregnant women should also practise food safety and be sure to avoid foods that could be contaminated (see Chapter 9).

✓ Get the extra nutrients needed. A woman's need for iron, calcium, and folic acid increases during pregnancy. Focus on choosing reliable sources of these nutrients every day.

Getting Enough Iron

✓ Iron helps carry oxygen from mom to baby. Iron is also essential for the development of the baby's blood system and brain. Iron-rich foods include red meats, seafood, dried fruit, iron-fortified cereals and pasta, dark-green leafy vegetables, and legumes (dried beans, peas, or lentils).

✓ When a pregnant woman eats vegetables, fruit, and grains, she is consuming foods rich in vitamin C that help her body absorb the iron in these plant-based foods.

✓ Iron deficiency (anemia) is a serious but relatively common problem during pregnancy. A health-care professional may recommend an iron supplement to ensure that a pregnant woman gets enough iron.

Getting Enough Calcium

✓ Calcium maintains strong, healthy bones and teeth.

✓ Pregnant women should aim to take in three to four servings of milk products (milk, cheese, or yoghurt) or fortified soy beverage each day to meet their increased needs.

✓ Cheese is a good source of calcium, protein, and other nutrients needed during pregnancy. However, it is important for pregnant women to read the labels on cheeses to ensure the milk used to make the cheese has been pasteurized. Health Canada recommends that pregnant women not eat unpasteurized cheese. Although most cheeses sold are safe to eat, make sure that the ingredient list clearly shows that the milk was pasteurized.

Getting Enough Folic Acid

✓ Folic acid (folate) is a vitamin essential for the development of a baby's brain and spinal cord during the very early stages of pregnancy.

✓ All women who are pregnant or planning to become pregnant should take a daily folic acid supplement.

✓ Folic acid is found in leafy dark-green vegetables, broccoli, dried peas and beans, oranges and orange juice, and breads, cereals, and pasta made with enriched flour.

Weight Gain During Pregnancy

Gaining weight is a normal and important part of a healthy pregnancy. Pregnant women usually eat more than they did before becoming pregnant, but the notion that they are "eating for two" is not true. Gaining too little or too much weight can be harmful to both mother and baby, so pregnant women need some guidelines about weight gain. Women with a healthy weight before pregnancy should gain 11.5–16 kg (25–35 lb). Women who are underweight will need to gain more; those who are overweight will not need to gain as much.

Once the baby is born, breastfeeding mothers should continue the healthy eating patterns and habits they practised while they were pregnant. Breastfeeding mothers should consume an average of 500 extra calories a day. They need to follow the same advice as when they were pregnant and ensure that they eat a wide variety of foods from all four food groups. Breastfeeding women may also find themselves thirsty. Because of their body's increased demand for liquids to produce milk for the baby, breastfeeding women should drink water and juices whenever they are thirsty. Breastfeeding women should avoid caffeine and alcohol.

It is interesting to note that recommendations about foods to avoid during lactation vary by culture. Research shows that family or cultural preferences are transferred to the infant through the mother's breast milk. By following her normal diet and eating the foods she is familiar with, a breastfeeding mother is passing on these traditions to her infant.

FIGURE 7-2 Why is it important for breastfeeding mothers to continue the healthy eating patterns and habits they practised during pregnancy?

ATHLETES

In the chapter introduction, you met Catrina, a high-performance athlete. Catrina trains and works out every day, so her energy needs are higher than most people her age. Research shows that the performance of athletes is related to the quality of food that they eat as well as their training and talent.

Athletes need more energy because they burn more energy. Meeting energy needs in a healthy way should be a top priority for any athlete. According to the Dietitians of Canada, the main source of fuel used by the body during exercise is carbohydrates, which come from grains, vegetables, and fruit. Carbohydrates are stored in muscles as **glycogen**, which is a form of sugar. During exercise, individuals use up their stored glycogen, so it is important to replace this between periods of exercise. For athletes to do this, they need to consume a diet high in carbohydrates. When athletes do not have enough stored glycogen, they can run out of energy during a performance. Ensuring that they have enough energy can improve their performance and improve overall strength and endurance.

It may be difficult for athletes to get all the energy they need by eating only three meals a day. Athletes should eat healthy snacks to ensure that their energy requirements are met. Athletes who are training and competing will do best to eat in the high end of the food guide range. Some athletes and coaches consult with a registered dietitian for advice on meal and menu planning.

Athletes in high-endurance sports such as the biathlon need a lot of carbohydrates, while those in power sports, like the bobsled, require high-protein meals.

FIGURE 7-3 All athletes must be sure that they consume enough carbohydrates to be able to maintain their performance. Which foods will support their energy needs?

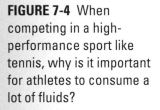

FIGURE 7-4 When competing in a high-performance sport like tennis, why is it important for athletes to consume a lot of fluids?

Staying hydrated during exercise and competition is also very important. Your body is designed to sweat in order to keep cool. When you exercise you tend to sweat a lot. The problem is that if you sweat too much, you get dehydrated. Being dehydrated can reduce performance, so it is crucial for athletes to stay hydrated. For peak performance, drink plenty of fluids before, during, and after activity to replace fluids lost due to sweating. If your activity will last less than an hour, then you are fine with plain water. If your activity will last longer, then you may need to consume a sports drink to gain the carbohydrates needed to replenish the glycogen stores in your muscles.

Dietitians of Canada states that research has shown that the protein needs of most athletes can be met by eating a healthy diet. It is not necessary for athletes to supplement their diet with protein products. By following *Eating Well with Canada's Food Guide*, athletes can obtain other nutrients as well as protein. Protein is important to repair tissues after exercise. Athletes who are strength training and play endurance sports need more protein than others, but with good protein choices, these needs can be met by following the recommended number of food guide servings. Good sources of protein include meat, fish, poultry, milk, cheese, and eggs.

Fat provides the body with energy as well as fat-soluble vitamins, and athletes also need to ensure that their diet has sufficient fat content. Eating too little or too much fat is not healthy. Good choices for fat include lean meats, poultry, fish, legumes, and lower-fat milk products.

When an athlete eats a well-balanced diet, vitamin supplements will not improve performance, according to Dietitians of Canada. Athletes are encouraged to eat a wide variety of foods from all four food groups so that they do not develop vitamin or mineral deficiencies.

A **risk factor** is something that increases the chance that a particular condition will occur. Female athletes should pay close attention to their iron intake, because iron deficiency is a risk factor for female athletes. To increase iron intake, they should choose meat, legumes, vegetables, and grains; eat foods that contain vitamin C to increase iron absorption; and avoid drinking coffee or tea with meals because they interfere with iron absorption.

Sport-enhancing supplements, such as protein shakes, are not supported by Dietitians of Canada. The organization states that the effectiveness of supplements has not been scientifically proven and advises caution in the use of any supplement.

Hayley Wickenheiser, Hockey Champion

Hayley Wickenheiser was born in Shaunavon, Saskatchewan, in 1978. She has often been described as the greatest female hockey player in the world. She was first chosen for the Canadian Women's National Team when she was 15. Since then, she has been a major contributor to the four gold medals earned at the Women's World Hockey Championships as well as two Olympic gold medals in Torino and Salt Lake City, and a silver Olympic medal in Nagano.

Hayley lives in Calgary, Alberta, with her partner Tomas and son Noah. She is currently training and playing hockey for the Calgary Oval X-Treme and is the new captain of the Canadian team for the 2007 World Women's Hockey Championship. Her future includes playing more hockey, getting ready for the Olympics, and promoting women's hockey around the world. She would like to eventually pursue a degree in medicine and become a doctor.

Hayley is involved with a charitable organization called Right To Play. This organization helps children in war torn and impoverished countries through sport and play. She went to Rwanda with three other athletes to experience and help with the work of Right To Play firsthand. Here in Canada, Hayley is involved in public awareness and fundraising for this worthy cause. She also works with Dreams Take Flight, Kidsport, and Spread the Net. These charities help improve the daily lives and health of disadvantaged or ill children in Canada and other countries.

Being an athlete means making careful food choices. Hayley relies on a balanced diet with a focus on whole grains, vegetables and fresh fruit, and chicken or fish for protein. She avoids highly-processed foods and tries to eat organic foods whenever she can. She drinks lots of water and believes that four or five smaller meals a day help her stay fit. Before a hockey game, she usually eats brown rice or whole wheat pasta with steamed vegetables, salad, and chicken, beef, or fish. Hayley avoids saturated and trans fats, and gets the fat she needs from nuts, seeds, and fish oils. She is very careful to stay away from junk food because it is high in calories and low in nutritional value. Her favourite snacks are popcorn and carrots with hummus. When Hayley treats herself to something extra special, her favourites are peanut butter and jam on toast or dark chocolate.

Hayley encourages teens to "Be active and disciplined, stay away from fast food, and focus on eating well. Carry a water bottle to school and drink lots of water. Healthy snacks during the day will help keep your energy up. Don't go longer than three or four hours without eating, and make sure you eat breakfast every day!"

"Be active and disciplined, stay away from fast food, and focus on eating well. Carry a water bottle to school and drink lots of water."

FIGURE 7-5 These children are playing soccer, thanks to Right to Play.

VEGETARIANS

Almost 1 million Canadian adults say that they are vegetarian. As a nation, Canadians are becoming more and more interested in their health and the role that nutrition plays in it. More than one-third of Canadians serve meatless meals on a regular basis.

Vegetarian styles of eating exclude animal products to varying degrees. It is very important to understand that healthy eating for a vegetarian involves more than simply eliminating a piece of meat from a meal; it means substituting other foods to replace the nutrients found in animal products. A vegetarian diet comprises mostly fruits, vegetables, cereals, grains, nuts, seeds, and legumes. There are several types of vegetarian:

- **Vegans** exclude all animal products.
- **Lacto-vegetarians** include dairy products.
- **Ovo-vegetarians** include eggs.
- **Lacto-ovo vegetarians** eat both eggs and dairy products.
- **Pesco-vegetarians** exclude red meat and chicken but do eat fish and seafood.

FIGURE 7-6 What special occasion foods might not be included in a vegetarian lifestyle?

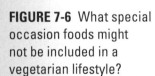

Some people who call themselves vegetarians will occasionally eat poultry or fish, or make exceptions on certain occasions.

People choose vegetarian diets and lifestyles for a variety of reasons, including

- Religious—some religions and cultures prohibit the consumption of some or all animal products.
- Ethical or moral—some people do not believe it is ethical to consume animal products.
- Health—some people choose vegetarian diets because they are lower in saturated fats.
- Environmental—some people believe that it is better for the environment if land is used to grow food rather than for raising animals.
- Economic—it costs less to eat a vegetarian diet than a diet that includes animal products.

Regardless of the reason, vegetarians must pay careful attention to their diet to ensure that they are not putting their health at risk by missing essential nutrients normally found in animal products.

Considerations with Vegetarian Diets

It is essential that vegetarians maintain an adequate intake of certain nutrients, which may be limited unless care is taken to choose reliable sources. These nutrients include protein, vitamins D and B_{12}, calcium, iron, and zinc.

- *Protein.* Vegetarians can meet their protein needs by choosing a variety of protein-containing foods. Good sources of protein are assorted legumes, tofu and other soy-based foods, grains, cereals, nuts, peanut butter, and other veggie "meats," such as veggie burgers, which are usually soy-based products. Consuming a variety of protein sources throughout the day will provide the essential amino acids (the building blocks of protein) to meet the body's requirement. Some interesting combinations include mixed beans on a tortilla, split pea soup and whole-grain crackers, black beans and rice, vegetarian chili with whole-grain bread, or Asian tofu stir-fry. Remember that essential amino acids must be eaten in combination with other foods to meet protein requirements.

- *Vitamin D.* The body produces vitamin D when the skin is exposed to direct sunlight. Light-skinned people can produce adequate vitamin D by exposing their face and forearms to the sun during the warm months for 10 to 15 minutes daily; those with dark skin require longer exposure. Remember that clouds, sunscreen, windows, and smog will block the ultraviolet rays that produce vitamin D. In winter months, dietary sources of vitamin D or dietary supplements should be used. Vitamin D is added to fortified soy and rice beverages, fluid milk products, and margarines, but it is not found in yoghurt or cheese. Check the labels before making purchases.

- *Vitamin B_{12}.* This important vitamin is derived from bacteria. Vitamin B_{12} of bacterial origin is present in animal products such as eggs and dairy products. Soy beverages and veggie "meats" that are fortified with vitamin B_{12} (check the labels) provide an adequate amount of the vitamin. If a vegetarian does not eat fortified products then a supplement should be considered.

- *Calcium.* Dairy products and many other foods make calcium readily available to your body. People who avoid milk, cheese, and yoghurt products can rely on fortified soy beverages that contain the same amount of calcium as milk. Other good sources of calcium include calcium-set tofu, certain dark-green vegetables (broccoli, kale, mustard greens, collards, Chinese cabbage, and okra), almonds, tahini (a smooth paste made from sesame seeds), beans, figs, blackstrap molasses, and calcium-fortified orange juice. A calcium supplement is recommended for those who

Research results show that people who eat a well-planned vegetarian diet have a 50 percent reduction in their risk of heart disease and have a longer life expectancy.

FIGURE 7-7 When carefully planned, a vegetarian style of eating can provide health benefits. What are they?

might not meet their calcium needs, particularly children, teens, pregnant and lactating women, and seniors.

- *Iron deficiency.* This is a common problem in vegetarian and non-vegetarian diets. Though abundant in plant foods, iron from plant products is less well absorbed, so vegetarians should consume about twice the recommended amounts to compensate for this difference. Good sources of iron include tofu, beans, assorted legumes, figs and dried fruit, nuts, fortified cereals and breads, enriched pasta, or dark-green leafy vegetables. Iron is better absorbed when these foods are consumed with vitamin C-rich foods (citrus fruits, tomatoes, and broccoli).

- *Zinc.* Whole-grain breads and cereals as well as brown rice contain **phytates**, a compound that interferes with the absorption of zinc. As a result, vegetarians require 50 percent more zinc than non-vegetarians. Men and women who follow vegetarian diets should have 16.5 mg and 12 mg (respectively) of zinc each day. Eating assorted legumes, as well as tofu, cashews, almonds, and fortified veggie "meats" increases zinc intake.

Benefits of Vegetarian Diets

When vegetarians take into consideration the above precautions, their diet is very healthy. Some of the benefits of being vegetarian include

- A diet that is low in saturated fat and cholesterol. Sources of fat include nuts, seeds, nut and seed butters, avocado, olives, coconut, oils, eggs, and dairy products if used, as well as the fats and oils used in preparing foods.

- Reduced saturated fat and cholesterol intake, combined with the high fibre content of plant foods, often results in lower blood cholesterol levels as well. Many vegetarians are also close to their ideal body weight. These two factors, as well as the abundance of protective phytochemicals in plant foods, may help to lower vegetarians' rates of certain diseases. These include obesity, type 2 diabetes, certain cancers, high blood pressure, heart disease, gallbladder disease, osteoporosis, and kidney stones.

- Leading a healthy lifestyle. Vegetarians tend to include regular physical activity in their lives and are usually non-smokers.
- Following a well-planned diet that is rich in vitamin C, vitamin E, and beta-carotene, which act as antioxidants. Antioxidants play a role in staying healthy and possibly in disease prevention. Vegetarian diets are also high in folic acid (another B vitamin), fibre, and phytochemicals (plant compounds with biological activity that may have health benefits). These may help protect against certain cancers.
- There are economic benefits to eating a vegetarian diet since plant products tend to cost less than animal products.

Planning Vegetarian Meals

Planning a healthy vegetarian diet doesn't have to be complicated.

1. Start by planning meals and snacks for several days.
2. Ensure that the meal plan includes sources of protein, iron, and calcium each day.
3. Follow up by buying the foods that are needed to put your plan into action.
4. Choose a variety of foods from each of the four food groups in *Eating Well with Canada's Food Guide* to help meet nutrient needs.
5. Experiment with different whole grains, such as quinoa (a South American grain with a crunchy texture) or spelt (a grain with light red kernels).
6. Try new vegetables and prepare them in new ways.
7. Pour fortified soy milk on your cereal at breakfast.
8. Enjoy protein-rich beans, peas, lentils, or other legumes in soups, salads, and stir-fries instead of meat.
9. Consult a good vegetarian cookbook or get tips from vegetarian friends.
10. Eat at a vegetarian restaurant, or, when eating out, look for vegetarian choices on the menu. Many restaurants now offer several vegetarian choices. Ask whether nutrition information is available for the foods you order.

EATING FOR A HEALTHY HEART

Have you heard the term *heart healthy*? This is a term the Heart and Stroke Foundation uses to describe strategies that people can take to keep their heart healthy. Research has shown that healthy eating habits combined with healthy activity are key factors in the prevention of cardiovascular disease. The Heart and Stroke Foundation has developed some excellent tools for people to use to improve their heart-healthy habits. From meal planning to recipes to the Health Check symbol, the Foundation is working hard to help all Canadians improve their overall health and the health of their cardiovascular systems.

A heart-healthy eating plan follows the basic principles of good nutrition outlined in *Eating Well with Canada's Food Guide*. The Heart and Stroke Foundation states that

Nutritious, balanced meals and healthy snacks may reduce your risk of heart disease and stroke by helping you increase your intake of heart-healthy nutrients, manage your weight, keep your blood pressure down, control your blood sugar levels, and lower your cholesterol.

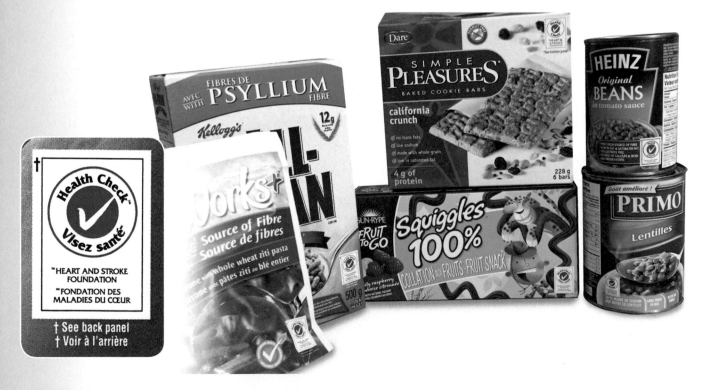

FIGURE 7-8 The Health Check symbol was designed to show consumers products that contribute to an overall healthy diet. Currently there are over 700 products with the symbol on them. Check out the food in your kitchen at home to see if your foods have the Health Check symbol.

✓ TIPS FOR A HEALTHY HEART

To achieve a healthy heart, there are many things you can do as a consumer. Below is a list of tips.

For Cooking

✓ Reduce portion size. Most people eat more than one food guide serving at a meal. Know what a serving size is.

✓ Cut the fat. Remove visible fat from foods before cooking. Do not add fats or oils while cooking, and use seasoning instead of butter or margarine on vegetables.

✓ Change ingredients to healthier ones. For example, use plain low-fat yoghurt instead of sour cream, or use lower-fat sour cream.

✓ Break the salt habit. Use herbs and spices to flavour foods, try to reduce your salt intake, and avoid processed foods because of their high salt content.

When Eating Out

✓ When choosing appetizers, go for salads with dressing on the side and other vegetables, instead of deep-fried foods or nachos loaded with cheese and sour cream. Choose a broth-based soup instead of a cream-based one.

✓ For main courses, look for low-fat methods of cooking. Terms such as *baked, barbequed, broiled, charbroiled, grilled, poached, roasted, steamed,* or *stir-fried* indicate lower-fat methods.

✓ Avoid foods that are high in fat, such as those labelled *Alfredo sauce, au gratin, cheese sauce, battered, breaded, buttered, creamed, crispy, deep-fried, en croûte, fried, hollandaise, pan-fried, pastry, prime, rich, sautéed, scalloped, gravy, mayonnaise,* or *thick sauce.*

✓ For dessert, choose fruit. If you want to indulge in a rich dessert, share it with your tablemates.

For Snacks

✓ Make snacks a part of your healthy eating. Plan for healthy snacks.

✓ Buy healthy choices and keep them stocked in your cupboard and refrigerator.

✓ Choose sliced vegetables, fresh fruit, plain popcorn, unsalted nuts, dried fruit, trail mix, and single servings of lower-fat yoghurt, cottage cheese, and puddings. At school, keep easy-to-store snacks, such as canned fruit, whole-grain crackers, seeds, lower-salt pretzels, or raisins.

Web connection

To learn more about keeping your heart healthy, go to this Web site and follow the links.

www.mhrfoodforlife.ca

Risk Factors for Cardiovascular Disease

There are numerous known risk factors for cardiovascular disease. These include

- High blood pressure (hypertension)
- High blood cholesterol
- Diabetes
- Being overweight
- Excessive alcohol consumption
- Physical inactivity
- Smoking
- Stress
- Age
- Women have some unique risk factors: Smoking and using birth control pills after the age of 35, pregnancy, and childbirth increase the rate of stroke, usually because of a pre-existing condition. Menopause increases the risk of stroke because of reduced estrogen levels.
- Gender: Men over the age of 55 and post-menopausal women are at higher risk.
- Heredity: Having a close family member who has suffered a stroke or heart attack increases your risk.
- Ethnicity: First Nations peoples and those of African or South Asian descent are more likely to have high blood pressure and diabetes and, therefore, are at greater risk of heart disease and stroke than the general population.

It is important to make healthy changes to your lifestyle. Both diet and activity reduce your risk.

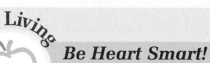

Healthy Living

Be Heart Smart!

Cardiovascular (heart and artery) disease is the number-one killer in Canada. People usually think that only older people get heart disease, but poor eating habits early in life can lead to irreversible health problems even for young adults.

One way to improve your heart health is to change a high-fat diet to a low-fat diet. First, you need to understand the difference between healthy fats and unhealthy fats.

FIGURE 7-9 Many teens eat fast foods that are loaded with fat and salt. What effect might these foods have on their heart and arteries?

- *Unsaturated fat.* Small amounts of unsaturated fats are healthy. Liquid vegetable oil, oil from seeds and nuts (except palm and coconut oil), and the fat found in fish oil (omega-3) all help to lower your risk of heart disease by reducing the level of LDL cholesterol in your blood.

- *Saturated fat.* Most saturated fat in your diet comes from meat and dairy products such as cheese and butter. It can also be found in many commercially baked products like cakes and cookies. Saturated fat is not healthy. It increases the level of LDL cholesterol in your blood and contributes to heart disease.

- *Trans fat.* This type of fat is created by the food-processing industry. Liquid vegetable oils are chemically treated to become solid (like some kinds of margarine) and then are used in many packaged foods. This increases the shelf life of the baked products. Unfortunately, although this is convenient for the food industry, trans fat has proven to be very unhealthy. Trans fat not only raises LDL cholesterol, but also lowers HDL cholesterol, which is the type you want to have in a healthy body. New laws are coming into place that limit or forbid the use of trans fat in many products due to the health problems that they cause.

What can you do? Check food labels carefully and choose foods with less fat. In particular, limit foods that have higher amounts of saturated fat and avoid all foods (many packaged snack foods) that contain trans fat. Choose low-fat dairy products and lean cuts of meat. Trim off visible fat, such as the skin from poultry. Cook with small amounts of healthy oils, such as peanut, olive, or canola oil, and eat more foods with natural or added omega-3 fatty acids. In restaurants, avoid fried food, especially french fries and battered items. **Your heart will thank you.**

Literacy in Your Life

Before Reading

1. Read the title of the article below. Notice the subtitle, which gets you ready for one part of the main idea. Read all the italicized headings and the information in the sidebar and guess what the BC government is going to tell you. Jot your predictions in the K column of a KWL organizer like the one below.

K (What I Know)	W (What I Want to Know)	L (What I Learned)

During Reading

1. Use the italicized headings to fill in "What I Want to Know "on your KWL chart. This is a very good way to organize new ideas when you are reading for information.

How Sweet It Is!

What Schools Need to Know About Sugar and Artificial Sweeteners

What's the big deal with sugar?
A little bit is fine when it's used to make nutritious foods. But sugar provides "empty calories" that can displace healthier choices. For example, pop drinkers are more likely to have a low intake of calcium and other nutrients. Students who sip sugary drinks or graze on sugary foods also have a higher risk of tooth decay.

How much is a lot of sugar?
The World Health Organization recommends that no more than 10 percent of our calories come from added sugars. For younger students, that can mean as little as 10 teaspoons worth. That leaves very little room for sugary drinks or candies, but it is ample for kids to enjoy nutritious foods with some sweetening.

How do we know if a drink is real juice or flavoured sugar-water?
Read the label and check the ingredient list. In Canada, only 100 percent juice can be labelled "100% juice." Words like *drink, blend, beverage, cocktail, splash*, or *contains/made with 100% juice* usually mean sugar is added. Don't be fooled by drink names, labels, or container shapes. These are carefully designed to attract children, and small amounts of juice or herbs might be added to entice adults. Don't be fooled by "natural" names like honey, cane syrup, or rice syrup either. These are all just different names for sugar.

Is fruit juice better than other sweet drinks?
Fruit juice contains some of the natural vitamins, minerals, and fibre found in fruit, so it is a better choice. However,
- It is too easy to drink two to four fruit's worth of juice, which means too many calories.
- Fructose, the sugar found in fruit, has less of an effect on our appetite than other sugars.
- Juice has the same effect on teeth as other sugary drinks.

What about fruit?
Eating a piece of fruit provides vitamins, minerals, and fibre along with fructose. Eating fruit is healthy.

Does sugar affect behaviour?
Studies tell us "no," but teachers and parents tell us "yes!" Is it just because children feel gleeful when they get a treat? Are some children sensitive to the colours or flavours in most sugary items? Are they sensitive to the caffeine in chocolate and some drinks?

Does sugar really affect the brain?
A student's brain needs glucose (sugar) to fuel its thinking processes. Both complex carbohydrates and sugars are digested to create glucose to fuel the brain. Sugar by itself provides a short burst of brain fuel. This is why children might get tired or grumpy soon after having a sugary snack.

Protein, fat, or fibre eaten with carbohydrates or sugars gives the brain a steadier energy supply for a longer time. This might explain why a child who just ate a healthy snack seems better behaved than a child who just had a sugary snack.

What about artificial sweeteners?
There are a lot of rumours and myths about artificial sweeteners. Health Canada has approved their use in small amounts for school-age children. At school, artificial sweeteners are best used to enhance the flavour of nutritious foods. To help prevent children from getting used to sweet-tasting, non-nutritious items, schools should minimize sales of diet pop and diet candy.

What does a "small amount" of artificial sweetener look like?
The acceptable daily intake (ADI) for aspartame for children ranges from 640–2680 mg/day (1–41 grains/day), depending on their body weight. One tablet or packet of aspartame contains 15–35 mg (.2–.5 grains) of aspartame and could be considered a "small amount" for most children. Diet pop has the equivalent of 4 to 9 packets/tablets of aspartame in a 355 mL (11 oz) can, or 6–15 packets/tablets in a 600 mL (21 oz) bottle.

This represents a larger portion of the ADI for children and is one reason the Guidelines for Food and Beverage Sales in BC Schools (2005, BC Ministry of Education) recommends minimizing access to diet drinks. For other foods and drinks, read the labels to find out how much artificial sweetener was added and compare it to the ADI.

FIGURE 7-10 Do you think that sugar-filled drinks affect children's behaviour?

After Reading

1. Finish your KWL chart by filling in the answers in the "What I Learned" column. Do they answer the questions in your "What I Want to Know" column?

2. Sugar exists in other forms, such as fructose, glucose, honey, cane sugar, golden sugar, and so on. List your favourite snacks. Read the labels on the snacks and list all the sugar products in your food. Did you know that ingredients are listed in the order of their content in the product? If sugar is listed first, it means there is more sugar in the product than any other ingredient.

Sugar Maximum: 10% of Calories

Years of Age	Boys	Girls
	cubes or teaspoons	
4–8 years	11	10
9–13 years	14	13
14–18 years	20	15

DIABETES

Diabetes is a disease that affects the ability of the pancreas to produce insulin. More than 2 million Canadians have diabetes.

What Are the Symptoms?

Signs and symptoms of diabetes include the following:

- Unusual thirst
- Frequent urination
- Weight change (gain or loss)
- Extreme fatigue or lack of energy
- Blurred vision
- Frequent or recurring infections
- Cuts and bruises that are slow to heal
- Tingling or numbness in the hands or feet

It is important to recognize, however, that many people who have type 2 diabetes may display no symptoms.

There are three types of diabetes:

- *Type 1 diabetes* is usually diagnosed in children and adolescents and occurs when the pancreas is unable to produce insulin. Insulin is a hormone that ensures that the energy needs of the body are met. Approximately 10 percent of people with diabetes have Type 1 diabetes.
- *Type 2 diabetes* occurs when the pancreas does not produce enough insulin or when the body does not effectively use the insulin that it produces. Type 2 diabetes usually develops in adulthood, although increasing numbers of children in high-risk populations are being diagnosed. Approximately 90 percent of the diabetic population has Type 2 diabetes.

People who have any of the prediabetic symptoms described in the list above should make lifestyle changes in order to reduce their chance of developing Type 2 diabetes. Research has shown that making lifestyle changes, such as increasing exercise and following a healthy diet plan, reduces the risk of progression to Type 2 diabetes and can, in fact, return blood glucose levels to normal.

- *Gestational diabetes* is a temporary condition that occurs during pregnancy. It affects approximately 3.5 percent of all pregnancies and increases the risk of developing diabetes for both mother and child.

FIGURE 7-11 People who are of First Nations, Hispanic, Asian, South Asian, and African descent are at higher risk of getting diabetes. Are you one of these people?

Risk Factors for Diabetes

Understanding the risk factors that could lead to diabetes is important. The risk factors for developing Type 2 diabetes include

- Having a parent or sibling who already has diabetes
- Being a member of a high-risk population, such as people who are of First Nations, Hispanic, Asian, South Asian, or African descent
- Already having some evidence of the complications of diabetes, such as eye, nerve, or kidney problems
- Having heart disease
- Having a history of gestational diabetes
- Having high blood pressure or high cholesterol
- Being overweight, especially around the abdomen

Diabetes and Insulin

Insulin is considered the most important Canadian medical discovery of the 20th century. Worldwide, it has saved the lives of people who otherwise would have died from diabetes. For millennia, many people suffered from the so-called "sugar disease."

Both the Ancient Egyptians and the Hindus recorded a number of remedies for the passing of too much urine (polyuria) as far back as 1500 BCE. In the *Ayurveda,* Hindus documented cases where flies and other insects were attracted to some people's urine because the urine was sweeter. The Hindus associated this with disease.

By 1000 BCE, Susrata, a Hindu, diagnosed diabetes mellitus (DM). Aretaeus, a Greek, defined the difference between DM and diabetes insipidus (DI), a rare disease where one passes large amounts of urine and suffers from intense thirst.

In 230 BCE the Greeks named the illness *dypsacus* (diabetes). At that time they associated the illness with the kidneys. Throughout the centuries, all kinds of cures were tried. These included the use of herbs, certain vegetables, wines, vinegars, various juices, diets, and opiates. By 1501, researchers began to measure the intake and output of fluids and noted that people with diabetes lost more water than they took in. They did not know why.

In the 19th century, scientists realized the connection between the pancreas and diabetes. The discovery of insulin in the early part of the 20th century was a combined effort. It was the work of a four-person research team that included physician Frederick Banting, graduate student Charles Best, professor of physiology J.J.R. Macleod, and biochemist J.B. Collip. In recognition of the discovery of insulin in 1923, the Nobel Prize in Physiology and Medicine was awarded to Frederick Banting and J.J.R. Macleod, who then shared the prize with Charles Best and J.B. Collip.

It is interesting to note that Dr. Collip's name is also associated with protein chemistry. He made insulin safe for human use. In 1941, Collip started the first Endocrine Research Institute at McGill University and is considered the pioneer of endocrine research.

Insulin is not a cure for diabetes. However, thanks to Canadian researchers, it continues to save lives in all parts of the world.

FIGURE 7-12 Charles Best (left) and Frederick Banting, two of the discoverers of insulin. What does insulin do for people with diabetes?

Reducing the Risks

Following a healthy eating pattern, engaging in regular physical activities, and maintaining your weight will all improve your quality of life, whether you are diabetic or living with a risk factor for diabetes.

The following tips for planning healthy eating will benefit both groups:

- Take a few minutes each week to plan your menus.
- Cruise the grocery store with a list, buy only what you need, and do not add high-sugar, high-fat snack foods.
- Choose seasonal produce and pick the brightest colours that you can find. Fruits and vegetables provide lots of vitamins and minerals to keep you healthy at a very modest calorie cost. In general, the darker the colour, the higher the nutrients (think bright-red peppers or dark-green broccoli).
- Equip your kitchen for low-fat food preparation by having the equipment needed to cook in low-fat ways, such as a grill or non-stick frying pan.
- Use cooking methods that do not add extra fat to the dish, such as steaming vegetables and broiling or grilling meats. Baking and barbecuing are other lower-calorie cooking methods.
- Reduce or eliminate high-fat ingredients from your favourite recipes.
- Learn to use spices and herbs to improve the flavour of food.
- Go vegetarian for one night each week.
- To control your portion size, think of the "space on your plate." A well-balanced plate comprises one-quarter protein (for example, chicken or fish), one-quarter starch (for example, rice, pasta, or couscous), and one-half vegetables. Drink milk and eat fresh fruit for dessert and you are well nourished at a moderate expense of calories.
- Double-check serving sizes. The serving sizes people normally eat are often larger than those recommended by *Eating Well with Canada's Food Guide.*

FIGURE 7-13 The portions in this meal are close to the ideal serving sizes for protein, starch, and vegetables. What do you notice about the proportions of the foods on the plate?

Research has shown that the total amount of carbohydrates a diabetic eats has an impact on his or her blood glucose level. Paying attention to the total amount of carbohydrates they consume in a day is an important part of a diabetic's lifestyle. Carbohydrate counting can be a challenge at first. Most people with diabetes meet with a dietitian when first diagnosed to talk about meal planning and carbohydrate counting. With practice and support, most diabetics learn to monitor their carbohydrate intake and maintain their blood glucose levels.

 ## Meat and Mushroom Pie

Ingredients

1½ lbs (750 g) lean ground beef
3 cups (750 mL) mushrooms, sliced
2 cups (500 mL) onion, chopped
¼ cup (50 mL) all-purpose flour
2 tsp (10 mL) dried thyme
¼ tsp (1 mL) each salt and pepper
2 cups (500 mL) low-sodium, fat-free beef broth
1 tbsp (15 mL) bottled steak sauce
1 cup (250 mL) frozen peas
½ frozen puff pastry sheet (397 g package), defrosted

Preparation

- Preheat oven to 450° F (230°C).

- In a heavy skillet over medium-high heat, brown beef, mushrooms, and onion until beef is no longer pink, breaking it up as it cooks, about 5 minutes. Sprinkle mixture with flour, thyme, salt, and pepper. Stir. Add beef broth and steak sauce. Cook, stirring, for 10 minutes or until mixture has thickened. Stir in peas. Spread mixture in 11 x 7 in. (28 x 18 cm) baking dish. Let cool slightly.

- On a lightly floured surface, roll out pastry slightly larger than top of baking dish. Place over filling. Tuck under any pastry beyond rim. Press to inner rim.

- Bake until pastry is puffed and golden brown, about 15 minutes.

Servings: 6

OSTEOPOROSIS

Osteoporosis is a condition that results in a loss of bone density. In aging adults, it can cause painful fractures, disability, and deformity. While heredity and bone size affect the development of osteoporosis, it is often possible to prevent, delay, or reduce bone-density loss through healthy living.

The risk of developing osteoporosis is higher for women that for men. One in four women over the age of 50 suffers from bone-density loss, while only one in eight men of the same age group is affected. Making changes in diet and lifestyle prior to the age of 50 can reduce the risk of developing this painful condition.

Risk Factors for Osteoporosis

- A family history of osteoporosis
- Low body weight
- A diet low in calcium
- Smoking
- Low levels of physical activity
- A woman having her ovaries removed or having an early menopause (before the age of 45) without hormone replacement
- Being past menopause
- Having a vitamin D deficiency
- Excessive caffeine intake (more than four cups a day of coffee, tea, or cola) or excessive alcohol intake (more than two drinks a day)
- Long-term oral use of some medications, such as cortisone, prednisone, or anticonvulsants

Food for Thought

About 99 percent of the body's calcium is contained in the bones and teeth. Consuming calcium-rich foods is important for everyone but especially for mature adults, who may be at risk for osteoporosis.

FIGURE 7-14 Why is maintaining an active lifestyle important for bone health?

Reducing the Risks

Reducing potential causes of osteoporosis is important if you have any of the risk factors listed earlier. The sooner you begin, the better the health of your bones will be. Here are some tips.

- Include calcium in your diet. As you age, your body doesn't absorb calcium as well, so calcium-rich foods are important, especially when you are younger and building up calcium storage. Foods include milk and milk products, salmon and sardines with bones, beans, sunflower and sesame seeds, broccoli and other greens, figs, and rhubarb.
- Get enough vitamin D. Calcium is not easily absorbed by the body without vitamin D. Sunlight is its main source, but consider taking a supplement, especially during winter months or if you wear sunblock.
- Be active every day. Bones become stronger with increased activity. Include regular, weight-bearing exercise such as dancing, walking, hiking, or tennis in your daily routine. Exercise that improves balance and coordination, such as yoga, tai chi, swimming, and flexibility exercises will help reduce the incidence of falls and prevent fractures. Try several activities until you find the one that's right for you.
- Avoid smoking. Smokers have faster rates of bone loss and a higher risk of fractures than non-smokers. Women who smoke also tend to begin menopause at an earlier age than non-smokers. This means more rapid bone loss takes place at an earlier age.

Food for Thought

British Columbia has the highest incidence of people with Crohn's disease in the world. Crohn's disease is a type of inflammatory bowel disease the exact cause of which is not known, but diets high in sweet, fatty, or refined foods may play a role.

INFLAMMATORY BOWEL DISEASE

Inflammatory bowel disease (IBD) is a condition in which there is chronic inflammation of the bowel. It is usually diagnosed in people under 30. There is no cure for the disease, but lifestyle changes can help to manage it.

Certain foods are easier for the body to digest. Most people with inflammatory bowel disease need to avoid highly spiced foods, high-fibre foods, and very fatty foods. Not all people with IBD will be sensitive to the same foods; some are sensitive to lactose, while others will find acidic fruits irritating. Since one of the side effects of IBD is that the body does not absorb nutrients well, IBD sufferers must to be sure that they are getting enough nutrients by maintaining a healthy diet.

FIGURE 7-15 People who suffer from inflammatory bowel disease should avoid spicy foods. Do spicy foods bother your system?

FOOD SENSITIVITIES

A **food sensitivity** is an adverse reaction to a food that other people can safely eat. Food sensitivities include food allergies, food intolerances, and chemical sensitivities.

Food Allergies

Many Canadians suffer from food allergies. According to Health Canada, **food allergies** are sensitivities caused by a reaction of the body's immune system to specific proteins in a food. Current estimates are that food allergies affect as many as 6 percent of young children and 3 to 4 percent of adults.

In allergic individuals, a food protein is mistakenly identified by the immune system as being harmful. The first time the individual is exposed to such a protein, the body's immune system responds by creating antibodies called **immunoglobulin E (IgE)**. When the individual is exposed again to the same food protein, IgE antibodies and chemicals such as histamine are released. A **histamine** is a powerful chemical that can cause a reaction in the respiratory system, gastrointestinal tract, skin, or cardiovascular system. In the most extreme cases, food allergies can be fatal. Although any food can provoke an immune response in allergic individuals, a few foods are responsible for the majority of food allergies.

Allergies can be life threatening. You have probably heard of a peanut or other nut allergy, but there are many other types of food allergies as well. People who have specific food allergies must plan ahead. The following is a list of strategies for people with food allergies.

- When purchasing ingredients for recipes, always check the ingredient list on food packages before buying it. Most food manufacturers include a toll-free number on their packages that you can call if you are still in doubt.

FIGURE 7-16 Many people have food allergies to such things as peanuts, dairy products, or seafood. Do you know anyone with a food allergy?

- The most common food allergens are wheat, milk, eggs, peanuts, tree nuts, seafood, sesame seeds, soy, and sulphites (a food additive). All of these food ingredients are avoidable with careful planning.
- When cooking for your family, see if you can adapt recipes to avoid the five most common food allergens (wheat [flour], milk, eggs, peanuts, and tree nuts [walnuts, pecans, etc.]).
- If a recipe calls for an ingredient that you should avoid, such as peanuts, be creative and simply substitute an alternative ingredient like raisins or fresh or frozen fruit—or simply leave the ingredient out if it will not affect the outcome of the recipe.
- For those recipes that require specific ingredients, like egg whites for an angel food cake, there is no known substitution. However, many cakes do not require eggs.
- For more information on food allergies, contact the Allergy/ Asthma Information Association.

Web connection

To learn more about food allergies, go to this Web site and follow the links.

www.mhrfoodforlife.ca

The Top Food Allergies

Some food allergies are more common than others. The following is a list of the top food allergies. Do you know someone with one of these allergies?

- *Wheat.* A wheat allergy occurs when proteins in wheat react with antibodies in the body. Wheat comprises proteins such as albumin, globulin, gliadin, and gluten. Allergic reactions can happen when a person eats wheat-containing foods or inhales flour that contains wheat. A wheat allergy is different from celiac disease, which is an intolerance. (You will learn more about celiac disease later in the chapter.)
- *Milk.* A milk allergy occurs when the body's immune system reacts to proteins found in milk of animal origin, the most common being cow's milk. The two main allergenic proteins are casein and whey. Some common foods that have milk ingredients are cream, cheese, butter, ice cream, and yoghurt. There are some hidden sources of milk ingredients in many processed foods; therefore, it is important to know the names of milk ingredients and to read food ingredient labels if you have a milk allergy.

    Milk provides many nutrients required for a healthy body. Two main micronutrients of concern for a person who does not consume milk are calcium and vitamin D. As you have learned, calcium is needed to build healthy bones and teeth and for muscle contractions. Other good sources of calcium include green vegetables, seafood, and fish with soft, edible bones such as salmon. Vitamin D helps the body absorb and use calcium. Foods that have vitamin D include eggs and organ meats. Sunlight exposure can also provide vitamin D, but because Canada is a northern country, dependence on sunlight for adequate vitamin D is unreliable between the months of October and April.

- *Eggs.* An egg is made up of many different proteins, all of which are potential allergens. The proteins found in the egg white are different from the proteins that make up the egg yolk. The majority of people who are allergic to eggs are most likely allergic to the proteins in the egg white. However, caution is still advised, and an egg allergy means avoiding all parts of the egg.
- *Peanuts and tree nuts.* Peanut and tree-nut allergies occur when the body's immune system reacts to the proteins in peanuts or nuts. It is important to note that tree nuts (pecans, walnuts, almonds, etc.) are from a different food family than peanuts. Peanuts are legumes that grow in the ground like peas and beans; they are not tree nuts. As with other food allergies, it is important to read food labels. If a food product says "may contain nuts," then avoid it if you are allergic.

Food Intolerances

A **food intolerance** is a food sensitivity that does not involve the individual's immune system. Unlike food allergies or chemical sensitivities, where a small amount of food can cause a reaction, a food intolerance generally takes a more normal-sized portion to produce symptoms of food intolerance. While the symptoms of food intolerance vary and can be mistaken for those of a food allergy, food intolerances are more likely to originate in the gastrointestinal system and are usually caused by an inability to digest or absorb certain foods or components of those foods.

Lactose Intolerance

An intolerance to dairy products is one of the most common food intolerances. Known as **lactose intolerance**, it occurs in people who lack an enzyme called *lactase*, which is needed to digest lactose (a sugar in milk). Symptoms of lactose intolerance may include abdominal pain and bloating, diarrhea, and flatulence. People who have lactose intolerance must avoid products that contain lactose and instead drink milk substitutes such as a soy beverage.

CELIAC DISEASE

Celiac disease is a hereditary condition in which a person has an allergic reaction to gluten, a protein found in cereals such as oats, wheat, barley, and rye. This sensitivity damages the lining of the small intestine so that it cannot absorb nutrients from food. Celiac disease affects about 1 in 3000 people in North America. It rarely affects people of Asian or African ancestry.

Causes

The lining of a normal small intestine is covered with finger-like projections called *villi*. The villi are covered with tiny hair-like endings called microvilli, which trap and absorb nutrients from food. In celiac disease, the villi flatten out or disappear due to the allergic response to eating foods containing gluten. The loss of shape in the villi and microvilli results in damage to the intestinal lining.

Symptoms

A person with celiac disease isn't able to absorb the nutrients from food. This problem of malabsorption can cause vitamin and mineral deficiencies. Iron deficiency from malabsorption causes anemia, which is a reduction in red blood cells. This can lead to fatigue and tiredness. Symptoms of celiac disease can include serious diarrhea, bloating, and cramps.

FIGURE 7-17 A person who has celiac disease cannot eat gluten, which is found in grain products. If you were diagnosed with celiac disease, which grain would you find most difficult to give up?

People with celiac disease often lose weight because their bodies can't absorb the much-needed nutrients from the foods they eat. Lack of vitamins and minerals may lead to many different complications, including:

- Swollen legs from lack of protein
- Bleeding gums from lack of vitamin K
- Trouble thinking or concentrating because of nerves that are affected
- Dry skin or sore lips and tongue
- Osteomalacia (softening of bones) due to nutritional deficiencies

Treatment

People with celiac disease must avoid eating gluten-containing foods, such as bread products made with wheat, rye, or barley. Gluten is also found in many prepared foods, such as pasta or chicken fingers. People with celiac disease have to carefully check the labels on processed foods for gluten. They should also check if any vitamins and medications they take contain gluten. Fortunately, more gluten-free food options are now available.

Keeping the body hydrated is important. Taking vitamin and mineral supplements may help compensate for malabsorption. Once a person begins to follow a gluten-free diet, the bowel begins to heal and the problem of malabsorption may disappear. Because it can be difficult to follow a completely gluten-free diet, it is important that the person get a definite diagnosis of celiac disease. If the disease is diagnosed, a gluten-free diet must be followed for the rest of the person's life.

CHEMICAL SENSITIVITIES

Chemical sensitivities occur when a person has an adverse reaction to chemicals that naturally occur in, or are added to, foods. Examples of chemical sensitivities are reactions to caffeine or the flavour-enhancer monosodium glutamate (MSG).

Getting Help

Treating food sensitivities is very important. If you experience adverse reactions to food, consult your family doctor and a dietitian to help you to determine if you have a food allergy, intolerance, or other food sensitivity.

Connecting to the Community

In each Connecting to the Community activity you will find out more about your local community by completing one of two assignments. This section forms one part of your Connecting to the Community for Unit 2. For this activity you will create one product from a choice of the following products:

Chapter 7 Choices

1. For this chapter, develop a script for a health talk show, providing information about two groups of people with special needs discussed in the chapter. Include the following information:

   ■ How many people are affected in the country, province, and local area
   ■ Specific nutrient requirements
   ■ Foods to avoid
   ■ Foods to seek out
   ■ Meal planning suggestions
   ■ Other considerations specific to the group

OR

2. Create an awareness campaign to help people to understand one of the considerations discussed in the chapter. Include the following information:

   ■ How many people are affected in the country, province, and local area
   ■ Specific nutrient requirements
   ■ Foods to avoid
   ■ Foods to seek out
   ■ Meal planning suggestions
   ■ Other considerations specific to the group

Chapter 7 Summary

In this chapter you looked at special food considerations for

- Pregnant and lactating women
- Athletes
- Vegetarians
- Children with special needs
- People with
  - Cardiovascular disease
  - Diabetes
  - Osteoporosis
  - Inflammatory bowel disease
  - Food sensitivities, including allergies and food intolerances
  - Celiac disease

Activities

1. Why should women who are considering getting pregnant be concerned about healthy eating?

2. Make a tip sheet for athletes. Include
   - Energy needs
   - Hydration needs
   - Protein and fat consumption
   - Vitamin and mineral requirements

3. Use *Eating Well with Canada's Food Guide* to plan a meal for each of the different types of vegetarians discussed in the chapter. Make sure that you include foods from all four food groups.

4. Investigate one of the special needs discussed in the chapter. Visit a support group or association for this special need to find out information on feeding and nutrition. Make a tip list to share with parents and other caregivers.

5. Your grandfather had heart disease and suffered a heart attack when he was only 64. He consumed a diet high in fat, salt, and sugar. He preferred his meat fried and loved french fries. You and your dad are now concerned about your risks of heart disease. Make a list of things that you can do to help avoid it.

6. What is the difference between Type 1 and Type 2 diabetes? How can people reduce their risk of developing Type 2 diabetes?

7. What is a risk factor? What are three risk factors for osteoporosis? What can a person do to reduce the risk?

8. What is the difference between a food allergy and a food intolerance? Give an example of each.

CHAPTER 8

Body Image and Lifestyle Choices

Key Concepts

- Body image
- Factors influencing body image
- Media influence on body image
- Body types and body image
- Changing views of beauty
- Healthy body weight
- Recognizing unhealthy eating patterns
- Finding help

Key Terms

body image
eating disorder
ectomorph
endomorph
mesomorph
obesogenic culture
self-confidence
self-esteem
self-image

This chapter focuses on achieving a healthy body image and a healthy body weight. It also examines the influence of the media on body image and changing perceptions of what a beautiful body is. Healthy and unhealthy eating patterns are also discussed.

Steve and Jake are looking at Steve's sister's magazines. The boys notice that most of the models in the magazines are extremely thin. Jake asks Steve if he has seen the latest photograph of a young singing star. He said he was surprised to see it because when the star was still in her teens, she looked really healthy and fit, and seemed to be a good role model for teenaged girls. Jake said that in the most recent photo, however, she looked extremely thin. They both think she looked better at 16 than she does now at 20. Jake says that even with photo retouching, she still has dark circles under her eyes.

Steve and Jake both agree that the pressures of the media and a celebrity lifestyle must have affected her. Steve worries

about what these images might do to the self-esteem of young girls like his sister. Jake is sure that that girls who don't see how impossible it is to look as good as in a digitally-enhanced photograph could form an unrealistic image of how they should look.

BODY IMAGE

When you look in the mirror, what do you see? Do you see the same person your friends see? Your parents see? Your teachers see? Your **body image** is the mental image and the thoughts and feelings you have about your body. Other people have different thoughts and feelings about you and often have a more realistic view of your body than you do. Your view of your body is influenced by not only what it looks like, but also how you feel about it and what you believe about it. This can make your body image different from the image that other people have of you.

Understanding the factors that create body image is important. Some factors that can influence your body image are

- How the culture you live in defines beauty
- How your family defines beauty
- How your peers define beauty
- How you feel about yourself in general
- Whether you value your health more than being in fashion
- Changes in your body, especially during puberty
- Media images and definitions of beauty

Let's explore some of these more thoroughly.

Culture

In Western culture, thin is beautiful; in other cultures, being thin is not necessarily considered beautiful. In countries where food is scarce, people who are overweight are seen as wealthy and are envied because they are able to buy enough food to be overweight. Historically, different cultures have had different views of beauty. Many women who were considered beautiful during the Renaissance, for example, would be considered overweight today.

FIGURE 8-1 If you were living in this society and culture that said that this was the ideal body type, how would it affect your body image?

The Corset

The first written accounts about corsetry are from Crete and other parts of Greece. Women wore a leather band to define their waist and hips.

During the Middle Ages, corsets disappeared as the fashions changed. Then, at the beginning of the 16th century, Spanish woman wore iron corsets that gave the body a smooth, flat outline underneath gowns. In the 17th century, clothes were softer and more flowing. The heavy iron corset was replaced by one that emphasized the waist and hips and the full skirts that were in fashion.

By the early 1800s women were attempting to enhance their bust lines and hips. During this period, corsets were made wider to accommodate the body more. They were made with less boning than those that were used later. A busk, or bone, was stitched into the centre of the corset to push up the bust.

In the 1860s, corsets returned as a fashion craze. The original corset was made from cotton sateen twill for the outer layer and linen batiste for the lining. Whalebone, wood, and flexible metal were covered in strips of casing cut from the same fabric. The corset had at least 14 bones. A drawstring was encased in the upper edge. The corset laced up in the back only. Later, metal loops and studs were added to do up the front. This undergarment could narrow an adult woman's waist to less than 30 centimetres (12 inches), depending on how tightly it was pulled. Women who worked in the fields wore corsets that were "boned" with rope, which made them more flexible and easier to move in.

The corset shaped the Victorian woman by elevating the bust, flattening the stomach, narrowing the waist, and smoothing her figure. The result created what was known as the "hourglass" look. Corsets were also worn by men to flatten their stomachs, providing a smoother body shape or acting as back support.

The severe lacing on corsets and restricted movement damaged internal organs and impaired women's health. Canadian physicians started to write about and document the perils of tight lacing. *The Manual of Obstetrics, Gynæcology, and Pediatrics*, written by Professor Kenneth N. Fenwick (1852–1896) of Queens University, blamed the corset for "compressing the abdominal organs, causing muscle atrophy, leading to congestion of blood in the pelvic organs and displacement of the uterus."

Criticism of tight lacing led to the formation of an organization in 1881 called the Rational Dress Society. The reformers focused their attention on the "emancipation bodice" as a replacement for the corset.

By 1913, the first modern brassiere was invented and corsets were no longer popular. Today, the corset has made its way back into some fashion circles. Madonna has worn them as a fashion statement during concerts. Goths are also fond of corsets as outer wear.

FIGURE 8-2 Victorian women wore corsets to attain an hourglass figure, while men wore them to achieve a flat stomach. What other effects would these corsets have on a person's body?

FIGURE 8-3 How did Madonna change the purpose of a corset?

FIGURE 8-4 How much of an effect do you think your family has on your self-image?

Family

Family members are the first people in a child's life to play a major role in forming his or her body image and self-esteem. Sometimes the way your family sees you is different from the way you see yourself. For some children and teens, parents set high expectations that their children feel are impossible to reach. This can lead to a poor self image. For other children, their families see all their good qualities, and help their children see them too. Sometimes it helps to see yourself through your family's eyes; sometimes it does not. It is important that parents and other family members provide children with positive messages about developing a healthy body and body image. Ridiculing or demeaning a child about his or her body can lead to a poor body image and unhealthy and disordered eating. As discussed earlier, role-modelling is also essential. A parent who is never satisfied with his or her own body image can make children more critical of theirs as well.

Peers

Peers also have a strong influence on how you see yourself, including your body image. If a friend tells you that you are too thin or overweight, you will likely believe him or her. The influence of peers on teens can be especially powerful. Having friends with realistic, healthy views on body image can have a very positive impact on your own.

Self

Self-image, the concept you have of yourself; **self-confidence**, the assurance you have in yourself and your powers and abilities; and **self-esteem**, the confidence or satisfaction you have in yourself, all contribute to how you see yourself. If these concepts of self are negative, they will have a negative impact on your body image; if they are positive, they will have a positive influence on how you feel about yourself.

Changes in your body occur at different stages in your life. As you grow and change, your body image changes as well. A teen who was a tall and gangly child may grow into a tall and attractive teen but may still have the body image of a gangly child. Puberty causes great changes in body type as a person goes through growth spurts and hormone changes. Facial and body hair grow and "baby fat" disappears.

Your body changes shape as well, and you no longer look like a child. Incorporating these changes into your body image is not always easy for teens. Not all changes are positive. For some, puberty is a time of acne and other frustrations associated with hormonal changes, and dealing with these changes can make some teens very unhappy. Having a healthy body and body image going into puberty will help teens deal with changes that occur during these exciting but challenging years.

UNDERSTANDING MEDIA IMAGES

People are constantly exposed to media images of the North American, or Western, concept of beauty. You cannot stand in the checkout line at a grocery or convenience store without seeing attractive celebrities and other media images of beauty. Watching television at any time of day will expose you to commercials that show ideals of beauty as well as products that promise to make you more attractive.

The media uses technology to digitally enhance photographs so that any celebrity can achieve an ideal form that cannot be achieved in real life, even for the celebrity! Using these images as a standard for the rest of us to live up to is not realistic and leads only to disappointment.

By age 21, the average person in North America will have watched 1 million TV commercials. About one in four commercials gives a message to viewers about what is and is not attractive.

FIGURE 8-5 (a) and (b) Are you surprised by how much being professionally made up and groomed improves Sienna Miller's image?

Web connection

To see more examples of photo retouching of models and celebrities, go to this Web site and follow the links.

www.mhrfoodforlife.ca

Thinking Critically | What Is Beauty?

There are different views of beauty. Some are more realistic than others. You have learned that the media and the beauty industry will touch up photographs to make models reflect unrealistic standards of beauty.

Have you seen the Dove Campaign for Real Beauty? It is a series of ads designed to help all people, but especially women, see that real beauty comes in all shapes and sizes. One of the campaign's main features is a set of short films about the pressures women and young girls experience trying to meet the standards of beauty set by the industry. The other feature of the campaign is the "self esteem fund" with messages encouraging self-esteem, such as "Let's change the definition of beauty." Dove is trying to improve the self-esteem of young girls to help them withstand the pressure to meet an impossible standard of beauty.

Some people applaud the company and the campaign because it attempts to bring a more realistic and healthy view of beauty to our society.

Others feel that it is a clever attempt by the beauty industry to achieve brand loyalty.

Go to the Web connection below and follow the link to the Dove Web site. Search that site and view some of the video clips.

Questions

1. Do you think the videos are effective at getting across the messages about self-esteem and a healthy body image? Why or why not?

2. Do you think that this type of campaign will succeed in helping women have a more positive view of their bodies? Why or why not?

3. Do you think this campaign would be more effective if it weren't run by a company involved in the beauty industry? Why or why not?

Web connection

To find out more about the Dove Campaign for Real Beauty, go to this Web site and follow the links.

www.mhrfoodforlife.ca

Media and Fashion Models

In recent years, there has been much attention paid to the unhealthy body types of runway models. In 2006, officials of Spain's biggest fashion show in Madrid turned away models they thought were too thin. The officials said that they wanted the models in the show to portray an image of beauty and health, and they would not promote the gaunt, emaciated look seen on other runways. The regional government encouraged the organizers to use healthier-looking women. The government believes that fashion shows are like mirrors for many young women, and unhealthy role models should be discouraged. Many people are concerned about how the distorted images of beauty influence the health and eating habits of young women.

All these factors—culture, family, peers, self, media—have an impact on your body image, which will be positive, negative, or someplace in between.

FIGURE 8-6 Do you think that fashion shows should ban unhealthy-looking models? Do you think they set a poor example for young men and women?

- You have a *positive body image* when you feel comfortable and satisfied with your body. You feel confident and have positive thoughts about it.
- You have a *negative body image* when you do not feel comfortable with your body. You are dissatisfied with it and often pick parts of it that you dislike, such as your hair, teeth, or stomach.

During the teenage years, most young people are somewhere between having a positive and a negative body image. It is helpful to understand what a healthy body looks like when forming an opinion of your own.

FIGURE 8-7 Look at this image of Nicole Richie. How would you describe her body image?

Safety Check

Recognizing Unhealthy Body Images
The media bombards people with images of "perfect" bodies. How can you recognize the difference between healthy and unhealthy images? If a model or celebrity is very thin and has very little fat, this is a sign that the person is not healthy. A healthy body has a protective layer of fat over its bones, such as the chest bones and the radius and ulna in the lower arm. Bones of the lower arms are normally not clearly visible.

BODY TYPES

Your body type may have an effect on the image you have of your body. But body types are difficult to change. It is best to come to accept your body type and appreciate it for what it is. Too often, people want what they cannot have—tall people would like to be shorter and short people would like to be taller. People are happier if they accept who they are.

One theory holds that there are three basic body types: the **ectomorph**, the **endomorph**, and the **mesomorph**. Some of us are a mixture of types. Which type are you most like?

Three Body Types

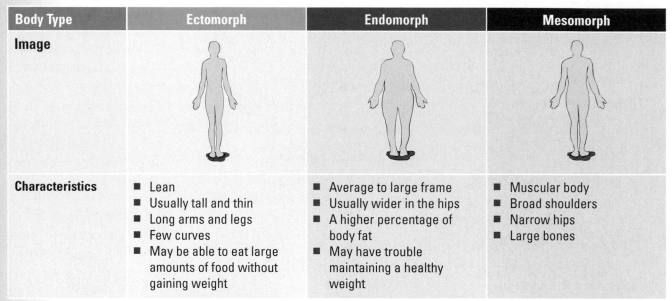

Body Type	Ectomorph	Endomorph	Mesomorph
Image			
Characteristics	■ Lean ■ Usually tall and thin ■ Long arms and legs ■ Few curves ■ May be able to eat large amounts of food without gaining weight	■ Average to large frame ■ Usually wider in the hips ■ A higher percentage of body fat ■ May have trouble maintaining a healthy weight	■ Muscular body ■ Broad shoulders ■ Narrow hips ■ Large bones

FIGURE 8-8 Model Kate Moss is an example of a person with an ectomorph body type.

FIGURE 8-9 Actor Jack Black is an example of a person with an endomorph body type.

FIGURE 8-10 The actor known as The Rock is an example of a person with a mesomorph body type.

ACHIEVING A HEALTHY BODY IMAGE AND A HEALTHY BODY WEIGHT

Healthy Eating and Activity

Healthy eating and healthy activity are two very important things that you can do to achieve both a healthy body image and a healthy weight. Healthy eating means that you eat from all four food groups and make healthy choices. You know that you might need to include snacks in your healthy eating strategies, since it is difficult to fit all of the recommended number of servings into just three meals, and it is best to give your body a constant supply of food. You also know that healthy eating involves balance. To achieve optimal health, you need to balance your diet, which can be done by choosing a variety of foods from *Eating Well with Canada's Food Guide.*

In Chapter 6: Good Nutrition throughout the Life Span, you learned that healthy physical activity, and being fit, is important at all ages. It is best to be active every day. Healthy activity allows your body to burn off any extra calories you may consume. Staying fit also keeps your muscles strong, including your heart and lungs.

Unhealthy Eating Patterns

There are many different types of unhealthy eating patterns. They range from eating too much or too little, to eating foods that are not healthy for you. Unhealthy eating patterns have an effect on a person's overall health. How much these eating patterns affect a person's health depends on his or her overall lifestyle.

Most people have times in their lives when they do not feel like eating and will eat very little. They also have times when they eat beyond being full. These times do not signal an unhealthy eating pattern as they are not part of the person's normal eating routine. A person who continually overeats and does not get any exercise will gain weight and become obese. This eating pattern is unhealthy because the weight gain is hard on the body, as you learned earlier in this unit. On the other hand, people who limit their food intake are also limiting their nutrient intake and this puts them at risk for nutrient deficiency diseases.

Other unhealthy eating patterns occur when someone eats enough food but the food is lacking in nutrients. Someone who lives on a high fat, high-sugar diet is putting his or her health at risk.

Most people know someone who is on a diet or has been on a diet. Playing the dieting game is often dangerous, and studies show that dieting can actually lead to weight gain. According to the Dietitians

In a study that tested healthy men's ability to taste salty, sweet, and other types of solutions, the researchers found that when the men skipped a meal, their taste buds were more receptive to sweet and salty flavours but not to bitter ones. Researchers suspect that our bodies may have been hardwired since ancient times to associate "sweet" and "salty" with "safe to eat," so these flavours may be more likely to trigger eating, especially when the body needs energy. This is a good reason to eat three complete meals and a couple of snacks each day.

Healthy Living

Fast-Food Facts

Fast food has become routine in North America. The 2004 Statistics Canada health survey found that, on average, one-quarter of Canadians and one-third of Canadian adolescents consume fast-food products daily. Here are some things to consider the next time you crave a burger and fries.

Fast-food restaurants cater to children and adolescents through a lot of expensive advertising, **gimmicks**, toys, and **new products**. Fast-food restaurants also charge small amounts of money for substantially increased serving sizes, making people feel like they are getting a good deal.

According to Wendy's Nutrition Facts Web site, a ¾ lb (.34 K) triple burger with cheese, a large fries, and a large Frosty give you:

- 2060 calories—close to what most people should have in an entire day.
- 99 grams of fat—The daily maximum is 75 grams a day.
- 2880 milligrams of sodium—The daily maximum should be no more than 2000 milligrams.

In general, fast food is **high in calories**, very **high in fat**—especially saturated fat—and extremely **high in sodium**. Regular consumption of these foods is bad for your body weight, heart, and blood pressure.

People are starting to realize that there are other options available at most fast-food restaurants, and many fast-food companies are recognizing the need to provide healthier alternatives as well as accessible nutrient information. If you check a restaurant's Web site, you can find its nutritional calculator and look at the nutrient breakdown of the food. So, before heading out for a quick meal, get informed and keep the following information in mind:

- Go to fast-food places less often. Once a week is reasonable.
- Choose fast-food restaurants that offer **healthier choices**. Salads, sandwiches, wraps, chili, baked potatoes, and vegetarian choices are becoming much more common at many popular restaurants.
- **Order small**. Your body never needs a triple-patty cheeseburger! The Wendy's Triple with cheese is 980 calories, while the ¼ lb single without mayonnaise is 390 calories.
- **Avoid all fried items**, including onion rings, fries, or battered chicken or fish. Choose grilled items instead. The McDonald's Web site reports that the Filet-O-Fish is 410 calories (20 g fat) and 10 McNuggets are 520 calories (31 g fat). Instead, try the Grilled Chicken Snack Wrap with Honey Mustard at 240 calories (and only 8 g fat) or a Chicken McGrill sandwich at 370 calories (15 g fat).

Remember, fast food should be an occasional treat, not a regular eating habit. Make sure you make smart choices and enjoy a better meal.

FIGURE 8-11 What aspects of this meal are bad for your health?

of Canada, real and sustainable weight loss can be achieved only through good, long-term, healthy eating and activity patterns. In Canada, we live in an **obesogenic culture**, which means there is constant pressure to eat too much. This pressure can create unhealthy eating patterns.

Some of the problems with dieting are

- Diets don't change your long-term eating patterns, so when you stop dieting, you usually gain all the weight back, and sometimes more.
- Diets promote rapid weight loss, but when you lose weight too quickly, you lose muscle as well as fat. This is counterproductive, since muscle burns more calories than fat.
- When you severely restrict calories, you put your body into "survival mode" and burn fewer calories doing the same activities. When you try to return to normal eating patterns, you gain weight because of your slowed metabolism.
- Diets create an unhealthy relationship with food, which can lead to deprivation, binge eating, and ultimately weight gain.

FIGURE 8-12 Have you noticed a public fixation with weight loss in your community?

These tips will help you develop healthy eating patterns instead of dieting.

1. *Eat less.*
   - If you consume more calories than you burn, *you will gain weight.*
   - Most Canadians eat 30 percent more food than they need.
   - Use a smaller plate to help reduce serving sizes.
   - Share appetizers and desserts when eating out.
   - Take half the meal from a restaurant home to eat the next day.
2. *Listen to your body.*
   - When you don't feel hungry anymore, stop eating. You can finish the rest of your meal or food later, when you are hungry again.
3. *Eat healthy and nourishing foods.*
   - Avoid high-fat and high-sugar foods that provide empty calories.
   - Avoid highly-processed foods.
   - Avoid junk foods.
   - Try to eat fresh vegetables and fruit.

FIGURE 8-13 Why would someone whose sport is wrestling be more likely to develop an eating disorder?

imperfections of their body, and they categorize foods as good or bad. Their relationship with food and weight is unhealthy.

A clinical eating disorder is one that is severe enough that the person who has it must get medical help. These disorders include anorexia, bulimia, and binge eating. Eating disorders tend to affect more females than males. Only about 10 percent of people with eating disorders are males. However, since people tend to think of females when they think of eating disorders, they often fail to recognize an eating disorder in a male. Most often, males are focused on both weight and an athletic-looking body. Because of this, people tend not to see the eating disorder for what it is.

People who do certain sports and physical activities are known to have a higher incidence of eating disorders than others. For girls, these sports and activities include figure skating, ballet, and gymnastics, for which a slim body is the ideal. For boys, eating disorders tend to be associated with sports where weight is important, such as wrestling and football. For both boys and girls, the ultimate goal is winning, and achieving that goal may depend on weight or body size.

Anorexia

People with anorexia, or anorexics, have an intense fear of being fat. When people have anorexia, they hardly eat at all, and the small amount of food they do eat becomes an obsession. Anorexics may weigh food before eating it or compulsively count the calories in everything they eat. It is not unusual for anorexics to also exercise excessively in an attempt to lose weight.

Anorexics feel a need to be thin and have very little body fat. Often, you can see the bones of their bodies. Anorexics have an altered body perception. Even though they might be shedding pounds at a dangerous rate, they don't see themselves as thin. On the contrary, people with anorexia look in the mirror and see a fat person. They cannot admit how underweight they are. They usually do not realize that their health is at risk and that they need professional help to overcome this illness. It is estimated that 10 to 15 percent of anorexics will die from the disorder.

FIGURE 8-14 Anorexia is a clinical condition that makes a person think he or she is fat when in fact he or she is very thin. What are the risks to the anorexic's health?

Anorexia

Warning Signs	Effects on the Body
■ Excessive weight loss ■ Denial of hunger ■ Excessive exercise ■ Feeling fat when actually thin	■ Lower heart rate and blood pressure ■ Lower body temperature ■ Menstrual periods become irregular or stop ■ Body hair or "baby hair" grows on the face and back ■ Hair loss on head ■ Skin becomes dry and pasty looking ■ Swelling and puffiness around the ankles, fingers, and face ■ Constipation ■ Hearing problems, osteoporosis, and brain damage may develop ■ Children and teens may experience stunted growth

Bulimia

People with bulimia are also obsessed with their weight, but they differ from people with anorexia in that they do eat. Bulimics usually consume large amounts of food and then rid their body of it quickly by taking laxatives or vomiting. This is called *binging and purging*. Both are very hard on the body and can lead to serious health issues. Bulimics eat to control emotions and are usually not hungry. They usually hide their emotions and give food a special significance, such as for a reward, or as punishment, comfort, or an expression of love or anger. It is not always easy to tell if someone is bulimic just by his or her apperance because most are in the normal weight range.

Bulimia

Warning Signs	Effects on the Body
■ Fluctuation in weight, gaining and losing weight often ■ Making excuses to go to the bathroom immediately after a meal ■ Eating large amounts of food but not gaining weight ■ Frequent use of laxatives ■ Withdrawing from social activities	■ Fatigue and low energy ■ Headaches ■ Dehydration ■ Diarrhea ■ Constipation ■ Bloated and painful stomach ■ Sore throat ■ Eroding tooth enamel ■ Electrolytes imbalanced ■ Hands and feet swell ■ Liver and kidney damage ■ Bowels collapse ■ Esophagus torn ■ Esophagus ulcers ■ Heart attack

Binge-Eating Disorder

People who have a binge-eating disorder, also called compulsive eating, consume large amounts of food on a regular basis. They do not recognize when they are full, and often eat in secret. Usually when people binge eat, they feel out of control while eating and powerless to stop.

Binge eaters overeat to comfort themselves when they feel stressed, angry, upset, or hurt. While they are eating, they are comforted, but later they often feel guilty and upset that they have eaten so much. Binge eating is a way of dealing with or avoiding emotions. The difference between binge eating and bulimia is that binge eaters do not get rid of the food they have consumed. As a result, most binge eaters are overweight.

Medical causes of binge eating could be that the hypothalamus, the part of the brain that controls appetite, fails to send proper messages about hunger and fullness, or that levels of seratonin, a chemical in the brain that affects mood, lead to compulsive behaviour. Other causes include habits developed in childhood stemming from being rewarded and punished with food, or from being given food to soothe, comfort, or show affection.

Binge Eating

Warning Signs	Effects on the Body
■ Eating more rapidly than others ■ Eating past the feeling of fullness ■ Eating large amounts of food even when not hungry ■ Eating alone because of embarrassment ■ Feeling disgusted, embarrassed, or guilty after a binge-eating episode ■ Gaining excessive weight	■ Obesity and related issues, such as diabetes, stroke, and heart disease ■ Depression ■ High blood pressure ■ Osteoarthritis ■ Gastrointestinal problems ■ Sleep apnea (often stops breathing while asleep) ■ Sleep problems

FIGURE 8-15 Why is it important for people with eating disorders to seek help?

Helping People with Eating Disorders

A combination of different therapies is usually most helpful for people with eating disorders. Each person will have an individual plan. The different types of help available are

- Medical attention to monitor health
- Counselling, to help change harmful thinking and beliefs about oneself, and to instill the will to live and recover
- Nutritional education to develop healthy eating patterns
- Support groups to help individuals and their families

Jennifer Eld, Counsellor for Eating Disorders

The Calgary Counselling Centre is a non-profit organization that began an eating disorders program in 1995. This program has offered specialized counselling to thousands of clients suffering from bulimia, anorexia, and binge eating.

Jennifer Eld is one of 60 full-time staff members who provide counselling for clients, including those diagnosed with eating disorders. Her own interest in eating disorders stems from her personal body-image struggles as a teenager. This led her to Mount Royal College where she obtained a diploma in Social Work. She then went to the University of Calgary for a Bachelor of General Studies and a Bachelor of Social Work.

Jennifer now works with clients suffering from eating disorders as well as people who excessively use diet pills, laxatives, exercise, and restrictive diets to reduce their weight. She sees bulimic behaviour most often, and usually works with female clients between the ages of 18 and 40.

During a typical day, Jennifer will work individually with up to four clients. For each client, she explores the person's history to try to find the root cause of the eating disorder. This is the most difficult part of her job, since the development of an eating disorder may be the result of many psychological and physical factors. Jennifer then works with the client to determine how much change he or she can manage. She also teaches clients skills such as healthy emotional expression, coping strategies, and building self-esteem. For each client, Jennifer keeps updated files, including plans, progress, and setbacks. She is also involved in a number of special projects, such as the development and delivery process of the "Towards Healthy Eating Group," a group in which counsellors enrol interested clients, offered at the Calgary Counselling Centre. The clients are people struggling with anorexia, bulimia, or an eating disorder not otherwise specified.

When working with teenagers, Jennifer strongly believes they need to hear the right message about healthy eating. Teens need to be very aware of the impact of the media on our society. Images of beauty, success, happiness, and love are communicated through the media by means of advertising and entertainment. It is vital that people remain critical of the media's goals and recognize their substantial impact on people in society. Unrealistic expectations are set by the media, and people who believe these expectations but cannot reach them are at risk of developing poor self-esteem. An even greater problem results if friends, family, or peers have these unrealistic expectations as well. Unrealistic expectations can lead to long-term damage, often well into adulthood.

It is extremely important for young people who are struggling with body image, an eating disorder, and/or low self-esteem to reach out for support. Early intervention can help make recovery successful. Jennifer suggests that people seeking help contact their physician or local hospital to be referred to an appropriate professional.

"Unrealistic expectations are set by the media, and people who believe in these expectations but cannot reach them are at risk of developing poor self-esteem."

Connecting to the Community

In each Connecting to the Community activity you will find out more about your local community by completing one of two assignments. This section forms one part of your Connecting to the Community for Unit 2. For the activity you will create one product from a choice of the following products:

Chapter 8 Choices

1. Look in your community for agencies and non-profit organizations that offer help and support to people with eating disorders. For each group, include the following information:

   ▪ Name of organization
   ▪ Contact information
   ▪ Target age group
   ▪ Type of organization
   ▪ Services offered

OR

2. Create an awareness campaign to help people understand the influence the media has on body image and/or contact local media to discuss the influence they have on young people and how the media can work with the community to create a positive message.

Chapter 8 Summary

In this chapter, you looked at some of the factors involved in achieving a healthy body image and a healthy body weight. These included

- Body image and the influences that affect it
- Media representations of beauty and their influence on people
- Healthy eating patterns
- Unhealthy eating patterns

Activities

1. What is body image and how does it affect your self-image, self-concept, and self-esteem?

2. Look at pictures in an art history book to see how the view of beauty has changed over the centuries. Make a timeline of beauty. Predict what people might want to look like in 10, 20, and 30 years.

3. Find copies of different types of magazines (fashion, entertainment, homemaking, teen, sports), and find pictures of women and men. Compare the pictures from different magazines by completing the following chart using the images and an explanation.

Magazine	Images of Women	Images of Men	Healthy Images	Unhealthy Images
Flare	Thin and young	Muscular and young	Few	Many thin people

4. Name three unhealthy eating patterns and identify how they put a person's health at risk.

5. Write an advice column on the problems resulting from dieting and explain how to develop healthy eating patterns.

6. What are eating disorders? Choose one of the eating disorders discussed in the chapter and provide the following information about it:
   - Define it.
   - Describe the signs of the disorder.
   - Outline the possible causes.
   - Describe the effects it can have on the body.

7. What are some ways to help a person who has an eating disorder?

Connecting to your community is an important part of being a good citizen. Everyone has a responsibility to one another. Both the Connecting to the Community at the beginning of each unit and the Connecting to the Community activity at the end of each chapter are designed to help you find out more about your own community.

Throughout the text you will be asked to consider your community and how it connects to you. A variety of activities will be presented and you will be offered choices as to how you want to present the information you have learned about your community. The choices for Unit 3 are as follows:

- Chapter 9: Food Safety
  - Choice 1: An awareness campaign about the principles of food safety—"clean, separate, chill, and cook."
  - Choice 2: Locate and describe places in your community where consumers can find information about food safety.
- Chapter 10: Kitchen Safety
  - Choice 1: A means of educating people about kitchen safety.
  - Choice 2: Locate and describe places in your community that offer first aid courses.
- Chapter 11: Kitchen Appliances, Equipment, and Tools
  - Choice 1: Make recommendations to someone setting up a kitchen, giving basic inventory and costing.
  - Choice 2: Describe basic kitchen tools and equipment, including their uses, care, styles and models available, and commercial examples.
- Chapter 12: Kitchen Literacy and Numeracy
  - Choice 1: Adapt an old recipe from a cultural group so that the product is healthier.
  - Choice 2: Compare a recipe for institutional use to a similar one for home use.

Putting It All Together

At the end of Unit 3, you will have completed *four pieces of work*—one for each chapter. Follow these steps to complete your product.

- Read over and edit your work from the chapters.
- Ask a peer or a parent/guardian to edit your work as well.
- Write an introduction to your product that pulls all the pieces together. Edit this as well.
- Type or write a good copy, as required.
- Find pictures to enhance your pieces of writing.
- Decide on a title for your product.
- Design how the product will be set up. Draw a rough design on blank paper before you put the product together.
- Put the product together.

Assessment

The following rubric will be used to assess the work you do on Connecting to the Community for Unit 3.

Criteria	1	2	3	4
Shows knowledge of kitchen basics	Shows limited knowledge of kitchen basics	Shows some knowledge of kitchen basics	Shows considerable knowledge of kitchen basics	Shows a high degree of knowledge of kitchen basics
Conducted research on the different factors related to kitchen basics for members of the community	Conducted research on the different factors related to kitchen basics for members of the community with limited effectiveness	Conducted research on the different factors related to kitchen basics for members of the community with some effectiveness	Conducted research on the different factors related to kitchen basics for members of the community with considerable effectiveness	Conducted research on the different factors related to kitchen basics for members of the community with a high degree of effectiveness
Use of critical and creative thinking processes	Limited use of critical and creative thinking processes	Some use of critical and creative thinking processes	Considerable use of critical and creative thinking processes	Uses critical and creative thinking processes with a high degree of skill
Communicates for different audiences and purposes	Communicates for different audiences and purposes with limited effectiveness	Communicates for different audiences and purposes with some effectiveness	Communicates for different audiences and purposes with considerable effectiveness	Communicates for different audiences and purposes with a high degree of effectiveness

Food Safety

Do you know of someone who has had food poisoning? Have you heard a warning from the Canadian Food Inspection Agency not to eat a certain food because it is contaminated? Food safety is essential to providing food for people. If people, especially those who work in the food industry, do not practise the principles of food safety, then others may get sick or food may have to be recalled. In this chapter you will learn about the many factors that you need to be aware of in order to keep food safe.

After school on Tuesday, Abhi and Kiah are watching a cooking show on television. They notice that when it comes to food safety, the celebrity chef does many of the things that Mr. Chevers, their food and nutrition class teacher, has warned them not to do. Abhi notices that the chef uses the same knife and cutting board for chicken and broccoli. Kiah points out that the chef stirs the food with a wooden spoon, then tastes the sauce, adds spices, and stirs with the same spoon. After watching the program for 15 minutes, they both agree that the TV chef would not pass the food-safety part of Mr. Chever's kitchen-ready test.

At school the next day, Abhi and Kiah tell Mr. Chevers about the show. The class decides to make a checklist for food safety and use it to evaluate cooking shows they see on television. During the rest of the week, everyone in class watches at least one

Key Concepts

Factors to consider about food safety:

- Foodborne illness and its causes
- Principles of food safety—clean, separate, chill, and cook
- Food spoilage
- Food preservation
- Safety and sanitation laws in commercial food establishments

Key Terms

cross-contamination
enzymes
food safety
foodborne illness
micro-organisms
oxidation
pathogens
perishable foods

show. At the beginning of the next week, students compared their results and were surprised at how many food safety mistakes they noticed. Mr. Chevers contacted the local newspaper and the students' observations made the front page! Abhi and Kiah are both amazed that they were in the news just because they watched television and applied what they learned in their food and nutrition class.

FIGURE 9-1 Do you know who Bac is? He represents bacteria that can spread to food when people do not use the principles of food safety.

Food for Thought

Research shows that more than half of food poisonings happen at home. Raw poultry and meats are often contaminated with salmonella, E. coli, and campylobacter bacteria, which can make you very sick or worse. Use separate cutting boards for meats and other foods and disinfect them after each use.

Food safety involves a number of principles or practices that help prevent foodborne illness and keep food safe to eat. According to statistics from the Canadian Partnership for Consumer Food Safety Education, each year, between 11 and 13 million Canadians suffer from foodborne illnesses.

Foodborne illness occurs when a person eats food that has been contaminated with a harmful micro-organism or pathogen. This condition is often called "food poisoning."

Many cases of foodborne illness go unreported because their symptoms are attributed to "stomach flu." Symptoms of foodborne illness include nausea, vomiting, diarrhea, and fever. If you or someone you know has these symptoms and do not begin to feel better within 24 hours, see a health-care professional. When seeking treatment, try to remember the foods and the places where you have eaten recently. If the health-care professional believes that foodborne illness is the cause, he or she will report it to the proper authorities. If you believe that you have eaten or purchased contaminated food, you can contact the Canadian Food Inspection Agency directly and report it. The organization will investigate if it thinks there is a chance that you are suffering from food poisoning.

Most people recover fully from foodborne illness, but some people will become seriously ill, some will develop chronic health conditions, and some, especially older people and children, will die. Complicating conditions such as chronic arthritis and hemolytic uremic syndrome, which may lead to kidney failure, have long-term consequences for people afflicted. Consumers must take care so that their food-handling practices do not lead to foodborne illness. Food safety is an important part of feeding people.

Food can be contaminated at any step along the way to your table. Everyone involved in getting food to your table must take precautions to ensure that their food-handling practices will not lead to foodborne illness.

Canada's food supply is increasingly global, which means that our food-safety practices, as well as those of other countries, affect the safety of the food we consume. Our food is also more processed now than it used to be, so that each time a food is handled at a different stage of processing, the chances of contamination increase. Bacteria may be passed from one food source to another. This is called **cross-contamination**. Cross-contamination can result from something as simple as using the same knife or cutting board for meats as for vegetables and forgetting to clean them. It can be as difficult to track

Producer

Distributor

Market

Home

Food for Thought

The "five second rule"—that food that has been dropped on the floor for five seconds or less is still safe to eat—has no basis in science. A study at the University of Illinois at Urbana-Champaign found five seconds is plenty of time for bacteria such as E. coli to stick to any food.

FIGURE 9-2 Do you know what food-safety practices are used to keep food safe during the trip from the farm to your table?

down as when bacteria from pet treats contaminate foods because a pet owner did not wash his or her hands after handling the treat.

There are also new strains of bacteria entering Canada and causing problems. The E coli O157-H7 bacterium has been found in unpasteurized apple juice, and cyclospora has been linked to imported berries, alfalfa sprouts, and bean sprouts. In the case of the sprouts, the seeds were contaminated before they were imported into Canada to be grown. It is crucial that everyone along the food chain practises the principles of food safety.

Foodborne illness is caused by **pathogens**—disease-causing agents —such as bacteria, parasites, viruses, and toxins. The following pages show a table of the most common pathogens that contaminate food.

Web connection

To find out more about foodborne illness or to report a case of it, go to this Web site and follow the links.

www.mhrfoodforlife.ca

The Most Common Pathogens That Contaminate Food

Pathogen	Description	Source	Symptoms
Clostridium botulinum	■ Does not make people ill by itself, but the toxins produced by the pathogen make people ill and may even cause death in up to 10% of cases	■ Canned (especially home canned) low-acid foods ■ Sometimes in aged meats from marine mammals	■ Double vision ■ Nausea ■ Vomiting ■ Fatigue ■ Dizziness ■ Headache ■ Dryness of the throat and nose ■ In extreme cases, symptoms may progress to respiratory failure
Campylobacter	■ Bacteria commonly found in the intestines of poultry, cattle, swine, rodents, wild birds, and household pets such as cats and dogs ■ Can also be found in untreated water	■ Undercooked poultry ■ Raw milk or non-chlorinated water	■ Fever ■ Headache ■ Muscle pain followed by diarrhea, stomach pain, nausea, and Guillain-Barré Syndrome
Cyclospora	■ A microscopic parasite that infects the small intestine of humans	■ Food or water contaminated by infected feces ■ Not naturally found on fresh fruits and vegetables, but contamination may occur during cultivation, harvest, packaging, or transportation through contact with contaminated water or workers	■ Diarrhea ■ Loss of appetite ■ Weight loss ■ Nausea ■ Gas ■ Stomach cramps ■ Muscle ache ■ Vomiting ■ Low-grade fever
E. coli (Escherichia coli O157:H7)	■ Bacteria that live in the intestines of animals such as cattle, pigs, sheep, and poultry. Despite precautions, when these animals are butchered, the bacteria can spread to the outer surfaces of the meat. When the meat is ground, the grinding process can spread bacteria through the meat.	■ In undercooked meat and poultry ■ On raw fruits and vegetables, including sprouts ■ In untreated water, unpasteurized milk, raw-milk cheeses, unpasteurized apples, juices, and ciders ■ At petting zoos	■ Minor flu-like symptoms to more severe stomach cramps, vomiting, fever, and even kidney failure ■ May cause death in small children and older adults

Listeria	■ Bacteria often found in soil, vegetation, animal feed, and human/animal feces	■ In dairy products, vegetables, fish, and meat products that are contaminated with the bacteria	■ Flu-like nausea, vomiting, cramps, and fever ■ Severe symptoms can result in a brain or blood infection, either of which can lead to death ■ A woman developing listeriosis during the first three months of pregnancy may miscarry. If she develops listeriosis later in pregnancy, her baby may be stillborn or acutely ill.
Clostridium perfringens	■ A spore-forming bacterium that produces a toxin in the intestinal tract of people who have eaten food containing high levels of the bacteria	■ In high-protein or starch-like foods, such as cooked beans or gravies ■ Especially likely to be a problem in improperly handled leftovers	■ Very gassy diarrhea ■ Cramps ■ Headache
Salmonella	■ Bacteria found in the intestines of animals ■ Bacteria may be present in foods or environments contaminated with animal waste ■ Also found in a low percentage of unbroken raw eggs	■ Most commonly in raw poultry, but also in raw and undercooked meats, unpasteurized milk, and eggs ■ Fruits and vegetables may also contain the bacteria if they have been in soil contaminated with animal waste, non-composted animal waste, and organic fertilizer	■ Mild diarrhea ■ Abdominal cramps ■ Vomiting and fever ■ Severe dehydration

Staphylococcusaureus	■ Bacteria found on or in food that has been contaminated by unclean food handling, or in contaminated milk or cheese	■ Most commonly passed by unsanitary conditions
		■ Toxins are heat resistant
		■ Found in 40% of general population (in noses, throats, infected sores)
			■ The following symptoms appear quickly:
			  – Nausea
			  – Vomiting
			  – Cramps
			  – Diarrhea

Toxoplasma	■ A microscopic parasite that may infect a wide variety of birds and mammals, including humans ■ Infection occurs when the oocysts or tissue cysts found in some raw meats are eaten	■ Improper handling of meat ■ In undercooked meat ■ In fruits and vegetables from gardens contaminated with cat feces	■ Slight fever ■ Enlarged lymph nodes and other flu-like symptoms ■ People with weak immune systems may develop more severe symptoms, such as pneumonia

FOUR STEPS TO FIGHTING FOODBORNE ILLNESS

There are four basic steps people can take to avoid most foodborne illness—clean, separate, chill, and cook. Let's look more closely at each step.

Clean

Being clean is key to preventing the spread of pathogens that can cause foodborne illness. You should wash your hands for at least 20 seconds before preparing food and again when you switch from one type of food to another. Working surfaces should be thoroughly cleaned before and after food preparation.

The Japanese have the highest incidence of foodborne illnesses in the world because of their high consumption of raw fish and seafood.

✓ TIPS ON KEEPING CLEAN

✓ To help reduce the risk of foodborne illness, wash hands before and after handling raw meat and seafood; after using the washroom; after changing diapers; after blowing your nose, coughing, or sneezing; and after touching pets.

✓ To wash your hands properly, wash them for at least 20 seconds using soap and warm water and rubbing your hands together. (A good way to ensure that you are washing your hands for at least 20 seconds is to sing the Happy Birthday song twice.)

✓ You can't tell if a food is contaminated by harmful organisms by looking at it, smelling it, or tasting it. When in doubt, throw it out!

✓ After you use tongs to handle raw food, wash the tongs and all utensils to prevent transferring harmful organisms from one food to another food.

✓ If you touch raw meat or seafood, wash your hands with soap and warm water for at least 20 seconds while rubbing them together.

✓ Raw meat and seafood should not be washed before cooking, since this could spread harmful organisms to kitchen surfaces and to other foods (cross-contamination).

✓ Before you open canned food, wash the lid of the can to prevent dust, dirt, or harmful organisms from getting into the can.

✓ Properly wash can openers after each use to keep them clean, since the can opener can cross-contaminate the next can you open.

✓ Prevent cross-contamination from cutting boards used for raw meat and seafood before using them for other purposes. Wash cutting boards thoroughly with soap and hot water, then sanitize them with a mild bleach mixture (5 mL [1 tsp] bleach to 750 mL [3 cups] water) or a commercial kitchen cleaner, or have two separate cutting boards.

✓ You can put plastic and glass cutting boards in the dishwasher to clean them. Set the cycle for a full wash. Your dishwasher should wash at a hot enough temperature to kill harmful organisms.

✓ Wash fresh fruits and vegetables with clean running water to remove any surface dirt, sand, and harmful organisms.

- ✓ Fruits and vegetables that have firm, rough surfaces, such as melons or potatoes, should be washed and scrubbed using a clean produce scrub brush before preparing or eating them.

- ✓ When washing fruits and vegetables, cut away any damaged or bruised areas since harmful organisms can grow there.

- ✓ Detergents are not intended for use on foods since they can be absorbed by produce or leave a surface residue. Use only clean running water and a produce scrub brush, if necessary.

- ✓ If you are on a picnic, hiking, or camping, bring clean water with you. Try to wash fruits and vegetables ahead of time.

- ✓ Always wash fruits and vegetables that have rinds that you can peel, such as squash, melons, pineapple, bananas, and oranges, before peeling, even though you do not eat the rind. This prevents any contaminants on the skin from being pushed into the produce when you cut or peel it.

FIGURE 9-3 Why is it important to wash produce?

Separate

Cross-contamination is a major source of foodborne illness. One of the biggest dangers is when raw meat and seafood cross-contaminate a food that will not be cooked. To prevent cross-contamination, never use the same surface, utensil, or cloth to clean or work on different foods.

✓ TIPS TO AVOID CROSS-CONTAMINATION

- ✓ Keep raw food separate from cooked and ready-to-eat food.

- ✓ When shopping, put raw meat and seafood in separate plastic bags and place them away from other items in your grocery cart.

- ✓ Defrost raw foods in covered containers on the bottom shelf of the refrigerator so they cannot touch or drip on other food.

- ✓ Do not use raw meat marinade on your cooked food unless it is boiled and stirred for one minute. Eating raw meat marinade can cause foodborne illness.

- ✓ To prevent foodborne illness, do not use the same plate or utensils for raw and cooked meat. Harmful organisms that may be in raw meat can contaminate cooked food.

Almost 40 percent of people admit to "double dipping"—dipping their veggies or appetizers into sauces and dips after they have taken a bite—which means that their germs end up in your dip! Spoon dip onto your plate or avoid any dips that aren't served this way.

Healthy Living

How Clean Is Clean?

Imagine being able to prevent 8.5 million Canadians from getting sick each year. According to the Canadian Restaurant and Food Services Association, that is the number of people in Canada who develop food-borne illnesses every year. Believe it or not, the most likely place to be exposed to bacteria that cause these illnesses is in your very own kitchen.

The kitchen is home to more germs than any other room of the house, including the bathroom. Viruses and bacteria are easily passed to family members when kitchens are not cleaned carefully. The tips below will help ensure your kitchen is really clean.

- **Kitchen sponges carry and spread more germs** than any other article in your home. The little holes surrounded by moisture pick up bacteria and provide the perfect humidity and temperature for rapid bacterial reproduction. One bacterium can become more than 8 million in less than 24 hours, and wiping the sink and counter with that sponge spreads them all over. The solution is to sanitize sponges by wetting them and then microwaving them for 2 minutes to kill the germs. If you use dish cloths instead of sponges, make sure they completely dry out between uses. Put them in the washing machine and a hot dryer between uses.

- **Washing your hands** before and during all food preparation will also help keep the germ count down. You can pick up viruses and bacteria from any damp surface, and they are easily transferred to foods if you are not careful. Warm or hot water, soap, and a thorough scrubbing are required before you touch any food.

- **Washing food** is also crucial to keeping your kitchen clean. Bacteria like salmonella and E. coli can live on raw meat, eggs, fresh fruit, and vegetables. Pesticides might also be on the surface of some fruit and vegetables. Even foods you peel first should be carefully washed.

- **Keep one cutting board for fresh produce and a separate cutting board for raw meat.** Wash cutting boards with warm or hot soapy water after each use, and make sure they are completely dry before storage. Plastic or glass cutting boards can be put into a dishwasher.

- **Use clean utensils.** Tasting food with a spoon and then stirring the food with the same spoon spreads your germs to everyone who eats that dish.

Follow these tips to keep your kitchen clean and your family healthy while you enjoy the foods you prepare at home.

FIGURE 9-4 When tasting food during preparation, what rule must you follow to ensure that you are not spreading germs?

Chill

Keeping foods cold slows the growth of bacteria. It is important to refrigerate or freeze **perishable foods** (foods that will spoil) within two hours or less of preparation. Perishable foods purchased at the store should be stored in the refrigerator as soon as you return home. The more time they are out of cold temperatures, the more time bacteria has to grow.

✓ TIPS FOR CHILLING FOODS SAFELY

✓ When marinating food in the refrigerator, always keep the food covered. Keeping food cold (at or below 4°C [40°F]) slows bacterial growth, which helps reduce the risk of foodborne illness.

✓ Do not defrost food at room temperature. The safest way to defrost food is to thaw it in a covered container on the bottom shelf of the refrigerator.

✓ Refrigerate or freeze perishables, prepared foods, and leftovers within two hours or less. Keeping food cold slows bacterial growth.

✓ To cool leftovers, such as chili or soup, divide the leftovers into shallow containers for quicker cooling.

✓ To keep food in the refrigerator cold, do not overfill the refrigerator. Leaving some room allows the cold air to circulate around the food and keeps it cold.

✓ When travelling with food on a hot day
  – Keep food in the refrigerator or freezer until you are ready to leave.
  – Use ice or frozen gel packs in the cooler where the food will be placed.
  – Carry the ice-filled cooler inside the car, not in the hot trunk.

✓ As an added precaution, put a refrigerator thermometer in with the food to check that the temperature is cold enough.

✓ When shopping at the grocery store, purchase perishable foods last.

✓ Store eggs in the main part of the refrigerator where it is coldest. Do not place eggs in the refrigerator door.

✓ Store a perishable lunch in the refrigerator or in an insulated lunch bag with a frozen gel pack.

✓ Partially thawed meat and seafood can be refrozen, but only if the food still contains ice crystals and feels refrigerator-cold.

It is estimated that 25 percent of the produce the average North American family buys goes bad and has to be thrown out. That amounts to 216 kg (475 lb) of food per household a year!

FIGURE 9-5 Why is it important not to overfill a refrigerator?

Cook

Food must be cooked at the proper temperatures to kill the bacteria that can cause foodborne illness. If food is undercooked, bacteria may still be alive and could make you sick. Once the food is cooked be sure to keep it out of the danger zone of 4°C–60°C (40°F–140°F) by serving it immediately. Cooked food should be kept at a temperature of 60°C (140°F) or above. Be sure you know the safe internal temperatures for different foods by checking the chart below and using a food thermometer to test whether food is cooked to a safe temperature.

Safe Cooking Temperatures

Meat	Temperature
Ground Meat	
Beef, pork, veal	71°C (160°F)
Chicken, turkey	80°C (176°F)
Fresh Beef	
Rare	63°C (145°F)
Medium	71°C (160°F)
Well done	77°C (170°F)
Rolled beef roasts or steaks	71°C (160°F)
Beef minute steak	71°C (160°F)
Fresh Pork	
Pork chops	71°C (160°F)
Roasts	71°C (160°F)
Fresh cured ham	71°C (160°F)
Cooked ham (reheated)	60°C (140°F)

Meat	Temperature
Poultry	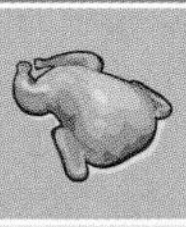
Chicken, turkey—whole, stuffed	82°C (180°F)
Chicken—whole, unstuffed	82°C (180°F)
Turkey—whole, unstuffed	77°C (170°F)
Chicken, turkey—pieces	77°C (170°F)
Stuffing	
Cooked alone	74°C (165°F)
Eggs and Egg Dishes	
Egg casseroles, sauces, custards	71°C (160°F)
Leftovers	
Reheated	74°C (165°F)

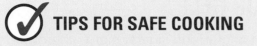

✓ TIPS FOR SAFE COOKING

✓ Hot food should be kept at a minimum of 60°C (140°F) to prevent the growth of harmful organisms. Use a food thermometer to check the temperature.

✓ Cold food should be kept at or below 4°C (40°F). Use food and refrigerator thermometers to check the temperature.

✓ Keep perishable food out of the danger zone by keeping it at or below 4°C (40°F) or by keeping it at or above 60°C (140°F) to slow the growth of harmful organisms.

✓ The best way to tell if a hamburger is cooked is by measuring its temperature with a food thermometer. For a burger, insert the thermometer sideways into each patty. The burger is done at 71°C (160°F).

✓ Cooking food to safe internal temperatures destroys harmful organisms that may be present and helps prevent foodborne illness.

✓ Hamburgers and all foods made with ground beef, such as meatloaf, lasagna, and meatballs, should be cooked to a minimum internal temperature of 71°C (160°F).

✓ It is unsafe to eat hamburgers rare. All foods made with ground beef must be cooked to a minimum internal temperature of 71°C (160°F) to prevent foodborne illness.

✓ To check the temperature of a food, insert a food thermometer into the thickest part of the food, away from fat, bone, or gristle.

✓ Leftovers, such as soup, stew, sauce, gravy, and chili, should be heated to a full rolling boil. Once the leftovers have boiled, cool the food until it's comfortable for you to eat.

✓ It is safe to eat steaks rare, since any harmful organisms that may be on the raw steak are only on the surface and are killed by the temperatures reached during cooking.

After losing millions of dollars in lawsuits because E. coli was found in burgers that were not cooked enough, fast-food restaurants are now some of the safest places to eat hamburgers. These restaurants now cook hamburgers to safety standards.

FIGURE 9-6 Why is it safe to eat steaks rare but not hamburgers?

Web connection

To learn more about fighting bacteria, go to this Web site and follow the links.
www.mhrfoodforlife.ca

WHERE CAN YOU GO FOR HELP?

While most people are concerned about food safety, many do not fully understand how to practise it. There are many people and places that consumers can visit to find information on food safety, including:

- Public health unit
- Grocery store
- Doctor
- Nutritionist
- Home economist
- Commodity groups, such as
  - Chicken farmers
  - Turkey producers
  - Dairy farmers
  - Pork producers
  - Beef Information Centre
- Government agencies, such as
  - Canadian Food Inspection Agency
  - Health Canada or a provincial health agency
  - Non-profit organizations (e.g., the Canadian Partnership for Food Safety Education)

FIGURE 9-7 Do you know how to recognize food that has spoiled?

FOOD SPOILAGE

All foods will spoil eventually. There are three main reasons for spoilage:

1. **Enzymes**, chemical substances within foods, speed changes within the food. In fruits and vegetables, enzymes are responsible for ripening and overripening, which leads to food spoilage.

2. **Micro-organisms**—including various bacteria, yeast, and mould—are visible on the surface of food and are a clear sign that the food is no longer fit to eat. Yeast grows in warm temperatures with sugar as its fuel. You can recognize yeast spoilage by the bubbles it produces on top of liquids such as pasta sauce. Moulds on bread and cheese take different forms. Bacteria is the most dangerous cause of food spoilage, as discussed earlier on page 208.

3. **Oxidation**, or the exposure of food to oxygen, shows as discolouration and a softer texture. Oxidation can also cause dehydration of the food.

Nelson Fok, Public Health Inspector

For over 20 years, Nelson Fok has been involved with food and public health. From his early beginnings cleaning up a grocery store to his current position as the Associate Director for Public Health Services in Edmonton, Alberta, Nelson has made food safety a priority.

"The best part of my job is the continuous challenge to learn."

Nelson's post-secondary education is impressive. He has an undergraduate degree in biochemistry, a diploma in environmental health, certification as a public health inspector, and a graduate degree in environmental science.

A health inspector's day includes listening to people who call about food health concerns. Often, people call the public health inspector for advice about food safety, such as food in a freezer that has been unplugged or tinned food past a "best before" date. In these cases, it is the inspector's job to educate the caller with accurate information and advice.

Other callers might complain about getting sick after eating at a restaurant, question the safety of their home tap water, or report the uncleanliness of a daycare centre. The inspector tries to resolve the issue over the phone and often follows up with a visit to the place in question.

Inspections might be routine, instigated by a complaint, or a follow-up from a previous inspection. First, the inspector will try to educate people at the establishment about proper food handling. The establishment might be ordered to throw away certain foods or store foods in a different manner. In severe cases, a restaurant might be closed down or the inspector might have to press charges against the owners for not complying with the *Public Health Act.* Inspectors also conduct foodborne-illness-outbreak investigations, tracing the cause and path of food poisoning.

The most important aspect of Nelson's job is communicating the correct information about public safety to people and organizations. Nelson's current position includes more health issues than just food safety. Although food is one significant area, this field also includes indoor air quality, drinking and recreational water, disease and injury control, housing, and other environmental health issues. Ensuring that the information given out to individuals and organizations is accurate and up to date means constantly learning about new researches and new dangers. Nelson says that "the best part of my job is the continuous challenge to learn."

SAFE FOOD STORAGE

All food has a limited time for which it can be stored and still maintain its quality. The length of time food can be stored depends on

- The type of food
- The packaging
- Storage temperature
- How the food was handled

Check the expiry dates on your packaged food. For example, mould forms in pancake mix that has expired and can cause a life-threatening allergic reaction.

✓ FOOD STORAGE TIPS

Follow these guidelines to retain the quality of stored food:

✓ Do not buy more food than you need.

✓ Use older food first. Store new food behind old food.

✓ Read the "best before" date, which is the date beyond which the full nutritional value of the food is no longer guaranteed.

✓ Make note of the "packaged on" date, which is the date the item was packaged for sale.

✓ Record the date you purchased the food on the package if "packaged on" and "best before" dates are not indicated.

✓ Clean storage areas and remove older food and food that has started to spoil.

Storing Food at Room Temperature

Store unopened dry foods, canned goods, and highly acidic items (e.g., ketchup, mustard, and vinegar) in a clean, dry place where the temperature is neither too hot (above 40°C [100°F]) nor too cold. After opening, refrigerate any food that should be kept cool (check the label). Do not use food from cans or jars that are damaged, since they may contain bacterial growth such as botulism.

FIGURE 9-8 Why shouldn't you eat food from a damaged can?

Storing Food at Cold Temperatures

It is important to know how long foods can safely be stored in the refrigerator or the freezer. Check the following chart to ensure that you are storing foods safely.

Cold Storage Chart

	Refrigerator 4°C (40°F)	Freezer –18°C (0°F)
Fresh Meat		
Beef—Steaks, roasts	2–4 days	10–12 months
Pork—Chops, roasts	2–4 days	8–12 months
Lamb—Chops, roasts	2–4 days	8–12 months
Veal Roasts	3–4 days	8–12 months
Ground Meat	1–2 days	2–3 months
Fresh Poultry		
Chicken, Turkey—Whole	2–3 days	1 year
Chicken, Turkey—Pieces	2–3 days	6 months
Fresh Fish		
Lean fish (e.g., cod, flounder)	3–4 days	6 months
Fatty fish (e.g., salmon)	3–4 days	2 months
Shellfish (e.g., clams, crab, lobster)	12–24 hours	2–4 months
Scallops, shrimp, cooked shellfish	1–2 days	2–4 months
Ham		
Canned ham	6–9 months	Do not freeze
Ham, fully cooked (half and slices)	3–4 days	2–3 months
Bacon and Sausage		
Bacon	1 week	1 month
Sausage, raw (pork, beef, turkey)	1–2 days	1–2 months
Pre-cooked smoked links or patties	1 week	1–2 months

Cold Storage Chart (continued)

	Refrigerator 4°C (40°F)	Freezer −18°C (0°F)
Leftovers		
Cooked meat, stews, egg in vegetable dishes	3–4 days	2–3 months
Gravy and meat broth	1–2 days	2–3 months
Cooked poultry and fish	3–4 days	4–6 months
Soups	2–3 days	4 months
Hot Dogs and Lunch Meats		
Hotdogs	2 weeks	1–2 months
Hotdogs—opened	1 week	Do not freeze
Packaged lunch meats	2 weeks	1–2 months
Packaged lunch meats—opened	3–5 days	1–2 months
Deli Foods		
Deli meats	3–4 days	2–3 months
Store-prepared or homemade salads	3–5 days	Do not freeze
TV Dinners/Frozen Casseroles		
Keep frozen until ready to serve		3–4 months

	Refrigerator 4°C (40°F)	Freezer −18°C (0°F)
Eggs		
Fresh—in shell	3–4 weeks	Do not freeze
Fresh—out of shell	2–4 days	4 months
Hard cooked	1 week	Does not freeze well
Egg substitutes	10 days	1 year
Egg substitutes—opened	3 days	Do not freeze

	Refrigerator 4°C (40°F)	Freezer –18°C (0°F)
Dairy Products		
Milk	Check "best before" date	6 weeks
Milk—opened	3 days	
Cottage cheese	Check "best before" date	Does not freeze well
Cottage cheese—opened	3 days	Do not freeze
Yoghurt	Check "best before" date	1–2 months
Yoghurt—opened	3 days	Do not freeze
Cheese—soft	1 week	Does not freeze well
Cheese—semi-soft	2–3 weeks	8 weeks
Cheese—firm	5 weeks	3 months
Cheese—hard	10 months	Up to a year
Cheese—processed	Several months	3 months
Cheese—opened	3–4 weeks	Do not freeze
Butter—salted	8 weeks	1 year
Butter—unsalted	8 weeks	3 months
Butter—opened	3 weeks	Do not freeze
Commercial Mayonnaise		
Refrigerate after opening	2 months	Do not freeze

Think twice about spooning an old condiment onto your plate, since spores could be growing inside the bottle, even though you cannot see them. Mouldy spores can cause diarrhea and other illnesses. Also, essential nutrients such as vitamin C deteriorate within four weeks of opening a jar.

	Refrigerator 4°C (40°F)	Freezer –18°C (0°F)
Vegetables		
Beans, green or waxed	5 days	8 months
Carrots	2 weeks	10–12 months
Celery	2 weeks	10–12 months
Lettuce, leaf	3–7 days	Do not freeze
Lettuce, iceberg	1–2 weeks	Do not freeze
Spinach	2–4 days	10–12 months
Squash, summer	1 week	10–12 months
Squash, winter	2 weeks	10–12 months
Tomatoes	Not recommended	2 months

Root Cellars

Before people had refrigeration or access to canned foods, they relied on other methods of keeping food safe to eat. The early pioneers, homesteaders, and First Nations peoples used root cellars, or cold cellars, to store many fruits and vegetables.

The ancient technology of the root cellar is believed to have originated with native Australians more than 40 000 years ago. They developed the technique of burying their produce for future use. Underground storage facilities were used by many cultures, including the Etruscans, who stored wine underground until it matured. During the 17th century the British built what were known as walk-in root cellars.

Early immigrants to Canada built many root cellars. Elliston, Newfoundland, is considered the Root Cellar Capital of the world. It has over 135 root cellars, and some are 200 years old! Different types of cellars were made depending on the area's terrain; for example, a hatch cellar, a hillside cellar, and even an above-ground cellar. Most had shelves that were at least 8 cm (3 in.) away from the walls to allow air circulation. An exhaust pipe in the ceiling allowed hot air to escape.

All root cellars require a humidity of 80–90 percent to keep fresh vegetables firm. A dirt floor provided the best conditions, since it held moisture. If the humidity was too low, water was poured on top of the soil to increase the moisture. A well-insulated root cellar could keep food 40 degrees cooler than the outside summer temperature. In the winter, the temperature was slightly above freezing, which slowed deterioration and rot.

Turnips, carrots, potatoes, cabbage, apples, smoked meats, and dried fish were all stored in root cellars. Pioneers even kept their homemade preserves, milk, butter, eggs, and cheese in the root cellar. Pumpkins and squash had to sit outside for a couple of weeks to harden their rinds, and potatoes needed to dry off, before being put into the cellar. Onions and garlic were cured in the sun before they were strung up to hang in the underground room. Only the best of the crop was stored, otherwise rot or mould would set in and could ruin all the food. It was also important to keep fruit separate, since apples, plums, and pears release ethylene gas once in storage. This can cause other vegetables, such as carrots, to become bitter. The approximate storage time for fruits and vegetables in the root cellar was four to six months.

Root cellars are making a comeback in many communities. The Tl'etinqox Reserve in British Columbia uses 20 root cellars to store the produce from its network of 60 gardens. The cellars are part of their Healthy Eating and Active Living (HEAL) program.

FIGURE 9-9 What type of root cellar do you think these are?

FOOD SAFETY IN RESTAURANTS AND FOOD-SERVICE ESTABLISHMENTS

In Canada, all restaurants and food-service establishments must adhere to food-safety principles. Restaurants and food-service establishments are inspected by provincial governments, regional municipalities, or regional health authorities. Who does the inspection varies by province and territory, but inspections take place across the country to ensure that food is handled safely.

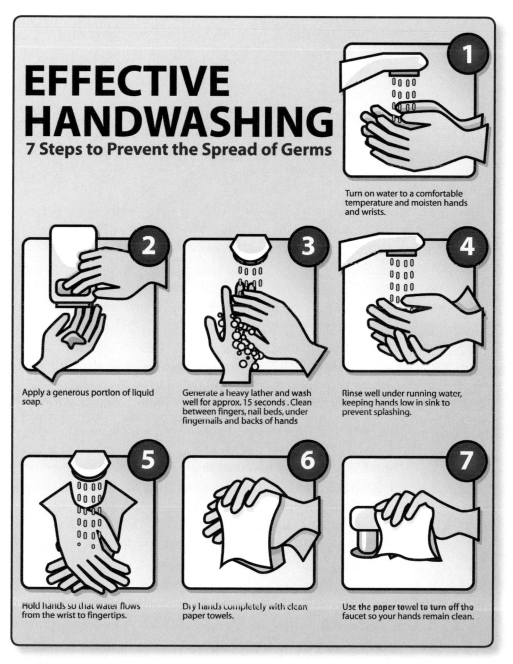

EFFECTIVE HANDWASHING
7 Steps to Prevent the Spread of Germs

1. Turn on water to a comfortable temperature and moisten hands and wrists.

2. Apply a generous portion of liquid soap.

3. Generate a heavy lather and wash well for approx. 15 seconds. Clean between fingers, nail beds, under fingernails and backs of hands

4. Rinse well under running water, keeping hands low in sink to prevent splashing.

5. Hold hands so that water flows from the wrist to fingertips.

6. Dry hands completely with clean paper towels.

7. Use the paper towel to turn off the faucet so your hands remain clean.

FIGURE 9-10 Do you follow these rules when washing your hands in the food and nutrition classroom?

Special Certifications for the Food Industry

Safe Food Handling Certificate

People who work with food in food-service establishments may be required to take a course to achieve their Safe Food Handling Certificate. Contents of the courses include the following topics:

- *Food-Safety Overview*
  Learn why food safety is so important to the food-service industry.
- *Safety Legislation*
  This section explains the role and authority of inspectors regarding the safe handling of food and how to recognize food-safety regulations that act as standards for inspections and for safe food handling in the workplace.
- *Microbiology*
  The microbiology section focuses on three types of microbes and their role in food contamination: recognizing common disease-causing bacteria, the conditions in which they multiply, and how they can be a danger to the food-service industry.
- *Foodborne Illness*
  Questions about foodborne illness (FBI) are answered: What is it? What causes it? How can it be prevented in the workplace? Who is most susceptible to it? How are FBI complaints best addressed?
- *Food Sensitivities*
  This section teaches about the seriousness of food allergies and life-threatening food anaphylaxis incidents, as well as preventing and handling these situations.

  - *Personal Hygiene*
    Learn how to prevent food contamination through appropriate personal hygiene, including sanitary hand-washing methods, correct use of gloves, and knowing when to report illness in the workplace.
  - *Purchasing*
    The Flow of Food concept begins with purchasing. Students examine the qualities of reputable food suppliers and purchasing guidelines for food items.
  - *Storing and Receiving*
    The correct ways to store foods safely, how to inspect deliveries, and how to clean and maintain storage areas are explained.
  - *Thermometers*
    Misuse of thermometers in the workplace is common. This section deals with how to prevent mistakes by learning how to correctly use and calibrate food thermometers.

FIGURE 9-11 In an anaphylaxis reaction to a food allergen, the person rapidly becomes unable to breathe due to swelling around airways, and may lose consciousness. These incidents can be fatal if not treated immediately.

- *Preparing, Cooking, and Holding*
  This section outlines preparing foods safely, correct cooking temperatures of high-risk foods, and safe hot and cold holding methods.
- *Serving and Dispensing*
  This section explores appropriate methods for safely serving and dispensing food to customers.
- *Cleaning and Sanitizing*
  How to clean and sanitize utensils and equipment safely is outlined by focusing on both mechanical and manual methods, such as the three-compartment sink.
- *Cooling and Reheating*
  Improper cooling is the most common cause of foodborne illness. This section deals with how to cool and reheat foods safely to prevent FBI in the workplace.
- *Pest Control*
  What are the signs of pest infestation in food premises? This section stresses the importance of preventing and controlling pests in food establishments.
- *Hazard Analysis and Critical Control Points (HACCP)*
  Students learn what HACCP is and how it is used in the workplace.

Hazard Analysis and Critical Control Points

Hazard Analysis and Critical Control Points (HAACP) is a risk management system that identifies, evaluates, and controls hazards related to food safety throughout the food supply chain. It looks at biological, chemical, and physical risks to food safety. There are seven principles of HACCP:

1. Identify food hazards and the necessary risk control measures.
2. Identify food-safety Critical Control Points (CCPs).
3. Determine the critical limits for each CCP.
4. Establish monitoring procedures for CCPs.
5. Plan and take corrective action when critical limits are exceeded.
6. Establish verification procedures for the HACCP Food-Safety Management System (FSMS).
7. Establish documentation and record keeping for the HACCP FSMS system.

Whether you are working in the kitchen of a fast-food restaurant, a food-service kitchen, the kitchen in the food and nutrition classroom, or at home, practising food safety is important to your health and the health of those around you.

Connecting to the Community

In each Connecting to the Community activity you will find out more about your local community by completing one of two assignments. This section forms one part of your Connecting to the Community for Unit 3. For this activity you will create one product from a choice of the following products.

Chapter 9 Choices

1. Create an awareness campaign for "clean, separate, chill, and cook." Include the following for each principle:

- A description
- Why it is important
- A list of 5–10 tips
- A graphic illustration

OR

2. Using the Yellow Pages™ or your community directory, find places in your community where consumers can get information on food safety. Include the following information for each source:

- Contact information (address, phone number, Web address)
- Type of service offered
- Hours of operation
- Three key messages about food safety that the source provides

Chapter 9 Summary

In this chapter you learned about food safety and the principles of food safety, including:

- Foodborne illness
- Pathogens that cause foodborne illness
- Safe food storage
- Food-safety principles and practices for restaurants and food-service establishments

Activities

1. Define the terms *food safety, foodborne illness*, and *cross-contamination*. Why should people pay attention to these concepts?

2. Make a checklist for food safety using the principles of clean, separate, chill, and cook. Watch a food-preparation television show and rate the chef on how safe his or her food-handling practices are.

3. Choose three of the pathogens listed in the chart Most Common Pathogens That Contaminate Food on pages 210–11 and create a brochure that explains
   - Health risks
   - Symptoms
   - Strategies to avoid contamination

4. Give a brief description of clean, separate, chill, and cook and provide a tip for each one.

5. Create a poster to hang in your kitchen at home to show proper food storage. Include:
   - Room-temperature storage
   - Refrigerator storage
   - Freezer storage

6. Restaurants and food-service establishments have to follow food-safety guidelines and undergo inspections to ensure that they are following procedures. Why do you think this is important? Explain your answer in a letter to the editor of your local paper.

7. Review the components of the Safe Food Handling Certificate program. Do you think everyone who works in the food industry should be required to have one? Justify your answer in a 500-word article for the school newspaper.

CHAPTER 10

Key Concepts

Practising kitchen safety, including

- General safety guidelines
- Prevention of fires, burns, falls, and cuts
- The safe use of electrical equipment
- The safe use of household chemicals
- The safe use of stoves and microwaves
- Special considerations for accident prevention involving children and people with special needs
- First aid treatment for bleeding, burns and scalds, poisoning, choking, and eye injuries

Key Terms

hazard symbols
– corrosive
– explosive
– flammable
– toxic
Heimlich manoeuvre

Kitchen Safety

I n this chapter you will learn about safe practices related to procedures and equipment in the kitchen. You will also learn about accident prevention and first aid.

Mallory, Jenelle, and Deirdre have been in the kitchen all day making healthy muffins for the school bake sale. When Deirdre's mom, Mary, comes home, she is appalled at the mess and the obvious lack of kitchen safety practised by the girls. There are cupboard doors open, a tea towel has been used to take the muffins out of the oven, the oven is still on although there is no one in the room, and an electrical cord is hanging in the sink. Mary is amazed that no one has fallen because there is muffin mix and milk spilled on the floor. She shakes her head, because all three girls earned good marks in their food and nutrition class. It's too bad that they have not put their knowledge of kitchen safety into practice in their own home kitchens.

SAFETY GUIDELINES

When you walk into a kitchen to prepare a meal, do you see all the potential hazards? Probably not. Most people never think about the potential for harm that may be in their own kitchens. It is very important to be aware of the various types of kitchen hazards, preventive measures to take to avoid them, and what to do in case of an accident or injury.

FIGURE 10-1 Do you know how to work safely in a kitchen?

Have you ever had an accident in the kitchen at home? At school? Could the accident have been prevented? In this chapter you will focus on safety in the kitchen not only to prevent accidents but also to learn what to do if there is one.

General Rules

There are many kitchen safety factors to remember. First, let's examine the general rules that apply to working in a kitchen.

1. Work with a purpose in a safe and orderly manner. Never run in the kitchen, and look out for people moving around you.
2. Prepare to work safely in the kitchen. Tie back long hair, remove jewellery, and tie up apron strings. Roll up sleeves. Do not wear loose-fitting clothing in the kitchen because it can touch an element and catch fire.
3. Keep the kitchen clean and free of clutter. Pick up anything that falls on the floor to prevent people tripping or slipping.
4. Keep the kitchen tidy. When finished with a utensil or ingredient, put it away to allow more workspace.
5. Keep pot handles turned toward the centre of the stove so pots and pans will not be knocked off by someone passing by.
6. Keep cupboard doors and kitchen drawers closed to prevent people from bumping into them.
7. When not in use, turn off and unplug small appliances.
8. Turn off burners when they are not in use. Make sure you have turned on the correct burner when you are ready to cook.

FIGURE 10-2 Why is keeping kitchens clean and free of clutter an important part of kitchen safety?

9. Use safe equipment. Never use a pot with an insecure handle, broken or chipped glassware, or damaged oven mitts.

10. Take the time to find the right tool for the job. In a kitchen, haste can cause accidents.

11. Store heavier items on lower shelves so they can be reached safely.

12. Clearly label household chemicals and store them in a cool, dry place out of the reach of children and pets.

Fire Prevention in the Kitchen

Fires are a serious hazard in the kitchen. Follow these simple rules to prevent fires from igniting during food preparation.

1. Keep paper away from the cooking surface. If you are using a recipe card or work sheet, tape it onto a cupboard so that no paper can come into contact with the stove.

2. Do not wear loose-fitting clothing, especially long or loose-fitting sleeves, near the stove.

3. When cooking with fat, do not leave the food unattended, and keep an eye on the temperature. When fat is heated to a high temperature, it may catch fire. If smoke is rising from the fat, then turn down the heat.

4. Use only heat- and flame-proof oven mitts and pot holders. Tea towels and aprons can come into contact with burners and catch fire.

5. Do not hang curtains over a stove as they too can catch fire.

Safety Check

Care of Oven Mitts and Potholders
Oven mitts and potholders are needed to protect your hands and arms from hot pots and pans during cooking. Check periodically that they are in good condition. If they are worn or have holes, they will not protect you. Replace them immediately, if necessary.

Most kitchen fires in homes and restaurants happen because someone heating fat or oil forgot about it. Oil gets hotter and hotter, smokes, bursts into flames, and becomes the fuel for the fire.

6. Only use fire-safe plastics near a stove. Some plastics are highly flammable and give off toxic fumes when burning.

7. Keep the oven clean. Spills and crumbs can catch fire.

8. Never use electrical equipment that has frayed or broken cords. They can cause a shock, a short, or a fire. They should be repaired before use.

9. When using an electrical appliance with a detachable cord, plug the cord into the appliance *before* plugging it into the outlet. When finished using the appliance, unplug the cord from the outlet *before* unplugging the appliance.

10. Fires require oxygen to burn, but you need to know what type of fire you have in order to smother it safely.

How to Extinguish Different Types of Fires

Type of Fire	How to Extinguish
Paper	Use water or an asbestos fire blanket to put out the flames.
Fabric	Use water or an asbestos fire blanket to put out the flames. If clothing is on fire, have the person wearing it stop, drop, and roll in the blanket.
Fat and oil	Never use water to put out a fat or oil fire. Water will spread the fire, which could ignite something else. Use baking soda, salt, or a fire extinguisher to smother the flames. Point the fire extinguisher at the base of the fire.
Oven	With oven fires, do not open the oven door. Opening the door allows oxygen in to fuel the fire. Leave the door closed and turn off the oven.
Electrical	Use a fire extinguisher and aim it at the base of the fire.

FIGURE 10-3 Do you know how to use fire safety equipment in the kitchen?

Preventing Burns in the Kitchen

People usually associate getting burned with fire, but there are many other ways to get burned in a kitchen. You can be burned by a hot pot or element; an oven rack; steam from something cooking; or by being splattered with hot oil, food, or liquid. Knowing how to prevent burns is an important part of kitchen safety.

Follow these tips to avoid being burned in the kitchen:

1. Use appropriate heat protection, such as oven mitts or potholders.
2. Do not use wet potholders. When heat combines with the moisture in the potholders, steam can be created and burn you.
3. When removing the lid from a pot, tilt the lid away from your body, allowing the steam to flow away from you.
4. Be careful when removing covers from foods cooked in the microwave. To avoid steam burns, tilt the lid or cover away from your body, making sure that steam does not come into contact with your hands or face.
5. When trying to reach food inside the oven, always pull out the oven racks instead of putting your arms into the oven. Use oven mitts to handle both the rack and the food.
6. Keep pot handles turned toward the centre of the stove to avoid knocking the pan over.
7. Keep children away from hot liquids. A child could easily knock over a pot of hot liquid and get seriously burned.
8. Turn off the stove when you are not using it.
9. Be careful when opening the oven door since hot air will rush out.

FIGURE 10-4 Do you know how to safely remove the lid from a pot full of steaming liquid?

Preventing Falls in the Kitchen

To protect people from falls in the kitchen, clean up spills immediately. When trying to reach higher shelves in a kitchen, use a stepstool or ladder. Do not use a chair or an open drawer or climb onto the counter. Make sure your shoes are tied to avoid tripping over laces. Keep throw rugs out of the kitchen unless they are slip-proof.

FIGURE 10-5 Do you always clean up spills quickly to prevent people from slipping?

Preventing Cuts in the Kitchen

Cutting tools and other sharp objects in the kitchen that can cause serious cuts. This includes sharp knives, can openers, skewers, and broken glass. Follow these tips to avoid cuts in the kitchen.

1. Store sharp knives in a safe place. Use drawer dividers to separate knives or use a knife rack.
2. Keep sharp knives sharp. Dull knives are more likely to slip and cause cuts.
3. When placing knives in or removing knives from the dishwasher, use the handles.
4. Never put knives in a sink filled with dishwater; you may reach for the knife and grasp the blade instead of the handle.
5. If you drop a knife, do not attempt to catch it.
6. When cutting something horizontally, cut with the blade turned away from you.
7. Use the correct knife for the job. See Chapter 11: Kitchen Appliances, Equipment, and Tools, p. 261.
8. If you break a glass, clean it up immediately. You may need to pick up the larger pieces first using a wet paper towel (not your bare fingers) and then sweep up the smaller pieces.
9. Wrap broken pieces of glass in layers of paper and throw them in the garbage.
10. If you break glass in the food and nutrition classroom, tell your teacher as there may be special glass disposal procedures in your school.
11. You can also cut yourself on the sharp edge of an open can, a can lid, or on a grater. Handle these with care.

FIGURE 10-6 Do you know how to store, wash, and use knives and other sharp tools safely?

Using Electrical Equipment Safely

There are usually numerous types of electrical tools and equipment in a kitchen. Improper use of electrical equipment can cause shocks, which can cause death. Careful use of electrical equipment in the kitchen is an important part of kitchen safety. Follow these tips:

1. Follow the manufacturer's directions for all electrical appliances.
2. Do not use electrical appliances when your hands are wet or when you are standing in water or on a wet floor.
3. Keep electrical appliances away from water.
4. Keep cords away from water and sinks.
5. If an electrical appliance falls into water, unplug the appliance before touching it.
6. Do not use small appliances in water unless the manufacturer's instructions say you can.
7. Do not use appliances with damaged cords.
8. Do not unplug an appliance by pulling the cord. Pull the plug itself from the outlet.
9. Do not overload an outlet. This can cause a fire.
10. If a new plug will not fit into an older outlet, do not try to make it fit. Replace the outlet or buy an adapter.
11. If an appliance has a detachable cord, unplug the cord from the outlet before you unplug it from the appliance.
12. Never put your fingers or utensils into an appliance while it is plugged in.
13. Do not let cords dangle off the counter. The cord can get caught and the appliance dragged off the counter.
14. Turn off small appliances when not using them.

Web connection

To find out more about the safe use of small appliances, go to this Web site and follow the links.

www.mhrfoodforlife.ca

FIGURE 10-7 Why is this unsafe?

Healthy Living

Kitchen Chemicals

Today when you go home, look to see how many **toxic chemicals** are stored in your kitchen. Look for the following items: spray cleaner, scouring powder, drain cleaner, bleach, window cleaner, dishwasher detergent, air freshener, floor cleaner, and oven cleaner. All of these products contain powerful chemicals that can be dangerous unless they are stored, handled, and used properly.

Commercial cleaners contain chemicals that may irritate the skin and eyes on contact. Many cleaners are sprayed as a mist or an aerosol, enabling the chemicals to spread into the air in fine particles that can damage the nose, throat, and lungs when inhaled. Silica, ammonia, chlorine, acetone, bleach, turpentine, lye, hydrochloric acid, sulphuric acid, phosphates, and fragrances are just some of the hazardous materials that make up the wide range of home cleaning products. When people clean their kitchens, they usually use several products: **combinations** of these chemicals dispersed into the air can create even greater hazards.

FIGURE 10-8 Can you smell the odour of chemical cleaning products in your home long after they've been used?

There are several simple things people can do to reduce the risk while using chemical products. First, cleaning products of any kind should not be stored under the sink where **younger children** or pets can reach them. Cleaning products should be placed in a high cupboard that is separate from all food. Over half of all Canadian **poisoning reports** involved children under four, and nearly half of the products involved were intended for household use.

Next, replace many or all chemical cleaners with less-toxic products. This will reduce your family's exposure to the chemicals and be better for the environment. Simple, inexpensive materials such as **vinegar** and **baking soda** can do many cleaning jobs. Baking soda can be used with a plastic scrubber to scour the sink and stove top, while vinegar can be used to wipe down washed counters and microwaves. Be sure surfaces are completely dried to slow the growth of bacteria. **Borax** (a laundry product) can be combined with baking soda for stubborn stains. Commercial environmentally friendly cleaners are available for tougher jobs such as floors.

Finally, read the instructions on all cleaning product labels. Follow instructions exactly, including proper disposal methods. ***Never mix cleaning products together***, especially anything containing ammonia. Mixing products can release dangerous gases. For example, toilet bowl cleaner mixed with bleach produces chlorine gas.

Next time you reach for a cleaner, think about yourself, your family, and the environment, and **try to find a less-toxic substitute**.

Safe Use of Household Kitchen Chemicals

There are hundreds of different chemicals used in kitchens. Most kitchen chemicals are safe, such as dishwashing detergent; others can be dangerous if used improperly. Understanding the safe use of chemicals is vital to your own and others' safety.

Kitchen chemicals that can be hazardous include

- Oven cleaners
- Disinfectants
- Bleach
- Drain cleaners

The following **hazard symbols** have been developed to provide a universal language for the safe use of chemicals. Understanding what the hazard symbols mean is crucial to using chemicals safely, particularly household cleaners used in the kitchen.

Web connection

To find out more about chemical hazards, go to this Web site and follow the links.

www.mhrfoodforlife.ca

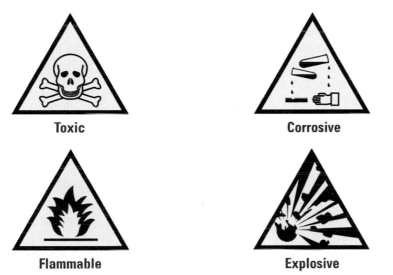

Toxic Corrosive

Flammable Explosive

FIGURE 10-9 Have you noticed any of these symbols on products you've handled in your home? Did you know what the symbols meant?

Once you know what the hazard symbols mean, follow these tips to help you use household chemicals safely:

1. Read the label and follow the instructions carefully.
2. Dispose of containers according to the directions.
3. Never transfer a chemical product from its original container to another container. The original container has government-approved safe-use messages. It is also designed to be safe for the containment of the specific chemical. Other people may not realize that the container holds a different chemical.
4. Do not mix chemicals. The fumes can be dangerous.
5. Store household chemicals safely out of the reach of children and pets.
6. Store flammable products away from heat.

Food for Thought

There are an estimated 650 000 hazardous chemical products in existence and as many as 1000 new ones are produced every year. Only 2 to 3 percent of them have been tested for the threat they may pose to humans and animals. There is mounting evidence that many of these chemicals can alter sexual and neurological development, impair reproduction, cause cancer, and harm the immune system.

Literacy in Your Life

Language
Extension

Environmentally friendly and *nature friendly* are terms used to refer to goods and services considered to cause minimal harm to the environment. These products generally save energy, produce less waste, reduce the use of toxic substances, and therefore save money in utility and disposal costs.

Before Reading

1. Have you ever had a job that included cleaning? What products did you use? Are you aware of any controversy surrounding these products? This article is on creating and using cleaning products that are easily obtained and safe for you and the environment.

During Reading

1. Read the article headings and decide whether it will be necessary to convince others in your home to use these recipes. Visualize the information in your mind. Can you create a picture of the suggested routines?

Recipes for Homemade Cleaning Products

Taken a trip down the cleaning aisle at the supermarket lately? If you believe the ad hype, you can't keep a clean house without loading your shopping cart with a different cleaner for each surface, floor, and sink in the house. Hogwash! Simple recipes using products from your pantry make effective household cleaning solutions. An added plus: these natural products are more environmentally friendly than commercial alternatives.

Stock your cleaning tool tote with these homemade cleaning sprays and solutions to make short work of household grime—without harsh chemicals or irritating fumes. Try these easy recipes to clean your home faster, better, and cheaper.

White Vinegar

Mildly acidic white vinegar dissolves dirt, soap scum, and hard-water deposits from smooth surfaces, yet is gentle enough to use in solution to clean hardwood flooring. White vinegar is a natural deodorizer, absorbing odours instead of covering them up. (And no, your bathroom won't smell like a salad! Any vinegar aroma disappears when the vinegar dries.) With no colouring agents, white vinegar won't stain grout on tiled surfaces. Because it cuts detergent residue, white vinegar makes a great fabric softener substitute for families with sensitive skin.

Try these recipes to harness the cleaning power of white vinegar:

Homemade Spray Cleaner Recipe
Mix in a sprayer bottle 250 mL (1 cup) white vinegar and 250 mL (1 cup) water. In the kitchen, use this spray to clean countertops, lightly soiled range surfaces, and backsplash areas. In the bathroom, use the spray to clean countertops, floors, and exterior surfaces of the toilet. For really tough bathroom surfaces, such as shower walls, pump up the cleaning power by removing the sprayer element and heating the solution in the microwave until warm. Spray shower walls with the warmed solution generously, allow to stand for 10 to 15 minutes, then scrub and rinse. The heat helps soften stubborn soap scum and loosens hard-water deposits.

Undiluted White Vinegar

Undiluted white vinegar makes quick work of tougher cleaning problems involving hard-water deposits or soap scum.

Use undiluted white vinegar to scrub the inside of the toilet bowl. Before you begin, pour a bucket of water into the toilet to force water out of the bowl and allow access to the sides. Pour undiluted white vinegar around the bowl and scrub with a toilet brush to remove stains and odour. Use a pumice stone to remove any remaining hard water rings.

Clean shower heads clogged with mineral deposits with undiluted white vinegar. Place 50–125 mL (¼–½ cup) vinegar in a plastic food storage bag, and secure the bag to the shower head with a rubber band. Let stand for two hours or overnight, then rinse and buff the fixture to a shine.

Add 250 mL (1 cup) of undiluted white vinegar, instead of commercial fabric softener, to the laundry rinse cycle. White vinegar softens clothes and cuts detergent residue—a plus for family members with sensitive skin.

Baking Soda

Baking soda's mild abrasive action and natural deodorizing properties make it a powerful replacement for harsh commercial scouring powders.

Sprinkle baking soda onto a damp sponge to tackle grimy bathtub rings, scour vanities, or remove food deposits from the kitchen sink. For tougher grime, make a paste of baking soda and water, apply to the tub or sink, and allow to stand for 10 to 20 minutes. Dirt, soap scum, and deposits soften and are easier to remove.

Slow-running drains? Keep bathroom drains running freely by pouring 125–200 mL (½–¾ cup) baking soda into the drain, and dribbling just enough hot water to wash the solution down. Let stand for two hours to overnight, then flush thoroughly with hot water. The deodorizing effect is an added bonus! (Do not use this method on blocked drains.)

Furniture Polish

Most people no longer use hard-to-apply furniture wax but rely on oil-based polish to keep furniture protected and shiny. The "salad dressing" version below avoids the danger of silicone oil, found in most commercial polishes and sprays. Silicone oil can penetrate tiny cracks in furniture finish and enter the wood, causing problems if refinishing is ever needed. Lemon juice dissolves dirt and smudges, while olive oil shines and protects the wood.

Furniture Polish Recipe
Mix in a sprayer bottle 250 mL (1 cup) olive oil and 125 mL (½ cup) lemon juice. Shake well and apply a small amount to a flannel cleaning rag or cleaning cloth. Spread evenly over furniture surface. Turn cloth to a dry side and polish dry.

FIGURE 10-10 Which homemade, environment-friendly cleaning products could you use in your bathroom?

After Reading

1. Make a list of some of the cleaning products in your house and include the ingredients in each. Should you be concerned if the ingredients are not listed? Are there warnings about toxicity? What do the hazard symbols tell you?

2. Explain some ways the environment will benefit if people switch to non-toxic cleaning products.

CHILDREN IN THE KITCHEN

Kitchens can be dangerous places for children. Small children like to be with adults and to imitate them. Doing this in a kitchen, children could get burned or cut, or they could fall. Children like to be at an adult's level and will climb on things to get there. If they climb onto the stove, they could get seriously hurt. Many kitchen fires involve children climbing to reach cereal boxes stored above a stove and their clothing catching fire. Are the cereal boxes stored in a safe place in your home?

Never leave small children alone in the kitchen. Cupboard doors should have childproof locks or safety latches. If children want to help in the kitchen, provide them with child-size, safe utensils and a safe place to work. Do not let children sit on a counter, since they can easily fall off. Young children should not use knives or work at or near the stove because they can easily get hurt. As discussed earlier in the text, one way children learn is by modelling what adults do. Model safe kitchen practices for children.

FIGURE 10-11 What hazards are a threat to children in the kitchen?

Early Remedies

Many early settlers from Europe brought herbs with them to Canada to grow for medicinal purposes. There were very few doctors at that time. Herbs are any plant with leaves, seeds, or flowers used for flavouring, food, medicine, or scent. The roots and bark of many herbs are beneficial in healing various ailments. The pioneers used herbs as benefits, to prevent illness, and as simples, to relieve pain caused by a sickness. Benefits could be compared to modern-day vitamins, whereas simples were used to relieve a specific pain, such as arthritis. Garlic, considered a herb, was used as a benefit to stimulate the digestive system and as a simple to provide relief for asthma.

Pioneer women gathered medicinal herbs in the fall and hung them to dry. The dried herbs were used for infusions and to make plasters and poultices. Plasters were mixtures made into a paste and applied directly to the area where there was pain or congestion; for example, to the chest for a cold. Poultices were made from bread, milk, herbs, and even onions. Poultices were placed on cuts and sores to speed their healing.

First Nations peoples eventually taught the settlers about native plants. They showed the settlers how to use spruce pitch for dressing wounds and as a poultice on boils to draw out infection. Chewed willow bark was used to help relieve pain. Today, Aspirin is made from the same chemical. Slippery elm bark was used for stomach upset.

First Nations peoples on the West Coast recognized the medicinal properties of the Pacific yew. Teas or infusions were made from its needles and bark for treating colds, infections, rheumatism, and other illnesses. Crushed needles were placed on wounds to speed healing. In 1971, researchers discovered a chemical compound in the Pacific yew called paclitaxel, which is now used to treat some cancers as well as AIDS.

FIGURE 10-12 Why would this herb doctor probably have made a good living in Montréal, Québec, in 1859?

Eventually, the most commonly-used medicines were tonics. These were taken to prevent or alleviate the symptoms of disease and to treat such things as weight loss, fatigue, colds, coughs, and fever. Tonics were prepared from a variety of plants, including spruce, wild cherry, and dogwood, which were made into **teas**. By the early 1900s, it was more common to buy a tonic from the local drug store than to make it at home. Many tonics were manufactured in Canada.

By the 1950s, more trained medical doctors were available, and people no longer had to rely on themselves for treatment. However, many of the herbs used by the early settlers and First Nations peoples are still very valuable to medicine today.

SAFETY CONSIDERATIONS FOR PEOPLE WITH SPECIAL NEEDS

Most kitchens are not designed for people with special needs. People who have physical challenges need special equipment or design features in the kitchen to be able to work safely. The type of accommodation needed depends on the person's special need. Below is a list of special needs and possible aids in the kitchen.

- **Vision Impairment**
  - Have a magnifying glass in the kitchen for reading small print.
  - Put larger labels on items to make them easier to read.
  - Ensure lighting is bright.

- **Physical Disability**
  - Store frequently-used equipment in easy-to-access places.
  - Use non-breakable dishes and glassware.
  - Put easy-to-use handles on cupboards and drawers.
  - Purchase a stove with knobs at the front.

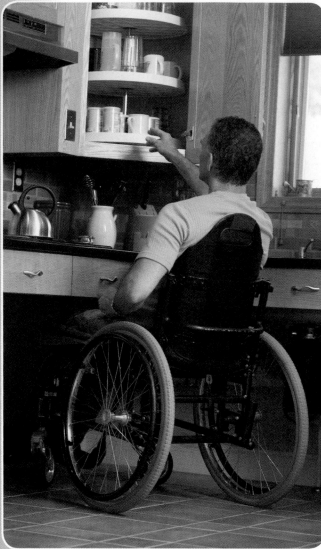

FIGURE 10-13 What special alterations have been made to this kitchen to make food preparation possible for this person?

FIRST AID

Accidents happen in the kitchen even if you have learned how to prevent them. This section will help you treat someone who has been hurt in a kitchen accident. Remember, if someone becomes ill or is injured in the food and nutrition classroom, you must tell the teacher immediately.

General Rules of First Aid

Taking a first aid course is a good way to learn about how to treat injuries anywhere. First aid courses are offered in your community by St. John Ambulance, the Canadian Red Cross Society, and by some community groups.

First aid guidelines include:

- Learn the basic principles of first aid.
- If 911 is not in your area, post telephone numbers for an ambulance, the police, and the fire department near the phone.
- Keep the number of your doctor near the phone.
- Make sure that there is no further danger to yourself or the victim before you treat him or her.
- Keep a first aid kit in the kitchen.

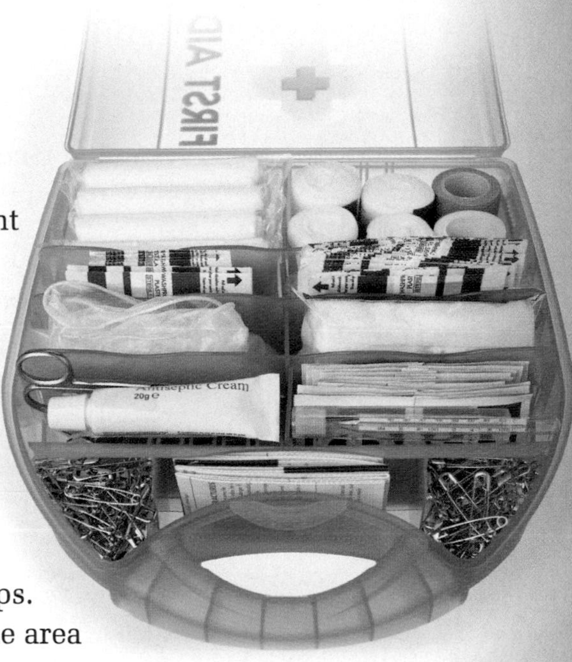

- **Bleeding**
  - Cover the wounded area with a sterile cloth.
  - Apply direct pressure.
  - Continue to apply pressure until the bleeding stops.
  - If there is no evidence of broken bones, elevate the area that is bleeding.
  - If an object is embedded in a cut, do not remove it. Get medical assistance.

- **Burns and Scalding**
  - Cool the area by placing it under cold running water.
  - Apply ice to relieve the pain.
  - Do not open blisters.
  - Do not put ointment or greasy substances on a burn.
  - If the burned area is deep or larger than the size of a quarter, seek medical treatment.

- **Poisoning**
  - Call 911 or the Poison Control Centre immediately.
  - Identify the type of poison, if possible, and have the container handy when you make the phone call.
  - If poison is swallowed, follow the treatment instructions given on the label and by medical personnel.
  - If poison has made contact with the skin, flood the area with cold running water for at least 15 minutes.
  - If poison has made contact with the eyes, gently rinse them with cold water for 15 minutes. Do not let the injured person rub them.

- **Choking**

  The **Heimlich manoeuvre** was developed as a safe way to help victims who are choking. The following section explains how to use the manoeuvre on adults, infants, and yourself. It is now recommended that before you begin the Heimlich manoeuvre, you should call 911 for support, if possible.

FIGURE 10-14 Do you know where the first aid kit is in your classroom? Do you have one in your home kitchen?

Web connection

To find out more about first aid, go to this Web site and follow the links.

www.mhrfoodforlife.ca

The Heimlich Manoeuvre for Victims of Choking

A choking victim can't speak or breathe and needs your help immediately. Follow these steps to help a choking victim:

1. From behind, wrap your arms around the victim's waist.
2. Make a fist and place the thumb side of your fist against the victim's upper abdomen, below the ribcage and above the navel.
3. Grasp your fist with your other hand and press into the victim's upper abdomen with a quick upward thrust. Do not squeeze the ribcage; confine the force of the thrust to your hands.
4. Repeat until object is expelled.

FIGURE 10-15A If conscious, victim should be in standing position

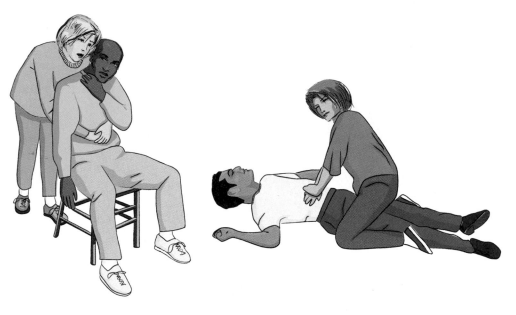

FIGURE 10-15B Positioning when rescuer cannot reach around victim, or victim is unconscious

For an unconscious victim, or if you can't reach around the victim, follow these steps:

1. Place the victim on his/her back.
2. Facing the victim, kneel astride the victim's hips.
3. With one of your hands on top of the other, place the heel of your bottom hand on the upper abdomen below the rib cage and above the navel.
4. Use your body weight to press into the victim's upper abdomen with a quick upward thrust. Repeat until object is expelled. Do not slap the victim's back. (This could make matters worse.)
5. If the victim has not recovered, proceed with CPR. If the rescue is successful, the victim should see a physician immediately.

Follow these steps to help a choking infant.

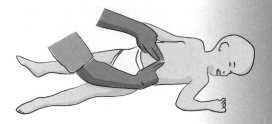

1. Lay the child down, face up, on a firm surface and kneel or stand at the victim's feet, or hold infant on your lap facing away from you.
2. Place the middle and index fingers of both your hands below child's ribcage and above the navel.
3. Press the victim's upper abdomen with a quick upward thrust; do not squeeze the rib cage. Be very gentle. Do not slap the victim's back. (This could make matters worse.)
4. Repeat until object is expelled.
5. If the victim has not recovered, proceed with CPR. The victim should see a physician immediately after rescue.

Follow these steps to save yourself from choking.

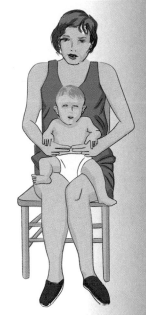

1. Make a fist and place the thumb side of your fist against your upper abdomen, below the ribcage and above the navel.
2. Grasp your fist with your other hand and press into your upper abdomen with a quick upward thrust.
3. Repeat until object is expelled.

Alternatively, you can lean over a fixed or horizontal object (table edge, chair, railing) and press your upper abdomen against the edge to produce a quick upward thrust. Repeat until object is expelled. See a physician immediately after rescue.

FIGURE 10-16 The Heimlich manoeuvre for infants who are choking

FIGURE 10-17A The Heimlich manoeuvre, using your hands to help expel object when you are choking

FIGURE 10-17B The Heimlich manoeuvre, using a chair to help expel object when you are choking

Connecting to the Community

In each Connecting to the Community activity you will find out more about your local community by completing one of two assignments. This section forms one part of your Connecting to the Community activity for Unit 3. For the activity you will create one product from a choice of the following products,

Chapter 10 Choices

1. Create a means of educating people about kitchen safety. Include information on the following:

- General safety
- Prevention of cuts, burns, falls, and fire
- Safe use of kitchen electrical equipment
- Safe use of kitchen chemicals

OR

2. Find places in your community that offer first aid courses. Create awareness of these courses among people in your school and community. Be sure to include at least the following information about each place:

- Location
- Duration
- Certification
- Cost

Chapter 10 Summary

In this chapter, you learned about kitchen safety, including

- The prevention of fires, burns, falls, and cuts
- Special considerations in the kitchen for small children and people with special needs
- First aid, including the Heimlich manoeuvre, and what to do in the case of an accident

Activities

1. Create a poster for the work area of your food and nutrition kitchen, highlighting the general safety rules for working in a kitchen.

2. Write a 500-word article on fire safety for your local paper to be printed during fire-safety week.

3. Working in a small group, write a skit that shows how to avoid one of the accidents discussed in the chapter and what to do in case such an accident and/or injury occurs.

4. Your best friend is going to babysit a family of three small children. He will be making supper for them every evening because their parents work shifts. He has e-mailed you for advice on working in the kitchen with small children. Create a list of five to 10 key pieces of advice you would give him.

5. Design a checklist for barrier-free kitchens. Use your checklist to evaluate the kitchen in your food and nutrition classroom.

6. Create a first aid poster for your classroom. Use graphics to make your poster effective, attractive, and eye catching.

CHAPTER 11

Kitchen Appliances, Equipment, and Tools

Key Concepts

- Major kitchen appliances
- Small kitchen appliances
- Kitchen equipment and tools
- Specialized kitchen equipment for commercial use
- Managing in the kitchen
  - Time- and labour-saving devices
  - Technology
  - Making the most of tools and equipment to satisfy individual needs

Key Terms

bakeware
convection oven
cookware
induction

In this chapter you will learn about the equipment, appliances, and tools that are used in the kitchen. These include major and small appliances, specialized equipment, and other tools that help people manage their time in the kitchen safely and effectively.

Jordan and Sophia are in the small-appliance section of a department store. They are trying to pick out a really cool present for their father's 40th birthday. It has to be a special gift because 40 years is a milestone. Their dad loves to cook and has a large collection of gadgets to show for it. It is difficult for Jordan and Sophia to decide what to get their dad that he doesn't already have. Luckily, they took a food and nutrition course this year and have a better understanding of what some of these kitchen tools can do.

Jordan and Sophia have narrowed down their choices and call their mom to help them make a final decision. After talking to their mom for awhile, they choose an espresso coffee maker. They know how much their dad loves his specialty coffee!

Jordan and Sophia are very happy with their decision and can't wait to see the look on their dad's face when he opens his gift! They'll remember their other three choices as back-ups for Father's Day. They know that any of their choices would make their dad happy.

KITCHEN EQUIPMENT

When people walk into a strange kitchen for the first time, they usually have trouble finding all the things they need. This is because we use so many different tools in our kitchens every day. A good knowledge of kitchen tools and their uses can make work in the kitchen easier.

Kitchen equipment is divided into three main categories: major appliances, small appliances, and tools.

Major appliances include

- Cooking: stove, cooktop, oven, microwave
- Cleaning: dishwasher
- Storing: refrigerator, freezer

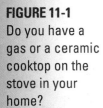

FIGURE 11-1
Do you have a gas or a ceramic cooktop on the stove in your home?

Cooking Appliances

Most people in Canada have a stove in the kitchen that is a combination of both a cooktop and an oven. There are two basic types of cooktops: gas and electric. Both have advantages and disadvantages. Gas is a quick heat source that cools quickly. Electric heat takes a little longer to warm up and cool down. Gas is not always available in homes, so sometimes you have no choice but an electric cooktop.

Some kitchens are equipped with a separate cooktop and wall oven. You may have seen this set-up in a cooking show on television. Like the cooktop of a stove, separate cooking units can be either gas or electric. Wall ovens tend to be electric, though. A **convection oven** uses a fan to circulate air around the space in the oven. When the air is circulated in this manner, the heat is more evenly distributed. This results in more even cooking which

FIGURE 11-2 Do you know someone who has a cooktop and wall oven instead of a stove?

results in a better quality product. Convection cooking is faster than a regular oven and requires less energy.

The cost of a microwave oven has decreased dramatically with advances in technology, and many homes now have one. Microwave technology heats the food but not the container, though the container may become hot due to the heated food. As a result, food can be cooked much faster in a microwave oven than in a conventional oven. Microwaves use 50 percent less energy than a stove. Many people use microwaves to reheat food and cook convenience meals and foods, often called "microwave dinners." Can you think of a product that was designed solely for cooking in a microwave?

There are two precautions you must take when using a microwave oven: You can never put metal into one, as this may cause a fire (see Cooking Equipment later in the chapter) and you cannot run the microwave when it is empty, since the waves can damage an empty microwave oven.

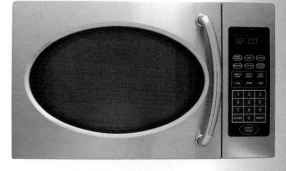

FIGURE 11-3 How often do you use a microwave oven?

Cleaning

Dishwashers are a convenience and a time saver in many homes. There are different types of dishwashers. Some sit on the counter, are portable, and move to the sink in order to be connected to a water source while in use. Others are built in and are permanently connected to the water source and drain. Both types offer different features, such as pot scrubbing and waste food disposal. In an effort to conserve energy, some have energy-efficient cycles. Still others have a two-drawer design so that you can wash only one drawer at a time, thus saving energy. With all types of dishwashers, you still need to scrape large food waste from the dishes before putting them in the dishwasher, and always use detergent designed for dishwashers.

FIGURE 11-4 Do you have a dishwasher in your kitchen? If so, what kind is it?

Cold Storage

The refrigerator is a standard appliance in most homes. Refrigerators come in various sizes from small bar fridges to large double-door types. People need refrigerators to keep perishable foods from spoiling. Most refrigerators have a freezer compartment as well. Beginning in the early 2000s, manufacturers started to put the freezer compartment on the bottom of the refrigerator, making it easier for consumers to see the food in the refrigerator section, since that is the part used more often.

Many families also have a stand-alone freezer. This could be a chest freezer or an upright model. Having a separate freezer allows families to store much more food. Families can buy in bulk, take advantage of sales, or easily store produce that they have grown.

FIGURE 11-5 Is the freezer of your refrigerator on the top or bottom?

Small Appliances

Several small appliances are frequently used in the kitchen. We will look at some of the more common ones as well as some of the newer technologies.

Toaster

The toaster is appropriately named, since its main function is to toast bread. Historically, the slots on most toasters were designed to fit the average slice of bread. In the past decade, manufacturers have redesigned toasters by widening the slots to enable bagels and other thicker breads to be toasted.

Toaster Oven

A toaster oven toasts breads and other products just like a toaster, and it can also broil and bake. It is an ideal small appliance for someone who wants to heat up food such as frozen pizza, which gets soggy when cooked in the microwave. Toaster ovens also have an energy-efficiency advantage, since you are heating a smaller space than a conventional oven.

FIGURE 11-6 Do you know the difference between these two small appliances?

Electric Mixer

There are many types of electric mixer available, from small hand-held wands to larger hand-held models with double beaters, to heavy-duty standing models. All accomplish the same goal of mixing ingredients, but each has its own advantages. The lightweight wands and other hand-held mixers are quick, easy to store, and easy to clean, but they cannot tackle the heavy mixing that standing models can.

Blender

A blender is also used to mix ingredients, but unlike the mixer, it has blades. The blades of a blender enable it to chop and grind food as well as blend ingredients. Countertop blenders have lids, so food can be mixed at high speeds without spraying it all over the kitchen.

Food Processor

A food processor can combine, chop, and grind like the two appliances mentioned above. The food processor is often more powerful than either the blender or the mixer and also has more functions. Its variety of blades and other attachments enable it to perform numerous jobs; for example, kneading dough, slicing vegetables and meat, and grinding meats. It can also purée fruits and vegetables and make juice.

The first mechanical bread mixer is said to have been invented in the first century BCE by Marcus Vigilius Euryasaces, a freed slave. It consisted of a large stone basin in which wooden paddles, powered by a horse or donkey walking in circles, kneaded the dough mixture of flour, leavening, and water.

FIGURE 11-7 What jobs do each of these appliances do? Are there advantages to having all three?

FIGURE 11-8 Each of these small appliances cooks food. Do you know which one would be best for cooking a stew?

Electric Frying Pan or Skillet

Electric frying pans have a thermostat that allows for precise heat control. This means that they can be used to fry, sauté, simmer, and panbroil. If the pan is deep enough, you can also cook a small roast. Electric frying pans usually have a nonstick surface, which makes cleanup easy.

Electric Grill

With people's quest for low-fat cooking these days, electric grills have become popular. These appliances use less or no fat to cook meats and grill vegetables. Many people now cook most of their meat on an electric grill. The grills tend to be small for easy storage and have a nonstick coating for easy cleanup.

Slow Cooker

Slow cookers have a crockery pot inside a metal shell. The shell contains a heating element. Slow cookers can simmer food for hours at a time. A slow cooker is an ideal appliance for people who want to start cooking their main meal before they leave for work so it will be ready when they come home. There are many cookbooks with excellent slow-cooking recipes.

Changing Trends

As times change and people's needs change, small appliances also change. Some small appliances that are quite popular now were not used by many only a few years ago. An espresso coffee maker is a good example. With the popularity of specialty coffees, these appliances are now found on many kitchen counters.

FIGURE 11-9 Do you know a family who has its own espresso coffee maker?

KITCHEN TOOLS

There are many other kitchen tools available that are used for a variety of purposes. We will take a closer look at tools for cutting, mixing, measuring, and cooking food.

Cutting Tools

Many different types of tools can be used for cutting. All cutting tools should be handled with extreme care. They are sharp, and can cause injuries if not used properly. Remember what you learned about the prevention of cuts in Chapter 10: Kitchen Safety. The table below shows some cutting tools.

Cutting Tools

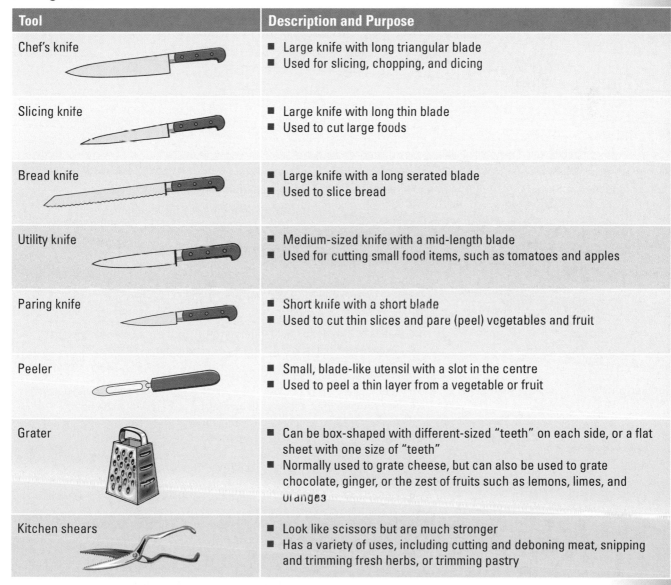

Tool		Description and Purpose
Chef's knife		▪ Large knife with long triangular blade ▪ Used for slicing, chopping, and dicing
Slicing knife		▪ Large knife with long thin blade ▪ Used to cut large foods
Bread knife		▪ Large knife with a long serated blade ▪ Used to slice bread
Utility knife		▪ Medium-sized knife with a mid-length blade ▪ Used for cutting small food items, such as tomatoes and apples
Paring knife		▪ Short knife with a short blade ▪ Used to cut thin slices and pare (peel) vegetables and fruit
Peeler		▪ Small, blade-like utensil with a slot in the centre ▪ Used to peel a thin layer from a vegetable or fruit
Grater		▪ Can be box-shaped with different-sized "teeth" on each side, or a flat sheet with one size of "teeth" ▪ Normally used to grate cheese, but can also be used to grate chocolate, ginger, or the zest of fruits such as lemons, limes, and oranges
Kitchen shears		▪ Look like scissors but are much stronger ▪ Has a variety of uses, including cutting and deboning meat, snipping and trimming fresh herbs, or trimming pastry

Mixing Tools

Most mixing is done using small appliances, but there are several other tools that you can use to mix ingredients. Read the chart below to find out more about different mixing tools.

FIGURE 11-10 Each of these mixing tools has a specific purpose. Do you know when to use each one?

Mixing Tools

Tool	Description and Purpose
Mixing spoons	■ Available in a variety of materials—wood, plastic, or metal ■ Used to mix ingredients
Hand-operated rotary beater	■ Used to mix or whip foods quickly ■ Faster than using a spoon
Whisk	■ Made of wire loops held together by a handle ■ Used for mixing, stirring, beating, and whipping
Mixing bowls	■ Made of a variety of materials—glass, metal, ceramic, or plastic ■ Some come with a handle to hold while mixing and some have rubberized bottoms to keep them stationary
Spatula	■ Made from rubber or soft plastic ■ Used to scrape food from bottom and sides of bowls and pans ■ Helps to make sure that all ingredients are well mixed
Sifter	■ Has a fine wire screen at the bottom with a blade that forces dry ingredients through the screen ■ Used to smooth and blend flour, sugar, and baking soda

Measuring Tools

Careful measurement is an important part of successful cooking, especially when baking. To measure accurately, you need the appropriate tool. You will learn more about measurement in Chapter 12: Kitchen Literacy and Numeracy, but here you will be introduced to the tools and their purposes.

Measuring Tools

Tool	Description and Purpose
Liquid measuring cup	■ Made of transparent glass or plastic so quantities can be seen ■ Available in different sizes: 1 cup (250 mL), 2 cup (500 mL), and 4 cup (1000 mL) ■ Used to measure liquids (e.g., oil or milk, or for the displacement method)
Dry measures	■ Usually made of plastic or metal ■ Available in several sizes, ranging from ¼ cup (50 mL) to 1 cup (250 mL) ■ Used to measure dry ingredients (e.g., flour or sugar)
Small measures	■ Six connected spoons of different sizes, ranging from ¼ tsp (1.25 mL) to 1 tbsp (15 mL) ■ Used to measure small amounts of dry and liquid ingredients

COOKING EQUIPMENT

Cooking equipment can be divided into **cookware** and **bakeware**. Equipment that is used for cooking on the stovetop is called cookware; equipment that is used for cooking inside the oven is called bakeware. Both come in a variety of materials including glass, metal, and pottery or ceramic. If using a microwave oven, you must use specialized bakeware. Only "microwave-safe" materials should be used in a microwave to prevent arcing, electrical sparks, melting, damage to the microwave, and fire.

Cookware

Equipment	Description and Purpose
Saucepan	■ Has a long handle and a lid ■ Used for cooking sauces and small amounts
Pot	■ Larger and heavier than a saucepan ■ Usually has two small handles, one on either side ■ Most pots come with lids ■ Usually used to cook larger amounts of foods (e.g., vegetables or pasta)
Skillet/frying pan	■ Circular- or square-shaped with a long handle ■ Comes in various sizes ■ Used to brown, sauté, or fry foods
Double boiler	■ Two saucepans; one fits inside and on top of the other ■ Boiling water in the bottom pan gently cooks food in the top pan
Dutch oven	■ Heavy-gauge pot with a tight-fitting lid ■ Can be used on top of the stove or in the oven ■ Often used to cook pot roast
Steamer	■ Basket-like container that sits over pot of boiling water ■ Steam from boiling water rises and cooks food
Pressure cooker	■ Heavy-gauge pot with a lid that locks into place ■ Creates a very high cooking temperature ■ Cooks food more quickly than in an ordinary pot

Cookware

Shopping for new cookware is a daunting task, given the wide variety of materials, coatings, and prices available. Next time you choose a pot or pan, think about the advantages and disadvantages of each type of material and how it will perform on the stove or in the oven.

Copper cookware is generally the most expensive. Copper conducts heat easily and evenly, making it attractive as a cooking material. Copper pots should be lined with stainless steel so that foods don't react with the copper. Taking care of copper is time consuming because the shiny surface quickly gets marked and dulls.

FIGURE 11-11 Can you identify the different materials from which these cookware items are made?

Aluminum cookware conducts heat quite well, but scratches easily and can react with food unless it is lined with stainless steel. Sometimes aluminum is sandwiched between stainless steel layers, or *anodized*, which alters the aluminum surface so that it won't react with foods.

Stainless steel cookware is durable, lightweight, and non-reactive to foods but does not conduct heat easily or evenly. Higher-quality stainless steel pots often have a thick layer of copper on the bottom.

Cast iron cookware is known for its ability to retain and distribute heat evenly and is excellent for browning foods. It is very heavy, though, and needs to be seasoned before it is used for the first time. To season cast iron, rub a thin coating of oil over the pan, and then bake the pan in an oven for about an hour. Some cast iron cookware can be purchased pre-seasoned.

Non-stick cookware has been coated with a non-stick material. This coating prevents food from sticking and makes cleanup easy. It also means very little oil needs to be used during cooking. The coating on inexpensive non-stick pots and pans wears off and scratches very easily. More expensive products have the coating bonded onto the surface and are more durable.

Glass and ceramic cookware can be used in a microwave oven, as well as in a conventional oven, unlike some other materials, particularly metal. However, only some types can be used on top of the stove. Glass and ceramic can be difficult to clean and pots could break if they are dropped; food can be served directly from the oven to the table in this cookware, which saves on washing serving dishes.

Silicon bakeware is relatively new. Flexible mats, cake pans, and muffin tins made of silicon are used in the oven. The mats can be used when baking cookies, or as a non-stick layer for fish and meat. They are quite expensive, but food does not stick to this cookware and it cleans very easily.

Bakeware

Equipment	Description and Purpose
Cookie sheet	■ Large, flat rectangular pan ■ Used to bake cookies and other products
Cake pan	■ Comes in various shapes and sizes, including specialty pans ■ Used to bake cakes
Loaf pan	■ Deep rectangular pan ■ Used to bake bread or loaves
Pie plate	■ Circular, shallow pan ■ Used to make pies, tarts, and quiches
Muffin tin	■ Usually a rectangular pan with individual deep circular holes for muffins ■ Used to bake muffins or cupcakes
Roasting pan	■ Large heavy pan, usually with lid ■ Usually oval or rectangular in shape ■ Used to roast meat or poultry
Casserole dish	■ Comes in a variety of materials and sizes ■ Available with or without lid ■ Used for baking and serving main dishes and desserts

COOKING TOOLS

There is a wide variety of tools used for different cooking purposes. Some basic tools include the following:

- Turner or spatula for lifting and turning flat foods in a skillet
- Tongs for gripping and lifting hot items from a pan
- Baster for suctioning juice from a pan, then basting meat
- Ladle for spooning hot liquids from a pan
- Cooking thermometer for checking the temperature of foods while cooking
- Brush for brushing foods with sauce or glaze
- Skewers for threading pieces of food to cook and serve
- Baking racks for cooling freshly-baked goods

FIGURE 11-12 Can you identify the cooking tools in this photograph?

West Coast Fish Canneries

For centuries, the West Coast First Nations peoples enjoyed the abundance of fish that the Pacific coastline held. When the transcontinental railway was built in the 1880s, everything changed. European and Asian immigrants arrived and new coastal communities developed. Fishing boats and canneries opened up jobs for thousands of workers.

At first, the canneries were labour intensive. Everything was done manually. The fish was salted and put in barrels to cure over the winter months. The cans were handmade from large tin sheets that were cut and shaped into cans during the winter. The employees spent long hours gutting, cleaning, cooking, and canning predominantly salmon. The early cans of salmon were almost exclusively sent to England. The tins had pictures of the mounted police, maple leaves, beavers, and other images of Canada.

By the 1890s steam engines were used for cooking the cans of salmon as well as cleaning the cannery machinery. Charcoal was used as the fuel to fuse and seal the bottoms and tops onto the cans. At first, the charcoal was imported, but by the late 1890s it was made by Japanese immigrants along the British Columbia coastline. Charcoal-making was an important industry until 1908. After that time, the canneries began to use coal for fuel.

During the early 1900s, teams of up to 30 Chinese men manually butchered 15 000 to 20 000 salmon during a 10-hour shift. Eventually, the workers were replaced by a "fish butchering" machine invented by Canadian Edmund A. Smith (1878–1909). This machine could butcher one fish per second, which increased cannery profits but put thousands of people out of work.

FIGURE 11-13 Beginning in the 1890s, many Chinese men were employed by West Coast fish canneries to butcher and can thousands of Pacific salmon. Why was there such a demand for the fish?

Throughout the Depression in the 1930s, salmon canning stopped as fortunes collapsed and the industry was forced to consolidate into fewer buildings. The canneries became raw fish depots. By the start of World War II in 1939, the canneries were re-opened due to the demand for canned fish to feed Canadian troops who fought overseas.

All through the 20th century, fishing and canning were important industries on the West Coast.

COMMERCIAL FOOD PREPARATION EQUIPMENT

Whether you are working in a food and nutrition classroom or in your home kitchen, you use appliances and equipment made for home use. Much of the kitchen equipment used in homes has been adapted to withstand the heavy use of the commercial food industry. Some appliances that are used in the commercial food industry are seldom used in home kitchens. Below are some examples.

Web connection

To find out more about commercial kitchen equipment, go to this Web site and follow the links.

www.mhrfoodforlife.ca

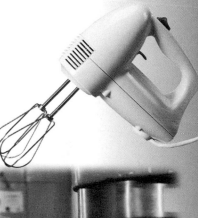

FIGURE 11-14 Some people buy an electric griddle to cook foods on, while most commercial food establishments have a large griddle as well as a grill. Why would commercial users need both?

FIGURE 11-15 Why do commercial mixers have to be heavy duty?

FIGURE 11-16 Even though many people might like to have a steam table and a warming oven, they are luxuries that few home kitchens have. Why are they necessary pieces of equipment in commercial kitchens?

MANAGING YOUR KITCHEN

There are literally hundreds of appliances, tools, and equipment used in kitchens, both at home and commercially. Combined, they enable people to achieve the best results. Now we will examine kitchen management in terms of

- Time- and labour-saving devices
- Technology
- Making the most of your equipment

Time- and Labour-Saving Devices

Many tools in kitchens are designed to save cooks time and labour. An electric blender works faster and more efficiently than a hand beater. The key to using these devices effectively is knowing when to use them.

Let's use beating an egg and a cake batter as examples. Both can be mixed using a fork, a whisk, a hand beater, or an electric mixer. For an egg, the fastest and probably the most time-efficient means is to use a whisk, especially given the cleanup and set-up time needed with a blender. A cake batter, however, will take longer to mix effectively with a whisk. You would save time and create a better product by using a hand or electric mixer.

Be careful that you are not drawn to an appliance or tool because you are told that it saves time, when in fact, it is more than you need for the job.

Technology

We live in an age of constantly changing technology, and the kitchen is no exception. Some of the small appliances that are now more commonly found in home kitchens were once only for commercial food establishments, mainly because of their cost. An example is the espresso coffee maker discussed earlier. The cost of these machines has been reduced because advances in technology have allowed less-expensive machines to be produced.

Another advance in technology is the speed with which we can cook our foods. Now there are ovens that combine both microwave technology and conventional oven technology to cook foods faster, like a microwave, while keeping the flavour and quality of conventional cooking. **Induction** cooktops employ a non-contact method of heating that uses magnetic fields to transfer energy directly to

Food for Thought

The coffee maker is the most popular kitchen appliance around the world.

Food for Thought

In 1945, the microwave oven was patented, and in 1947, the first microwave oven, called the "Radarange," was built. It was the size of a refrigerator, weighed 340 kg (750 lb), and cost $5000. By 1975, sales of microwave ovens exceeded those of gas ranges.

the cookware. The induction element stays cool while the target object heats rapidly for extremely efficient heating. When the element is turned on, it will not heat up until there is a pot on it, and only the area where the pot is sitting heats up. This technology is not only efficient, but also safer, since the area around the pot stays cool. Spills will not bake onto the surface and thus cleanup is also much easier.

FIGURE 11-17 What advantages are there to induction elements that only heat the area where a pot is sitting?

Easy Cauliflower and Broccoli Au Gratin—Conventional Method

Ingredients

1 lb (500 g) cauliflower, large florets
1 lb (500 g) broccoli, large florets
½ cup (125 g) cream cheese, cubed
½ cup (125 mL) milk
½ cup (125 mL) sour cream
1 ½ cups (375 mL) cheddar cheese, grated
10 small snack crackers, crushed
3 tbsp grated parmesan cheese

Preparation

- Preheat oven to 350°F (175°C).

- Cook broccoli and cauliflower in large pot of boiling water for 5 minutes or until tender. Drain and place in 8 cup (2 L) baking dish.

- In medium saucepan, stir cream cheese and milk over medium heat until mixture is blended and smooth. Remove from heat; stir in sour cream. Pour over vegetables; sprinkle with cheddar cheese.

- Mix cracker crumbs and parmesan cheese. Sprinkle over vegetables.

- Bake 20 to 25 minutes or until cheese is melted.

Servings: 10

Easy Cauliflower and Broccoli Au Gratin—Microwave Method

Ingredients

1 lb (500 g) cauliflower, large florets
1 lb (500 g) broccoli, large florets
½ cup (125 mL) water
½ cup (125 g) cream cheese, cubed
½ cup (125 mL) milk
½ cup (125 mL) sour cream
1 ½ cups (375 mL) cheddar cheese, grated
10 small snack crackers, crushed
3 tbsp grated parmesan cheese

Preparation

- Place cauliflower and broccoli in 8 cup (2 L) microwaveable dish. Add water; cover. Microwave on high for 10 minutes or until vegetables are tender; drain. Set aside.

- Microwave cream cheese and milk in 2 cup (500 mL) microwaveable measuring cup or medium bowl for 1 minute or until cream cheese is melted and mixture is well blended when stirred. Add sour cream; mix well. Pour over vegetables; sprinkle with cheddar cheese. Microwave for 2 minutes or until cheese is melted.

- Mix cracker crumbs and parmesan cheese. Sprinkle over vegetables.

Servings: 10

Making the Most of Your Equipment

The following list of tips will help you manage your kitchen and your tools and equipment more effectively:

- Choose the right tool for the job.
- Keep tools stored safely.
- Store tools in a way that makes them easily accessible in the area where they are used. For example, keep cooking tools near the stove; keep mixing tools and equipment near your food preparation area.
- Do not store heavy items on high shelves.
- Plan your cooking. Read the recipe and plan time-saving steps. For example, get all ingredients from the fridge or spice rack at once instead of making several trips.

One key to success in any kitchen is knowing the capabilities of your tools and equipment, and using them to the best advantage.

Adell Shneer, *Canadian Living* Test Kitchen Food Specialist

Imagine writing recipes for a living. That is what Adell Shneer, test kitchen food specialist, does for the *Canadian Living* Test Kitchen. She begins her work day with the magazine editor, deciding on topics, themes, and recipe ideas. Ideas might be seasonal, but planning for each issue of the magazine happens well in advance, so winter holiday ideas will have been determined the previous spring, and summer food ideas will have been put together in the winter.

Once a topic is chosen, Adell must then create appropriate recipes. She gathers together ingredient ideas, similar recipes, and possible methods. Calling upon her cooking experience, recipe skills, and a sophisticated computer program, Adell then creates the recipes. This is all done before any cooking takes place.

In the test kitchen, Adell tries out her creations, keeping in mind that readers of *Canadian Living* magazine must be able to re-create the recipes at home. When a recipe has been completed, three people taste the result and the recipe is adjusted to incorporate comments and criticism from the tasters. When Adell is satisfied with the modifications, the recipe is made and tasted again, but this time by a different test kitchen food specialist.

Adell isn't always in the test kitchen. She also attends the Good Food Festival, a large consumer trade show in Toronto, for *Canadian Living*. There, she participates in many live food demonstrations. At times, Adell also attends media events to learn about new food ventures and ideas.

In the past, Adell has been the food stylist and recipe coordinator for *Party Dish*, a program on Food Network Canada. She has also been a cooking teacher and baker for Dish Cooking Studio. She won the Taste of Canada Gold Medal for Special Occasion Cakes in 1984.

Adell has always loved food and cooking. Both her father and maternal grandmother worked in her family's restaurant in Edmonton, Alberta, when she was growing up. Adell spent hours with her grandmother making Turkish delight, strudels, and knishes. When Adell attended post-secondary school, she was not planning a career in food. She went on to York University and received an Honours Degree in Graphic Design. When she began doing freelance work for *Canadian Living,* she decided to go back to school to take food courses. She attended the Culinary Institute of America in New York and George Brown College in Toronto.

"I feel extremely lucky to have been able to turn a passion into a career."

Connecting to the Community

In each Connecting to the Community activity you will find out more about your local community by completing one of two assignments. This section forms one part of your Connecting to the Community for Unit 3. For this activity, you will create one product from a choice of the following products:

Chapter 11 Choices

1. Do an inventory of all the equipment and tools in your food and nutrition classroom or in your home kitchen. Divide the list into headings similar to these.

   - Major or small appliances
   - Cutting tools
   - Mixing or measuring tools
   - Cookware and bakeware
   - General tools

   Find out how much it would cost to replace the equipment and tools in the kitchen. Make recommendations to someone who is going to set up a kitchen, based on your inventory and costing. Take into consideration

   - Essential tools and equipment
   - Cost-saving suggestions
   - Time-saving equipment
   - Other concerns

OR

2. Look at the lists and descriptions of equipment and tools in the chapter, then choose one category from the list given in Choice 1. For each item

   - Describe how to use and care for it
   - Describe the different styles available
   - Find the prices of different models
   - Find the latest technology
   - Find a commercial example, if possible

Chapter 11 Summary

In this chapter you learned about

- Major and small appliances
- Cutting, mixing, and measuring tools
- Mixing tools
- Cookware and bakeware
- General tools
- Commercial food preparation tools
- Time- and labour-saving devices
- Technology in the kitchen
- Making the most of your equipment

Activities

1. Choose one of the small appliances in your food and nutrition classroom. Using the manual, learn how to use the appliance safely. Demonstrate how to use the appliance to the rest of the class.

2. Create a poster or flyer on the safe use and storage of cutting tools. You may refer to Chapter 10: Kitchen Safety for safety tips.

3. Plan a meal for your family. First, find recipes that you want to use for the meal, then complete the following chart listing the equipment needs for the recipes.

Equipment	Recipe Requirements
Major appliances	
Small appliances	
Cutting tools	
Mixing tools	
Cookware	
Bakeware	
Other tools	

4. Identify three different types of equipment or tools commonly used in kitchens. Do a comparison between the household versions and the commercial versions.

5. Choose a recipe that can be made using hand tools or small appliances. Make the recipe both ways. How much time did using technology save you? Write a 200-word report on this experiment.

Kitchen Literacy and Numeracy

Key Concepts

- Recipe literacy
  - Language
  - Instructions
- Characteristics and functions of common baking ingredients
- Preparation
  - Setting out ingredients
  - Preparing pans
- Adapting recipes
  - To increase fibre
  - To decrease fat
  - To decrease sodium
  - To increase or decrease quantity
- Evaluating products
- What to do when a recipe fails

Key Terms

active format
gluten
kitchen literacy
kitchen numeracy
leavening agent
narrative format
standard format
water displacement method

In this chapter you will learn the language of recipes and what instructions mean. You will investigate the characteristics and functions of common baking ingredients, preparations necessary before beginning a recipe, and ways to adapt recipes to suit specific dietary needs. You will also learn how to evaluate a product and what to do if it fails.

Anita and Mike are working in the kitchen. They are very carefully following the directions of a recipe they are preparing. They don't want to repeat the mistake of missing a key ingredient, as they did in their food and nutrition class. When they made carrot muffins, they missed the flour and could not figure out what went wrong. The rest of the class had muffins that looked and smelled really good. Their cooking group had nothing. Anita and Mike have brought the recipe home to make it for their family.

They laugh about their friends Shayla and John, who put in all the ingredients but did not pay attention to the amounts. They put in 50 mL of salt instead of 5 mL and their muffins tasted so salty! The whole class learned the importance of double-checking to make sure that you have the correct amounts.

When they were talking about their lab the next day, and the problems they'd had making muffins, Ms G told them that she always uses a low-cost recipe for their first lab, so mistakes like these are not so expensive. The class agreed that this was a good idea and that they would all be more careful in the future. Learning sometimes happens when you make mistakes.

Have you ever had an experience like the one the two people in the story had? Many of us have. When we talk about **kitchen literacy**, we mean being able to read and interpret instructions to be successful in the kitchen. **Kitchen numeracy** means being able to work with numbers in the kitchen, including amounts used in recipes. If you were to interpret 50 mg as 50 g, you would not get the expected result.

THE LANGUAGE OF RECIPES

When you look at a variety of reading materials, you know that even though you can still read them, they have different formats and languages. Think about reading

- A comic book
- An instruction manual
- A novel
- A graphic novel
- A textbook
- A greeting card

Each one has a different format, but you still know how to read them. The format of a reading material allows the reader to make the best use of it. Recipes and cookbooks are formatted so that people can get all the information they need from them. Most recipes are tested before they are published to ensure that they can be recreated successfully by the people who will use them.

Recipes have common elements to them, including, but not limited to

- *An ingredient list.* This is a list of the ingredients that you will need to complete the recipe.
- *Yield.* This is the amount of food the recipe will make.
- *Time and temperature information.* This information varies, but most will at least tell you how long it takes the item to cook and at what temperature. Some recipes will also include the amount of preparation time.
- *Directions.* The quality of the directions in recipes varies. Some will include detailed, step-by-step information, while others will provide more limited direction. The more detail that is included, the easier the recipe is to follow.
- *Other information.* This includes such things as nutritional content, ways to adapt the recipe, helpful hints, an equipment list, and any other necessary information.

Look at the recipes included in this textbook. What information do they contain?

Instructions

As discussed above, directions for recipes come in different formats, and each format has its advantages and disadvantages. Also, each style appeals to a different type of person. Just as people enjoy different types of books, people also have different preferences when it comes to instructional formats. No matter what the format, you should always read the recipe through completely before you begin to cook to make sure you understand the directions that you are supposed to follow.

The most common types of recipe formats are

- **Standard format**, which has a list of ingredients and a list of instructions
- **Active format**, which has instructions for each set of ingredients
- **Narrative format**, which is written in paragraph form and includes the ingredients within the instructions

Carrot Raisin Cake

Standard Format

This format is most often used because it is easy to follow and takes the least space to print. Cooks can determine easily if all ingredients are on hand. Ingredients are listed in the order they are used and the step-by-step method of combining them follows.

1 ½ cups (375 mL) whole wheat flour
1 tsp (5 mL) baking powder
1 tsp (5 mL) baking soda
1 tsp (5 mL) salt
2 tsp (10 mL) cinnamon
1 tsp (5 mL) cloves
1 tsp (5 mL) nutmeg

4 eggs
½ cup (125 mL) sugar
½ cup (125 mL) vegetable oil
1 ½ cups (375 mL) shredded carrots
1 cup (250 mL) raisins

1. Stir measured dry ingredients together.
2. Beat eggs with sugar in a large bowl until fluffy.
3. Gradually beat oil into egg mixture.
4. Add dry ingredients to wet ingredients.
5. Stir in carrots and raisins.
6. Pour into a greased 22-cm (9-in.) round cake pan or a bundt pan.
7. Bake at 180°C (350°F) for one hour or until cake tests done.

Active Format

This format is popular and easy to follow, but it takes more space. Checking at a glance for the necessary ingredients is not as convenient.

Measure and stir together:
1½ cups (375 mL) whole wheat flour
1 tsp (5 mL) baking powder
1 tsp (5 mL) baking soda
1 tsp (5 mL) salt
2 tsp (10 mL) cinnamon
1 tsp (5 mL) cloves
1 tsp (5 mL) nutmeg

In a large bowl, beat together:
4 eggs
½ cup (125 mL) sugar

Gradually beat in:
½ cup (125 mL) vegetable oil

Stir in:
1½ cups (375 mL) shredded carrots
1 cup (250 mL) raisins

Pour batter into greased 22-cm (9-in.) round cake pan or a bundt pan. Bake at 180°C (350°F) for one hour or until cake tests done.

Narrative Format

This format is written in paragraph form giving the ingredients along with the method of combining them. It works well for short recipes with few ingredients. This recipe would be very hard to follow using this format.

Measure and stir together 1½ cups (375 mL) whole wheat flour, 1 tsp (5 mL) baking powder, 1 tsp (5 mL) baking soda, 1 tsp (5 mL) salt, 2 tsp (10 mL) cinnamon, 1 tsp (5 mL) cloves, 1 tsp (5 mL) nutmeg. In a large bowl, beat together 4 eggs and ½ cup (125 mL) sugar. Gradually beat in ½ cup (125 mL) vegetable oil. Add prepared dry ingredients to wet ingredients. Stir in 1½ cups (375 mL) shredded carrots and 1 cup (250 mL) raisins. Pour batter into greased 22-cm (9-in.) round cake pan or a bundt pan. Bake at 180°C (350°F) for one hour or until cake tests done.

Tea Biscuits

Ingredients

2¼ cups (550 mL) cups all-purpose flour
2 tbsp (25 mL) granulated sugar
1 tbsp (15 mL) baking powder
½ tsp (2 mL) salt
½ cup (125 mL) cold butter, cubed
1 cup (250 mL) milk
1 egg, lightly beaten

Preparation

- In a large bowl, whisk together flour, sugar, baking powder, and salt. Using a pastry blender or 2 knives, cut in butter until mixture resembles coarse crumbs. Pour milk over top and stir with a fork to form soft, slightly sticky dough.

- Turn out dough onto a lightly-floured surface. With lightly-floured hands, knead gently about 10 times. Gently pat out into ½ inch (1 cm) thick round. Using 2 inch (5 cm) floured cutter, cut out rounds. Place on ungreased baking sheet. Gather up scraps and repat dough; cut out more rounds, press remaining scraps into last biscuit.

- Brush tops of biscuits with egg. Bake at 425°F (220°C) oven for 12–15 minutes or until golden. Place pans on rack to cool.

Servings: About 12

Variations

Cheese Tea Biscuits: Omit sugar. Add 1 cup (250 mL) shredded cheddar cheese after butter has been cut in.

Tips

Treat biscuit dough gently. Do not overmix. Keep the kneading process to a bare minimum.

Literacy in Your Life

Before Reading

1. Read the title. Can you think of a different word to use than "most"?

2. What kinds of problems could result if you do not read the *whole* recipe before you start cooking?

During Reading

1. Read the headings and make up questions for yourself, such as, "How do you follow a recipe?". Answer these questions as you read the sections. What new information did you learn about how to follow a recipe?

Getting the Most from Recipes

Although most recipes are kitchen tested, how well they turn out can hinge on how well they are followed. Here are some tips for getting good results, including how to read a recipe properly. (If you do nothing else, read it through from start to finish before getting started.)

How to Follow a Recipe

- Before you start preparing, read the recipe from start to finish so there are no surprises.
- Before actually starting to cook or bake, gather all the necessary ingredients and equipment. Prepare the ingredients according to the directions in the ingredient list. (See "Watch Those Modifiers," below, for more on this.)
- To determining doneness, always rely first on the recipe's sensory descriptor, such as "cook until golden brown." Consider any times given in a recipe as merely guides for when to start checking for doneness.

Watch Those Modifiers

A recipe ingredient list contains words such as "diced" and "chopped" that tell you how to prepare each ingredient for the recipe. The placement of these "preparation modifiers" in the ingredient line is as important as the modifier itself. Take, for example, the following two similar lines that you may see in a recipe ingredient list:

1 cup rice, cooked
1 cup cooked rice

The first line is telling you to take 1 cup of rice and cook it; the second line is calling for 1 cup of rice that has already been cooked. The first line of directions will result in two cups of cooked rice, while the second line means only one cup of cooked rice. Misreading these instructions can make a big difference in the outcome of a recipe.

A Pint Isn't Necessarily a Pound

Don't confuse fluid ounces with ounces. Fluid ounces are a measure of volume; ounces are a measure of weight. For example, 8 fluid ounces (1 cup or .24 litre) of honey weighs 12 ounces (340 g). The only time you can be positive that fluid ounces and ounces are equal is when you are measuring water.

Use the Right Measuring Cup

To measure flour or other dry ingredients, stir the flour and then lightly spoon it into a dry measuring cup (these are usually metal) and level it with a knife. Do not shake or tap the cup. Be sure to measure liquids in glass or plastic liquid measuring cups, which have extra space above the measurement line to prevent spillage.

Give Your Oven Plenty of Time to Heat Up

Do not rely on your oven's preheat signal; it can often go off prematurely. Instead, let your oven heat for at least 20 minutes before baking anything.

Calibrate Everything

- To check that your oven is heating properly, keep an oven thermometer inside it.
- To check the accuracy of your thermometer, take the temperature of ice water (1°C–2°C [33°F–34°F]) and of boiling water (100°C [212°F] or less, depending on altitude).
- To check the accuracy of your kitchen scale, weigh a known quantity, such as a 4-ounce (12-mL) chocolate bar or pound of butter.

What You Can Assume about Ingredients

Here is a list of what you can assume (unless otherwise noted) for the most commonly-used ingredients in these recipes.

- Black pepper is always freshly ground.
- Butter is unsalted.
- Eggs are large (about 2 oz or 60 g each).
- Flour is bleached, all purpose. (Do not sift unless directed to.)
- Sugar is white, granulated.
- All produce, including fresh herbs, is washed and dried.
- Garlic, onions, and fresh ginger are peeled.
- Citrus zest comprises only the top, coloured part of the peel (not the bitter white pith beneath); make wide strips with a vegetable peeler; use a rasp-style grater for grated zest.
- Toasted nuts are nuts toasted in a dry skillet or in a hot (191°C [375°F]) oven until lightly browned.
- Fresh breadcrumbs mean homemade; make them by pulsing torn, slightly stale bread in a food processor until you get the size of crumb desired.
- Chicken broth is low salt.

After Reading

1. Are there other aspects of your life where following instructions is key to success?

2. Read the recipe on page 281 and jot down the key words that you will need to pay attention to and understand.

UNDERSTANDING INGREDIENTS

When we cook food we are causing a chemical reaction that changes the food's chemistry. Understanding what the different ingredients do is an important part of cooking, especially baking.

Here are some common baking ingredients and their functions.

FIGURE 12-1 When you get ready to cook, how organized are you?

Common Baking Ingredients and Their Functions

Ingredient	Function
Baking powder	■ Is a **leavening agent**, an ingredient or combination of ingredients that makes a flour mixture rise and become light and porous ■ Made from an acid compound, usually bicarbonate of soda and starch ■ When it is moistened, it releases carbon dioxide ■ Single-acting baking powder has only one active ingredient, while double-acting baking powder has two active ingredients ■ Cook batter as soon as possible after the liquid is added to ensure that the effect of the leavening is maximized
Baking soda	■ Is a leavening agent ■ Has to be combined with an acid, such as buttermilk, sour milk, sour cream, yoghurt, or lemon juice ■ Some recipes will call for both baking powder and baking soda

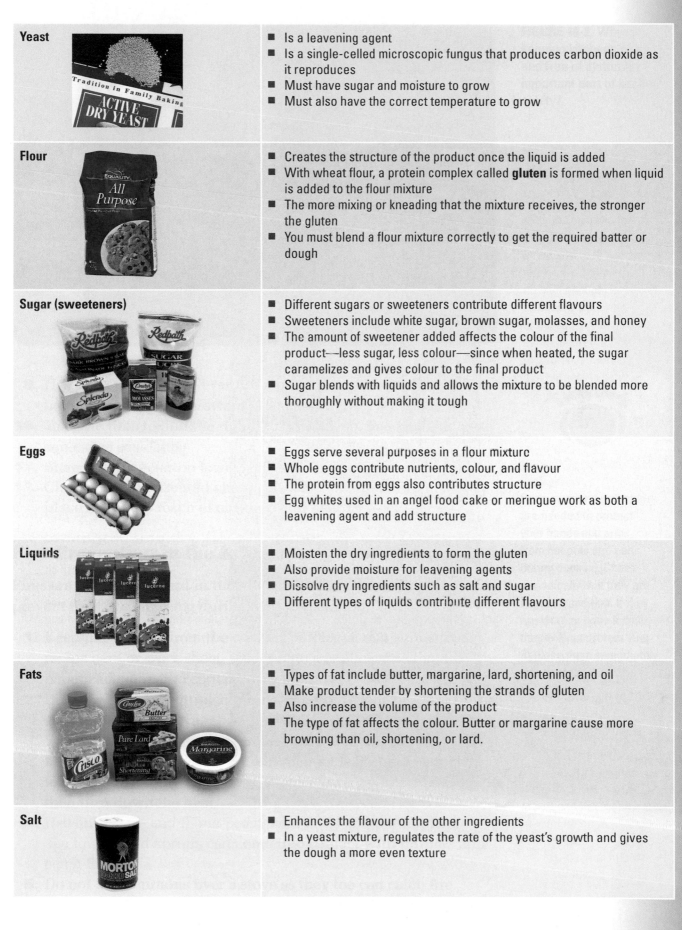

Yeast
- Is a leavening agent
- Is a single-celled microscopic fungus that produces carbon dioxide as it reproduces
- Must have sugar and moisture to grow
- Must also have the correct temperature to grow

Flour
- Creates the structure of the product once the liquid is added
- With wheat flour, a protein complex called **gluten** is formed when liquid is added to the flour mixture
- The more mixing or kneading that the mixture receives, the stronger the gluten
- You must blend a flour mixture correctly to get the required batter or dough

Sugar (sweeteners)
- Different sugars or sweeteners contribute different flavours
- Sweeteners include white sugar, brown sugar, molasses, and honey
- The amount of sweetener added affects the colour of the final product—less sugar, less colour—since when heated, the sugar caramelizes and gives colour to the final product
- Sugar blends with liquids and allows the mixture to be blended more thoroughly without making it tough

Eggs
- Eggs serve several purposes in a flour mixture
- Whole eggs contribute nutrients, colour, and flavour
- The protein from eggs also contributes structure
- Egg whites used in an angel food cake or meringue work as both a leavening agent and add structure

Liquids
- Moisten the dry ingredients to form the gluten
- Also provide moisture for leavening agents
- Dissolve dry ingredients such as salt and sugar
- Different types of liquids contribute different flavours

Fats
- Types of fat include butter, margarine, lard, shortening, and oil
- Make product tender by shortening the strands of gluten
- Also increase the volume of the product
- The type of fat affects the colour. Butter or margarine cause more browning than oil, shortening, or lard.

Salt
- Enhances the flavour of the other ingredients
- In a yeast mixture, regulates the rate of the yeast's growth and gives the dough a more even texture

Dr. Doug Goff, Food Scientist

Doug Goff is a professor in the Department of Food Science at the University of Guelph, in Guelph, Ontario. His interest in food science began at an early age while working for his father's company in the dairy industry. He pursued this interest by first taking a diploma in agriculture in Nova Scotia, then a bachelor's degree at the University of Guelph, then a Master's and Ph.D. in science at Cornell University in New York. While in Guelph, Doug also held a part-time position with Professor Sandy Pearson, a renowned Canadian ice-cream expert.

Doug became a professor in the Department of Food Science in 1987. He teaches a variety of courses, such as Dairy Processing, Food Chemistry, Food Engineering, Nutrition and Food Science, and the well-known Ice Cream Technology Course, which has been offered at the University of Guelph since 1914.

Doug supervises numerous research projects, particularly those related to dairy products and frozen food. Ice cream is one product that has received considerable attention, and Doug's research on it has achieved international recognition. For example, Doug uses electron microscopy to study the molecular makeup of ice cream.

Doug and his research team have determined that a protein in winter wheat can be added to ice cream to act something like antifreeze, preventing the formation of large crystals. This helps keep the ice cream smooth and gives it a longer shelf life.

Doug speaks at conferences several times a year, provides academic counselling for undergraduate students, and supervises many Ph.D., M.Sc., and post-doctoral researchers. He is the author of numerous research papers, and the recipient of several teaching awards, including the Kraft Foods Teaching Award.

Doug also works closely with the food industry, usually on a daily basis.

FIGURE 12-2 A B, AND C These close-up views of ice cream show ice crystals (i), air bubbles (a), the unfrozen serum phase rich in sugars (s), and globules of fat on the air bubbles (f). Bar (shown in C) = 100 μm in A, 30 μm in B, and 7.5 μm in C.

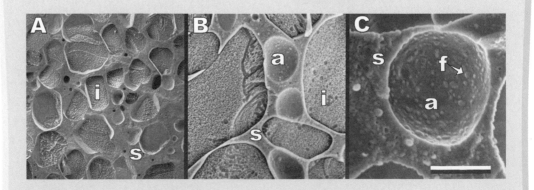

PREPARING TO COOK

When you are cooking, the better organized you are, the smoother the process will be. Organizing your workspace, equipment, ingredients, and time will help to ensure that you create a tasty product.

When working in the kitchen, it is important to have a good workspace. Clearing counters to allow sufficient space is an important first step. Having the correct equipment is also important to success. When you choose a recipe, double-check to make sure that you have all the equipment you need. If you want to use small appliances or other equipment, make sure that they are in good working order. It can be very frustrating to find out something does not work in the middle of preparing food. Once you know you have the equipment you need, take it out in preparation for cooking.

Some equipment needs special preparation for cooking. Cake pans, for example, may need to be properly prepared to make sure that the batter does not stick to the surface and the cake comes out easily. Some recipes are not specific about pan preparation, while others are very specific. Some recipes will tell you to grease the pan and then flour it. When making muffins, you may be told to grease the pan or to use paper liners. To grease a pan, you can take a paper towel and dip it in fat (butter, margarine, or lard) and wipe it around the inside of the pan, or use an oil-based cooking spray on the cooking area of the pan. Many cooks will do this before they even start food preparation so they are sure that the pans will be ready when the time comes.

Once you have your equipment set out, the next step is to gather your ingredients and get organized. Read over the recipe again. Many cooks like to measure out the ingredients while doing this so they only have to assemble them while following the recipe. This is a good way to be sure you have not missed an essential ingredient.

Food for Thought

Baking and cooking are two different skills. When you bake, you must follow the recipes exactly and measure the ingredients carefully. When you cook, the recipe is more of a guide and you will be able to make substitutions for some of the ingredients when you are more experienced.

FIGURE 12-3 Some equipment needs special preparation before cooking. Do you prepare muffin and cake pans before or after you begin a recipe?

ACCURATE MEASURING

Some professionals develop and test recipes to be sure that they work. Following a recipe precisely guarantees that you will have the same success the developers and testers did.

Part of being successful in following a recipe is to measure accurately. As discussed in Chapter 11: Kitchen Appliances, Equipment, and Tools, make sure you use the right tool for the job. Use a liquid measure for liquids and a dry measure for dry ingredients. For each measurement, follow the tips outlined in the chart below.

Tips for Measuring

Liquid	Dry	Small Measures
■ Set the measuring cup on a solid surface. ■ Pour the liquid into the cup. ■ Read the measurement at eye level for accuracy.	■ Do not measure ingredients while you are holding the measure over the mixing bowl. If you do, any excess ingredient may fall into the bowl. ■ Fill the measure to overflowing, then scrape off the excess with a flat-edged tool, such as a knife.	■ Choose the correct size of measure. ■ Follow the directions for liquid or dry ingredients, depending on what you are measuring.

Measuring Fats

There are a few ways to measure fats such as butter, margarine, and shortening. Some fats are packaged in sticks, which make them easy to measure; others have measures marked on the package and you simply have to cut off the correct amount. You can also measure solid fats using the **water displacement method** explained below.

1. Subtract the amount of fat from the total volume of a liquid measure. In this example, you want to measure 75 mL (⅓ cup) butter in a 250 mL (1 cup) measure. Subtract 75 mL from 250 mL. The result is 175 mL (⅔ cup).
2. The difference between the amount of fat and the total volume is the amount of water you need to put into the cup. Pour 175 mL (⅔ cup) water in the cup.
3. Spoon the fat in until the water rises to the full volume of the cup.
4. Pour off the water. (Do not forget to do this or you will have more liquid than you need in the mix.)
5. Remove the fat with a rubber spatula and add to the mixture.

The Water Displacement Method

TECHNIQUES FOR COMBINING INGREDIENTS

After you have accurately measured the ingredients, you combine them using the correct technique. There are several ways to combine ingredients. Read the recipe to find out which method to use. Different methods call for different speeds and intensities of motion. If you use the wrong method, you will not get the desired results.

- *Stir.* When you are asked to stir in a recipe, you are being asked to mix with a utensil, usually a spoon. Sometimes recipes will ask you to stir with a fork, a whisk, or another utensil. Stirring has many purposes: to mix ingredients, to prevent separation of ingredients, or to prevent sticking or burning of foods while they are cooking.

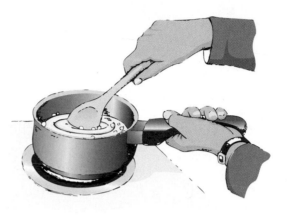

- *Beat.* Beating is generally used to mix together ingredients that tend to separate, and to add air to the mixture. Beating is a faster, more vigorous movement than stirring. You can beat with a fork, a whisk, a rotary beater, or an electric mixer. Remember to scrape the ingredients from the sides of the bowl regularly so that all ingredients get mixed in.

- *Whip.* Whipping is done to incorporate air into a mixture. It is a very rapid form of beating. Whipping is done with a whisk, a rotary beater, or an electric mixer.

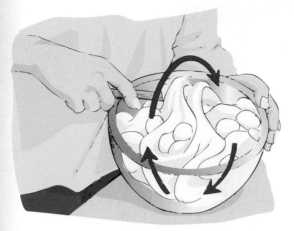

- *Fold.* Folding is a gentle combining of ingredients. A vertical motion is used to fold the ingredients from the top down and then over again. This is best accomplished by tipping the bowl and pulling a spoon or spatula across the bottom of the batter and then back over the top. Rotating the bowl every few strokes helps to distribute the ingredients more evenly. When folding, the goal is to work gently.

- *Cream.* Creaming is used to turn a solid fat into a smooth mixture. The fat is mashed by using the back of a spoon, then stirred and beaten into the side of a bowl to soften it and add air. The friction breaks down the structure of the fat. You can also cream a fat by using an electric mixer at a low speed or by using the back of a spoon. When you cream a solid fat, it is easier to combine it with other ingredients. Sugar is often creamed into a fat mixture. Melting the fat does not give good results.

- *Blend.* In a recipe, when you are asked to blend, you are being told to thoroughly mix ingredients together. Depending on what you are asked to blend, it may take a short time or a longer time. Many recipes will give you a suggested time for blending ingredients. You can use a spoon, a whisk, or an electric mixer to blend.

Web connection

To find out more about different cooking methods, go to this Web site and follow the links.

www.mhrfoodforlife.ca

HISTORICAL PERSPECTIVES

Multicultural Influences on Breads

Bread is a food made by baking a mixture of flour and water called *dough*. Flour is made by grinding cereal grain into a powder. There are several types of flours, including wheat, rye, barley, oat, maize (corn), sorghum (a cereal grown in hot climates), and brown rice. Some bread is leavened with *yeast*, a fungus, to make it rise. Leavened bread is light and airy. **Unleavened bread** is heavier and dense and is often called *flatbread*.

First Nations peoples taught early settlers in Canada how to make **frybread** and **bannock**. Both breads could be prepared quickly. After the dough was mixed together, it was kneaded, shaped into a flat circle, and cooked in a heavy cast-iron frying pan.

Eventually, the pioneers began to bake their own breads. They used ground wheat, rye, oats, and barley. At first, a Dutch oven was used to bake the bread in a fireplace. A Dutch oven is a large cast iron pot with a lid. It was placed on hot coals, and more hot coals were put on top of the lid so the bread would bake evenly. In time, the settlers built ovens alongside their fireplaces. Once the family had an indoor stove and could regulate the temperature of the oven, several loaves of bread could be baked at one time.

The pioneers were familiar with **sourdough**, the oldest and original form of leavened bread. The Egyptians made sourdough bread as far back as 1500 BCE. It was probably discovered by accident. If you combine flour with a liquid, such as water or milk, and let it sit in the open air, wild yeasts in the air will convert the natural sugars into lactic acid, giving the dough a sour taste. A sourdough culture is kept active by adding flour to a small portion of the raw dough, which is then set aside and fed regularly to provide a sourdough starter for the next batch. Sourdough bread was also called "cellar biscuits" and "yeast dough," while German immigrants knew it as "saurteig" and African-Canadians called it "most."

Pita bread, which originated in the Middle East, is a yeast-leavened flatbread. It is baked in a very hot oven, which causes two layers to separate during baking. The hollow centre that is formed makes a pocket that can be opened at one end to fill for a sandwich. Pita bread is now available at most grocery stores. **Naan** is flatbread originally found in India, Afghanistan, Pakistan, and Iran. It is used for dipping or can be rolled around a variety of meats and vegetables. Mexicans use the **tortilla**, a thin, unleavened flatbread made from finely ground corn. *Bing* is a Chinese flatbread similar to the tortilla or Indian **roti**. Some breads, like Ukrainian **paska**, are made for specific occasions, such as Easter. Canada is a multicultural country, and the influences of many cultures have made it possible for us all to enjoy a wide variety of breads.

FIGURE 12-4 How many of these breads have you tasted?

ADAPTING RECIPES

Sometimes we need to adapt the recipes we have. Some of the reasons for adapting recipes include

- Not having all the ingredients
- Wanting to substitute a healthier ingredient
- Disliking one ingredient and wanting to substitute a different one
- Being allergic to an ingredient

Regardless of the reason for the substitution, you need to know how to do it properly to create a successful product. Let's look more closely at a few adaptations.

Increasing Fibre

You can increase fibre in a recipe by using whole-grain flour instead of white flour. However, keep in mind that some recipes do not adapt well to whole wheat flour. It is better to use whole wheat in a muffin mix rather than in a cake mix, for example. If a recipe calls for white rice, you can substitute high-fibre brown rice. You can also add fibre as a topping in the form of nuts, seeds, or beans. Cereal grains such as oats, bran, or wheat germ can be added to cookies or used in ground meat mixtures.

Decreasing Fat

Most recipes can be adapted to reduce the fat. One simple way to reduce fat when cooking is to change the cooking method. Instead of frying meat, try grilling it or broiling it. Use low-fat or no-fat versions of ingredients such as milk and yoghurt. Use low-fat mayonnaise and low-fat salad dressings, or substitute lemon juice or flavoured vinegar for salad dressings. Change meat choices from high fat to lower fat. Substitute two egg whites for a whole egg, or use a lower-fat egg substitute. All these methods will help reduce the amount of fat in recipes.

Decreasing Sodium

Look for lower-sodium choices of ingredients. Soup bases or broths are available in lower-sodium versions. Reading the label will enable you to determine the better choice. Instead of using salt to enhance flavour, try using spices or herbs. Never add uncalled-for salt to foods during cooking. If people want more salt in their meals, they can add it themselves at the table.

Food for Thought

Whole wheat flour can be substituted for white or unbleached flour by up to one-half of the amount in a recipe, but it will produce a denser result. It is not advisable to use whole wheat flour in cake or pastry recipes as it will affect the texture.

Changing Quantity

Recipes are designed to produce a certain quantity or yield. Sometimes that quantity is too much or too little for your purpose. Most recipes can easily be doubled, but it is more difficult to cut back a recipe, especially one involving baking. Follow these simple steps to change the quantity of a recipe.

1. Decide what quantity you want to make.
2. Multiply or divide the amount of each ingredient using the same formula. If you want more, then you multiply; if you want less, then you divide. For example, if you wanted half as much, all ingredients would be divided by two. If you wanted twice as much, all ingredients would be multiplied by two.
3. Be sure to change the size of the equipment you will be using as well. Choose the appropriate-sized pan for the job. Because baking times will vary, adapt pan sizes only when necessary. For example, if you are doubling a recipe, use two of the pans recommended for the original quantity, rather than one larger pan.

FIGURE 12-5 Do you know how to adapt a recipe to feed a large crowd?

Healthy Living

Altering Recipes

Some people cook by following recipes exactly; others use recipes as only guidelines; and still others cook with no recipe at all. However, using a recipe means that you can rely on what has worked for others as well as repeat something you have made before. Often, the recipe yield makes a meal for four or six. This might be a problem if you are trying to feed a crowd or want only enough for two. Other recipes might have ingredients that you are allergic to, while still others might have too much fat or sugar to be healthy. Here are some factors to consider when adjusting recipes for any of these reasons.

- Many recipes can be doubled to create twice as many servings; however, **do not double cake or cookie recipes.** Make a second batch instead. Other recipes, especially soups, casseroles, chilies, pastas, and stews, double or even triple easily, but **be careful with salt and spices** such as hot peppers. Do not double or triple spices. Use the original amount and add more, if necessary, when the recipe is done. Remember that **a greater quantity of food will likely take longer to cook.**

- **If you are trying to make a smaller number of servings, most ingredients should be reduced accordingly.** To divide an egg, beat it and then measure half the egg and use that. Remember that a smaller amount of food will cook in a shorter length of time, so be sure not to overcook the food.

- When adapting recipes to lower calories, you can often **substitute a low-fat version of the high-fat ingredient.** For example, cream can often be replaced with low-fat evaporated milk, and cream cheese can be replaced with low-fat ricotta cheese or quark.

- When baking, **some substitutions can be made for health reasons.** For example, up to one-half cup of oil can be replaced with an equal amount of applesauce or low-fat yoghurt to create a healthier product. Often, the amount of salt called for in a recipe can be reduced (but not usually eliminated). Ingredients that are higher in fibre can also be used; for example, whole wheat flour instead of white flour.

- **If you are altering a recipe because it has ingredients to which you or a family member or guest are allergic,** take considerable care. Wheat allergies pose difficulties because rice- and potato-based flours do not act the same way in recipes. It is best if you find recipes specifically without wheat or gluten. There are, however, many new brands of rice pasta that cook and taste almost the same as wheat pasta.

FIGURE 12-6 What might each of these ingredients replace in a recipe to make a healthier product?

EVALUATING PRODUCTS

When you have completed a recipe and created a product, you evaluate it. Some of the criteria to use are

- Appearance
- Taste
- Smell
- Texture
- Weight

The better the evaluation, the more likely you are to make the recipe again. You will not want to reuse all the recipes you try. Most people have taste preferences and will keep a collection of favourite recipes that suit their tastes and needs. Sometimes, you may enjoy a product but find that cooking it takes too much time or energy for you to want to make it again. The criteria you use to evaluate a product and a recipe will vary, depending on the circumstances.

WHAT TO DO WHEN A RECIPE FAILS

Every cook has made something that did not turn out well. When a recipe fails, ask yourself the following questions:

- Did you read the recipe carefully and use the proper amount of each ingredient?
- Did you forget to add an ingredient?
- Did you use the correct technique?
- Did you use the correct cooking temperature?

By identifying any mistakes you may have made, you can avoid making them again in the future. Remember that recipes have been developed to be successful, but they are only successful if they are followed correctly, and if you like the taste of the result.

FIGURE 12-7 Have you ever had a failure in the kitchen? Could you salvage the product?

Connecting to the Community

In each Connecting to the Community activity you will find out more about your local community by completing one of two assignments. This section forms one part of your Connecting to the Community activity for Unit 3. For this activity you will create one product from a choice of the following products.

Chapter 12 Choices

1. Find an older recipe that reflects your cultural heritage or another cultural group in your community. Determine whether the recipe can be adapted to make it healthier by increasing fibre or reducing salt or fat. Make the adapted recipe. Compare the results of the adapted recipe to the original. Write a report on the process and your findings.

OR

2. Volunteer to help in your community at a place that serves meals to the needy or to other large groups (e.g., a shelter, a community group, a seniors' home, a daycare centre). Ask to see the recipes the kitchen staff use. Take one of the recipes and find a similar recipe to try at home. Compare the recipes using the following criteria:
   - Ingredients
   - Equipment needed
   - Instructions/directions
   - Yield
   - Time needed
   - Cooking/baking
   - Nutritional information provided

Evaluate the nutritional value of each recipe.

Chapter 12 Summary

In this chapter you have learned

- The definitions of recipe literacy and numeracy, as well as the language and instructions specific to recipes
- About the characteristics and functions of common baking ingredients
- Aspects of preparing to cook, including setting out ingredients and preparing pans
- How to adapt recipes to increase fibre, decrease fat and sodium, and increase or decrease quantity
- What to look for when evaluating products
- What to do when a recipe fails

Activities

1. Compare the way a recipe is set up (i.e., the format) to another type of writing (e.g., a report or an essay). How do you account for the differences? How is each set up, or formatted, to work effectively for readers?

2. Find a recipe that you would like to make. Identify and label the following elements in it:
   a) Ingredient list
   b) Yield
   c) Time and temperature information
   d) Directions
   e) Other information (e.g., nutrient content)
   f) List of equipment you will need
   g) List of techniques you will use

3. What is the difference between a liquid measure and a dry measure? Give examples of what you should measure with each type of measure. Explain how to use each type of measure.

4. Find a recipe for a casserole or other main-course dish. Make note of the yield of the recipe. Complete the following chart to change the yield.

Original Ingredients and Quantity	Recipe Halved (Quantity of Ingredients Divided by Two)	Recipe Doubled (Quantity of Ingredients Multiplied by Two)

Providing Healthy Food

Overview

In this unit you will be introduced to consumer issues related to food and nutrition. You will gain an understanding of the marketing strategies used to entice you to buy products. You will learn how to use your food dollar wisely and become a smart shopper, and see how reading food labels can help you to make informed purchases. You will also become familiar with food additives. Once you have discovered how to shop wisely, you will practise some basic meal planning skills. This will include factors to consider when planning meals, such as family composition, health concerns, and culture.

Connecting to your community is an important part of being a good citizen. Everyone has a responsibility to one another. Both the Connecting to the Community at the beginning of each unit and the Connecting to the Community activity at the end of each chapter are designed to help you find out more about your community.

Throughout the text you will be asked to consider your community and how it connects to you. A variety of activities will be presented and you will be offered choices as to how you want to present the information you have learned about your community. The choices for Unit 4 are as follows:

- Chapter 13: Becoming a Wise Consumer
  - Choice 1: A product that can help shoppers to be wise consumers
  - Choice 2: A product that can be given to users of a local food support program to help them to make the healthiest food choices
- Chapter 14: Meal Planning and Preparation
  - Choice 1: Report on how an institution, such as a day care centre or seniors' residence, plans its menus
  - Choice 2: Report on how an institution, such as a school or a hospital, provides food that is healthy and appropriate for the people it serves

Putting It All Together

At the end of Unit 4, you will have completed *two pieces of work*—one for each chapter. Follow these steps to complete your product.

- Read over and edit your work from the chapters.
- Ask a peer or a parent/guardian to edit your work as well.
- Write an introduction to your product that pulls all the pieces together. Edit this, as well.
- Type or write a good copy, as required.
- Find pictures to enhance your pieces of writing.
- Decide on a title for your product.
- Design how the product will be set up. Draw a rough copy on blank paper before you put the product together.
- Put the product together.

Assessment

The following rubric will be used to assess the work you do on the Connecting to the Community for Unit 4.

Criteria	Level 1	Level 2	Level 3	Level 4
Shows knowledge of how to shop wisely for food and how to plan meals for families	Shows limited or no knowledge of how to shop wisely for food and how to plan meals for families	Shows some knowledge of how to shop wisely for food and how to plan meals for families	Shows considerable knowledge of how to shop wisely for food and how to plan meals for families	Shows a high degree of knowledge of how to shop wisely for food and how to plan meals for families
Use of critical and creative thinking processes	Uses critical and creative thinking processes with limited or no effectiveness	Uses critical and creative thinking processes with some effectiveness	Uses critical and creative thinking processes with considerable effectiveness	Uses critical and creative thinking processes with a high degree of effectiveness
Communicates for different audiences and purposes	Communicates for different audiences and purposes with limited or no effectiveness	Communicates for different audiences and purposes with some effectiveness	Communicates for different audiences and purposes with considerable effectiveness	Communicates for different audiences and purposes with a high degree of effectiveness

Becoming a Wise Consumer

I n this chapter you will learn about a number of issues that consumers need to be aware of in order to make wise choices. You will gain an understanding of food marketing, smart shopping, and store layout, and how they affect our shopping habits. You will also come to understand the information that you find on a food label. Sources of reliable information on food and nutrition will be discussed, as well as food grading and food additives.

Mikel and Peiter are in the grocery store. They have to buy the groceries for their family this week since their parents are out of town and their grandparents, who are staying with them, speak limited English and are not comfortable shopping.

Mikel and Peiter are bringing a shopping list, which they prepared ahead of time. They also had lunch before they came, because their food and nutrition teacher, Mrs. Singh, told them never to shop for food on an empty stomach because "you may buy more than you set out to get." Mikel and Peiter made their grocery list by planning menus for the week, checking to see which ingredients they already had, and adding the foods they need to their list.

Money is tight in their family, so they looked through the grocery store flyers before making their menus to take advantage

Key Concepts

- Food marketing
- Shopping smart
- Store layouts
- Food labels
  - Mandatory information
  - Voluntary information
  - Interpreting information
  - Finding nutrition information and reading the label
- Reliable nutrition information
- Grading of foods
- Food additives

Key Terms

candling
diet and health claims
food additives
grading
marbling
market garden farm
nutrition facts table
nutrition labelling
nutrient content claims
unit pricing

of sale items. Mrs. Singh also advised them to look for store-brand products to save even more money. The boys also know they should stay away from displays that are set up at the grocery store to entice them to buy things they don't need. Mikel reminds Pieter that they can taste all the samples, but they cannot buy the products. They are eager to do the weekly grocery shopping and put what they have learned in their food and nutrition class into practice.

COMMON PRACTICES IN FOOD MARKETING

Can you imagine how much money is spent on food in Canada every day? If the family of every student in your class spent $100 on food per week, how much money would be spent by all the families in your school? Providing food for families is a big business. Food marketing is an industry that generates thousands of jobs. As consumers, we need to be aware of the techniques organizations use to market food so that we can make food choices based on facts and not clever advertising.

FIGURE 13-1 Do you know how to avoid the pitfalls of food marketing?

When you understand food marketing practices, you can see through them to make wise food choices. In any type of marketing, producers and companies must

- Know their consumers
- Market their product to their target audience
- Advertise

Let's consider each of these more thoroughly.

Knowing the Consumer

Companies know they must understand their consumers and manufacture products that meet consumers' needs and wants. They have to meet consumers' demands or else the product will not sell. To do this, companies spend plenty of time and money researching what consumers want. Many people have participated in some form of market research, such as

- Taste-testing a product at a booth in a store or mall
- Challenge tests (a company pits its product against another to show consumers that its product is better)
- More formalized testing involving a detailed questionnaire and product testing
- Surveys conducted in various formats (e.g., on-line, through the mail, or by telephone)

Food companies use this information for many purposes, including

- Deciding which products to make
- Establishing popular flavours
- Testing new ingredients to see if consumers will like them
- Determining consumer preferences and current trends in food habits and patterns
- Looking at lifestyles and how companies can create products that meet consumers' demands

Market to Your Target Audience

One of the keys to marketing success is knowing your target market. Each target market requires different strategies. Understanding the people in that market and the strategies that will entice them to purchase the product are key to successful marketing. Marketers have to decide which messages to use to promote a product in a way that appeals to their target. Here are a few examples.

- **Parents**
  When targeting parents, marketers will emphasize
  - Healthy food choices for growing bodies
  - Making children happy
  - Foods that children will like to eat

FIGURE 13-2 Have you ever participated in market research by sampling a food product?

FIGURE 13-3 Even though young children do not buy the groceries, they do influence many family food decisions. Did you ever convince your parents to buy a food because you saw it in a marketing campaign?

- **Children**

  When marketing to children, marketers will emphasize
  - Taste
  - Fun
  - The toy or prize included with the food

- **Teens**

  When marketing to teens, marketers will emphasize
  - Coolness
  - Trends in popular culture
  - Increasing their popularity

These are only a few examples. Marketers will break down their marketing strategy even further for all groups. Have you noticed any other marketing strategies on television, in magazines, or on the Internet?

Advertising

Advertising is one of the main methods marketers use to make their products known to consumers. There are many different types of advertising, including

- Television
- Radio
- Internet
- Billboard
- Public transportation vehicles and stations
- Store flyers

Food manufacturers spend billions of dollars in advertising. Most of this advertising focuses on highly-processed and heavily-packaged foods, which tend to be consumed in large quantities in North America.

FIGURE 13-4 How do marketers advertise to you?

- Vending Machines
- Newspaper inserts
- Calendars
- Recipe booklets
- Packaging

All these forms of advertising promote the product and deliver the marketers' key messages. Marketers decide which form of advertising to use based on the target market. If they are using television advertising, they will air advertisements during programs that their target market watches. For example, if young children and their parents are the target audience, marketers will advertise during children's programming. Newspapers tend to be read by adults, so ads there will be for that target market. Ads on the Internet will be placed on sites frequented by the target market, or entire Internet sites may be developed to market a product. Many recipe booklets have been designed solely to showcase a product or a group of products. Some of them are produced annually; others are produced seasonally. These appeal to different groups of consumers. Regardless of the means of advertising, knowing the target market ensures success for marketers.

Impulse Buying

Food marketers know that if people see something that is attractive, they may buy it on impulse. Some of the factors that influence impulse food purchases are

- An attractive display
- Coupons
- Sale price
- Free samples
- Smell of the product
- Effective, frequent advertising

Everyone buys on impulse occasionally, and most of us have bought a food product for one of the reasons above. However, if you are on a tight food budget or have health issues, you may have to control your impulse buying.

Don't go shopping when you are hungry, frazzled, or feeling down as you will be prone to impulse buying.

FIGURE 13-5 When was the last time you bought something because it was made attractive to you? Impulse buying is common, and marketers rely on it for part of their sales.

The General Store in Pioneer Times

When the first settlers arrived in Canada, there weren't any stores. If the settlers were lucky, they could buy some supplies at trading posts. These were originally built as depots for First Nations peoples to sell furs in exchange for supplies.

Eventually, railroads were built, opening up the wilderness to settlers. As communities grew, retailers and their families began opening general stores that sold all-purpose goods and other supplies. Most general stores were built as two-storey structures; the shop was on the main floor and the family lived above it. Larger pieces of farm equipment, building supplies and tools, stoves, and sewing machines were stored in a shed nearby.

The front of the store had windows that displayed some of the things for sale. Inside were long counters, shelves, display cases, barrels, baskets, sacks, drawers, and bins that held the many items available. Every bit of space, including the ceiling and walls, was utilized.

The general store was often the hub of the community. Farm families enjoyed their trips into town to go to the store because they met other people, played board games like checkers, and shared local news. In small towns the store often served as a post office or bank as well.

Home-grown fruits and vegetables were sold at the general store alongside other homemade goods. Items that weren't available locally were delivered from the larger cities. Groceries such as tea, sugar, coffee, spices, rice, cheese, and dried meats were for sale along with household items such as blankets, brooms, pots, and pans. Dry goods, including fabrics and sewing supplies, boots and shoes, clothing, and leather gloves, were sold as well as miscellaneous goods such as paper, pens, and ink.

FIGURE 13-6 Have you ever seen a store similar to this in your community or when you were on holiday? How did you feel about it, compared to the stores you use now?

Most early pioneers relied on the bartering system, which meant exchanging goods and services without using money. When money was short, the settlers bartered with the storekeeper in exchange for needed goods. Sometimes settlers traded what they grew or did odd jobs for the general store owner. The storekeeper kept records of what the settlers brought to and took from the store to keep track of what was owed or available as credit. First Nations peoples also bartered at the general store, often trading baskets, moccasins, meat, or furs for other supplies.

Today, general stores have all but disappeared, but some big box stores still sell the variety of items that once were sold at general stores.

BEING A SMART SHOPPER

You are now more aware of the ways in which food marketers try to entice you into buying their products. In the next section of this chapter, we will look at things that you and your family can do to ensure that you are spending your food dollar wisely.

Avoiding Food Marketing

The first step to avoiding food marketing is to understand marketers' techniques. Once you know how marketers attempt to influence your purchasing decisions, then you can avoid the pitfalls. Let's take a closer look at their techniques.

Avoiding Food Marketing

Marketing Technique	Your Strategy
Knowing the consumer	■ Be aware that marketers have spent time and money researching your age group's needs and wants.
Marketing to target audience	■ Be aware that marketers are targeting you as a specific market group. ■ Know what you need before you spend money on food.
Advertising	■ Be aware that advertising is meant to sell a product. ■ Find out the whole story behind advertising claims. ■ Do not allow an ad to convince you that you need a food product.
Impulse buying	■ Be aware that marketers know that many people buy on impulse. ■ Know the strategies that marketers use to persuade you to buy on impulse.

Many strategies help people make better food purchasing decisions. You and your family may already practise some of these strategies; others may be new to you. Consider the following tips:

- **Plan Ahead**
  - Plan menus for a week, then check to see which ingredients you already have and which ones you need to purchase.
  - Check over your menu plan to ensure that you are providing yourself and your family with a healthy diet as recommended by Health Canada in *Eating Well with Canada's Food Guide*.
  - Check grocery store flyers and on-line ads for specials on the foods you need. You can also do this prior to making your menus and then plan your meals around the specials for that week.

FIGURE 13-7 Does your family make a list before going grocery shopping?

- Make a list of the foods that you need and specify quantities. You could arrange the list by food group or according to the layout of the store you are visiting.
- Eat before you go shopping. You will be better able to resist impulse buying.

■ **At the Store**

- The fresh foods, such as vegetables, fruits, milk and alternatives, grains, and meat products are located around the perimeter of a grocery store.
- Take your list, read it, and check off the foods as you pick them up. Do not buy foods that are not on your list.
- If you find a food item on sale that can be substituted for an item on your list, be flexible enough to purchase it.
- Look for store-brand and name-brand choices. Compare their prices and the **unit pricing** information. Unit pricing tells you how much a specified unit or amount (e.g., 100 g) of a product costs. This helps you to make legitimate comparisons.
- For staple foods, such as flour, sugar, and cereals, larger quantities usually cost less per unit. If you have the storage space at home, you may decide to purchase these.
- If a staple is on sale and you know that you will need it soon, it may be wise to purchase it even if it is not on your list for this trip.
- Many stores sell large quantities of a variety of items for less than the cost of smaller amounts. If you know you will be able to use all of the product before it expires, buying in quantity may help you save money.
- Check for coupons that arrive in the mail or on-line. Also check for a coupon area at the store. Coupons can help lower your overall food costs.
- Be aware of the cost of convenience. A convenience food has been commercially processed to make it easier or more convenient for you to use. The more processing done ahead of time, the higher the cost to the consumer. You and your family must weigh the cost of convenience against the cost of your time, and determine how "convenient" the product really is.

FIGURE 13-8 The unit price is the cost per unit or specified amount. Do you compare prices using unit prices?

- Single-serving sizes, which are packaged to provide one serving of a food product, cost more per serving than larger sizes. Compare the unit pricing or cost per serving to be sure that you can justify the cost of the single serving. Buying the larger size and repackaging the contents into smaller servings is a good way to save money.

FIGURE 13-9 Have you compared the cost per serving of these items?

WHERE TO SHOP

When shopping for food, there are several places you can go. Each place offers different choices for consumers.

Farmers' Markets

Farmers' markets specialize in locally grown food, primarily vegetables and fruits. Depending on the market, you may also find a butcher, a baker, and specialty food products. Some markets are open only during growing season; others stay open year-round, selling fruits and vegetables that can be stored, as well as meats, baked goods, and other specialty foods.

FIGURE 13-10 Do you and your family shop at farmers' markets or market garden farms?

Literacy in Your Life

Before Reading

1. Read the article title. What things do you suppose grocery stores would prefer you not know?

During Reading

1. Ask yourself which of these things you knew about already and which ones present new information.

2. Item 2 in the article tells you to read labels carefully. What else should you look for besides the expiry date?

Ten Things Your Grocery Store Doesn't Want You to Know

By Sally Wadyka

"Market researchers have worked for years to come up with ways to make sure shoppers see as many products as possible, because the more they see, the more they buy," says Marion Nestle, author of *What to Eat: An Aisle-by-Aisle Guide to Savvy Food Choices and Good Eating*. To make yourself a smarter shopper, learn about the top tricks and other secrets lurking at the supermarket.

1. The shopping carts have cooties.

According to studies done on shopping carts, more than 60 percent of them are harbouring coliform bacteria (the sort more often associated with public toilet seats). "These bacteria may be coming from raw foods or from children who sit in the carts," says Chuck Gerba, Ph.D., a microbiologist at the University of Arizona. To avoid picking up nasty bacteria, Gerba recommends using sanitizing wipes to clean off cart handles and seats, and to wash your hands after you finish shopping.

2. Dates are open to interpretation.

Product information and instructions for proper storage are required for most foods that have a shelf life of 90 days or less, starting on the day the food was packaged for retail sale. Labels that give a "best before" date are more of a suggestion than a safety issue—the food will taste best if eaten by the date on the label but won't necessarily be unsafe if eaten soon after that.

3. Kid-friendly food is purposely placed within their reach.

"I always tell parents never to bring a kid to a store," says Nestle. "The packages with the cartoons on them are often placed on low shelves where even toddlers can reach for them." A trip down the cereal aisle will confirm this.

FIGURE 13-11 Why might a parent not want to bring his or her children grocery shopping?

4. They cut up food so they can charge more.

The produce and meat departments display luscious-looking slices of pineapple and melon, chicken breasts and beef, all ready to serve or cook. There's no denying that these precut foods can make life easier. But realize that you're also paying a tremendous premium—sometimes up to twice as much—compared to uncut versions of the same food.

5. Good-for-you foods require bending and reaching.

Not surprisingly, grocery store eye candy—those foods with enticing come-ons and delectable photos on the packaging—that aren't on your shopping list—are prominently placed to encourage you to reach for them.

6. End-of-aisle displays are there to distract you from your mission.

"Food companies pay the stores to place their products where they can be seen most easily—such as in a display at the end of an aisle," says Nestle. That prime real estate is likely to hold high-profit items or grouped items designed to inspire impulse buys.

7. Bargains aren't always a bargain.

Who can resist an offer like "buy five, get one free," or "three for $1"? Apparently, very few people can. "Any time you see numbers in a sign, you're likely to buy at least 30 percent *more* than you may have purchased otherwise."

8. You'll walk the store the way they want you to.

There's nothing haphazard about the layout of your grocery store. Walk in the front doors and chances are you're faced immediately with hard-to-resist items (not on your list) like fresh-cut flowers or just-baked loaves of bread. In fact, research has shown that 60 to 70 percent of what ends up in our carts is unplanned.

9. The ready-to-eat food section can make you sick.

Raw produce at the ready-to-eat section, premade salads at the deli counter, and other precooked prepared foods all have the potential for harbouring harmful bacteria (like E. coli, salmonella, and norovirus). "The biggest contributors to unsafe food are foods that are stored at unsafe temperatures, handling of food by individuals with poor hygiene, and refilling partially used containers of perishable food with fresh food," says Michael Doyle, Ph.D., director of the Center for Food Safety and Quality Enhancement at University of Georgia.

10. They don't always clean as often as they should.

Health inspectors routinely visit supermarkets to look out for the red flags that may signal unsafe conditions for your food, but you can do a little snooping yourself. Flies in the produce or meat departments could be depositing bacteria on raw food. Don't buy in stores where you can see pests.

After Reading

1. Which of the predictions you made in Question 1, based on the title, were discussed in this article?

2. Have you recently given in to impulse buying? Do you think that 60 to 70 percent of the items you buy are unplanned?

Direct from the Farmer

During the growing season, you might see roadside stands that sell fresh vegetables or fruits. In many areas, you can also go to a farm to pick your own produce. Many farmers have what they call a **market garden farm**, where they have a store on site, and consumers can pick their own produce or buy freshly-picked produce. Many market garden farmers also sell specialty products, such as jams, relishes, breads, and pies. Some consumers like to buy farm-fresh eggs as well, and have a weekly commitment to buy from a local farmer.

Specialty Stores

Specialty stores sell products that cater to a specific market. Some, such as bakeries and butcher shops, focus on a certain product or food group while others focus on certain cultural or religious food preferences, such as kosher or halal foods.

Convenience Stores

Many consumers count on nearby convenience stores when they run out of a food product rather than make the trip to a large grocery store or supermarket. Convenience stores offer the basics but do not have a wide variety. Their prices tend to be higher than a supermarket's, since you are paying for the convenience. Many convenience stores remain open around the clock.

Health Food Stores

Health food stores offer a wide variety of food products, some of which may not be found in a supermarket. These range from alternative foods to organic foods, to specialty products such as kelp. Some consumers include a trip to the health food store as part of their grocery routine.

Warehouse Stores or Bulk Food Stores

Warehouse and bulk food stores are set up to provide consumers with the best prices and very few frills. Most products are available in bulk or large quantities, which generally saves you money. You can also buy only the amount you need (e.g., nuts for a recipe) and this can save money as well. Consumers who have the storage space can save a considerable amount of money using these stores. However, do not expect to find conveniences at these stores—you may have to bag your own groceries.

Pete Luckett, "Canada's Favourite Greengrocer"

Pete Luckett first began working at a produce store when he was 16. Five years later, he opened "Pete's Frootique" in an open market in Nottingham, England. His was one of 20 stalls, and competition was fierce. After four successful years, Pete needed a change. He sold nearly everything he owned and travelled to the United States, Guatemala, Mexico, and Belize.

Pete eventually settled in Saint John, New Brunswick, in 1979. There, he stocked a tiny market stall with $300 worth of fruit and vegetables. With hard work, good organization, and people skills, Luckett built this small market stand into a thriving business. He was able to open a second Pete's Frootique in 1992 and another in 2004 in Nova Scotia. He expanded his fruit and vegetable displays to include a delicatessen, a gourmet butcher shop, a juice bar, a wine shop, and a British specialty food shop. Luckett also employs a registered dietitian to serve food samples and provide recipes and nutrition information. The dietitian also publishes a monthly newsletter with tips, advice, and newsworthy nutrition topics. As an added bonus for shoppers, Pete's Frootique also provides live entertainment on weekends.

Pete's Frootique has become a vibrant multi-million-dollar retail and wholesale operation. Pete's style, creativity, customer care, and dedication earned him the Canadian Independent Grocer of the Year Award in 1999, 2003, and 2005. His store has also been recognized with the Best Independent Specialty Grocery Store Award in Canada for the third time in 2005.

Luckett's enthusiasm and knowledge have also given him a place in Canadian television. For 12 years, Pete has been providing tips about exotic fruit and vegetables on the CBC show *Midday*. He now hosts his own food adventure series, *The Food Hunter*. This series premiered on Food Network Canada and Food Network U.S., and now airs in the United Kingdom, South Africa, and Scandinavia as well. For this show, Pete travels to exotic places all over the world, looking for new food experiences. He celebrates wonderful food and the unique cultures that produce and prepare it.

Pete has committed 20 years to providing people with the best produce and customer service possible, earning him the title "Canada's Favourite Greengrocer."

"Pete celebrates wonderful food and the unique cultures that produce and prepare it."

Grocery Stores or Supermarkets

Grocery stores and supermarkets are set up to sell consumers all their foodstuffs, from fresh produce to milk and alternatives, to prepackaged and fresh bakery items, to packaged and fresh meat and fish. They usually have large freezer sections where you can buy a wide variety of frozen foods. Grocery stores and supermarkets carry mostly canned and packaged foods, including fruits, vegetables, sauces, and pasta. They can also carry many other things such as toiletry items, over-the-counter medications, and paper products like tissue, paper towel, and toilet paper. Many of these stores now have large health food and organic food sections as well. Others offer items such as clothing and furniture, and are becoming multi-purpose stores.

FOOD LABELLING

If you know how to read a food label properly, you can find the information you need to make healthier choices when shopping. Understanding nutrition and health claims helps people decipher the information on food packages.

On January 1, 2003, Health Canada published regulations under the *Food and Drugs Act* regarding the labelling of food products in Canada. The regulations made **nutrition labelling** mandatory, put in place requirements for **nutrient content claims**, and permitted **diet and health claims** on food packaging in Canada.

Now labels in Canada contain

- An ingredient list that shows ingredients in order of their quantity in the food
- A nutrition facts table that provides per-serving information on nutrients in the product

Labels may contain some voluntary information as well, including

- Diet and health claims, which may or may not be provided by the manufacturer, but are governed by the nutrition labelling regulations
- Allergen warnings, such as "May contain nuts." to let people with food allergies know that the food may contain a particular food allergen. (Note: This legislation is under review and allergy labelling may become mandatory.)
- Organic certification to let consumers know that the food has been certified by the organic food industry
- Origin of the food, and if the product contains ingredients that were derived from biotechnology

Thinking Critically | Claims on Labels

Packaged food products often have health or nutrient content claims on them, which are designed to catch your eye and make you buy the product. Did you know that through the *Food and Drugs Act*, Health Canada regulates what can and cannot be claimed on a label? To help consumers make wise choices, Health Canada has defined the terms that companies may use. See the chart below to find out more.

Common Nutrient Content Claims and What They Mean	
Key Word(s)	**What They Mean**
Free	■ An amount so small that health experts consider it nutritionally insignificant
Sodium-free	■ Less than 5 mg sodium (salt)*
Cholesterol-free	■ Less than 2 mg cholesterol, and low in saturated fat (includes a restriction on trans fat)* ■ Not necessarily low in total fat
Low	■ Always associated with a very small amount
Low fat	■ 3 g or less fat*
Low in saturated fat	■ 2 g or less of saturated and trans fat combined*
Reduced	■ At least 25 percent less of a nutrient compared to a similar product
Reduced in calories	■ At least 25 percent fewer calories than the food to which it is compared
Source	■ Always associated with a "significant" amount
Source of fibre	■ 2 grams or more of fibre*
Good source of calcium	■ 165 mg or more of calcium*
Light	■ When referring to a nutritional characteristic of a product, the word "light" is allowed only on foods that are either "reduced in fat" or "reduced in calories." ■ An explanation is required on the label of what makes the food "light"; this is also true if "light" refers to sensory characteristics, such as "light in colour."**

* Per reference amount and per serving of stated size (specific amount of food listed in Nutrition Facts)

** Three exceptions that do not require an explanation are "light maple syrup," "light rum," and "light salted" with respect to fish. Note that a separate provision is made for the claim "lightly salted," which may be used when a food contains at least 50 percent less added sodium compared to a similar product.

Questions

Choose three different products that have health or nutrition claims on them. For each product, do the following:

1. Rewrite the wording on the claim so that it includes the information from the chart above. For example: "A good *source* of calcium" could be changed to "contains a significant amount of calcium."

2. Describe how the claim is a health benefit.

3. Do you think the claim could be misleading to consumers? Why?

Nutrition Facts Table

It is now mandatory for most packaged foods to have a **nutrition facts table** on the label. The information in these tables is designed to help consumers make healthier food choices. With this information, consumers can compare products and find information on

- Calories per serving
- Amount and types of fat, including saturated and trans fat
- Cholesterol content
- Sodium content
- Types and amounts of carbohydrates, including fibre and sugars
- Protein content
- Vitamin and mineral content

When you are able to compare this information, you can choose products that are higher in healthy nutrients and fibre and lower in less-healthy nutrients like sodium and fat, and calories.

When reading labels, carefully check the serving sizes. Often a serving is a smaller amount than what you would normally eat. For example, a serving of crackers may be listed as 11 crackers or 20 g, but you would normally eat more than 11. You have to adjust the amount

The nutrient information is based on a specified amout of food. Compare this to the amount you eat.

This number is the amout of the nutrient in the specified quantity of food.

The *Nutrition Facts* table will include this list of Calories and 13 nutrients.

The **horizontal format** may only be used when there is not enough room for the standard format.

The **linear format** may appear on smaller items.

The % Daily Value gives a context to the amount of the nutrient in the specified amount of food. The Daily Values are based on recommendations for healty eating.

Nutrition Facts
Per 125 mL (87 g)

Amount	% Daily Value
Calories 80	
Fat 0.5 g	1 %
Saturated 0 g + Trans 0 g	0 %
Cholesterol 0 mg	
Sodium 0 mg	0 %
Carbohydrate 18 g	6 %
Fibre 2 g	8 %
Sugars 2 g	
Protein 3 g	
Vitamin A 2 %	Vitamin C 10 %
Calcium 0 %	Iron 2 %

Nutrition Facts
Valeur nutritive

Per 1 bar (40 g)
pour 1 tablette (40 g)

Calories 220

* DV = Daily Value
VQ = valeur quotidienne

Amount / Teneur	% DV / % VQ*	Amount / Teneur	% DV / % VQ*
Fat / Lipides 13 g	**20 %**	**Carbohydrate / Glucides** 23 g	**8 %**
Saturated / saturés 5 g + Trans / trans 3.5 g	**42 %**	Fibre / Fibres 0 g	**0 %**
		Sugars / Sucres 20 g	
Cholesterol / Cholestérol 10 mg		**Protein / Protéines** 3 g	
Sodium / Sodium 70 mg	**3 %**		
Vitamin A / Vitamine A	2 %	Vitamin C / Vitamine C	0 %
Calcium / Calcium	6 %	Iron / Fer	4 %

Nutrition Facts per 1 cup (264 g): **Calories** 260
Fat 13 g (20 %), **Saturated Fat** 3 g + **Trans Fat** 2 g (25 %), **Cholesterol** 30 mg,
Sodium 660 mg (28 %), **Carbohydrate** 31 g (10 %), **Fibre** 0 g (0 %), **Sugars** 5 g,
Protein 5 g, **Vit A** (4 %), **Vit C** (2 %), **Calcium** (15 %), **Iron** (4 %).   % = % Daily Value

of nutrients you are receiving in proportion to the amount of crackers you eat. Also, when comparing two products, make sure that the servings are equal or your comparison will be flawed.

A few products are exempt from having to provide a nutrition facts label. They include

- Fresh fruits and vegetables
- Raw, single-ingredient meat and poultry
- Raw, single-ingredient fish or seafood
- Foods that contain insignificant amounts of the nutrients that appear on the label
- Products sold at retail outlets where they are prepared and sold
- Individual servings for immediate consumption

Web connection

Test your knowledge of nutrition facts tables by playing a nutrient label game; go to this Web site and follow the links.

www.mhrfoodforlife.ca

Nutrient Content and Diet-Related Claims

Nutrition labelling regulations now allow health claims to be put on food packages (e.g., "low calorie"). The regulations define and specify the exact conditions required for a food to qualify for a claim. These conditions are based on recognized health and scientific information. If there is no support for the claim, then the term cannot be used.

Health Claims

To Make a Health Claim About ...	The Food ...
Potassium, sodium, and reduced risk of high blood pressure	■ Must be low in (or free of) sodium ■ May also be high in potassium ■ Must be low in saturated fatty acids ■ Must have only limited amounts of alcohol ■ Must have more than 40 calories if the food is not a vegetable or a fruit ■ Must have a minimum amount of at least one vitamin or mineral
Calcium, vitamin D, and regular physical activity, and reduced risk of osteoporosis	■ Must be high (or very high) in calcium ■ May also be very high in vitamin D ■ Cannot have more phosphorus than calcium ■ Must have only limited amounts of alcohol ■ Must have more than 40 calories if the food is not a vegetable or a fruit
Saturated and trans fats and reduced risk of heart disease	■ Must be low in (or free of) saturated fat and trans fat ■ Must be limited in cholesterol, sodium, and alcohol ■ Must have more than 40 calories if the food is not a vegetable or a fruit ■ Must have a minimum amount of at least one vitamin or mineral ■ Must, if it is a fat or an oil, be a source of omega-3 or omega-6 polyunsaturated fatty acids
Vegetables and fruit and reduced risk of some types of cancers	■ Must be fresh, frozen, dried, or canned fruit or vegetable; fruit juice; vegetable juice ■ Must be limited in alcohol

FIGURE 13-12 Do you pay attention to health claims on food products?

The regulations also allow specific diet-related health claims on food. The permitted claims are about the following diet or health relationships:

- *A healthy diet low in sodium and high in potassium* may reduce the risk of high blood pressure.
- *A healthy diet adequate in calcium and vitamin D* may reduce the risk of osteoporosis.
- *A healthy diet low in saturated fat and trans fat* may reduce the risk of heart disease.
- *A healthy diet rich in vegetables and fruit* may reduce the risk of some types of cancer.

Using Labels to Improve Your Diet

Health Canada hopes that more nutrition and health information on labels will help Canadians make healthier choices. Do you and your family use this information to make decisions when purchasing food?

By reading the labels and health claims you can

- Reduce your consumption of less-healthy choices, such as those high in sodium, trans fat, saturated fats, calories, and cholesterol
- Increase your consumption of healthier choices, such as those that are high in fibre, protein, and vitamins and minerals
- Gain an understanding of how nutrition affects your health

RELIABLE NUTRITION INFORMATION

Finding reliable information about nutrition can be a challenge. We see and hear many different claims about food and nutrition on a regular basis. If you receive e-mail with information that sounds like it could be true, how can you know for sure? When considering a nutrition claim, keep these tips in mind:

1. Determine the original source of the information. Look at the institution or organization, and the qualifications of the people who did the research.
2. Be wary of research from unnamed sources.
3. Look for bias on the part of the people who performed the study or reported the information.
4. Read the whole story, not just the headlines. Headlines are designed to get your attention and seldom give enough information to make a wise decision.

5. Make sure that the information is solid. If the report is on initial findings or the researcher's initial hypothesis, there may not be enough evidence to support the theory or claim. Too often we receive information about a study to be done and assume that the hypothesis is based on fact. Look for the follow-up reports, which may discredit the initial reports.

6. Look at the design of the study. If the study was a clinical trial done on humans, the information is more reliable than studies done on animals since results are not always transferable.

FOOD GRADING

Food **grading** helps consumers be aware of the quality of a food product. Different types of foods have different grading systems, but each system helps consumers make informed choices. Grading systems vary for producers. Some get paid according to the quality of the food they produce, so the higher the grade, the more they earn. For example, Canada Extra Fancy apples command a higher price than Canada Commercial. For other foods, the grade determines how the food will be used. Using eggs as an example, table eggs (the ones you eat for breakfast) have to be of a higher grade than eggs used in making processed foods.

FIGURE 13-13 What do grading labels on fruits or vegetables tell the consumer?

Food grading is regulated under the *Canadian Agricultural Products Act* and the *Meat Inspection Act*, which are pieces of federal legislation. The *Canadian Agricultural Products Act* provides specific regulations for different types of foods or commodities. The Canadian Food Inspection Agency is responsible for enforcing the regulations and for ensuring that the product makes the grade. Some products also have provincial grades applied to them, which may be specific to foods sold only in the province or for foods sold outside the province.

The federal government has developed guidelines for labelling products that are graded. Here are some examples:

- A food product may be advertised with the price stated but, if this is done, the grade must also be stated. This way, consumers know the quality of the product they are getting for the price they will pay.
- Only legitimate grade names can be used when advertising a product.
- Grade names can only be used on the product they are intended for. A manufacturer cannot use the grade name for a different product. For example, a manufacturer couldn't use a triple A grade (which is for beef) on laundry detergent.
- If a food product is imported, then the grade used in the country of origin can be stated in advertising.
- If an imported food goes through part of its processing in Canada, then the Canadian grade can be used.

Product Variation

Grade names vary for different products. They differ for type of product—for example, vegetables or meats, and processing of products—for example, fresh or canned. Understanding the different grades will help you make more informed choices.

Fruits and Vegetables

There are different grading systems for different types of fresh fruits and vegetables as well as for processed fruits and vegetables. When you know how you are going to use the product you are buying, you can decide which grade to buy. If you are making applesauce, for example, you can save money by buying a lower grade of apple; if you want to eat the apple raw and whole, you might want the higher-grade fruit.

The tables on the following pages explain grading and what to look for when buying fresh fruits and vegetables.

Food for Thought

Frozen produce is a good choice. Fresh produce can sit in a truck or chilled storeroom for days, losing nutrients such as vitamin C. Frozen fruits and vegetables are often put on ice within hours of harvest, may be cheaper than fresh foods, and will not be wasted because they have gone bad before you have had a chance to eat them.

Grade Names of Fresh Vegetables

Product	Grade Name	When Buying, Look For ...
Asparagus	Canada No. 1 Canada No. 1 Slender Canada No. 2	Fresh, crisp, bright-green spears with tightly closed tips
Beans	No grade given for this vegetable under this regulation	Bright, crisp, young beans of uniform size, free of blemishes; avoid mature beans with swollen pods.
Beets	Canada No. 1 Canada No. 2	Applies only to beets that have no tops. Firm, uniform beets free of cracks or blemishes; attached leaves should be deep green and fresh looking.
Broccoli	No grade given for this vegetable under this regulation	Firm stalks with compact green bud clusters; avoid yellow florets.
Cabbages	Canada No. 1 Canada No. 2	Firm, heavy head with fresh outer leaves and good colouring
Carrots	Canada No. 1 Canada No. 2	Applies only to carrots that have no tops. Firm, clean, bright orange carrots that should be well-shaped. If tops are attached, they should be bright green and fresh-looking.
Cauliflower	Canada No. 1 Canada No. 2	Heavy, firm, creamy white heads with compact florets
Celery	Canada No. 1 Canada No. 1 Heart Canada No. 2	Crisp, rigid green stalks with fresh leaves; avoid limp or rubbery stalks.
Corn, Sweet	Canada No. 1	Cobs should have fresh-looking green husks and moist stems. Kernels should be juicy when pierced.
Cucumbers	Canada No. 1 Canada No. 2 (Applies to field cucumbers and greenhouse cucumbers)	Firm, well-shaped bright-green; avoid soft, over-mature, or yellowing ones.
Eggplant	No grade given for this vegetable under this regulation	Firm, purple eggplant that is heavy for its size, with glossy, unbroken skin
Lettuce, Iceberg	Canada No. 1 Canada No. 2	A crisp head with fresh outer leaves, free of brown spots and yellow leaves; it should be springy but firm to gentle pressure.
Mushrooms	No grade given for this vegetable under this regulation	Free of blemishes or slimy spots

Product	Grade Name	When Buying, Look For ...
Onions	Canada No. 1 Canada No. 1 Pickling Canada No. 2	Firm, small-necked onions with brittle outer leaves; avoid dark-spotted or sprouted bulbs.
Peppers, red, green, or yellow	No grade given for this vegetable under this regulation	Crisp, well-shaped, bright in colour with smooth skin
Potatoes	Canada No. 1 Canada No. 2	Clean, firm, and smooth, without sprouts, green areas, or blemishes
Spinach	No grade given for this vegetable under this regulation	Fresh crisp leaves with solid green colouring
Squash, Winter	No grade given for this vegetable under this regulation	Heavy for its size with a hard rind that is not shiny
Tomato	Canada No. 1 (Field) Canada No. 2 (Field) Canada No. 1 (Greenhouse) Canada Commercial (Greenhouse) Canada No. 2 (Greenhouse)	Smooth, well-formed, firm, heavy for size, and uniform in colour
Zucchini	No grade given for this vegetable under this regulation	Small, smooth-skinned, and bright-coloured; smaller ones are less seedy and more tender.

Grade Names of Fresh Fruits

Product	Grade Name	When Buying, Look For ...
Apples	Canada Extra Fancy Canada Fancy Canada Commercial Canada Hailed Canada Commercial Cookers Canada No. 1 peeled Canada No. 2 peeled	Well-shaped, smooth-skinned fruit free of bruises; brownish freckled areas do not affect flavour.
Apricots	Canada No. 1 Canada Domestic Canada Hailed	Plump, fairly firm fruit with as much golden orange as possible
Bananas	No grade given for this fruit under this regulation	Firm, unblemished fruit; yellow with brown speckles indicates a sweet, tender fruit.
Blueberries	Canada No. 1	Firm, plump, dry, dark-coloured berries with a powdery blue bloom

Grade Names of Fresh Fruits *(continued)*

Product	Grade Name	When Buying, Look For ...
Cantaloupe	Canada No. 1	Melon with a deeply-netted, yellow-gold rind; ripe fruit yields slightly to gentle pressure and has a musky fragrance.
Cherries	Canada No. 1 Canada Commercial Canada Orchard Run	Plump, bright-coloured fruit; the deeper the colour, the sweeter the fruit; avoid very soft or shrivelled fruit
Grapefruit	No grade given for this fruit under this regulation	Firm, well-shaped fruit that is heavy for size
Grapes	Canada No. 1 Canada Domestic	Plump fruits that are firmly attached to green stems; avoid wrinkled or sticky fruit
Kiwi fruit	No grade given for this fruit under this regulation	Evenly ripe fruit, free of mould or soft spots that yield to gentle pressure
Peaches	Canada No. 1 Canada Domestic	Fruit with yellowish (not green) background; ripe fruit yields to gentle pressure when squeezed in the palm, not with the fingers.
Pears	Canada Extra Fancy Canada Fancy Canada Commercial	Firm, well-shaped fruit; use fully-ripe fruit immediately. Minor scars and blemishes do not affect flavour.
Plums	Canada No. 1 Canada Domestic	Full-coloured smooth fruit; ripe fruit yields to gentle pressure.
Strawberries	Canada No. 1	Firm, plump berries that are fully red, with bright green caps; strawberries do not ripen once picked.
Watermelon	No grade given for this fruit under this regulation	A firm, symmetrical melon with fully rounded sides and a yellowish underside; if cut, select a melon with brightly coloured flesh.

Processed vegetables and fruits are graded according to processing. Canned vegetables and fruits are divided into three grades:

- Canada Fancy
- Canada Choice
- Canada Standard

Frozen vegetables and fruits are divided into two grades:

- Canada A
- Canada B

A very few frozen products can have a third grade of "Canada C," but these generally aren't available in grocery stores.

Meat Inspection

Meat sold in Canada has to be inspected. Once inspected, it is stamped with the stamp you see here on the left. The stamp means that the meat has met the food safety standards for Canada and is fit for human consumption. This stamp is not an indication of the grade of the meat.

Wild game is considered uninspected meat. As such, it can only be consumed by people who are part of the animal owner's household. It cannot be sold or given away. Selling or giving away uninspected meat is a serious offense and comes with a fine of up to $10 000.

Grading Meat and Poultry

Beef can be graded into 13 different categories. Most beef is divided into Canada Prime, Canada AAA, Canada AA, and Canada A product.

The main difference between these grades is the amount of **marbling** in the meat. Marbling refers to the fine white streaks of fat running through the flesh. It increases tenderness, juiciness, and flavour. The more marbled the meat is, the higher the price. Consumers should decide how they want to use the meat before deciding which grade to buy. Many stores now label meat according to cooking style, such as roasting, moist cooking, or stewing. The more moisture you cook with and the longer you cook meat, the less tender a grade of meat you need. For example, if you are using beef to make stew, you can buy a lower grade than if you were planning to grill the meat.

Poultry, including chicken and turkey, is divided into Canada Grade A, Canada Grade B, and Canada Grade C product.

The grade will appear on the label in a symbol shaped like a maple leaf. The grading system looks at the shape and quality of the carcass; the distribution of flesh and fat; and the general appearance, or dressing. The better the carcass scores, the higher the grade.

FIGURE 13-14 Do you know how to tell the difference between different grades of beef?

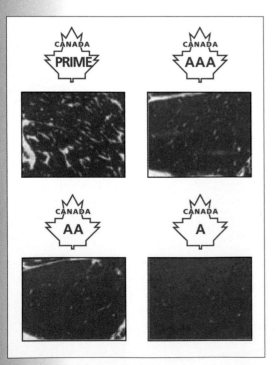

Fish and Seafood Inspection

The Canadian Food Inspection Agency (CFIA) is responsible for inspecting all fish and seafood for sale in Canada, including imported products. The CFIA verifies that suppliers are following appropriate product and processing standards that contribute to the acceptable quality, safety, and identity of fish and seafood products processed in federal establishments or imported into Canada. All facilities must be registered in order to sell fish and seafood. In order to protect the health of Canadians, the foods must go through the inspection process.

Grading Eggs

Eggs have to go to a registered egg-grading station to be graded. Eggs cannot be sold commercially unless they have been graded in a registered facility. Part of the process involves **candling** the egg. Eggs are put on a conveyor belt and pass over a strong light. The light makes the inside of the egg visible and reveals its quality. Only Grade A eggs can be sold in the retail market. Grades B and C eggs are sold for commercial baking and other processes.

The table below shows the differences among the three grades of eggs.

Making the Grade—Eggs

Grade A	Grade B	Grade C
■ Sold in retail stores for household use ■ The most commonly bought consumer egg	■ Sold for commercial baking or further processing ■ Can be sold at retail	■ Sold to commercial processors for further processing only
■ Firm white ■ Round, well-centred yolk ■ Clean, uncracked shell with normal shape ■ Small air cell (less than 5 mm deep)	■ Watery white ■ Slightly flattened yolk ■ Uncracked shell possibly with rough texture ■ May be slightly stained or soiled	■ Thin, watery white ■ Loose yolk ■ Possibly cracked shell and up to ⅓ stained
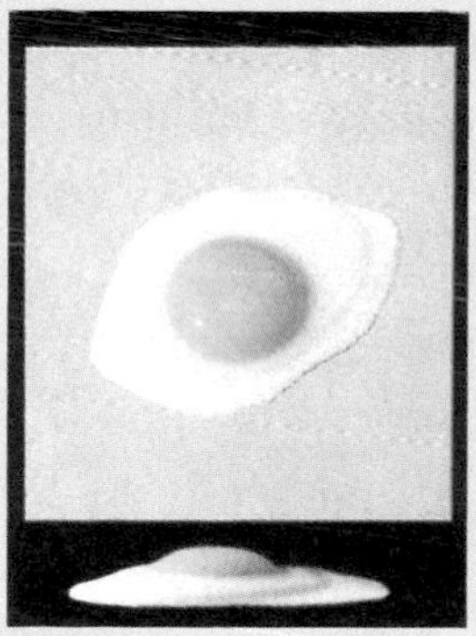 Grade A	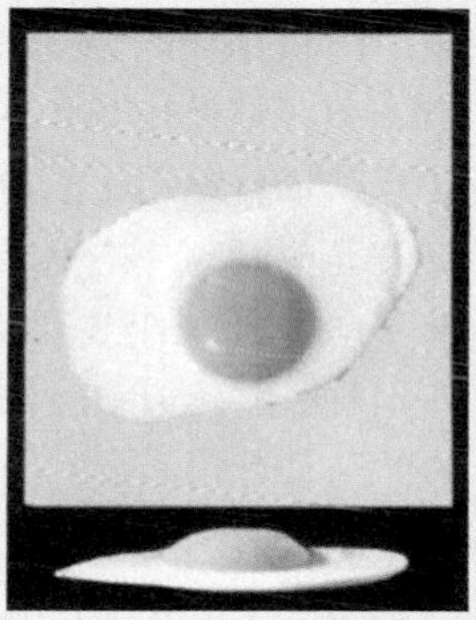 Grade B	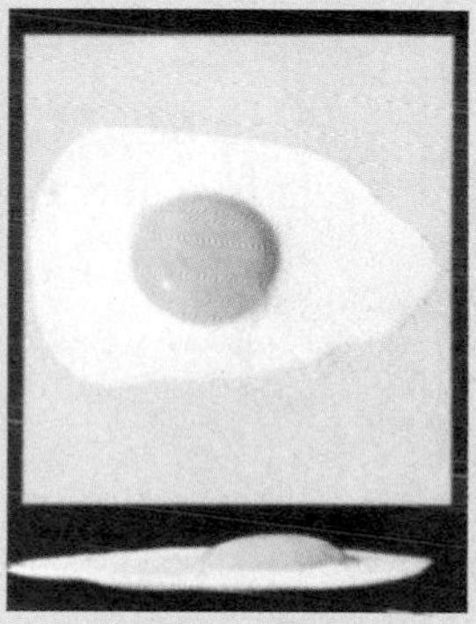 Grade C

FIGURE 13-15 Can you see the differences in these three grades of eggs?

Grading Milk

Liquid milk is not graded but must pass through a series of inspections and tests to be made available for sale in Canada. The same requirements have to be met for all liquid milk sold. Other milk products, such as butter and cheese, are graded. Butter, butter products, and cheddar cheese are graded Canada 1. Dry milk products, such as milk powders, can have a grade of Canada 1 or Canada 2.

FIGURE 13-16 Do you look for "packaged on" dates on the foods you buy?

SHELF LIFE OF FOODS

Another important consideration when grocery shopping is the shelf life of packaged foods. Reading labels regarding shelf life will help to make you aware of the quality of the food you are buying.

- "Best before" dates have to be put on foods that have a durable life of 90 or fewer days. This indicates the date before which the food product will still be good if kept unopened. If the food requires special storage to maintain its quality, then that information must be on the label as well.

- "Packaged on" dates tell you the date the food was packaged. They are also used for foods that have a durable life of 90 or fewer days. However, these foods are packaged at the retail store. Some of these packages will also contain a "Use before" date and safe storage information.

FOOD ADDITIVES

FIGURE 13-17 Many restaurants stopped using MSG when consumers began complaining. Do you know if your favourite restaurant uses MSG?

Food additives are substances added to food primarily to enhance flavour, appearance, and texture, or to preserve freshness. Their use is controlled by Health Canada under the *Food and Drugs Act*. Manufacturers have to get permission from Health Canada to use a food additive. They must submit a report that includes the results of safety tests, how the additive will be used, and the benefits of the additive to the consumer. Health Canada evaluates the report to see if the additive will do what the manufacturer claims and not pose a health risk to Canadians. Health Canada also considers other information about food additives from sources such as the World Health Organization and the United Nations Food and Agriculture Organization. Health Canada sets acceptable levels of food additives, which are reviewed as new information becomes available.

Some consumers do not want foods that contain additives and so are very careful about reading ingredient lists. Other consumers must read labels carefully because they are allergic to certain additives. For example, many people have an allergic reaction to the flavour enhancer monosodium glutamate (MSG).

Understanding food additives and the role they play in food can help you make informed decisions about them. Refer to the chart that follows to see some of the common additives found in food in Canada.

Food Additives

Additive	Function	Used in These Foods
Beta carotene, ascorbic acid (vitamin C), sodium ascorbate, phosphates, dextrose	*Artificial colourings and colour stabilizers:* Used to make food appeal to the eye	Candy, pop, gelatin desserts, margarine, shortening, non-milk whiteners, cereals, fruit drinks, cured meats, cheese, breakfast cereals, marshmallows
Mannitol, aspartame, sugar (sucrose), dextrose, sucralose, acesulfame-K	*Sweeteners*	Baked goods, chewing gum, soft drinks, gelatin desserts, diet foods, low-calorie foods, frozen desserts, sweetener packets, marshmallows, table sugar, sweetened foods
Alginate, propylene glycol alginate, carrageenan, corn syrup, gelatin, locust bean gum, xanthan, food starch—modified (corn)	*Thickeners, stabilizers:* Keep factory-made food mixed	Ice cream, cheese, candy, yoghurt, pop, salad dressing, drink mixes, chocolate milk, toppings, syrups, snack foods, imitation dairy foods, marshmallows, beverages, frozen pudding, cottage cheese
Alpha-tocopherol (vitamin E), ascorbic acid (vitamin C), BHA (butylated hydroxyanisole), citric acid	*Antioxidants:* Slow or prevent rancidity in fats, oils, and oil-containing foods, or browning of fruits or vegetables when cut and exposed to the air	Vegetable oil, cereals, chewing gum, potato chips, ice cream, vegetables and fruit
MSG (monosodium glutamate), HVP, salt, citric acid	*Artificial and natural flavourings, flavour enhancers:* Companies often keep the identity of "flavourings" such as these a secret	Pop, candy, breakfast cereals, gelatin desserts, soup, salad dressings, potato chips, restaurant foods, crackers, processed foods, popcorn seasonings
Ascorbic acid (vitamin C), vitamin A, E, D, ferrous sulphate (iron), niacin, riboflavin, calcium	*Nutrients*	Cereals, fruit drinks, cured meats, pasta, milk
Caffeine	*Stimulant*	Present in coffee, tea, hot chocolate, and coffee-flavoured products, such as yoghurt and frozen desserts; added to soft drinks, chewing gum
Calcium propionate, sodium propionate	*Preservatives:* Extend the shelf life of food	Breads, rolls, pies, cakes
Calcium (or sodium) stearoyl lactylate, sodium bicarbonate	*Dough conditioners, whipping agents, and leaveners:* Strengthen bread dough so it can be used in bread-making machinery; help produce a more uniform grain and greater volume	Bread dough, cake fillings, artificial whipped cream, processed egg whites
Monoglycerides and diglycerides, phosphates	*Emulsifiers:* Keep oil and water mixed; make bread softer; prevent spoilage; make caramels less sticky; prevent the oil in peanut butter from separating	Baked goods, margarine, candy, peanut butter
Silica gel, cornstarch	*Anti-caking agents:* Prevents lumping of powders	Popcorn seasonings, icing sugar
Glycerin	*Maintains water content*	Candy, baked goods, fudge

Connecting to the Community

In each Connecting to the Community activity you will find out more about your local community by completing one of two assignments. This section forms one part of your Connecting to the Community for Unit 4. For the activity, you will create one product from a choice of the following products.

Chapter 13 Choices

1. Throughout this chapter you learned about purchasing foods. Prepare a product that will help consumers to shop wisely. Include the following components:

   - Marketing strategies to be aware of and pitfalls to avoid
   - Good places to shop in your community
   - Tips for making wise choices while shopping

OR

2. In this chapter you learned about reading labels to make healthier food choices. Create a product that can be given to users of a local food support program to help them to make the healthiest food choices for their clients. Include the following information in your product:

   - What is on a label
   - Understanding nutrition facts tables
   - Ingredient lists
   - Health and diet claims
   - Comparing similar products and understanding serving sizes
   - Food grading
   - Food additives

Chapter 13 Summary

This chapter explored many aspects of shopping for healthy food. You learned

- About common marketing practices used to entice consumers to buy products
- How to be a wise consumer and make healthy food choices
- About places to shop for food
- About food labelling requirements
- How to finding reliable nutrition information and what to look for in terms of
  - Food grading
  - Food additives

Activities

1. Choose an age group or target market group. Look for food advertising geared to that group. Make a list of key messages in the marketing.

2. What are food additives and why are they added to our foods? Name three common food additives and their functions.

3. Name three common marketing practices used to entice consumers to purchase a product. Choose a food product and create an ad using these practices.

4. Go to a kitchen cupboard at school or at home and find two examples of a similar product, such as crackers or soup. Find the nutrition facts tables and mount or copy them onto paper. Compare the two products and determine which one is the healthier choice using the following criteria:
   - Amounts of less-healthy ingredients (e.g., fat, sodium, cholesterol, calories, and sugars)
   - Amount of healthier ingredients (e.g., fibre, vitamins, and minerals)
   - Serving sizes

   What conclusions can you draw from your comparisons?

5. Create a tip sheet for finding reliable information on nutrition. Use this sheet to evaluate information that you find in a newspaper, magazine, or on the Internet. Apply the following criteria in your tip sheet:
   - Source of information
   - The whole story
   - Findings of a study (initial or complete)
   - Design of the study

CHAPTER 14

Meal Planning and Preparation

In this chapter you will learn about meal planning and preparation. You will read about the factors to consider when planning meals for individuals and families. You will also look at related issues such as time, budget, special dietary needs, and food preferences.

Haruki and Hina are skimming through cookbooks. Next week their mom has to go to the hospital for surgery. She will be in the hospital for at least four days, and when she comes home, she will need a diet that is low in fibre, sodium, and fat. Haruki and Hina will be in charge of cooking the family dinners since their dad works evenings. Their dad will make breakfast and school lunches. Their mom wants Haruki and Hina to plan the evening meal menu for the next 10 days. When they finish, they will check the cupboards, fridge, and freezer to see which ingredients their mom should buy before she goes to the hospital.

Haruki is glad that he took food and nutrition last year. He has discovered that he remembers quite a few things from that class. He has already shown Hina how to read the Nutrition Facts tables on the foods they already have in the kitchen cupboard. Haruki and Hina are trying to make sure that the meals they are planning will meet their mother's new dietary requirements. Hina is still a little worried about how they are going to be able to keep their two younger siblings happy. Haruna doesn't like

Key Concepts

- Personal food choices
- Factors to consider when planning meals
- Meal planning basics
  - Food budgeting
  - Saving money on food
  - Managing time
  - Making a work plan
- Working as a team
- Balancing time and money
- Serving meals

Key Terms

budget
family service
plate service
serving pieces
table setting
tableware
time management
work plan
work schedule

very many vegetables—only carrots, beans, Brussels sprouts, and cabbage. This limits how creative they can be when cooking for the two of them. Luckily, Haruto eats more vegetables, but he is quite picky about meat and alternatives. He is a borderline vegetarian, so Haruki and Hina have to be sure that they make him meatless meals that will fulfill his protein needs.

Haruki and Hina never understood how creative their mom really was in the kitchen until they had to do the meal planning themselves. They just wish she had been more creative with their names and chosen some that didn't start with the letter H!

Who plans the meals in your family? Is it one person, or do several family members get involved? Are meals planned daily or ahead of time? A week at a time or more? Do you decide what to eat based on what is in the kitchen or what you feel like eating? Ask your friends how their families plan meals. Is it the same as or different from your family's method?

Different families plan meals in different ways. What suits one family's needs and requirements may not suit another's. Even though meal planning and preparation is something that is done by all families, each family finds a system that works for them. In this chapter you will consider different aspects of meal planning.

PERSONAL FOOD CHOICES

When planning meals for someone other than yourself, many factors must be taken into consideration. Personal food preferences is just one of them. Can you imagine what it would be like if the food you were served every day was never what you wanted to eat? Most people are offered foods they don't like once in a while, but people who plan and prepare food for others usually take into account the food preferences of the people they are feeding.

Living in a family does not mean that everyone likes the same foods. So planning meals for the whole family involves the personal food preferences of all family members. The larger the family, the more complicated meeting their preferences can become. Understanding food preferences will help you plan meals that your family will enjoy.

FIGURE 14-1 When you go out to eat with your family, does everyone eat the same types of food, or do people have different food preferences?

FACTORS TO CONSIDER WHEN PLANNING MEALS

There are several factors to take into consideration when you are planning meals for other people. As a teen, you may or may not take part in planning and preparing family meals. Some teens are responsible for much of the cooking for the evening meal, while others just get themselves a snack. Regardless of how much time you spend planning meals now, in the future you will probably be involved in meal planning at some times. Understanding the main factors of meal planning will help you provide for others more successfully. Let's look at these now.

- *Nutrition.* When planning meals, consider the nutritional needs of those for whom you are providing food. Balancing nutritional needs over the course of a day or a week is a key factor in meal planning.
- *Eating patterns* of those you are feeding are also a main consideration. Many families do not eat lunch at home on weekdays and thus eat light, packed, or purchased lunches. Consequently, their main meal is in the evening. Some families have a very light breakfast and then have a more substantial snack in the morning. Being aware of eating patterns can help you to plan meals more successfully.
- *Schedules* are like eating patterns: they are particular to a group of people. In some families, trying to schedule an evening meal together is not possible because family members have part-time jobs and other commitments. Some families spend the first meal of the day together instead of the evening meal, since this is often the time when all family members are at home. Shift work also affects meal planning. When a parent works shifts or leaves home very early to go to work, his or her schedule changes the way the family eats, which affects meal planning.
- *Budget* has a major impact on meal planning. If a budget is tight, many families cannot afford convenience foods because they tend to be more expensive. Meal planning often requires creativity in order to make the most of a food budget. Most families set a food budget and try to work within it.
- *The stage of the life cycle a person is in* also has an effect on meal planning. When a family has a variety of stages to plan for, it can be a challenge. For example, what if both grandparents and young grandchildren were living in the same house?

Safety Check

Taking a safe packed lunch to school

When planning, preparing, and packing school lunches, keep food safety in mind. An insulated lunch bag with an ice pack or frozen juice box is one of the safest ways to pack a lunch. Be wary of putting mayonnaise in a lunch bag that has to sit for a long time. If you pack a meat sandwich without mayonnaise, it can be frozen the night before and will thaw by lunchtime. Vegetable sticks packed in a container with an ice cube will stay fresher longer too. Regardless of what you pack, remember to keep cold foods cold and hot foods hot to avoid food-safety hazards.

Many people believe that it is best to have three meals each day—breakfast, lunch, and dinner. Most North Americans' lives are planned around these three meals. We have learned that breakfast is an important meal and that most of us start our day with breakfast of some kind. At work and at school, people have either a lunch or a dinner break. The evening meal is usually served at home, and for most North American families it tends to be the biggest meal of the day. At other times, we snack, although often our snacks are not our most nutritious choices.

Contrary to this popular eating pattern, new research is showing that it may be better to eat several small healthy meals a day rather than three larger ones. Health experts are suggesting that people would be better off eating an early-morning meal, a mid-morning meal, a midday meal, an afternoon snack, and an early-evening meal. None of these meals should be as large as the meals people currently eat. All these meals should comprise healthy choices. Health experts claim that by providing our bodies with a steady source of nutritious foods, we are laying the foundation for good health.

FIGURE 14-2 Would you rather eat three large meals a day or several small meals? Why? Why not?

Questions

1. Think about how many times a day you are hungry or want to eat. Do you want to eat more than the three large meals typical of North American culture?

2. When you snack, do you make nutritious choices? Do the times of day when you snack match the times suggested for small meals by the new research? How do you think this might affect your eating patterns?

Young children tend to have a more limited palate than adults. Adults should plan meals to introduce new flavours and textures to young children while still offering them foods that they enjoy. When meal planning for young children

- Plan meals that are easy to eat and easy to chew.
- Plan meals that allow children to feed themselves.
- Involve children in planning their meals.
- Plan fun and interesting meals, and make the presentation of them appealing.

Another group that presents meal planning challenges is older adults. Due to health reasons and changing tastes, older adults might have to change their diets. Some older adults find that their senses of taste and smell are diminished. This affects the appetite. When planning meals for older adults

- Plan meals that contain nutrient-dense choices.
- Remember to include foods that are rich in calcium.
- Make foods flavourful and attractive.
- Serve foods with a softer texture for adults who have difficulty chewing.
- Include good sources of fibre.
- Other considerations include food allergies and special diets, such as low fat, diabetic, or vegetarian diets, as outlined in Chapter 7: Living with Special Considerations. Cultural food preferences or restrictions are also key considerations. The activity level of each family member is also a contributing factor, since the more active a person is, the more energy he or she requires.

FIGURE 14-3 Do you have to consider how to meet the food needs of young children and older adults when meal planning?

As you can see, there are many different factors to consider when planning meals. You need to know quite a bit about the people you are feeding. Planning a meal for your family is easier than planning a meal for people whom you do not know well. Have you ever served food at a party only to find out that one of the guests cannot or will not eat the food you made? Asking guests ahead of time if there are any foods they cannot eat is a good way to avoid embarrassing situations.

Starting the Day with a Good Breakfast

Sometimes it is too easy to skip breakfast. The alarm didn't go off, the extra few minutes in bed were just too good to give up, it was one of those days when your hair took an extra 20 minutes, or you couldn't decide what to wear. Perhaps after reading this feature, you will want to make sure you **save a bit of time for the most important meal of the day**.

Your brain and body need a constant supply of fuel to work. If you don't eat breakfast, your body has to resort to stored carbohydrates to give your muscles and brain the energy they need. In the morning, your body is in a state of **temporary starvation** (it has been 12 or 14 hours since your last meal). Skipping breakfast has at least three unwanted effects. First, you can't think or move at your best. Second, your **metabolism** slows down, making you feel sluggish and tired. Third, later in the day **you are much more likely to overeat** and crave high-calorie foods to make up for those missed at breakfast.

In a number of different food studies, subjects were asked to perform various tasks after having eaten and not eaten breakfast. In general, these studies showed that eating breakfast regularly leads to **better memory** and ability to concentrate. Adults performed better at mental tasks and children performed better in academic and sport activities when they've had a good breakfast.

Like all meals, a healthy, well-balanced breakfast takes some planning. Ideally, breakfast should provide you with **about one-quarter of your caloric intake for the day**. However, grabbing a muffin, a croissant, or a donut may give you those calories but not the nutrients that will give you a good start to the day. Many donuts and croissants contain at least 350 calories each. Choosing the right breakfast foods is a crucial component of eating breakfast.

Aim to **include at least three of the four food groups in your breakfast,** and choose complex carbohydrates like whole grains to keep your energy level up until lunch. A traditional breakfast, such as whole-grain cereal with milk and some fresh fruit, covers three food groups. Add a small piece of cheese, an egg, or a slice of meat for **extra protein** and you have a breakfast that will start your day off with everything you need.

Often, people don't eat breakfast because they don't like cereal. Whole wheat waffles, multi-grain bagels, or toast topped with nut butter or fruit and cream cheese are all tasty, nutritious breakfasts. Another alternative is to build a healthy blender drink with fresh or frozen fruit and yoghurt. **Get creative and eat breakfast every day!**

FIGURE 14-4 All of these foods are healthy choices. Which ones would you choose for a healthy breakfast?

MEAL PLANNING BASICS

Meal planning basics can be applied to meals for just one or two people or for feeding a large gathering. Once you understand the fundamentals, you have the tools to plan successful meals.

When preparing to plan meals, first consider your resources. These include

- Time available for meal preparation
- Availability of seasonal foods and any specialty foods required
- Food already stocked in your kitchen
- Budget
- Skills required to prepare the foods
- Equipment needed to prepare the foods

Considering all your resources enables you to make informed decisions. Some people may have more time than money and therefore will choose to make food from scratch. Other people have limited time, and they may opt for convenience foods. Let's look at how to use your money and time wisely.

FIGURE 14-5 Could you plan a meal for a large group of people? Would you know where to begin?

Food Budgeting

Why do people budget for food? Because they have to eat! A **budget** is a plan for managing your money so that you have enough to purchase the food that you need. Food makes up a large portion of a family's spending. Families have to consider the cost of food, shelter, clothing, and transportation, and these four expenses usually take up the largest share of a family's budget.

There are several factors to account for when setting a food budget, including

- Income
- Other expenses, such as rent or mortgage payments, heat, and electricity
- Number and ages of the people who will be eating each meal
- Cost of food (e.g., food in season is less expensive than imported food out of season, foods on sale, coupons)
- Amount spent on take-out food and restaurant meals

- Time available to make food
- How often you want to cook meals
- Food storage capacity. Can you buy in bulk to save money?
- Food preferences and special dietary needs

A few simple guidelines will help you set up and follow a food budget:

1. *Track spending.* Keep track of the money you spend on food. Make sure that you track all food spending—at the grocery store, at work or school, meals out, snacks at places like the movies, and so on.

2. *Decide how much you will spend* in each category of food type. Many families have different categories in their food budgets. Some include a grocery budget, a lunch budget, an entertainment budget, and a special-occasions budget.

3. *Be realistic.* If you have budgeted too little, you may have to make changes. Keeping track of your spending after you have set a budget can help you determine whether your budget is realistic or not.

4. *Keep money in reserve.* Some weeks you will spend less than others. If that is the case, keep any unused money in reserve for weeks when food costs are higher. Often people spend more during weeks when there is a special cultural, religious, or family celebration.

5. *Re-evaluate.* After a couple of months, look at your spending and your budget and re-evaluate to see if the budget is working.

FIGURE 14-6 Does your family keep track of its food spending?

Saving Money on Food

Chapter 13: Becoming a Wise Consumer, looked at making wise and informed decisions when shopping for food. If you are on a budget, it is important that you also

- Check grocery store flyers for sales.
- Buy fresh produce in season and frozen or canned vegetables and fruit when they are out of season.
- Choose cuts of meat that are more economical and do any extra preparation yourself. For example, chicken that still has bones in it can be deboned at home and costs less, and a less-tender cut of beef can be slow-cooked with moist heat to tenderize it.
- Buy only what your family will eat. If you have leftovers, store them carefully and use them for another meal.
- Cook meals at home rather than going to a restaurant or buying prepared food.
- Use fewer convenience foods. The more processing that a food product undergoes, the more it costs.
- Be flexible, so you can take advantage of good deals.

FIGURE 14-7 Does your family use grocery store flyers to prepare your food budget?

Managing Time

Time management is one of the most important aspects of meal planning. Forgetting to keep track of time is one of the main reasons why new cooks have trouble in the kitchen. Being organized and knowing how long each step of your meal preparation will take is key to success. To do this, you need a plan.

MAKING A WORK PLAN

A good **work plan** takes into account all aspects of meal preparation, including

- Reading the recipe carefully
- Getting out the equipment
- Getting out the ingredients
- Preheating the oven, if necessary
- Completing all steps in the recipe

- Cleaning up
- Serving

For each step in your plan, estimate how much time it will take. Many recipes will actually give an approximate time for preparation and cooking. Look at the recipe for Speedy Spaghetti and Meatballs on the next page. You can see that it refers to

- Preparation time
- Roasting time
- Cooking time

FIGURE 14-8 When planning meals, do you think about how much time the whole meal will take including preparation, cooking, and cleanup?

Recipes with this kind of timing information help new cooks manage time more effectively. When your recipe does not include timing, you will have to determine how long things will take yourself. The more practise you have at cooking or making a particular recipe, the better you will be at assessing the time needed for preparation and proper cooking. As a new cook, or with a new recipe, you should allow more time than you think you will need so that you are sure to have enough time to complete all the tasks properly.

When setting up a work plan, determine whether any of the tasks can be done ahead of time. If you are making something that requires chopped vegetables, for example, they can be chopped earlier and refrigerated until needed. You can do some tasks, such as setting the table, ahead of time. Another time-saving technique is to do your cleanup while the food is cooking. In the recipe on page 339, you can see that the food will take 15 minutes to cook. During that time, you can usually take care of most of the preparation cleanup.

Once you have your work plan with approximate times on it, you can then turn it into a **work schedule** quite easily by adding the times of day to it. To do this, decide what time you want the food to be ready, then subtract the work plan time and start from there. Read over the following example of a work plan and schedule for a sandwich lunch that you want to have ready by noon.

Work Plan (Total time: 6 minutes)	Work Schedule (Eating time: 12:00 noon; Start time: 11:54)
- Get out ingredients: 1 minute - Wash hands and counter: 1 minute - Spread cream cheese on bread: 1 minute - Pour juice in glass: 1 minute - Clean up preparation area: 2 minutes	11:54: Get out ingredients 11:55: Wash hands and counter 11:56: Spread cream cheese on bread 11:57: Pour juice in glass 11:58: Clean up preparation area 12:00: Serve meal

Speedy Spaghetti and Meatballs

Preparation time: *10 minutes*
Roasting time: *20 minutes**
Cooking time: *15 minutes**

Ingredients

6 plum tomatoes or 4 regular tomatoes, cored and quartered
1 each red and green pepper, coarsely chopped
1 tbsp (15mL) olive oil
½ tsp (2 mL) each salt, black pepper, and dried oregano
20 frozen chicken or beef meatballs
½ (450 g) pkg spaghetti
1 cup (250 mL) tomato-based pasta sauce

Preparation

- Preheat oven to 450°F (230°C). Line a shallow-sided baking sheet with foil. In large bowl add tomatoes, peppers, oil, salt, pepper and oregano. Toss until evenly coated. Spread on baking sheet and scatter meatballs around vegetables. Roast in centre of oven, stirring occasionally, until meatballs are lightly browned, 18 to 20 minutes.

- As soon as you put the meatballs and vegetables in the oven, bring large saucepan of water to a boil. Add pasta to boiling water and cook according to package directions. Drain well, leaving pasta in colander.

- Add pasta sauce to saucepan. Heat over medium heat until hot, 2 to 3 minutes. Then add pasta, roasted vegetables, and meatballs. Stir until evenly mixed. If desired, sprinkle with grated parmesan.

* The roasting and cooking occur at the same time.

Servings: 4

Working as a Team

Often when you work in a kitchen, you are working with someone else. When you are part of a team, a good plan is essential for success. Planning how you will share the work will use your time, skills, and the workspace efficiently. When you are working as a group in the food and nutrition classroom, pay close attention to the time since your class time is limited.

In the food and nutrition classroom, jobs are often divided up among classmates. In some cases, the teacher may assign different job descriptions to individual students. These job descriptions are often changed for each class so that each student gets an opportunity to do each job. In other classrooms, the teacher will not assign specific job descriptions to students, but will let group members decide on who will do each job themselves. Regardless of how the job descriptions are assigned, there is still planning and organizing to do based on the specific requirements of the recipe(s) planned for the food lab.

To be effective in the food and nutrition classroom, each group must consider the following aspects of planning:

1. *Organization.* Make a work plan and schedule for each member of the group. When each member has a timed task list, multi-tasking can be done by the entire group.
2. *Support each other.* Each member of the group should complete his or her own task. When one person is finished, he or she can pitch in if another member needs help.
3. *Don't wait until all the cooking is finished to clean up.* Cleaning as you go helps avoid the last-minute rush to get to your next class on time.
4. *Reflect.* After you have finished, reflect on the success of the whole experience and propose strategies to improve the lab for the next time.

FIGURE 14-9 How do you organize your group in food and nutrition class?

Elias Minatsis, School Chef

Elias Minatsis is a well-known figure at Elphinstone Secondary School in Gibsons, B.C. He is responsible for not only ensuring that breakfast and lunch are ready for staff and students, but also for working with and supervising students in the kitchen.

Elias first wanted to become a cook two years after he finished high school. He had been working in a restaurant and realized it was something he was good at. To pursue his goal, he completed the Cook Certification course at Vancouver Community College in the Culinary Arts Program and then completed a three-year apprenticeship at La Folie Restaurant in White Rock, B.C. Upon completion, he received his Red Seal Journeyman's Certification.

Through working in a number of restaurants Elias developed a wide variety of cooking skills. He has prepared tapas and breakfast foods, done line cooking, and been part of an open kitchen visible to the restaurant clientele. He has worked a variety of food stations, as an entremétier (preparing vegetables), garde manger (preparing cold foods and completing all final food decorating), and saucier (preparing sauces, stews, and hors d'oeuvres).

Elias's current responsibilities at Elphinstone Secondary School include meal preparation; ordering, receiving, and storing food and supplies; setting menus; cleaning up; and organizing the kitchen.

Elias is dedicated to preparing healthy meals from scratch for the staff and students. Each lunch consists of a hot entrée, such as quesadillas, lasagna, shepherd's pie, or a stir-fry. Among other things, he also offers a soup of the day, sandwiches and wraps, and various salads. Soup of the day is a favourite, especially among staff members. Elias offers chicken noodle with vegetables, as well as more exotic soups such as carrot and ginger. A student request for "spicy thai chicken coconut soup" was also a hit. Vegetarian choices are regularly offered at lunch, and include quiche, spanikopita, pasta with tomato sauce, or meatless enchiladas and quesadillas. Elias also provides breakfast daily and cooks omelettes, scrambled eggs, and fried-egg sandwiches to go along with breakfast parfaits and muffins.

Elias enjoys working with students in the kitchen. Students who sign up for this elective work one hour a day in the kitchen preparing food and cleaning up. They are also required to help serve breakfast and lunch once a week. Elias says that "A positive attitude and sense of humour are necessary for running a smooth kitchen, and being able to work with the 15 students in the cafeteria elective."

"A positive attitude and sense of humour are necessary for running a smooth kitchen ..."

BALANCING TIME AND MONEY

Many people use convenience foods on a regular basis. Some have never tasted the homemade version of their favourite convenience food. Have you ever made any of these foods from scratch?

- Popcorn
- Pancakes
- Macaroni and cheese
- Spaghetti sauce
- Jam

FIGURE 14-10 Which foods do you make from scratch and which ones do you use mixes for?

- Pizza
- Meat patties
- Egg rolls
- Cake
- Muffins
- Cookies

Web connection

To find more recipes with preparation and cooking times, and other meal planning information, go to this Web site and follow the links.

www.mhrfoodforlife.ca

Convenience foods are widely available in Canada and range in price from inexpensive to moderately expensive to very expensive. Today, there are more dual-career and single-parent families than there are families with a stay-at-home parent or guardian. Many families need extra time more than they need extra money and so convenience foods fill an important need.

When buying any prepackaged food, remember what you learned about reading labels in Chapter 13: Becoming a Wise Consumer. Paying particular attention to the amount of sodium, types of fat, and cholesterol content will help you make healthier choices. Fresh, healthy choices supplemented with convenience foods can make for a healthy diet.

Some prepackaged foods offer a competitive price and save valuable time, while still offering a healthy choice. Complete pancake mix is a good example. You can purchase a one-kilogram (2.2 pound) box of mix for $2.15, and in 10 minutes or less have the pancakes ready to eat, with no more equipment than a mixing bowl, a fork or whisk, a measuring cup for liquids, and a griddle. To make pancakes from scratch, you must have flour, sugar, baking powder, eggs, milk, oil, and vanilla on hand. The time to prepare and cook from scratch is closer to 30 minutes. While some people may prefer the taste of homemade pancakes, when time is limited, the mix is an affordable option.

Another way to balance time and money is by combining convenience and fresh foods. If you look at the recipe on page 339, you will see that the sauce was made from scratch but the meatballs were frozen. Being creative can help you make healthy, delicious meals that meet the constraints of both time and money.

Convenience Foods

Today, the term "convenience food" describes a hot or cold dish that is intended to save the consumer time in the kitchen. Convenience foods are usually quick, require very little preparation, are packaged for a long shelf life, and can be purchased frozen, chilled, boxed, or canned. They thus require few cooking skills.

Canada has a long and interesting "convenience food" history. Before the invention of commercial food preservation methods, Canada's First Nations peoples relied on their own convenience food called *pemmican*. It was a very nutritious, portable, and long-lasting food. Dried meat was combined with berries and fat and stored in bison-skin bags called *parfleches*, which were sealed with melted lard. As the skins dried, they shrank, compressing the pemmican and creating a vacuum seal that kept the contents from spoiling. First Nations peoples sold pemmican as a convenience food to the Hudson Bay Company (HBC) in the 1820s. European fur traders bought it from the HBC to take with them on their travels.

Breakfast cereals are very familiar convenience foods. One of the first was Pablum, a nutritious, precooked, vitamin-enriched baby cereal that was fast and easy to prepare. Pablum was invented in 1930 by three Ontario doctors.

During World War II, much of the available food was sent overseas to feed Canada's military. This created a food shortage for civilians. The Canadian Government issued War Ration Books to each family to guarantee that everyone got a fair supply of staples like milk, cheese, sugar, butter, coffee, and tea. Home cooks had to make do with fewer ingredients and learn to make substitutions. Cookbooks, magazines, and government pamphlets introduced new meatless recipes as well as sugarless and eggless baking. In 1937, J.L. Kraft, originally from Ontario, introduced Kraft Macaroni and Cheese. His timing (during food shortages) had a lot to do with its success. Such convenience foods are very profitable and their development by manufacturers has been spurred on by their high sales potential.

After the war, convenience foods like cake mixes and dehydrated juices were introduced to the Canadian public. Prepackaged foods invented by the military were used to feed the post-war population boom. New products were developed at a rapid pace. In 1962, research scientist Edward Asselbergs, at the Department of Agriculture in Ottawa, had invented instant mashed potato flakes. They were sold worldwide as a packaged convenience food that could be reconstituted by just adding hot water or milk.

One hundred years ago the average grocery store had about 100 food items for sale. Thirty years ago there were approximately 8000 items available. Today's grocery stores have more than 17 850 convenience foods to choose from. Most Canadian households use convenience foods in one form or another.

FIGURE 14-11 This Canadian-invented baby cereal was one of the first convenience foods. Were you fed Pablum as a child?

SERVING MEALS

As discussed in previous chapters, families have different practices when it comes to sharing a meal. Some families get together to eat once a day, while others manage to eat together a few times a week. Some lifestyles today make sitting down to a meal difficult for some families. When people do get together to share a meal, they enjoy the time more if they dine in a pleasant atmosphere.

Table Setting

Some families like to set a formal table when they get together for a meal. Some parents use this opportunity to teach their children how to dine with a formal place setting.

Many families are more concerned about eating together and time constraints, and, consequently, set a much less formal table. Other families save time by making one-pot dinners like casseroles, which can be cooked and served in the same container. Still others do not use serving dishes at all and prefer to put the cooking pots on the table to save on cleanup time.

Regardless of how formally or informally a family chooses to set a table, the following components make up a basic **table setting**:

- **Tableware**, which includes anything people use to eat their food with or from (e.g., cutlery, chopsticks, plates, bowls, glasses, cups). This also includes linens, such as placemats, napkins, and tablecloths
- **Serving pieces**, which include platters, bowls, utensils, and, in some cases, cookware

How a table is set is also determined by culture and the foods that are to be eaten at each meal.

FIGURE 14-12 How does your family set the table at home?

Service Methods

There are two basic types of meal service, **family service** and **plate service**. Family service means the table is set and serving dishes are placed on the table. The serving dishes are passed around the table so that each person can take his or her own portion. Most families pass the serving dishes in one direction. Sometimes parents will fill the plates of younger family members.

For plate service, the table is set without the plates. Each plate is filled in the kitchen and then placed in front of each person who is dining. In this type of service, plates are usually filled from the containers in which the food was cooked or prepared. Plate service is most common in restaurants.

Some families use a combination of family and plate service. When there are several dishes, it is easier to use family service. However, serving soup from the pot or a casserole from the dish can be more convenient with plate service.

Salads are usually served separately, and most people like to eat from a salad bowl or plate. This prevents dressings from mixing with other food on the plate and helps keep hot and cold foods separate. Bread or buns usually have their own plate as well. Dessert is served on a new plate or in a clean bowl, most often after the dishes from the main meal have been cleared. Clean utensils are usually provided for dessert.

FIGURE 14-13 Does your family practise family service or plate service, or both?

Connecting to the Community

In each Connecting to the Community activity you will find out more about your local community by completing one of two assignments. This section forms one part of your Connecting to the Community for Unit 4. For the activity, you will create one product from a choice of the following products:

Chapter 14 Choices

1. Visit a place that prepares food for large groups, such as a seniors' residence, daycare centre, school cafeteria, hospital, or catering service. Find out how the establishment plans its menus. Use the following points to guide you:

   ■ Duration of the meal plan (e.g., daily, weekly, monthly)
   ■ Age(s) of people being served
   ■ Special considerations, such as health issues, specialized diets, food restrictions
   ■ Healthy choices for the age group
   ■ Budget
   ■ Seasonal purchasing

   Report on your findings.

OR

2. Visit one of the establishments mentioned in Choice 1. Find out how the establishment serves food. Include table settings and arrangement, service style, and other considerations. Create a report that includes drawings or photographs.

Chapter 14 Summary

In this chapter you looked at

- How personal food preferences can influence meal planning
- Factors to consider when planning meals
- Meal planning basics, including food budgeting, saving money on food, managing time, making a work plan, and working as a team
- Balancing time and money when planning meals
- Serving meals, including table settings and service methods

Activities

1. Look at the recipe on page 339 and make a work plan for it. Be sure to include time for preparation, cooking, and cleanup.

2. Choose a convenience food that your family enjoys and find a recipe for a homemade version of it. Calculate the cost per serving for each version as well as the time it takes to make them. Choose the version that is the better value in terms of time and money. Write a 200-word paragraph to justify your choice.

3. Survey six people to find out how their families set the table and serve family meals. Complete the following chart with the information from the survey. Compare the survey results to your own family's practices. Write a one-paragraph summary of what you have learned from this survey.

   Table Settings and Service Survey

Meal most often eaten together	
Formal table setting?	
Informal table setting?	
Family service?	
Plate service?	

4. Write an article for the local newspaper on how families can save both time and money when planning meals. The article should be at least 500 words long.

5. Discuss with your parent(s) or guardian(s) the factors that they consider when they plan meals for your family. Taking these factors into consideration and using *Eating Well with Canada's Food Guide,* plan the main meals your family will eat for one week. Include at least three of the four food groups in each meal.

Early Canadian, Regional, and Global Foods

UNIFYING CONCEPTS

- Food patterns and customs of First Nations, Inuit, and Métis peoples
- Foods patterns and customs in regions of Canada
- Food patterns and customs in cultures around the world
- Agriculture and food production in Canada

Overview

In this unit you will explore more fully the heritage of the foods that we eat in Canada. You will also come to understand how the wide variety of foods that we eat has been influenced by the wide variety of cultures in Canada, and discover some of the foods of particular cultures. Finally, you will learn where the food we eat comes from and gain an understanding of agriculture and food production in Canada.

Connecting to your community is an important part of being a good citizen. Everyone has a responsibility to one another. Both the Connecting to the Community at the beginning of each unit and the Connecting to the Community activity at the end of each chapter are designed to help you find out more about your community.

Throughout the text you will be asked to consider your community and how it connects to you. A variety of activities will be presented and you will be offered choices as to how you want to present the information you have learned about your community. The choices for Unit 5 are as follows:

- Chapter 15: Canadian Food Heritage
  - Choice 1: Interview a First Nations person about the role of regional foods in his or her cultural celebrations and spiritual ceremonies.
  - Choice 2: Plan a day's menu involving two or three recipes typical of your region, providing information about the food and its sources.
- Chapter 16: A Mosaic of Cuisines
  - Choice 1: Compare your family's weekly food consumption and expenditure with that of two families from other countries examined in the chapter.
  - Choice 2: Look into the cultural origins, traditions, and foods of immigrants in your community.
- Chapter 17: Providing Food for Canadians
  - Choice 1: Investigate one agricultural commodity in your region.
  - Choice 2: Create a product that will encourage people to buy locally.

Putting It All Together

At the end of Unit 5, you will have completed *three pieces of work*—one for each chapter. Follow these steps to complete your product.

- Read over and edit your work from the chapters.
- Ask a peer or a parent/guardian to edit your work as well.
- Write an introduction to your product that pulls all the pieces together. Edit this, too.
- Type or write a good copy, as required.
- Find pictures to enhance your pieces of writing.
- Decide on a title for your product.
- Design how the product will be set up. Draw a rough copy on blank paper before you put the product together.
- Put the product together.

Assessment

The following rubric will be used to assess the work you do on the Unit 5 Connecting to the Community.

Criteria	Level 1	Level 2	Level 3	Level 4
Shows knowledge of Canadian food heritage, cultural foods, and food production in Canada	Shows limited or no knowledge of Canadian food heritage, cultural foods, and food production in Canada	Shows some knowledge of Canadian food heritage, cultural foods, and food production in Canada	Shows considerable knowledge of Canadian food heritage, cultural foods, and food production in Canada	Shows a high degree of knowledge of Canadian food heritage, cultural foods, and food production in Canada
Uses critical and creative thinking processes	Uses critical and creative thinking processes with limited or no effectiveness	Uses critical and creative thinking processes with some effectiveness	Uses critical and creative thinking processes with considerable effectiveness	Uses critical and creative thinking processes with a high degree of effectiveness
Communicates for different audiences and purposes	Communicates for different audiences and purposes with limited or no effectiveness	Communicates for different audiences and purposes with some effectiveness	Communicates for different audiences and purposes with considerable effectiveness	Communicates for different audiences and purposes with a high degree of effectiveness

Canadian Food Heritage

I n this chapter you will learn about the heritage of food in Canada. You will see how the foods that were naturally available in different areas of the country became staples in the diets of First Nations peoples as well as Europeans who immigrated to these regions. You will also take a closer look at how geography influences Canada's regional foods.

Elisapie and Alasie are very excited that their friends are coming to the Arctic Food Festival. They met them when they went to the Aboriginal Youth Council meeting last summer. The girls decided they would get together each summer to experience each other's festivals. Since Elisapie and Alasie (Elizabeth and Alice in English) are sisters, they get to host the first meeting.

Their friend Jennifer lives in southern Alberta. She is from the Siksika or Blackfoot Nation. Her Siksika name is Isapoinhkyaki, which means "singing crow woman." Tina is from British Columbia and will receive her traditional name this summer at a potlatch, an important ceremony in her community. Anjij is from Nova Scotia. She is Mi'kmaq and her name is Annie in English.

Elisapie and Alasie shared the importance of Inuit dancing to the drum with their friends and enjoyed playing traditional Inuit music when they met at the council. They cannot wait for their friends to see them perform. For the traditional dance, the women sit in a circle and sing, and the men dance around them. Elisapie and Alasie are very excited to be part of the inner circle and have been practising their songs for weeks. Adults have their own personal songs and their father's song is about

Key Concepts

- First Nations peoples and their foods:
  - Northeastern Woodlands
  - Canadian Shield
  - Great Plains
  - Plateau
  - Northwest Coast
  - Western Subarctic
  - Arctic
- Canada's regional foods
  - Atlantic Canada
  - Québec
  - Ontario
  - Prairie Provinces
  - British Columbia

Key Terms

back bacon
bannock
colcannon
holubtsi
jerky
kolach
maple syrup
Oka cheese
pemmican
pluma moos
poutine
Montréal smoked meat
Tourtière

love. He will perform the drum dance during his song, and, as the song nears completion, Elisapie and Alasie will join in.

Elisapie and Alasie are also excited to have their friends try some of their traditional foods. Arctic char is a salmon-like fish. Their friends will be able to sample it smoked, dried, baked, and cooked in a stew. They will also sample caribou, which has a fine texture. Some other foods will not be cooked since many traditional foods were eaten raw because fuel for cooking was difficult to find in the Arctic. If Elisapie and Alasie's friends are really brave, they can try some specialty dishes made with whale and walrus meats.

FIRST NATIONS, INUIT, AND MÉTIS PEOPLES

In earlier chapters you read about how geography influences the food available to people in different parts of Canada and around the world. This was the same for First Nations peoples of Canada. There are many different First Nations in each region or reserve in Canada. Many share a common geography, and thus share food and other characteristics in common.

Historians group First Nations using three criteria:

- Regions of Canada—eight different divisions
- The languages spoken by the First Nation
- The cultures of the First Nations peoples—seven different divisions

This chapter uses the cultural divisions of First Nations to explain their foods and lifestyles. The divisions are

- The Northeastern Woodlands
- The Canadian Shield
- The Great Plains
- The Plateau
- The Northwest Coast
- The Western Subarctic
- The Arctic

Web connection

To learn more about First Nations, go to this Web site and follow the links.

www.mhrfoodforlife.ca

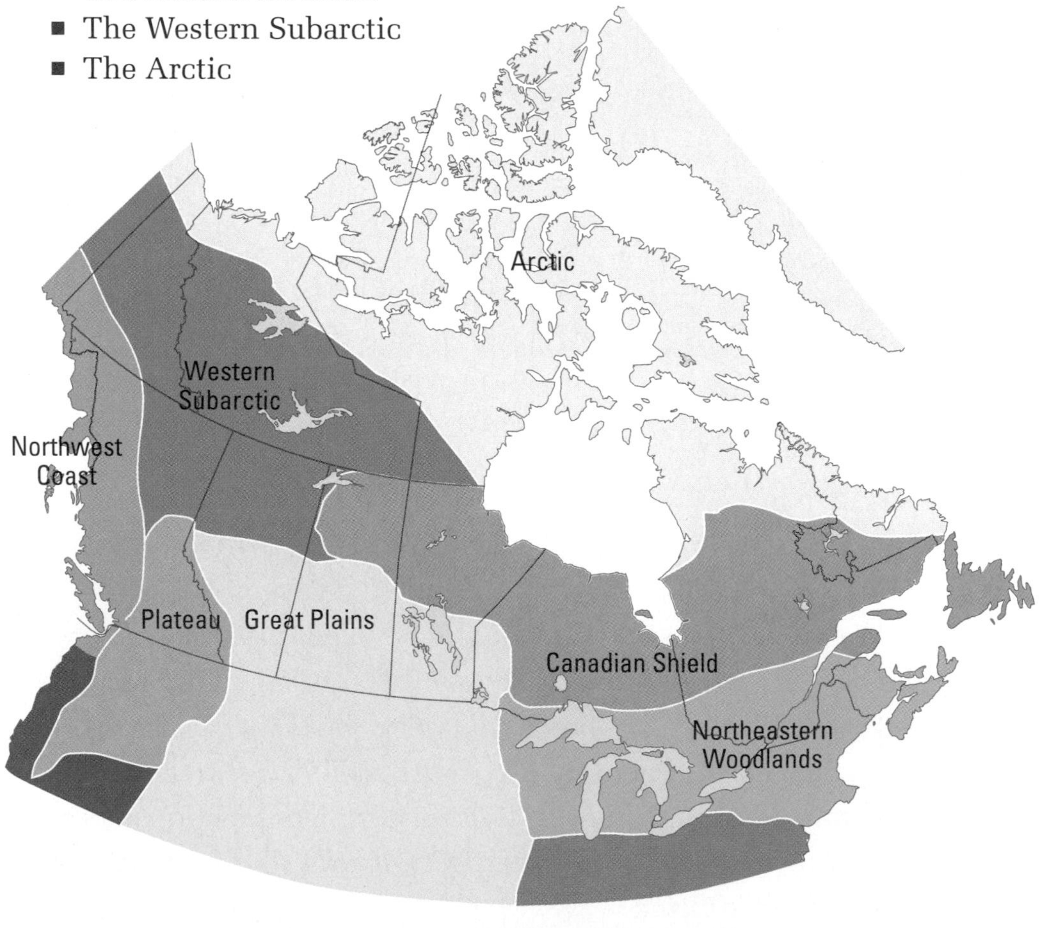

FIGURE 15-1 Which First Nations peoples do you live near?

Cultural Divisions of First Nations Bands

The history of each First Nations people was defined, in part, by where they lived in Canada, the food available, and their access to water. These factors had an impact on the lifestyle of the people in each region.

First Nations peoples were resourceful and learned to use the riches nature made available to them, no matter where they lived in Canada. They were the original environmentalists, since they took nothing for granted and used only what they needed. They had a deep respect for Mother Earth. First Nations peoples strove for balance in life as well as in nature. They knew the local plants and were able to determine which would provide them with food and which could be used for medicinal purposes.

The spirit of hospitality was very strong among First Nations communities. Their ceremonies were a time of celebration and giving. Many ceremonies included singing and dancing as well as ceremonial or traditional foods. Many First Nations legends involved food and were a way of imparting knowledge to younger generations.

Let's take a closer look at each of the First Nations groups.

The Northeastern Woodlands

The Northeastern Woodlands peoples lived in Eastern Canada. As you can see from the map, their territory stretched from Prince Edward Island in the east to the Great Lakes in the west. Among the Northeastern Woodlands peoples were the Algonquin, Cree, Mi'kmaq, Ojibwa, Mohawk, Oneida, and Beothuk.

Due to the abundance of wildlife and water, the Northeastern Woodlands peoples were experts at trapping, hunting, and fishing. In the spring, summer, and fall, they used the waterways to travel in lightweight canoes. In the winter, they travelled on snowshoes.

The Northeastern Woodlands peoples ate a wide variety of meat, including moose, deer, bear, caribou, goose, duck, muskrat, beaver, and hare. They also enjoyed a wide variety of fish and seafood, including cod, lobster, oysters, eel, Atlantic salmon, and scallops. They picked and ate wild plants and a variety of berries that grew in their region. To preserve food for the winter months, they dried meat, fish, and berries.

The region occupied by the Northeastern Woodlands peoples was naturally diverse. Those living in the Maritimes had access to seafood, including the sea vegetables dulse, Irish moss, and kelp.

FIGURE 15-2 What can you tell about the Northeastern Woodlands people from this illustration?

Groups that lived in the interior developed agricultural skills and were able to grow food to supplement their hunting and fishing. They grew corn, potatoes, sunflowers, pears, plums, tomatoes, squash, cotton, flax, and plants for medicinal use. They produced enough grain to process it and trade it with fur traders and more northern bands. They also gathered wild fruits and vegetables. Before the arrival of the Europeans, the agricultural knowledge of Northeastern Woodlands peoples included plant breeding, planting techniques, and methods of fertilization. When they cleared a field for planting, they would burn the underbrush and use the ashes for fertilizer. Since they did not leave fields fallow, the Northeastern Woodlands peoples would move on when their fields were depleted of nutrients.

The Canadian Shield

The peoples of the Canadian Shield lived in a land of long, cold winters and short, cool summers. Groups included Algonquin, Cree, and Chipewa. Forests covered the area of the Canadian Shield and provided shelter in the winter. Food was scarce so people lived in smaller groups and a nomadic lifestyle was necessary in order not to deplete the species living in the hunting territories. Homes had to be portable and light enough to be transported by dogs. These homes were made of hides stretched across poles.

A wide variety of food was available to the peoples of the Canadian Shield. They hunted caribou, moose, beaver, and bear. They also trapped and snared animals by determining the routes the animals commonly used and setting up their snares or traps appropriately. They used nets to capture geese.

The peoples of the Canadian Shield caught fish in weirs, which were fences or barriers built in a stream to trap fish but allow the water to flow through. These weirs were usually made of latticework tree branches and brush. Fish were dried, pounded, and mixed with oil for later use. The bands who lived in the more southern areas grew food such as corn and pumpkins, and gathered wild greens and berries. Wild rice was a staple for many groups. They also understood the value of plants for purposes other than food. Wintergreen, chokecherry, hemlock, sugar maple, sassafras, and sumac were dried and ground into tonics or preventive medicines.

FIGURE 15-3 Why did First Nations peoples use dogs to pull their loads?

Wild Berries in First Nations and Pioneer Cultures

There are more than 200 species of edible wild berries that grow in Canada. They can be broken down into different categories. A **drupe** is a fruit composed of three separate layers—an outer skin, a fleshy middle, and a hard, woody layer surrounding a seed. Cherries and elderberries are both drupes. A **pome** is a fruit that has a core surrounded by edible, fleshy receptacle tissue. The core is not usually eaten by humans. Saskatoon berries are pomes. **True berries** are smooth skinned and totally edible. Blueberries, currants, gooseberries, and cranberries are examples of true berries. **Aggregate fruits** are clusters of many ripened fruits produced from a single flower, such as blackberries and raspberries.

In the past, almost all of the edible wild berries were used by First Nations peoples across Canada. Wild berries added variety to their diet and played an important nutritional role, since they are rich in vitamins and minerals.

In the past, berries were gathered and stored in baskets made by First Nations women. The tradition of basket weaving, along with the various designs of each group, was handed down from one generation of women to the next. The Northwest Coast peoples made baskets from cedar and coloured them with berries and other vegetation. Each year the Northwest Coast peoples held special Berry Ceremonies. Wild berries, such as the huckleberry, also were part of the ceremonial food served at the First Salmon Celebration each spring. Wild berries collected by the Northwest Coast

FIGURE 15-4 What were some of the ways wild berries were used by the First Nations peoples and the pioneers?

peoples were mashed and cooked in bent wood cedar boxes until they thickened like a jam. The jam was poured over skunk cabbage leaves that lined cedar frames. The frames were dried over a slow fire. Finally, the fruit was rolled and stored for later winter use.

The Inuit preserved berries by freezing them in **caches** (places where food was safely stored away from predators or high temperatures) and drying, smoking, or preserving them in sealskin bags called **sea pokes**.

Early settlers enjoyed eating wild berries, too. They would often preserve the berries by drying them. When they wanted to use them, they would put the berries in water and cook them. Settlers also preserved berries in jams and jellies. They baked and steamed them in puddings and made fruit desserts like pies and cobblers. Settlers used wild berries in Christmas cakes, wines, and liqueurs.

The Great Plains

The Great Plains peoples included eight different tribes who spoke three distinct languages. The tribes included the Blackfoot, Blood, Peigan, Plains Cree, Saulteaux, Assiniboine (Nakota), Dakota, and Lakota. The Great Plains peoples lived from the land east of the Rocky Mountains in Alberta, to Lake Superior in Manitoba. The people who lived near the central plains of the Prairies were nomadic and followed the buffalo or bison. They travelled light and lived in teepees. The Great Plains peoples used all parts of the buffalo for many purposes. They cooked the meat on a spit over an open fire or they boiled it in a skin bag with stones to make soup. To store buffalo or bison meat, they dried it in very thin slices called **jerky**. They hunted only as many as they needed and respected the vital role the buffalo played in their survival.

The Great Plains peoples also ate a wide variety of berries. They enjoyed them fresh in season and dried them for out-of-season use. In the Historical Perspectives feature in Chapter 14, you learned about **pemmican**, a mixture of dried meat and berries mixed with fat. It was lightweight and nutrient dense and a perfect food for the nomadic peoples of the plains.

The peoples of the Great Plains supplemented their diet by hunting birds and gathering greens. The peoples who lived closer to the mountains and northern plains also ate moose and deer. The peoples in the north had more access to fresh water so they ate more fish, including smoked and dried whitefish, pike, and pickerel.

Bannock, a flat, round bread usually made from barley, rye, or oat flour, was quick and easy to make since it was not leavened. It was very nutritious and became a staple in First Nations diets after it was introduced to them by Europeans.

The Great Plains peoples collected a variety of wild plants and roots, including pigweed, rosehips, dandelions, Labrador tea, cattail roots, and mint. They used them for a variety of purposes, in soups, stews, and teas; others were used to make medicinal tonics.

Some of the symbolic foods of the Great Plains peoples included dried chokeberry paste and Saskatoon berries, which were served at the Abundance Ceremony, and sweetgrass, which was burned during the Flower Day Ceremony at ancestors' graves and on other important occasions.

Food for Thought

Head-Smashed-In Buffalo Jump in southern Alberta is the world's oldest, largest, and best-preserved buffalo jump. It has become a UNESCO World Heritage site. The Blackfoot had limited hunting tools 6000 years ago, yet devised a way to kill enough animals to feed and clothe their large communities. They herded the buffalo over the 10–18 metre (33–59 feet) cliffs, and then processed the carcasses to provide for their needs. The skeletal remains at the base of the cliffs are up to 11 metres (36 feet) deep. A nearby butchering area contains the preserved remains of meat caches, buffalo bones, and cooking pits.

FIGURE 15-5 Why did the Great Plains peoples adopt a nomadic lifestyle?

Fruits and Berries Used by the Great Plains Peoples

Crabapple  	CRABAPPLE: Picked in the fall, after the first frost. White blossoms on trees turn to yellow-green fruit. HOPA CRABAPPLE: Pink apple blossoms followed by fruit red all the way through. All recipes use the crabapple differently, so follow specific directions in each recipe. Make sure to always remove blossoms and stems. Cut out any bruised or wormy parts.
Cranberries 	CRANBERRY: Gather this fruit in October. Cranberries will stay on stem all winter long. The fruit is scarlet red; the stems are trailing and wiry. There are many ways to use cranberries, which will keep for months and months. Wash well in cold water 2 or 3 times. Pack in sterilized jars and refrigerate. To freeze, lay out on a tray and freeze for about 2 hours. When frozen, place berries in containers or in freezer bags. When needed, rinse out berries in cold water and use in any recipe calling for fresh cranberries.
Elderberries	ELDERBERRY: Pick in July to the middle of August. The berries are magenta-purple, almost black in colour, and grow in a single cluster. During June and July, clusters of tiny, creamy-white flowers bloom. These flowers are called elderblow. Both the berries and the flowers are edible. The Aboriginal Peoples used the stems as well. They made maple spiles (spouts), pea-shooters, and whistles with them. The berries are best when dried and good for use in pies, muffins, sauces, and juices. Always stew berries with a little sugar first; strain, and use in recipe. Elderberry has little acid and so is best mixed with other fruit. When using elderblow, simply remove any coarse stems and rinse. Use in favourite recipes.
Huckleberries and Blueberries 	HUCKLEBERRY: Is smaller and darker in colour than the blueberry and has a hard, seed-like berry. Gather these in July and August. BLUEBERRY: These are gathered in July and August also. The fruits are blue-black with a waxy bloom and many soft seeds. Simply pick through berries, removing all smashed or green berries. Place in a pot filled with water and skim off whatever floats to the top. Use in favourite recipes.
Wild raspberries 	WILD RASPBERRY: Pick in July or early August. The fruits are red (sometimes yellow) and juicy. Each is an aggregate of several tiny individual fruits. When the berries are ripe, they separate easily from the white central receptacle and fall off in a typical thimble form. Sort through berries carefully, removing any bruised or wormy fruit. Wash in cold water; drain, and let dry. Use in favourite recipes.
Stag sumac 	EDIBLE SUMAC BERRIES: Are hard and bright red in colour, covered with tiny hairs. POISONOUS SUMAC BERRIES: Are white and hang loosely. Sumacs are usually found in the same areas as the elderberry. They complement other less acidic fruits, such as the elderberry. Break off fruit in whole clusters, gathering before hard rains wash out most of the acids. Put heads in a large container and cover with water. Using a potato masher, pound and stir for 10 minutes. Always strain juice through a cloth several times to remove tiny hairs.

Cornmeal–Crusted Trout with Blueberry Chive Sauce

Ingredients

1 cup (250 mL) blueberries
⅓ cup (75 mL) minced red onion
2 tbsp (25 mL) red wine vinegar
2 tbsp (25 mL) honey
4 tbsp (50 mL) olive oil
4 large boneless rainbow trout fillets
¼ tsp (1 mL) each salt and pepper
1 cup (250 mL) cornmeal
¼ cup (50 mL) finely chopped chives

Preparation

- In small saucepan over medium heat, combine blueberries, onion, vinegar, honey, and 2 tablespoons of olive oil. Stir gently and bring to a boil. Reduce heat to low and simmer 5 minutes.

- Season fish with salt and pepper then coat both sides in the cornmeal. Coat evenly and shake off any excess. In large non-stick frying pan over medium heat, add remaining 2 tablespoons olive oil. When the oil is hot but not smoking, add the fillets. Panfry for 3 to 5 minutes per side or until golden brown and fish flakes easily with a fork.

- Stir chives into the warm blueberry sauce and serve immediately with the fish.

Servings: 4

The Plateau

The peoples of the Plateau lived in the interior of British Columbia. Ktunaxa (Kutenai) peoples lived along the Stoney Mountains (Rocky Mountains). Dakelh (Carrier), Okanagan, Secwepemc (Shuswap), Stl'atl'imx, Nlaka'pamux (Thompson), Tsilhqot'in, and Salishan peoples are all associated with the southern Plateau region. Dene Thah, Gitksan, and Athapaskan groups occupied the northern territories.

Food was plentiful for the Plateau, and salmon was a main part of their diet. They smoked and dried the salmon, then stored it in underground pits lined with birch bark. Like the Great Plains peoples, they also made pemmican, but used salmon instead of buffalo. Plateau peoples also ate a variety of other foods, including game, waterfowl, roots, greens, berries, and the inner bark of both evergreen and poplar trees. The women dried berries in the summer for use all year long. When hunting large game, the Plateau peoples used deadfall or pitfall traps covered with branches and twigs. An animal, such as a deer, would fall into the trap, and be captured for use as meat. The Plateau peoples also used nets to catch fowl, such as ducks in flight, by stringing a net between two poles.

Plateau peoples also ate a variety of wild greens and other plants, including clover, lamb's quarters, leeks, milkweed, common morels (mushrooms), stinging nettles, yellow pond lily, cattails, dandelions, and fiddleheads.

FIGURE 15-6 Why was salmon so important to the Plateau peoples?

Greens and Other Plants Used by the Plateau Peoples

Puffballs	PUFFBALL: All puffballs with white flesh are good for eating. Avoid picking the ones that are over-ripe. These will fall apart when touched or, if cut open, the centre will appear yellow to greenish-brown. In preparing, if the puffball is small, simply scrape off the soil, rinse, and wipe with a damp cloth. Large puffballs should be peeled. The flavour suggests that of a mushroom.
Common purslane	COMMON PURSLANE: This plant may be gathered all through the summer months. The stems are a reddish colour, the leaves are small and paddle-shaped, and the flowers are small, 5-petaled, and yellow. When using the leaves wash well and use raw in salads or cook. This is an excellent substitute for cucumbers. The seeds can be ground into meal and mixed with flour to bake breads or boiled and eaten as porridge.
Wild rose	WILD ROSE: This thorny plant grows in thickets 1.3 to 2 m (4 to 6 feet) tall and has oval-shaped, toothed leaves 5 cm to 10 cm (2 to 4 inches) long. The wild rose is a light red, 5-petaled flower. The fruit can be eaten raw and suggests the flavour of apples.
	To make a sweetener, the seeds must be pulverized, boiled, strained through cheesecloth to make a syrup.
	To make tea, steep flowers for 5 minutes in boiling water and sweeten with wild honey.
Water cress	WATER CRESS: The plant should be gathered in the spring and summer. The leaves are shiny, dark green with rounded lobes, and the flowers are white, and grow in clusters. Water cress is popular because of its superior taste compared to any kind of lettuce. In taste it resembles spinach. To cultivate, snip or pinch off at the water's surface. Do not pull up the entire plant. Wash thoroughly and use in salads or as a fresh or cooked vegetable.
Wood sorrel	WOOD SORREL: This plant should be picked in summer. The flower closely resembles clover, as the flowers are compounded in 3s and close at night. Flowers vary in colour from yellow to purple and always have 5 petals. The stems are long and juicy. The wood sorrel has a delicate, lemony flavour. Wash thoroughly and add to soups, stews, or mix in salads. The stems are full of moisture and, simply nibbled on, make a good thirst quencher.

David Wolfman, First Nations Chef and Cooking Show Host

Born in Toronto, David Wolfman is a Xaxli'p Nation member, a descendant of the Lillooet people of British Columbia. He is proud of his culture, and is constantly involved in projects to educate people about First Nations traditions. He has become world renowned for his inventive use of traditional foods.

David is best known for his highly successful cooking show, *Cooking with the Wolfman*, aired on the Aboriginal Peoples Television Network (APTN). He is the writer, host, and executive producer of the show. The program showcases traditional foods with a modern twist. Some of the traditional foods Wolfman uses include salmon, Arctic char, venison, caribou, moose, bear, rabbit, and prairie chicken, along with bannock, wild rice, corn, fiddleheads, and beets.

David is also involved in many community events. For "The Streets of Toronto" menu, he prepared sage-dusted venison with a roasted garlic and sweet potato bannock, accompanied by a cedar and maple jelly. This is a long way from his first memorable cooking experience. At nine years of age, he got in trouble for cooking bologna while being babysat by his older sisters!

David pursued his interest in cooking by attending George Brown College's School of Hospitality and Tourism. His knowledge of traditional First Nations foods was instrumental in his appointment as Team Captain of the Aboriginal Culinary Team. The team competed in the IKAHOGA Culinary Arts Olympics in Germany in 1992. They won an unprecedented seven gold, two silver, and two bronze medals!

David next became head chef with Marriott Management Services, where he stayed for eight years. After that, he decided to open Lillooet Catering, a company specializing in the preparation of natural and traditional Aboriginal cuisine. He has received several awards for his skill and dedication, including the Evian Health Menu Award in 1993 and an Outstanding Achievement Award in the Catering Division from the Canadian Council for Aboriginal Business in 1994.

David designed an Aboriginal Cuisine Program for George Brown College in 1994. This chef training program was the first of its kind in Canada. David is now a full-time professor in the School of Hospitality there, and teaches many basic and advanced courses, such as "Theory of Aboriginal Culture and Heritage."

David has since developed a training course for First Nations–owned restaurants. This program is taken to community health centres both on and off reserves. Often on a volunteer basis, David shares his knowledge of healthy and inexpensive cooking, using traditional foods in unique ways.

"David is a Xaxli'p Nation member, a descendant of the Lillooet people of British Columbia. . . He has become world renowned for his inventive use of traditional goods."

The Northwest Coast

The peoples of the Northwest Coast, including Haida, Nuxalk, and the Gitksan, lived along the coast of mainland British Columbia, and on the Queen Charlotte Islands and Vancouver Island. They were fortunate because they had plenty of food nearby, from the sea, land, and rivers. They did not need to live a nomadic life, so they developed settlements.

Access to water made them excellent fishers. They used nets and harpoons, and also trolled for fish. Their catch included salmon, herring, flounder, and halibut. They did not waste any part of the fish. Like the Plateau peoples, they smoked salmon, but the Northwest Coast peoples stored it in cedar boxes. They also barbecued salmon by soaking it in salt water, drying it in the sun, threading it onto cedar sticks, and then setting these upright in a fire.

The Bella Coola peoples caught *ooligan*, a saltwater smelt that they valued for its oil. They used the oil both as a flavouring and as a preservative. They also ate a wide variety of seafood, including mussels, clams, crab, and octopus. As well, the Bella Coola hunted seal and cultivated berries, including raspberries, huckleberries, soapberries, elderberries, and blueberries.

The peoples of the Northwest Coast also collected wild greens, including sheep sorrel, lamb's quarters, silverweed, fern, seaweed, cottonwood, mushrooms, and thimbleberries. Cow parsnip was an important part of their diet. Most of these greens were dried and stored for later use.

FIGURE 15-7 What enabled the peoples of the Northwest Coast to develop permanent settlements?

Food for Thought

For thousands of years the Northwest Coast First Nations harvested *ooligan* in the spring. These small fish were known as "salvation fish" because they were the first fish to arrive after the long cold winter when most of the peoples' food supplies were depleted.

The Western Subarctic

The peoples of the Western Subarctic followed different herds in different seasons. Food was scarce in this area and they were forced to adopt a nomadic way of life. Unlike the peoples of the Great Plains, they hunted a wider variety of animals, including moose, caribou, mountain sheep, and wood buffalo. Groups who had

FIGURE 15-8 First Nations peoples who lived in the Western Subarctic were great hunters and fishers. How do you think having to follow your food would improve your hunting skills?

more access to water lived on small game and fish. They dried fish and meat to store it for later use in soups and stews.

The hunters had to travel great distances to find food. In the summer months, they travelled by canoe; during the winter, they used sleds and snowshoes. Since food was so scarce, very strict rules and rituals were practised during the killing and butchering of game. The animals they hunted, including bear, lynx, wolf, and wolverine, gained special significance in many ceremonies. Meat was dry roasted or stone boiled in bark containers or root baskets.

Fishing methods depended on the season and the type of fish. In the winter months, the peoples of the Western Subarctic bored a hole through the ice and speared fish. In warm months, they placed traps in the rivers and streams. From kayaks, they hunted sea mammals such as walrus, beluga, and seals.

Although known for their hunting skills, the peoples of the Western Subarctic also gathered food. Edible berries, Labrador tea, wild roses, and fireweed are the most abundant plants in the Subarctic region. Migratory waterfowl, eggs, small game, fruit, and vegetables also contributed to their diverse diet.

The Arctic

As you can see from the Cultural Divisions of First Nations Bands map on page 358, the Arctic region extends from the west to the east coasts of northern Canada. The weather there is severe and extremely cold. The winter is eight months long and the summer is short. During the winter there is very little daylight; in the summer, the sun never sets. In winter, the Arctic peoples, the Inuit, had winter homes made of ice, called igloos. Bands included the Copper Inuit and the Dorset. Their summer homes were tents made of hides. These peoples used dogs harnessed to sleds to travel between their two homes.

The Arctic diet changed with the seasons. The summer hunting season focused on coastal animals and vegetation. Birds, seal, walrus, fish, beluga, and narwhal were hunted from the coastal tent camps. The autumn caribou migration provided food for the winter season. During the winter, primary food sources also included preserved summer supplies supplemented by seals, walrus, and bears caught during coastal hunting trips on sea ice. Whale and seal oil was used in food preparation and

FIGURE 15-9 How did the challenging living conditions of the Arctic help make Inuit peoples so self-sufficient?

food storage. The oil also provided fuel for soapstone lamps, which were vital during the eight winter months with little or no sunlight.

The Arctic peoples were very creative and developed unique tools to help them hunt. Ocean fishing and hunting were accomplished by the development of advanced watercraft designed for sea travel. Kayaks and umiaks, large flat-bottom boats used for carrying freight, were manufactured from sewn sealskin. Inuit technology is also credited with float harpoons, an inflated sealskin bag attached to the harpoon head, which prevented the animal from diving and getting away.

Web connection

To learn more about First Nations, Inuit, and Métis food and traditions, go to this Web site and follow the links.

www.mhrfoodforlife.ca

CANADA'S REGIONAL FOODS

The early settlers adapted the recipes they brought from their home countries to include foods available in their new homes. Their cuisine was also influenced by that of First Nations peoples who lived in the area. First Nations peoples taught the settlers which wild greens and other plants were edible and how to prepare them. They also told them which crops grew well in the region and how to cultivate the land.

FIGURE 15-10 Which region of Canada do you live in? Do you know what foods the region produces?

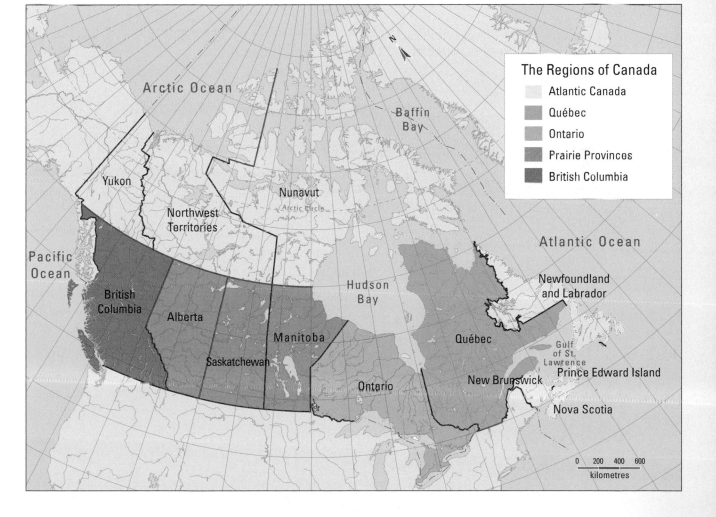

The Regions of Canada
- Atlantic Canada
- Québec
- Ontario
- Prairie Provinces
- British Columbia

Since the first settlers arrived in Canada, many other groups of immigrants have arrived. Our Canadian cuisine has been enriched by a wide variety of cuisines from other nations and cultures. Let us look more closely at the regional foods of Canada.

Atlantic Canada

The Atlantic provinces have a large coastline and, as a result, fish and seafood are mainstays of their diet. Cod has played a major role in the history of Newfoundland, being both a staple food and a major export and economic influence. However, due to depleted cod stocks, there are now limits on the amount of cod that fishers can harvest. Licenses are given to fishers to ensure the cod are protected, and some traditional fishing areas are now closed. Historically, salted cod helped Newfoundlanders survive the long cold winters. As time passed and cod stocks declined, the Newfoundland fisheries expanded to include tuna, herring, char, mackerel, turbot, ocean perch, and various shellfish, including snow crab, clams, shrimp, lobster, sea cucumber, and scallops.

Atlantic Canada is known for its seafood. People from around the world travel there for a traditional lobster dinner. All over Atlantic Canada, lobster dinners are served in church basements and community halls, allowing those from outside the region to enjoy the bounty of the sea and the hospitality of the people.

Prince Edward Island is famous for its lobster, blue mussels, Malpeque oysters, clams, scallops, and fresh fish. New Brunswick provides more freshwater fish, since it has good freshwater resources. Smelt and trout are favourites in New Brunswick. Nova Scotia has a long coastline as well as freshwater resources of fish and seafood. Cod, eel, mackerel, lobster, and herring are plentiful there.

Summers are short in the Atlantic provinces, which limits the growing season. Many different berries are native to the Atlantic provinces, including partridgeberries, blueberries, and rock cranberries. Nova Scotia and New Brunswick are two of the maple syrup–producing provinces in Canada. Canada is famous internationally for its **maple syrup**. In New Brunswick, fiddleheads are a local favourite, while Prince Edward Island is famous for its potatoes, which are also an important crop in New Brunswick, due to the influence of early Irish immigrants.

The Acadians, who settled in the Atlantic provinces, are of French descent and they have had a

FIGURE 15-11 Have you ever attended a lobster fest in Atlantic Canada?

strong influence on the foods in the region. Their style of cooking is simple and hearty, comprising dishes such as soups, stews, and casseroles. One famous dish is **poutine**, which is now enjoyed across Canada. Poutine consists of French fries topped with cheese curds and gravy. Another strong influence in the Atlantic provinces comes from the British Isles. Oats are a traditional Scottish contribution to many dishes. **Colcannon**, another favourite with both Scottish and Irish heritage, is made by mashing together potatoes, turnips, and cabbage.

Québec

Québec has maintained much of the influence of France and Europe in both its culture and its cuisine. The Québecois are very proud of their French heritage, and their food has a distinctly French flavour. Specialties include seafood soups, specialty cheeses, and French breads and pastries. Distinctly Québécois foods and flavours include smoked meat or brisket, and many delis sell **Montréal smoked meat** sandwiches. **Back bacon**, called Canadian bacon in the United States, is less fatty and has a milder flavour than side bacon. **Tourtière** is a meat pie made from ground pork, and is unique to Québec cuisine.

Québec also is a major producer and exporter of maple syrup, since the province has an abundance of maple trees. Like the lobster dinners in Atlantic Canada, maple syrup festivals in Québec attract visitors from around the world, who enjoy participating in the "sugaring off" process that produces maple syrup. Visitors can watch the process and then savour a meal of pancakes and maple syrup in a rustic restaurant to complete the experience. Maple syrup is sold as syrup or cooked further to make maple sugar or maple candy. Maple syrup was the

FIGURE 15-12 Have you ever been to Québec and experienced Québécois cuisine?

main sweetener used by the early Québécois, so it is used in many traditional recipes.

Québec is also world renowned for its cheeses. The first settlements had plenty of milk and dairy cattle, which supported the production of cheese. **Oka cheese** was first made by Trappist monks in 1893 and it is still made by them today.

Like the French, the Québécois love food and fine cuisine. As a result, Québec is known for its fine dining. Whether in large cities or small towns, visitors may be treated to wonderful food experiences. The imagination of Québécois cooks has created unique and tasty products including jellies made from flowers, exotic preserves, specialized sausages, apple cider, and fine wines.

Ontario

Ontario is the most heavily populated province in Canada. It produces a wide variety of agricultural products including beef, dairy foods, wild rice, poultry, eggs, and numerous fruits and vegetables. The Niagara region enjoys long, warm summers and is able to grow many tender fruits, including peaches, cherries, plums, and grapes. An abundance of freshwater lakes and rivers contributes to the variety of fish available. Berries such as strawberries, blueberries, and cranberries are also plentiful. Ontario is another large producer of maple syrup.

First Nations peoples of southern Ontario had a major impact on the agricultural practices of the first Europeans in the area. First Nations peoples showed settlers how to grow and use corn. They also helped them appreciate the wild greens that grew in the area. The first settlers

FIGURE 15-13 Which foods from different cultures have you eaten recently?

came to Ontario from Scotland, Ireland, and Great Britain. The influence of these groups can be seen in regional foods, such as potatoes, shortbread, and roast beef with Yorkshire pudding. Later immigration brought Swiss Mennonites who provided a German influence with foods such as sweet breads and a variety of sausages. In the Kitchener-Waterloo area, many Mennonites still live a traditional lifestyle.

Ontario attracts immigrants from all over the world. Consequently, cuisine in Ontario is heavily influenced by a wide variety of cultures. Toronto, the capital of Ontario, is one of the most ethnically diverse cities in the world. In Toronto, you can visit restaurants offering cuisine from almost any culture, including Indian and South Asian, Italian, Greek, French, Caribbean, Mexican, African, Arab and Middle Eastern, Balkan-Albanian, British, Irish, German, Jewish, Latin American, Eastern European, Western European, Chinese, Vietnamese, Japanese, Philippine, and Korean. There are also many specialty shops and markets selling ingredients so that you can make these cuisines yourself at home.

Prairie Provinces

Manitoba, Saskatchewan, and Alberta are Canada's Prairie Provinces. They are famous for wheat fields and cattle ranches. The First Nations peoples who lived on the Prairies were nomadic, following the buffalo and eating the wild greens that were available along the way. The first Europeans were traders who exchanged goods for furs with First Nations peoples. The Europeans settled around the trading posts established by the Hudson's Bay Company but later settlers were farmers and ranchers. The wide expanses of grazing land made cattle ranching a good choice for the West. Cattle were driven to market by cowboys who relied on chuckwagons for their food. Chuckwagons carried the food supplies for all the people on the drive. A cook rode in or drove the chuckwagon. When the cattle drive stopped, the cook would prepare food for the entire crew. The Calgary Stampede celebrates the West's history every summer with chuckwagon racing, one of the favourite events at the Stampede.

Shortly after Confederation in 1867, the Canadian government encouraged more European settlers to move to the West. The development of a hardy strain

FIGURE 15-14 Have you been to the Calgary Stampede? Is there an event in your area that reflects the heritage of your region or community?

Literacy in Your Life

Before Reading

1. Read the title. What do you think "fellowship meals" are?

2. Given the information about Mennonites in the sidebar and article, what do you think their approach to food for their families would be?

During Reading

1. As you read each heading, turn it into a question; while you are reading the section, answer your question.

2. Can you think of other groups of people mentioned in the text who place importance on food in their community events?

Who Are the Mennonites?
Mennonites are a religious group committed to non-violence, pacifism, non-resistance, and simplicity of life. Many Mennonites have moved to Canada from different parts of Europe and tend to live in rural areas.

Language Extension

The word *community* means "a group of people who live in the same area with a common background or with shared interests in a society." It comes from the root *communitat* which means "common."

Mennonite Fellowship Meals

By Derek Suderman

Studying eating habits can be an excellent starting place for discovering an ethnic or cultural group. Mennonites are no exception. As they have moved from place to place, Mennonites have developed many traditional foods. Since these traditions were greatly influenced by their contact with different peoples and the availability of different foods, Swiss and Russian Mennonite groups have distinct food traditions that reflect their migrations.

Importance of Food

One thing is certain, however; eating has been a very important part of Mennonite culture. More than just the food, meals have been and continue to be important community events. They provide chances for people to interact, catch up on and discuss local events and news, celebrate and recognize important happenings, and enjoy great food.

The importance of food in Mennonite culture tends to be connected to the culture's emphasis on **community**. Weddings, funerals, economic crises, and holidays all affect the larger community. Although especially true for Mennonites living in mostly rural areas, somewhat isolated from their non-Mennonite counterparts, community remains an important part of this tradition for those in cities. Fellowship meals continue to be held at weddings, funerals, meetings, and other gatherings.

Popular Culinary Traditions

Many culinary favourites are seasonal traditions, with specific recipes prepared for Christmas, New Year's, and Easter. Perhaps the most famous Mennonite culinary tradition is the *potluck*. Often held as congregational gatherings at church, each family brings enough food for their own members and more. Some people bring main courses; others bring salads, drinks, vegetables, fruit, and desserts. There is a great assortment, and plenty to go around.

Sometimes the recipes themselves reflect the importance of community. In the back of *The Mennonite Treasury of Recipes*, for example, is a whole section of recipes for 100 people or more. The following recipe from *The Best of Mennonite Fellowship Meals* is for *borscht*, a type of soup commonly found in Ukraine, which was adopted by Russian Mennonites during their time there.

Chicken Borscht

(70–75 servings)

23 lbs (10 kg) chicken
14 quarts (14 L) water
12 tsp (60 g) salt
24 cups (6 L) diced potatoes
24 cups (6 L) diced carrots
7 medium onions, diced
7 cups (1.75 L) cooked tomatoes
5 heads cabbage, shredded
12–15 peppercorns
3–4 bay leaves
12–15 whole allspice
chicken bouillon to taste

FIGURE 15-15 Eastern Pennsylvania Mennonite women prepare a hearty breakfast before setting out for a day of volunteer work.

Perhaps the most telling is the fact that literally hundreds of cookbooks with "Traditional Mennonite" recipes have been published. Since cooking has been an area dominated by women, old cookbooks can often give us a unique perspective into Mennonite culture.

New Traditions

The Mennonite church welcomes people of many cultures and backgrounds. This increasing diversity has brought many changes; rice, beans, and tortillas have joined shoofly pie, *vereniki* (cottage cheese dumplings), and summer sausage as "Mennonite food."

After Reading

1. Why do you suppose that when people gather together they have special meals or feasts?

2. What changes might you see in future publications of Mennonite recipe books?

3. What are the advantages of having a potluck at a gathering?

of wheat by Charles Saunders in 1904 allowed farmers on the Prairies to begin to produce wheat that would be sold around the world. Many people think of flowing wheat fields when they think of the prairies. However, canola is another important crop grown in this vast region. It is harvested for its oil, which is used in a variety of products. The flowers of the canola plant and other native prairie plants make Manitoba, Saskatchewan, and Alberta Canada's major producers of honey.

Manitoba, Saskatchewan, and Alberta also have freshwater sources of fish. Fishing goes on in both summer and winter, and ice fishing is particularly popular. Fish from the Prairies is exported around the world. Species include northern pike, pickerel, tullibee, whitefish, lake trout, and goldeye.

The agricultural heritage of the prairies is seen in farmers' markets, which are very popular. The produce sold at the markets reflects the culture and foods of the region. Different styles of baking, fruits and vegetables, and specialty meats, such as sausages, showcase their cultural diversity. There is a large Ukrainian community reflected in many specialty breads including **kolach**, a braided bread made for Easter and cabbage rolls, or **holubtsi**, another famous Ukrainian dish. Manitoba has a strong Mennonite community whose favourite foods include cabbage soup, farmer's sausage, and a fruit soup called **pluma moos**.

Many varieties of berries grow on the Prairies, including strawberries, Saskatoon berries, red currants, raspberries, and blueberries. Wild greens are enjoyed, such as cattails, fireweed shoots, Labrador tea, wild onion, wild rice, and wild mushrooms.

British Columbia

Salmon has always been a staple in the diet of British Columbians, beginning with First Nations peoples. As discussed earlier, salmon is an important part of First Nations culture, as can be seen in some bands' art and festivals. Smoked salmon from British Columbia is considered a delicacy worldwide. Other fish found in British Columbia include cod, halibut, tuna, and herring. British Columbia also exports fish. Shellfish from British Columbia include prawns, oysters, shrimp, clams, and mussels.

British Columbia is also known for the fruits grown in the Okanagan Valley. Apples, pears, cherries, peaches, nectarines, and apricots are enjoyed locally and are exported across the country and around the world. Grapes grown in the region are used for juices, jams, jellies, and wine.

The first immigrants to British Columbia were of British descent, and they brought their customs and foods with them. High tea is still served in some restaurants, and visitors can enjoy tea and scones in the late afternoon. The city of Victoria still shows a strong British influence.

In the mid-1800s, thousands of Chinese immigrants came to British Columbia during the Gold Rush and the building of the national railway system. Many of them settled in and around Vancouver, creating a large Chinese community there. Visitors to Vancouver can experience Asian food and culture in restaurants and at markets in Chinatown. British Columbia continues to attract immigrants from Asian countries and enjoys a vibrant Asian community.

Vancouver is a very cosmopolitan city. With its multicultural population it is known for its diverse cuisine. Many dishes that are now popular in the rest of Canada—sushi, for example—first became popular in Vancouver. The mix of cultures and the creativity of their chefs allow people living in and visiting the city to experience many culinary delights.

Web connection

To learn more about Canada's regional foods, go to this Web site and follow the links.

www.mhrfoodforlife.ca

FIGURE 15-17 How did immigration influence the foods of British Columbia?

Connecting to the Community

In each Connecting to the Community activity you will find out more about your local community by completing one of two assignments. This section forms one part of your Connecting to the Community for Unit 5. For the activity, you will create one product from a choice of the following products.

Chapter 15 Choices

1. Contact a local Native Friendship Centre or a local organization of First Nations peoples. Interview an individual about his or her culture. Find out about
   - Traditional foods
   - How food played and/or plays a role in cultural celebrations
   - How food played and/or plays a role in spiritual life
   - Traditional foods that grow in the region, and their use in the past and present

OR

2. Investigate the foods of your region. Find materials to present in a format that suits your Connecting to the Community choice for this unit. Include the following information:
   - Main food sources, foods produced and found in the region
   - Specialty foods specific to the region
   - Cultural influences on foods
   - A typical menu for a day
   - Two or three recipes using foods that are famous to your region

Chapter 15 Summary

In this chapter you explored:

- The foods of First Nations across Canada, including:
  - The Northeastern Woodlands
  - The Canadian Shield
  - The Great Plains
  - The Plateau
  - The Northwest Coast
  - The Western Subarctic
  - The Arctic
- Regional foods of Canada, including:
  - Atlantic Canada
  - Québec
  - Ontario
  - The Prairie Provinces
  - British Columbia

Activities

1. Describe three ways that First Nations peoples prepared foods to store them for the winter months.

2. Which everyday foods of First Nations peoples are still used today? Have you eaten any of them?

3. Which foods were common to all First Nations groups in Canada?

4. Using a chart like the one below, compare the regional foods of Canada.

Region	Meat and/or Fish	Fruits and Vegetables	Specialty Dishes or Specialized Cuisine

5. For which produce is your region of Canada best known? What is your favourite dish made with this food?

6. List the foods regularly eaten in your family.
   a) Which foods are from your region?
   b) Which foods are from other regions in Canada?
   c) Which cultures influence the food choices your family makes?

CHAPTER 16

Key Concepts

National foods and typical weekly groceries for sample families from

- Great Britain
- France
- Poland
- Italy
- Chad
- Egypt
- Kuwait
- India
- Japan
- United States
- Mexico
- Ecuador

Key Terms

beef bourguignon
bigos
chutney
coq au vin
de pollo
escargot
kielbasa
lomo salteado
mansat
meushti
mish
mole
perogy
polenta
pulses
seco de chivo
sushi
tempura
tortilla
zubaidi

A Mosaic of Cuisines

In this chapter you will read about the foods eaten by people in different countries around the world. You will see what the average family eats in a week and what they spend on food in a week. You will also explore some typical foods and dishes from a number of cultures.

Arturo and Brigida are excited to get home. They have been on a five-month student exchange in Germany. As they sit together on the plane, they reflect on their experiences.

Arturo remembers how much he missed Canadian food when he first arrived at the small town in the Bavarian Alps where he would be staying. He soon learned to love much of the German food, although he still found some of it quite heavy. He will miss the sausages, though. He had eaten German sausage in Calgary, but they did not have the same flavour as the ones he ate in Germany. Arturo also can't believe he would only eat white bread before he went to Germany. He is sure he will find it tasteless after eating the rich rye and pumpernickel breads his host family served. When he talked to his mom yesterday, he asked her to prepare an Alberta roast beef dinner for him when he gets home.

Brigida's German family made wonderful sweet breads, and often the father would have a freshly baked sweet bun ready for them when they got home from school. Brigida's favourite German food was streuselkuchen, coffee cake topped with a mixture of brown and white sugar, butter, and nuts. She stayed in the Hanover area,

in the north of Germany. On a cool winter day, she would look forward to the rich stews and soups her family prepared. It often made her homesick for her dad's cooking. Brigida asked her dad to make homemade soup for her when she gets home. Her dad loves to be creative, and uses lots of vegetables. He always serves soup with fresh bread from the bakery.

Both Brigida and Arturo are glad to be home and are looking forward to eating their favourite foods again. When they have picked up their luggage, they say goodbye to each other and head off to find their families.

Earlier you read about how both culture and geography influence the foods we eat. In this chapter, you will look more closely at the foods that some typical families in various countries eat in a week. You will be asked to look at the photo of each family and make a few observations.

- Do you see any foods that you and your family eat?
- Notice the amounts of fresh vegetables and fruits, packaged foods, convenience foods, and junk foods each family eats.
- Do you have any favourite foods in common with the family?
- How does the amount of money each family spends on food in a typical week compare to your family's weekly expenditure?

Countries to be Studied in Chapter 16

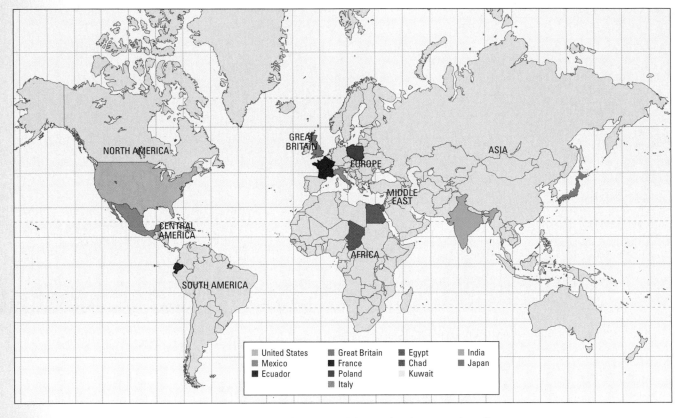

FIGURE 16-1 Have you ever thought about where in the world your food comes from?

EUROPE

Europe includes both the mainland continent and the British Isles. The first settlers to come to Canada were from European countries; as a result, many of our foods have a European flavour. In this section we will look at the foods of Great Britain, France, Poland, and Italy.

Great Britain

Great Britain is an island country off the coast of Europe. Traditional British food tends to be plain and simple. Food is cooked using basic methods and few sauces. In Britain, many people still eat four meals a day—breakfast, lunch, tea in the late afternoon, and dinner in the evening. A hearty breakfast is considered an important start to the day and usually consists of a combination of eggs, cereal, bacon or sausage, and toast with jam or marmalade.

Great Britain's main sources of protein are beef, mutton, pork, and fish. The British also eat a variety of game, including pigeon, quail, pheasant, and deer. Vegetables eaten regularly are potatoes, Brussels sprouts, parsnips, and spinach. Fruits include various berries, along with apples, plums, peaches, and apricots.

Some typical British foods would be

- Roast beef and Yorkshire pudding—Beef roasted in the oven with a popover-like pastry cooked in the pan drippings. The beef is usually served with horseradish or mustard.
- Shepherd's pie—Ground beef or lamb cooked with onions, garlic, and seasoning. It is layered with mashed potatoes and baked in a casserole dish.
- Plum pudding—A dense, cake-like pudding made with raisins, nuts, and flavourings, and steamed in cheesecloth. It is a traditional Christmas dessert.

FIGURE 16-2 The Bainton family of Collingbourne Ducis, Great Britain

Weekly Food for the Bainton Family

On the right is a photo of what the Baintons, a typical family in Great Britain, eat in a week. What are your observations on their choices of foods?

Bainton family food expenditure for one week: $253.15 CDN (155.54 British pounds)

Some of their favourite foods: Avocado mayonnaise sandwich, prawn cocktail, chocolate fudge cake with cream

France

As you can see from the map below, France is a large country with a variety of geographic influences. To the west, the Atlantic Ocean affects the cuisine by providing fresh seafood, and to the east are the French Alps. The climate in the north is quite a bit cooler than in the south. This has led to a variety of cuisines. Southern France is famous for its fine wines and seafood. Champagne is one of the most famous of all French wines.

When people think of French cuisine, they think of fine foods. French cuisine, like French fashion, is *haute*, meaning of the highest quality and standards. Some foods commonly associated with French cuisine are croissants, crêpes, quiche, omelettes, soufflés, pâté, mousse, custards, and cream puffs. Regional differences are also seen in French foods. For example, in the Burgundy region, you find rich sauces. **Beef bourguignon** and **coq au vin** are two famous dishes made with wines of this region. The French eat a wide variety of protein including beef, chicken, squab or pigeon, pork, veal, and rabbit, as well as fresh fish and seafood. *Escargot*, or snails, is a well known French specialty. The French are famous for a sophisticated palate and a talent for creating fine foods.

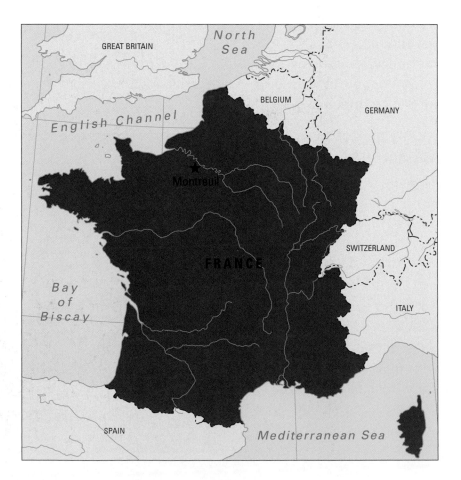

The French are renowned not only for their haute cuisine but also for their fine cheeses. French cheese-makers have been perfecting the art for centuries. Some famous French cheeses are Brie, Rocquefort, Camembert, and Emmental, which most people are familiar with, but there are many others as well. Various regions of France have developed different cheeses using different types of milk such as cow's milk, ewe's milk, and goat's milk, each giving each type of cheese a distinctive flavour and texture.

For centuries, France has celebrated and created food at the highest level. The French want their food to be fresh; they will often shop on the way home for the evening meal. Fresh bread, such as the baguette, is an essential part of any French meal. The French take their time to eat and enjoy their food.

Food for Thought

The French eat more cheese than any other country in the world, an average of 20.5 kilograms (45 pounds) per year.

Weekly Food for the Le Moines Family

The Le Moines live in Montreuil, in the north of France, near Paris. What are your observations on the foods they eat?

Le Moines family expenditure for one week: $419.95 CDN (315.17 euros)

Some of their favourite foods: Delphine Le Moine's apricot tarts, pasta carbonara, and Thai food

FIGURE 16-3 The Le Moines family of Montreuil, France

Poland

Poland is also located in central Europe, on the southern shore of the Baltic Sea. Poland has a strong agricultural base and produces potatoes, wheat, and a variety of livestock. Poles eat three meals a day, with the main meal usually served at midday. Lunch typically consists of three courses, including soup, a main course, and dessert.

Polish cuisine has been heavily influenced by other countries. As a result, some foods of German origin are also popular, including sausage, sauerkraut, and sauerbraten. Other influences on Polish food include Turkey, Hungary, France, Italy, and Jewish culture.

Meat, especially pork, is a staple in the Polish diet, including **kielbasa**, the Polish word for sausage. Poles also eat plenty of game and enjoy different noodles and dumplings in their meals. **Perogies** are small dumplings that are usually stuffed with cheese, but may also have potato, sauerkraut, cabbage, onion, or meat in them. The dough is rolled into a circle, stuffed, then folded into a half-moon shape. Bread

made of wheat, rye, or barley flour is the most popular side dish in the Polish diet. Vegetables are often pickled to preserve them—pickled cucumbers, beets, and sauerkraut are a few examples. Fish, such as herring, is also pickled. Many Polish recipes call for sour cream, curd cheese, and soured milk because maintaining freshness was a challenge in the past.

The national dish of Poland is **bigos**, a stew usually made with sauerkraut, meat, and other ingredients such as mushrooms, sausage, apples, and tomatoes. *Krupnik* is a soup made from barley and vegetables to which sour cream and dill are added for flavour. *Chlodnik* is a cold soup made from beets or fruit, and is served on warm days. *Makowiec,* or poppy seed cake, is a popular dessert and *kuita*, a small, square pasta topped with poppy seeds, nuts, raisins, and honey is often served at Christmas.

Food for Thought

Herring is a staple in the diets of many northern Europeans. These little fish are pickled in a variety of ways—marinated with vinegar, onions, sugar, cloves, and mustard, as well as other flavourings. Herring is served an an appetizer, for snacks, and for breakfast.

Weekly Food for the Sobczynscy Family

The photo below shows the Sobczynscy family, who live in central Poland. What are your observations about their food choices?

Sobczynscy family food expenditure for one week: $151.27 CDN (582 zlotys)

Some of their favourite foods: pig's knuckles with carrots, celery, and parsnips

FIGURE 16-4 The Sobczynscy family of Konstancin-Jeziorna, Poland

Perogies

This recipe will take two days to complete.

Day One
- Prepare the dough, cover with plastic wrap and leave overnight in fridge.
- Prepare mashed potatoes and put in fridge overnight.

Day Two
- Prepare potato filling
- Assemble perogies and prepare for cooking

Ingredients

Dough
3 cups (750 mL) all-purpose flour
1 ½ tsp (7 mL) salt
1 egg
¾ cup (175 mL) water, approx.
4 tsp (20 mL) vegetable oil

Mashed Potatoes
2 lb (1 kg) baking potatoes, peeled and cut in large chunks

Potato Filling
1 tbsp (15 mL) butter
½ cup (125 mL) onion, finely chopped
2 cups (500 mL) cold mashed potatoes
1 cup (250 mL) cheddar cheese, shredded
½ tsp (2 mL) salt

Preparation

Dough
In bowl, whisk flour with salt. In separate bowl, beat together egg, water, and oil; stir into flour mixture to make soft dough that holds together in a bowl. If necessary, add more water, 1 tbsp (15 mL) at a time. Be careful not to make the dough sticky. Turn out onto lightly floured surface; knead about 10 times, or just till smooth. Do not knead too much or dough will toughen. Halve dough; cover with plastic wrap. Let rest in fridge overnight.

Mashed Potatoes
Place potatoes in large saucepan and cover with water. Cover and bring to boil; reduce heat and boil gently for 15 minutes or until tender but not mushy. Drain well and place pot back over low heat for a minute or so to evaporate excess water. Mash potatoes with potato masher until smooth.

Potato Filling
Meanwhile, in skillet, heat butter over medium heat; cook onion for 3 to 5 minutes or until tender. Transfer to bowl; stir in potatoes, cheese, and salt.

Working with half dough at a time and keeping remainder covered to prevent drying out; roll out on lightly floured surface to about ¹⁄₁₆-inch (1.5 mm) thickness; with 3-inch (8 cm) round cookie cutter, cut out rounds. Place 1 tsp (5 mL) of the filling on centre of each round. Fold each round in half; pinch edges together with fingers to seal. The edges should be free of filling. Place on tea-towel-lined baking sheets; cover with damp tea towel to prevent drying out.

Cooking
In large pot of boiling salted water, cook perogies in batches, stirring gently to prevent from sticking together. Do not attempt to cook too many at a time. Continue boiling for 2–3 minutes or until they float to top. Perogies will be ready when they are puffed. Remove with slotted spoon to a colander and drain well.

To Serve
In large heavy skillet, melt 2 tbsp (25 mL) butter over medium heat; cook one sliced onion for about 5 minutes or until golden. Add perogies; toss to coat and warm through. Serve with sour cream on the side.

36 perogies

Italy

Italy is a peninsula on the southern tip of Europe. It has a rich history, and its food has been influenced by various cultures, especially during the Roman Empire. Besides its cuisine, Italy is famous for its art, music, and architecture.

Meals in Italy are seen as time to spend with family and are not rushed. There are usually three or four courses, which may include

- *Antipasto*—Meaning "before the hot food," may consist of salads, pickled vegetables, cheeses, and other appetizers
- *Primo*—The first course, usually pasta or rice
- *Secondo*—The second course, usually with meat
- *Ontorono*—A side dish
- *Formaggio e fruita*—Cheese and fruit
- *Dolce*—Dessert
- *Caffe*—Coffee or espresso
- *Digestivo*—Digestives such as liqueurs

Pasta is the dish most often associated with Italy. Different regions of Italy eat their pasta in different ways—some with a tomato sauce; others with an Alfredo, or creamy cheese sauce. Some areas prefer rice to pasta and would rather eat rice balls or risotto. Cornmeal is more common in the north than in the south of Italy. It is used to make **polenta**, a mush that is molded, sliced, and fried.

Italian food differs by region, due in part to the history of each area and the availability of ingredients. Northern regions were influenced by Germany and France, while most southern regions naturally favoured fish and seafood since they are surrounded by various small seas, as well as the Mediterranean. Italy's northern regions are mountainous and experience colder temperatures than in the south, which has a milder climate. Olive trees grow in southern Italy, so cooks there use plenty of olive oil; in the north, butter is preferred.

Italian beverages are also famous. Italian coffee, or espresso, is enjoyed worldwide, and some Italian wines are considered among the finest in the world. Italian cheeses, including Parmeggiano (parmesan), ricotta, mozzarella, Gorgonzola, and Asiago, are also popular internationally.

Food for Thought

The highlight of a traditional Italian Christmas is a 13-course meal enjoyed on Christmas Eve.

Web connection

To find more recipes from Great Britain, France, Poland, and Italy, go to this Web site and follow the links.

www.mhrfoodforlife.ca

Weekly Food for the Manzo Family

The Manzo family, seen in the picture below, live on the island of Sicily, the sunniest part of Italy. What are your observations about the foods they eat?

Manzo family food expenditure for one week: $260.11 CDN (214.36 euros)

Some of their favourite foods: fish, pasta with ragu, hot dogs, frozen fish sticks

FIGURE 16-5 The Manzo family of Sicily, Italy

AFRICA

The continent of Africa is divided into the northern, Sahara desert regions and the southern, sub-Saharan regions. As you might expect, the cultures of southern, sub-Saharan Africa are very different from those in northern Africa.

People in southern Africa define their culture through kinship ties. This is a centuries-old network of clans and peoples. Southern Africans lived together in large groups, and their food sources followed the social patterns of the groups. The climate in the sub-Sahara is mainly tropical or subtropical. The region has a variety of geographic features, including mountains, river valleys, coastline, rain forests, and desert. Each region has its own cuisine based on the foods available.

In northern Africa, some countries have access to water from both the Mediterranean Sea and the Nile River. Because of this, and the use of irrigation, more food is cultivated in this region than in some regions of southern Africa.

Chad

Chad is located in the middle of Africa. Since much of the country is desert, it is difficult for people to produce food. In the regions around Lake Chad, there is some agriculture and wildlife. Cereal crops are grown in the southernmost area of the country, while animals are raised on the pastures in central regions. Most of Chad's population is in the south.

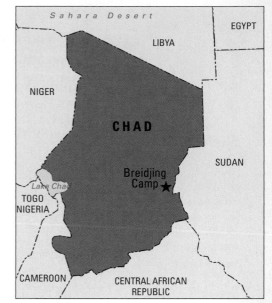

Unlike the countries previously introduced in this chapter, Chad is subject to food insecurity, according to the Food and Agriculture Organization of the United Nations, which monitors and reports on food security throughout the world. As you can see in the graph below, even though the situation in Chad is improving, a large percentage of the population is still experiencing food insecurity.

As a result of food insecurity in Chad, the country's cuisine is not as much of a focus as are its staple foods. These staples include vegetables and fruits such as mangoes, bananas, plantain, okra, yams, and corn. Chadians obtain protein from plant sources such as peas, beans, and lentils. Meat is not a regular part of their diet, especially in more rural areas. Some Chadians do not eat beef because it is sacred, and because the number of cattle one owns is a sign of wealth. Animals native to the area, including goat, sheep, oxen, and rodents, are more commonly consumed. Fish is usually eaten only by people who have access to freshwater resources. Breads are made from a variety of flours, including maize (corn), cassava, millet, wheat, and rice.

In rural areas, cooking can be done indoors and outdoors, usually over an open fire or in a pit that contains heated stones. Water in rural areas is scarce, and people must always take care that it is safe to drink. Most households store water in large jugs. In urban areas, technology is becoming more accessible and is changing people's diets as well as how they cook and store foods.

Number of Undernourished People in Chad, 1990–2004

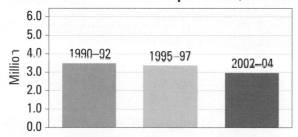

The prevalence of undernourishment in Chad is lower than in Central Africa but higher than in sub-Saharan Africa.

FIGURE 16-6 Compare the number of undernourished people in Chad with the number of food insecure people in your town or city.

Weekly Food for the Aboubakar Family

The Aboubakar family, shown in the photo below, live in east central Chad. What are your observations about the foods they eat?

Aboubakar family food expenditure in one week: $1.23 CDN. (685 CFA francs)

Some of their favourite foods: soup with fresh mutton

FIGURE 16-7 The Aboubakar family of Breidjing Camp, Chad

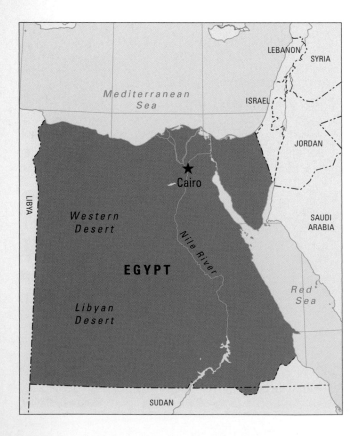

Egypt

Unlike Chad, Egypt has access to water through irrigation from the Nile River. Bread is a staple food in the Egyptian diet, and is usually made from corn, millet, or sorghum. Rather than forks and spoons, bread is often used to pick up other foods from a plate or bowl. Sources of protein include lentils, chickpeas, and ***mish***, a strong cheese made from skim milk. Many Egyptian dishes are vegetarian and use plant sources for protein.

Food security is not as critical an issue in Egypt as it is in Chad. Compare the statistics in the graph for Egypt on page 389 to the statistics for Chad on page 387. What differences do you see?

Egyptian food has had a strong Turkish influence, evident in foods such as stuffed vegetables called ***meushti***. Other foods, such as *shourba*—egg yolks mixed with lemon juice and whisked into clear soup stock—and the many varieties of honey-drenched and nut-stuffed pastries made with phyllo, show both Greek and Turkish influences on Egyptian cuisine. ***Mansat***, a Bedouin dish made of rice and lamb, is also popular.

Coffee, or *kaffa*, is believed to have originated in Egypt. It was first used as an energizer and stimulant. When Islamic countries began sharing their coffee with people in other countries, it became known as "the wine of Islam." Coffee is still a very important part of Egyptian culture. The innumerable coffeehouses all over the country are traditional meeting places.

Cotton is Egypt's main crop. Although used primarily to make cloth, cotton is still an important food crop because cotton oil is used for cooking. Egyptian farmers raise cattle, chickens, sheep, and goats. Since Egypt is primarily a Muslim country, pork production is rare. Milks from cattle, sheep, and goats are all used to make yoghurt and cheese.

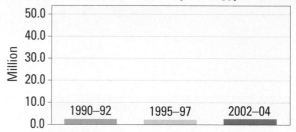

Number of Undernourished People in Egypt, 1990–2004

The prevalence of undernourishment in Egypt is lower than in other parts of North Africa and the Middle East.

FIGURE 16-8 Compare the number of undernourished people in Egypt with those in Chad. What conclusions can you draw?

Weekly Food for the Ahmed Family

The Ahmed family lives in Cairo, the capital, and largest city in Egypt. What are your observations about their choice of foods?

Ahmed family food expenditure for one week: $68.53 CDN (387.85 Egyptian pounds)

One of their favourite recipes: Okra and mutton

Web connection

To find more recipes from Chad and Egypt, go to this Web site and follow the links.

www.mhrfoodforlife.ca

FIGURE 16-9 The Ahmed family of Cairo, Egypt

World Food Day

October 16th of each year has been designated **World Food Day** by the Food and Agriculture Organization of the United Nations. This is an annual celebration that began in 1981 and is now recognized in 150 countries as a day for raising public awareness of **global food concerns**.

Each year, a different theme is presented. In 2007 the theme was **"The Right to Food."** The Universal Declaration of Human Rights of 1948 first recognized the right to food as a human right. Since then, people continue to see that, although we produce enough food for everyone in the world, a large percentage of developing countries have huge **food shortages and famine**. Worldwide, 850 million people are deprived of enough food to be healthy, and **6 million children die every year** as a result of malnutrition. The challenge of eliminating hunger is a question of equal distribution.

FIGURE 16-10 Does your community celebrate World Food Day?

What is Canada doing to help this situation? The **Canadian International Development Agency (CIDA)** has agreed to increase spending in agricultural aid to over $500 million by 2008. This aid is not intended to provide actual food but to assist developing countries with agricultural practices to provide ongoing, sustainable food production. For farmers in developing countries to be successful, they need access to markets, land, water, seeds, and tools. CIDA is committed to providing financial assistance to help make this happen.

Many complex trade laws interfere with the ability of developing countries to sell products for a reasonable profit. For example, Mozambique produces sugar at a very low cost. However, it cannot compete with the **European Union**, which heavily subsidizes its own sugar farmers. These European countries produce large amounts of sugar at **artificially low prices** thanks to this subsidy. Meanwhile, the European Union imposes a large tariff on imported sugar, making the price of sugar from developing countries **artificially high**. These laws will not change easily because powerful companies are making large profits from them.

A significant concern continues to be the **profits made by large corporations** involved in food production. Companies in the food industry show large profits every year. For example, in 1998 Philip Morris Inc. showed revenue of $109 billion, while the total revenue for all Canadian farmers was $29 billion. In 1975, a box of Corn Flakes™ sold for $0.55, with the corn farmer receiving $0.07. In 1998, the same size box sold for $2.98, and the corn farmer received $0.10 per box.

Small groups of people are making efforts to provide fair trade products. **Fair Trade** promotes the payment of a fair price for a product, with a fair profit going to the producer. At this point, neither Fair Trade nor World Food Day can significantly alter worldwide hunger, but they are important first steps towards changing attitudes.

THE MIDDLE EAST

The Middle East is located north of Africa between southeast Europe and southwest Asia. Most people in the Middle East are Arabs, with the exception of Israel, where many are Jews. Middle Eastern cuisine is heavily influenced by Arab culture. There are strong similarities between this cuisine and North African cuisine as well.

Kuwait

Kuwait is a tiny country in the Middle East. It is mostly desert, and the temperatures are extreme. As a result, there is very little agricultural production in the country. Kuwaitis rely on the importation of agricultural products from other countries. Since Kuwait is situated on the Persian Gulf, it does have a significant source of fish.

Due to its location on the Persian Gulf, Kuwait was on an international trade route for centuries and so its food was influenced by many cultures. Modern Kuwait is home to people from a variety of cultures, which also influence the country's cuisine.

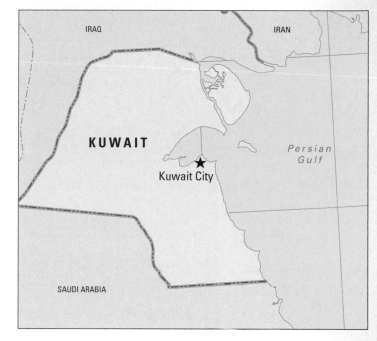

In early times, an entire meal was cooked in one pot. Meat or fish, vegetables, and spices were first browned at the bottom of the pot, then water was added along with either rice or wheat. The pot was covered and the dish was left to simmer. Spices are an important tradition in Kuwaiti cooking and include cardamom, cinnamon, cloves, coriander, cumin, ginger, nutmeg, black pepper, and paprika. These spices are used to flavour meat, rice, and fish.

The rich source of fish and seafood allows Kuwaitis to enjoy them several times a week. Common dishes include shrimp, *hamour* (grouper), *hamra* (red snapper), and the local favorite, **zubaidi** (pomfret). Chicken is also frequently on the menu. From the Bedouin tradition comes grilled, skewered meat, both cubed and ground. Traditionally, the meat would be mutton, but international trade has made beef more accessible.

Salads are usually made with romaine lettuce, cucumbers, tomatoes, radishes, and red onions, dressed with lemon juice and salt. Pickled turnips, tomatoes, and peppers are popular side dishes.

FIGURE 16-11 The Al Haggan family of Kuwait City, Kuwait

Weekly Food for the Al Haggan Family

On the left you see the Al Haggan family, who live in Kuwait City. What are your observations about the foods they eat?

Al Haggan family food expenditure for one week: $221.45 CDN (63.63 dinar)

A favourite family recipe: Chicken biryani with basmati rice

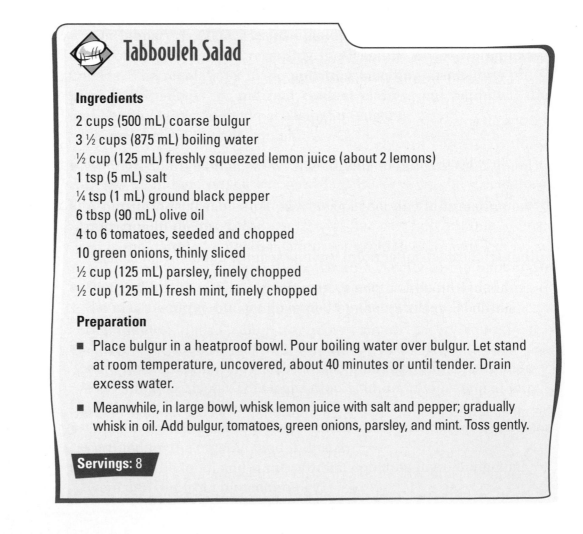

Tabbouleh Salad

Ingredients

2 cups (500 mL) coarse bulgur
3 ½ cups (875 mL) boiling water
½ cup (125 mL) freshly squeezed lemon juice (about 2 lemons)
1 tsp (5 mL) salt
¼ tsp (1 mL) ground black pepper
6 tbsp (90 mL) olive oil
4 to 6 tomatoes, seeded and chopped
10 green onions, thinly sliced
½ cup (125 mL) parsley, finely chopped
½ cup (125 mL) fresh mint, finely chopped

Preparation

- Place bulgur in a heatproof bowl. Pour boiling water over bulgur. Let stand at room temperature, uncovered, about 40 minutes or until tender. Drain excess water.

- Meanwhile, in large bowl, whisk lemon juice with salt and pepper; gradually whisk in oil. Add bulgur, tomatoes, green onions, parsley, and mint. Toss gently.

Servings: 8

ASIA

Asia is the world's largest continent, both in land mass and population. Asian cooking is known for its use of legumes, grains, and many fresh ingredients. South Asian food is characterized by curries, spicy stews made with a variety of meats and vegetables. The staple grain in Asia is rice. Soybeans are another mainstay of Asian cooking and are used to make soy sauce, tamari, and tofu. The basic cooking methods used in Asia are steaming, frying, and boiling. Main meals usually have only small amounts of meat or fish with steamed, stewed, or fried vegetables and a grain, normally rice or noodles. Food is cooked in bite-sized pieces, allowing it to be cooked more quickly and picked up easily with chopsticks or fingers. This style of cooking also uses less fuel, which was important historically because fuel was scarce in many areas.

Some Indians believe that milk proteins should not be eaten with meat because the combination could result in leucoderma, a loss of skin pigmentation.

India

As you can see on the map below, India is a large country in south Asia with a long ocean coastline—some 7000 kilometres. India's geography is quite diverse, and this is reflected in its food, which is divided into northern, southern, eastern, and western cuisines. The Himalayan Mountains in the northeast provide a cooler climate, while the southern regions are tropical. Access to the sea provides plenty of seafood, while the southern climate provides more tropical fruits and vegetables and is ideal for growing rice. In the northern mountain climate, sheep and goats are common sources of protein as both meat and dairy products.

When people think of Indian food, they usually think of spices. Indian cuisine is known for the ways in which spices are integrated into a meal to enhance flavours and to excite the senses of both smell and taste. Curry is the style of cooking most often associated with Indian cuisine. Various blends of spices are used to curry (stew or fry) meats and vegetables in many different ways. Curry spices include chilli pepper, black mustard seed (*rai*), cumin (*jeera*), turmeric (*haldi*), fenugreek (*methi*), asafoetida (*hing*), ginger (*adrak*), and garlic (*lassan*).

Chutney is another famous Indian food made from a variety of ingredients including

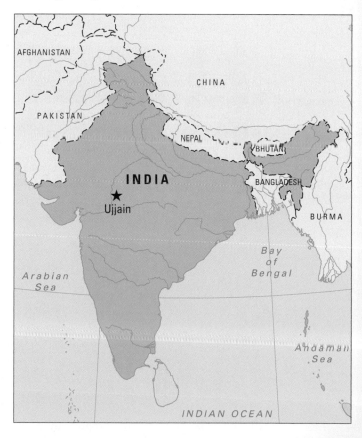

mangoes, limes, and ginger. The term "chutney" comes from the Hindu word *chatni*, meaning "for licking," as in savouring an appetizing taste. Chutneys are actually condiments that are used to awaken the taste buds and add flavour and variety to a meal.

Indian food has a long tradition of vegetarianism and a large proportion of Indian cuisine is still vegetarian. **Pulses**, or the edible seeds of crops such as peas, beans, and lentils, are an important part of the Indian diet as they provide a non-animal source of protein. For non-vegetarian meals, chicken, lamb, goat, and fish are most often cooked. Pork is not eaten for religious reasons. Grain sources include rice, and breads, called *roti*, such as *chapati*, *naan*, and *paratha*.

Food is an essential part of Indian culture and plays a major role in cultural events. Etiquette is also important. Food is commonly eaten without cutlery; only the fingers of the right hand are used. Sitting down to a family meal is customary in Indian society, and most meals have two or three main dishes accompanied by a variety of chutneys and pickles.

Weekly Food for the Patkar Family

The photo below shows the Patkar family, who live in central India. What are your observations on their choice of foods?

Patkar family food expenditure for one week: $39.27 CDN (1636.25 rupees)

A favourite family recipe: Sangeeta Patkar's Poha (rice flakes)

FIGURE 16-12 The Patkars of Ujjian, India

Chopsticks

It is believed the first chopsticks were developed in Ancient China about 5000 years ago, when some early people began using sticks to grasp and remove food from their cooking pots. By 500 CE, the use of chopsticks had spread to neighbouring countries such as Japan, Korea, and Vietnam.

Chopsticks were first made from a variety of materials including wood, bamboo, jade, ivory, gold, and silver. Each country developed a distinctive form. Chinese chopsticks were long and slim with tapered tips. Japanese chopsticks were originally in the shape of tweezers and were shorter and tapered to a point at one end. Korean chopsticks were short and flatter than both Chinese and Japanese chopsticks and were made of metal. Wealthy families at one time even used ivory chopsticks with silver tips. They believed that if the silver-tipped chopsticks touched poisonous food, the silver would warn them by turning black.

Canada's earliest relations with Asia began during the fur trade, but it wasn't until the late 19th century that people came from Asia to live and work in Canada. Thousands of Chinese people immigrated to work on the Canadian Pacific Railway. Once the railroad was completed, many workers stayed and opened small restaurants or worked in mines and canneries, often as cooks. In Vancouver and Victoria, as well as in many small communities in the West, Chinese food became a staple of local culture. Many British Columbians grew up using chopsticks as well as forks and knives.

FIGURE 16-13 What differences can you see among all these pairs of chopsticks?

The Japanese introduced *waribashi*, or disposable chopsticks, in 1868. During the 1890s, Fort Nelson, British Columbia had the largest chopstick manufacturing plant in the world. The Canadian Chopstick Manufacturing Company produced an average of 8 million disposable chopsticks a day and employed 200 workers. The *waribashi* chopsticks were made from B.C. and Alberta aspen. This, however, led to deforestation and the destruction of forest habitats as billions of disposable chopsticks were being thrown away every year after only a single use. The Canadian Chopstick Manufacturing Company was closed in 1997 due to these environmental concerns. Today, many Asian Canadians carry a personal set of chopsticks with them at all times.

Japan

As an island nation, Japan has always relied heavily on food from the sea, including fish, seafood, and sea vegetables such as kelp. Japanese food is nutritious, economical, and popular worldwide. Since Japanese people try to eat 30 different foods a day, most meals consist of small amounts of a variety of foods. Fish is consumed both cooked and raw as in **sushi**. Other staples of the Japanese diet are rice and various types of noodles. **Tempura**, a batter used to coat vegetables and fish before deep-frying, is a Japanese specialty. Food is usually chopped into small pieces so it will cook quickly.

Presentation is important to the Japanese, and great care is taken to ensure that the table is properly set and the food is attractively displayed for serving. Japanese tea is traditional with any meal.

Weekly Food for the Ukita Family

The Ukita family lives in Kodaira City, close to the East coast of Japan. What are your observations on the foods they eat?

Utika family food expenditure for one week: $317.25 CDN (37,699 Yen)

Some of their favourite foods: sashimi, fruit, cake, potato chips

Web connection

To find more recipes from India and Japan, go to this Web site and follow the links.
www.mhrfoodforlife.ca

FIGURE 16-14 The Ukita family of Kodaira City, Japan

NORTH AMERICA

The United States

Food in the United States has been influenced by the same factors as those that have influenced Canadian cuisine. Regional geography and the influence of both First Nations peoples and immigrants have all had an impact on the foods typically eaten around the country. Traditionally, in the north, root vegetables that store easily were a mainstay of the diet. Turnip, potatoes, sweet potatoes, corn, and carrots were necessary to survive during the cold winters. Berries were also important, including strawberries, huckleberries, raspberries, and elderberries. Other fruits, such as cherries, plums, apples, peaches, and crabapples, and nuts, such as pecans, hickory nuts, black walnuts, and acorns, were also traditional. Protein sources included wild game such as bear, mountain lion, and mountain goat, and small game such as rabbit, chipmunk, and possum. Due to numerous rivers and lakes, as well as long coastlines on both the Atlantic and Pacific oceans, a wide variety of fish and seafood has long been part of the American diet.

From early colonization, there has always been a difference between northern and southern cuisine in the United States. In the south, the climate is warmer and the growing season is longer. This means a greater availability of agricultural products, allowing fresh produce to play a large role in southern cuisine. A tropical climate produces tropical fruits, which also feature in the diet and cuisine of some southern states. Deep-fried foods are more popular in the south than in the north. Both the French and the English influenced the cuisine of the areas in which they settled. In Louisiana, for instance, African, Caribbean, and French influences are all evident.

An influx of immigrants into the United States in the last century has brought with it a wide variety of cooking styles and cuisines. As in Canada, you will find particular ethnic influences on foods eaten in certain regions and cities. Both Asian and Mexican cuisines are favourites in the United States, but the all-American hot dog, is actually adapted from German cuisine. Foods originally from many cultures are produced in the United States and imported from around the world to meet the needs of both the founding cultural groups and others who have come to live in the USA.

Weekly Food for the Caven Family

The Cavens live in southern California, where many foods that originated in other countries are now grown and exported around the world. What are your observations on the foods this family eats?

Caven family food expenditure for one week: $159.18 CDN

Some of their favourite foods: beef stew, berry yoghurt sundae, clam chowder, ice cream

FIGURE 16-15 The Caven family of southern California

CENTRAL AMERICA

Mexico

Mexican food has developed from the cultures of its First Nations peoples and that of their Spanish invaders. Cornmeal, rice, chilli peppers, and cooked dried beans are basic ingredients of Mexican cuisine. The contrast between the bland tastes of corn and beans are complimented by the spiciness of the peppers. The main source of carbohydrate is

the **tortilla**. It is used in various forms, such as tacos, quesadillas, and burritos. Mexican food is known for its unique and spicy flavours. The main sources of protein are beef, chicken, pork, and various types of beans. Due to Mexico's warm climate, fresh vegetables and fruits such as bananas and oranges are also common in the Mexican diet.

Regional diversity is evident in Mexican foods. In the north, more beef is eaten since cattle ranches are common there. In the south, chicken-based dishes with spicy vegetables are more typical. Seafood is a staple in areas that border the ocean. Choc-

Sue Singer, President of Pacific Institute of Culinary Arts

On January 2, 2007, Pacific Institute of Culinary Arts in Vancouver, British Columbia, celebrated its 10th year of operation. The institute is the result of the passion and dedicated work of Sue Singer, founder, president, and owner.

Sue graduated from Humber College in Toronto with a diploma in Business Management, and went on to work in the airline industry for 25 years. She moved to Vancouver in 1992 and accepted a position in a privately owned cooking school, where she says she "fell in love with the business of training." After consulting with her husband and daughter, Sue began the long process of opening her own culinary school. She wanted to be self-employed and knew there was a need for such a school in Canada.

Now, Pacific Institute of Culinary Arts has a faculty of 28 and a student body of 200. Students receive instruction in the fundamentals of classic French and international cuisine, including nutrition, kitchen efficiency, and preparation skills. Ninety percent of the curriculum is hands-on training by chef instructors. Students also operate an on-site restaurant, catering facility, bakeshop, and café.

The school has recently achieved North American recognition by receiving the Consumers' Choice Award in both 2006 and 2007. This prestigious honour recognizes business excellence in a trade school and has never before been awarded to a Canadian culinary school.

At work, Sue wears many different hats: admissions director, finance officer, and marketing director. On a typical day, she interviews student applicants, meets with her executive chef, does accounting, and works on marketing. She loves the work because, as she says, "No two days are the same here—ever." After 11 years she thinks she has seen it all, but she still enjoys going to restaurants or hotels to watch her graduates work.

Sue's vision for herself and her school is "to provide students with top-calibre training so that they are fully prepared for employment in the hospitality industry. We hope to see our graduates working in fine dining establishments around the world."

"We hope to see our graduates working in fine dining establishments around the world."

Web connection

To find more recipes from Mexico, go to this Web site and follow the links.

www.mhrfoodforlife.ca

olate is another favourite food in Mexico. It is enjoyed as both a drink and a sweet, and is the key ingredient in the national food of Mexico—chicken cooked in *mole*, a rich, dark chocolate sauce. Strong coffee is also popular.

Weekly Food for the Casales Family

The Casales family lives in Cuernavaca, in south central Mexico. What are your observations on their choice of foods?

Casales family expenditure for one week: $189.09 CDN (1,862.78 Mexican pesos)

Some of their favourite foods: pizza, crab, pasta, chicken

FIGURE 16-16 The Casales family of Cuernavaca, Mexico

SOUTH AMERICA

South American food has been influenced by many different cultures, including those of the First Nations peoples who originally lived there, the Europeans who settled there, and Africans who were brought there as slaves. Since it is a large continent, the climate and growing conditions vary greatly from very warm near the equator to cooler near the South Pole. Several mountain ranges also influence climate and growing conditions.

Ecuador

Ecuador is located on the northwestern coast of South America. It has a wide range of climates depending on where you are in the country. The coastal areas have a rainy season in the winter and a dry summer; the highlands have a cool and rainy season in the winter; and the Amazon region is rainy and humid from January to September. These varying climates allow different types of foods, from tropical foods like bananas and pineapples, to coffee beans. Agriculture has long been practised in

Web connection

To find more recipes from Ecuador, go to this Web site and follow the links.

www.mhrfoodforlife.ca

Ecuador. Centuries before the Spanish colonized the country, Ecuador's First Nations had well-established agricultural practices.

Ecuador is the world's largest exporter of bananas, and many other fruits are grown, eaten, and exported as well. The main sources of carbohydrates in Ecuador are potatoes and rice. The several varieties of potatoes are staples along with beans, lentils, and rice. Protein sources are chicken, beef, and pork as well as fish and seafood. Food is spicy and there are many variations of *aji*, traditional hot sauce. Soup is another favourite part of Ecuador's cuisine. Many soups are made with potatoes and other vegetables.

Some common Ecuadorean dishes include **de pollo** (stewed chicken accompanied by rice and avocado slices), **lomo salteado** (thin beef steak covered with onions and tomatoes), **seco de chivo** (goat stew served with a mound of rice), tortillas de maiz (thin corn pancakes), and choclo (barbecued Andean corn).

Weekly Food for the Ayme Family

The Ayme family lives in Tingo, in the heart of Ecuador. What are your observations on the foods they eat?

Ayme family food expenditure for one week: $31.55 CDN

One of their favourite recipes: potato soup with cabbage

FIGURE 16-17 The Ayme family of Tingo, Ecuador

Literacy in Your Life

Before Reading

1. Read the title and make some predictions about the subject of the article. What does the term "ethnic evolution" bring to mind? What do you think this article will be about?

2. Before you read, based on the title, choose one of the topics below as a possible main idea for the article:
   - One family's success in opening a restaurant
   - Foods from other countries are healthy
   - Nanaimo's response to foods from different countries

During Reading

1. Create a restaurant timeline from the article.

Language Extension

Evolution means "a gradual process of growth or development." It is a process during which something changes. It comes from *evolutus*, which means "to roll."

Ethnic Evolution

By Catherine Litt

Sitting at a booth in his Nanaimo restaurant, Chatterjit Parmar proudly points out he still has his turban. In 1991, when he told friends he was opening an Indian restaurant in Nanaimo, B.C., they said he'd lose everything—including his turban and his self-respect—when the venture failed.

His friends had good reason to warn Parmar. Other Indian restaurants had failed in Nanaimo. Ethnic cuisine hadn't yet blossomed into popularity, so there was little reason to think Parmar and his wife, Santosh, would succeed serving samosas, pakoras, and other seemingly exotic foods to a community weaned on meat and potatoes. "It was a big challenge," says Parmar. But the couple persevered and today, nearly 15 years later, their Gateway to India on Fourth Street is still open and Chatterjit is still proudly sporting his turban.

The Parmars are among a new generation of restaurant owners whose successful businesses are both a reflection of Nanaimo's increasing multicultural diversity and its willingness to explore cuisine beyond its borders. "I'm happy that other restaurants have opened since we have. It's good," says Parmar. "Now people know what a samosa is."

But it wasn't long ago that Nanaimo residents didn't know a samosa from a falafel. And it wasn't long ago that the idea of eating "ethnic food" meant going out for Chinese dinner. "Twenty years ago, it would have been a very different story," says Les Barclay, owner of Amazing Thai on Franklyn Street. "It was much more a meat-and-potatoes community." It was also a community with roots still tied to its coal-mining heritage. In the late 1800s, British miners were among the first customers of Nanaimo's restaurants. They dined where they boarded—in hotels such as the Grand, Royal, and Provincial, which were located downtown and had restaurants that boasted "first-class meals."

While British miners ate in hotels, the city's many Chinese coal miners ate traditional Cantonese meals cooked by family or neighbours in informal kitchens in Nanaimo's Chinatown district. As the Chinese population grew, so did the opportunities for businesses within Chinatown. By the 1940s, restaurants were a common sight in Nanaimo's last remaining Chinese district on Pine Street, serving customers from all ethnic backgrounds.

By the 1950s, Chinese restaurants began appearing outside Chinatown, but they no longer had Cantonese-sounding names. They had names like the Rendezvous, the Maple Leaf, and the Modern Café. "That was common throughout Western Canada at the time," says Christine Meuztner, manager of Nanaimo Community Archives. "It was an attempt to Anglicize them."

While Chinese restaurants moved toward mainstream acceptance with their new names, other ethnic restaurants made little effort to westernize their establishments. Johnny "The Jazz" Alvano's Venice Café on Victoria Crescent proudly advertised a taste of Italy with his ravioli and "Johnny Alvano's Venice Sauce."

A significant change in the restaurant industry came soon after Canada opened its borders with a new points-based immigration system in 1967. Soon the country was attracting more immigrants from places like the West Indies, Indochina, Hong Kong, and Taiwan than from Europe. Among the largest groups of newcomers were the Vietnamese. "The Vietnamese who came over here in the 1970s and 1980s as refugees began to change the tastes," says Barclay. "They opened up Nanaimo to a wider variety."

Today the city's restaurant landscape is like a mini-United Nations. Chinese, Vietnamese, Thai, Greek, Japanese, Indian, Mediterranean, and Latin dishes are among the many choices available to Nanaimo diners. "It's wonderful to have options in terms of where we go to eat, so in that sense it makes Nanaimo perhaps more cosmopolitan," says Terre Flower, diversity coordinator for the Central Vancouver Island Multicultural Society.

"We want to make Nanaimo a welcoming place, a place where you want to live," says Flower. "Those restaurants do that by raising the level of what we as a community have to offer."

After Reading

1. Go back to the "Before Reading" section. Do you want to change your choice?
2. Has there been a food evolution in your community? If you answered yes, what do you think caused this evolution?

Connecting to the Community

In each Connecting to the Community activity you will find out more about your local community by completing one of two assignments. This section forms one part of your Connecting to the Community for Unit 5. For the activity, you will create one product from a choice of the following products.

A display case?

A PowerPoint presentation?

A poster?

A bulletin board display?

A script?

A brochure?

A game?

Chapter 16 Choices

1. Compare your family's weekly food consumption and spending to that of two families from countries shown in the chapter. Include the amount of money that your family spends on food in a week and a list of the typical foods eaten in a week. Create a chart comparing the two families from countries explored in the chapter. Include how much each family spends, typical foods, fresh vegetables and fruits, packaged and convenience foods, and junk foods. Write a summary of what you have learned.

OR

2. Look into the different cultures and traditions in your community and explore

   ■ The countries the original and later immigrants in your area came from and their influences on the food-related traditions in your community.

   ■ The ethnic restaurants in your community and whether they reflect the community's desire for a more diverse choice of foods.

Chapter 16 Summary

In this chapter you learned about the cuisines of the following countries, as well as weekly foods and food expenditures of sample families from each country:

- Great Britain
- France
- Poland
- Italy
- Chad
- Egypt
- Kuwait
- India
- Japan
- United States
- Mexico
- Ecuador

Activities

1. Choose two countries and explain how geography influenced their food patterns and cuisine.

2. Compare one country from this chapter in which the profiled family spends a lot of money on food to a country from this chapter in which the profiled family spends very little on food. Look at the foods the families eat in terms of
   - Vegetables and fruits
   - Convenience and packaged foods
   - Junk food

   Write a one-paragraph conclusion about your findings.

3. Which of the countries profiled in this chapter have had the greatest influence on the foods
   - You eat
   - Your family eats
   - Your friends' families eat
   - Available in your community

4. Choose one of the countries profiled in the chapter or another one of your choice and find three traditional recipes. Choose one recipe and make it at home. Report back to the class on the experience, including
   - Common ingredients found or grown in that country
   - Common cooking techniques in that country
   - Ingredients unique to that country
   - Cooking techniques unique to that country

Providing Food for Canadians

I n this chapter you will explore agriculture in Canada. You will look at agriculture from a historical perspective, current trends in agriculture, and regional agriculture in Canada. You will also revisit food-safety strategies, only this time, as they are used in agriculture. Environmental farm practices, stewardship, and organic farming will also be discussed, along with global influences on Canadian products and the benefits of buying locally produced foods. The chapter wraps up with a look at Canada's rapidly-growing aquaculture industry.

Jenny and Mike have just returned from the National 4-H conference held for members of 4-H, a rural-youth organization. Both Jenny and Mike were nominated to go to the conference by their local club in Vermillion, Alberta. Jenny is interested in beef farming and lives on a ranch. Mike is an equestrian member and rides competitively. They both enjoyed meeting their peers from farms across Canada. They knew there was a great diversity of farming in Canada, but until the conference, they never really understood it.

Jenny and Mike also met Fred, who lives in the Okanogan Valley in British Columbia. His family grows fruit trees and is beginning to expand into grape-growing. The family wants to tap into British Columbia's growing wine industry. Fred is

hoping to go to the University of Saskatchewan to study agriculture and eventually travel to France to do a Master's degree in viticulture.

Lutz, from Saskatchewan, tells Jenny and Mike that he knows that people think of wheat fields when they think of his province. He says that wheat fields are gradually being replaced by other crops such as chickpeas and lentils, as well as cattle, goat and llama farms.

FIGURE 17-1 How much do you know about agriculture in Canada?

According to Statistics Canada, fewer than 1 percent of the Canadian population are farmers. Perhaps that is why so many Canadians have little understanding of modern agriculture in Canada. Agriculture is essential to this country's well-being. A country's capacity to provide food for its citizens is a vital part of its independence. In Canada, we are fortunate that our small agricultural community is strong enough to provide food not only for Canadians but also for other countries.

PUTTING AGRICULTURAL HISTORY INTO PERSPECTIVE

Some people think that the small farm disappeared only a few years ago. In reality, once Canadians started moving to cities in large numbers, farmers had to adjust their practices to grow enough food to feed these growing populations. In 1900, over half of Canada's population were farmers. Each farmer produced enough food to feed 10 people, and people spent an average of 50 cents of every dollar on food. Can you imagine how many farms like this it would take to feed the people in a city like Winnipeg, with its population of approximately 650 000 in 2006?

Another common perception about farming is that farming methods used long ago were not as hard on the environment as those used today. In fact, some historical practices were not environmentally

FIGURE 17-2 Many people have an idealized vision of farming, where farmers produce only enough food for their families. With large numbers of Canadians living in cities, how realistic is this view of agriculture?

friendly at all. People today know much more about the damage we can do to the environment and those involved in agriculture are no exception. Many practices that farmers currently use are much more environmentally friendly than some historical practices.

Prior to 1850, farmers grew wheat crops one year and left the land **fallow**, or without a crop, the following year. This system of growing one crop is called **monoculture**. It depletes the quality and fertility of the soil as the crops draw on the same nutrients time after time. When farmers left the land fallow, they cultivated it, but did not replenish the nutrients that the previous crop had used. This system also wasted the land since half of it was not in use, and this was hard on soil quality and fertility as well. Tillage (plowing) removed the crop's root systems and left the land vulnerable to **soil erosion**, since soil could be washed away by rain or runoff from melting snow, or blown away by the wind. Monoculture was widely practised until about 30 years ago.

Further education has since shown farmers that monoculture is unhealthy for the land and the environment since there is a build-up of disease and pests over time. However, crop rotation is now the norm. Early crop protection consisted of excessive tillage or plowing to destroy weeds that threatened the crop, and this led to further soil depletion and erosion. The use of harmful chemicals that are no longer legal, such as sulphur, mercury, and arsenic compounds, were also used to destroy pests. Research and understanding have resulted in the banning of many pesticides that are no longer considered safe.

B.C. Mushrooms

A mushroom is neither a plant nor an animal; it is a fungus. There are more than 38 000 types of mushrooms identified worldwide and 2000 varieties are edible. The consumption of mushrooms in Canada is one of the highest in the world, and British Columbians eat more mushrooms than anyone else in Canada. First Nations peoples have included mushrooms in their diets for more than 4500 years, often drying them for use during the winter months.

Ancient civilizations in China, Rome, and Egypt thought that wild mushrooms had magical healing and strengthening powers. The Romans were so convinced of this that they fed them to their soldiers before they went into battle. Egyptian pharaohs forbade common people from eating mushrooms, reserving them for the nobility only. Chinese pharmacology has included mushrooms for centuries.

Two types of mushrooms in Canada are fit for human consumption: those that are grown commercially and certain species of wild mushrooms. Commercial types include the white button, brown button, portabella, and specialty mushrooms, sometimes called "exotic" or "gourmet." Some specialty mushrooms are believed to have medicinal powers. Shiitakes, for example, are exported to Japan, where they are used in cancer prevention therapies as well as in cooking.

Wild mushrooms are harvested during their natural growing season. There is no human intervention in their growth or cultivation. Mushroom hunters and gourmet chefs alike highly prize these mushrooms. But harvesters must be trained to identify them correctly, as eating some wild mushrooms can be deadly.

The B.C. lower mainland is home to one of the widest varieties of fungi in the world. In 1975, the VanDusen Botanical Garden in Vancouver hosted the first Mushroom Fair, exhibiting many local wild mushrooms. Since then, the fair has become an annual event. In 1978, the Vancouver Mycological Society was formed. Its members share an interest in fungi.

The Queen Charlotte Islands of British Columbia (also known as Haida Gwaii) are the ancestral home of the Haida peoples. Chanterelle mushrooms are harvested annually there in second-growth timber. Up to 70 percent of the harvest takes place at Skidegate Lake. Two hundred pickers arrive every year in August to harvest the wild mushrooms, most of which are exported to Japan.

Mushroom biology is complicated, and the forest to mushroom connection is just beginning to be studied on Haida Gwaii and throughout lower mainland British Columbia.

FIGURE 17-3 Wild mushrooms are harvested by the Haida in B.C. Why must harvesters be specially trained to identify wild mushrooms?

CANADIAN AGRICULTURE IN THE 21ST CENTURY

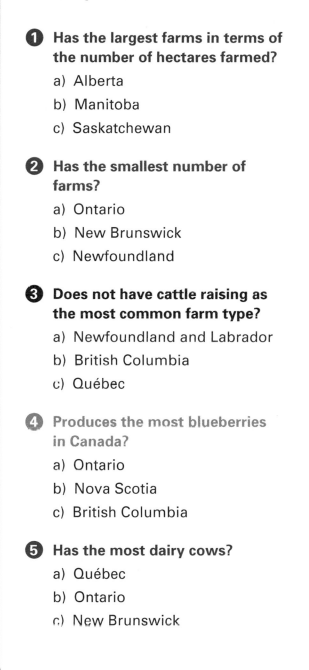

POP QUIZ

Which province ...

1 **Has the largest farms in terms of the number of hectares farmed?**
   a) Alberta
   b) Manitoba
   c) Saskatchewan

2 **Has the smallest number of farms?**
   a) Ontario
   b) New Brunswick
   c) Newfoundland

3 **Does not have cattle raising as the most common farm type?**
   a) Newfoundland and Labrador
   b) British Columbia
   c) Québec

4 **Produces the most blueberries in Canada?**
   a) Ontario
   b) Nova Scotia
   c) British Columbia

5 **Has the most dairy cows?**
   a) Québec
   b) Ontario
   c) New Brunswick

6 **Grows the most Christmas trees?**
   a) Nova Scotia
   b) New Brunswick
   c) British Columbia

7 **Raises the largest number of pigs?**
   a) Ontario
   b) Québec
   c) Manitoba

8 **Grows the most soybeans?**
   a) Ontario
   b) Alberta
   c) Saskatchewan

9 **Has the highest number of farms producing tree fruits (e.g., peaches and cherries) and berries?**
   a) Ontario
   b) British Columbia
   c) Nova Scotia

10 **Has the largest percentage of certified organic farms in Canada?**
   a) British Columbia
   b) Prince Edward Island
   c) Saskatchewan

Answers: 1. C 2. C 3. A 4. C 5. A 6. A 7. B 8. A 9. B 10. C

Now that you have taken the quiz on page 411, were you surprised by anything you learned about Canadian agriculture? Canadian agriculture is diverse. However, we tend to think of only one type of **commodity**, or agricultural product, when we think of certain provinces. Most of us identify wheat with Saskatchewan, fruit with British Columbia, beef with Alberta, and potatoes with Prince Edward Island. Look at the map below. Find your province and the provinces just mentioned. What did you learn about their agricultural production?

When you look at the big picture, you can see trends that may help you forecast the future of farming. We have already discussed the fact that fewer than 1 percent of Canadians are farmers. Other farm trends include

- Farm size is expanding but the number of farms is decreasing. The size of Canadian farms has been growing steadily over the last 100 years. In fact, between the 2001 and 2006 censuses, the number of farms dropped by 7.1 percent.
- Changes in farm practices and technical improvements, such as crop rotation and no-tillage technology, have reduced stress on the soil and improved productivity.

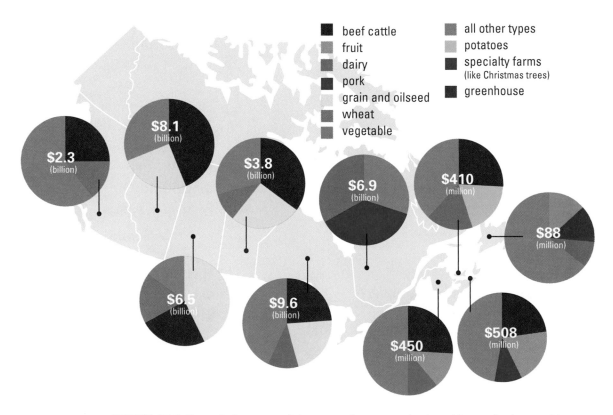

FIGURE 17-4 Canada has one of the most diverse agricultural bases in the world. This graph shows the proportions of farm types in each province, their dominant farm types, and gross sales.

- Improved practices and strategies, such as **integrated pest management**, a series of pest-control strategies that reduce the impact of pests and lessen their impact on the environment, have reduced the amount of pesticides sprayed on crops and added to fertilizer. In Ontario alone, pesticides applied to crops have been reduced by 50 percent in the last 25 years.
- Farmers are seeking a higher education; 38 percent of men and 48 percent of women farmers have post-secondary degrees.
- There are fewer young farmers. According to the 2006 census of agriculture, the average age of a Canadian farmer is 52, with only 9.1 percent of farmers being under the age of 35.
- Contrary to the media image, 98 percent of Canadian farms are owned by families.
- Today's farmer feeds 120 people, on average.
- Canadians spend about 12.5 cents for every dollar on food.

Factors That Affect the Canadian Food Supply

Now that we have looked at some trends in Canadian agriculture, let's consider some of the factors that are creating or affecting those trends.

Farmers Take a Thin Slice of the Food Dollar Pie

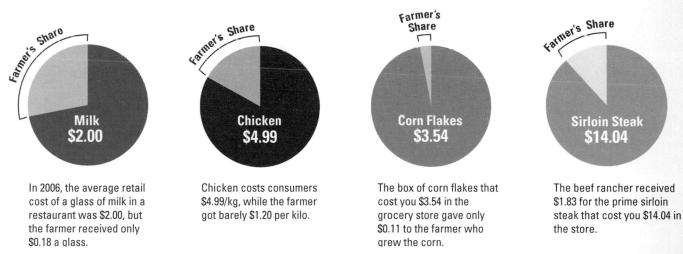

In 2006, the average retail cost of a glass of milk in a restaurant was $2.00, but the farmer received only $0.18 a glass.

Chicken costs consumers $4.99/kg, while the farmer got barely $1.20 per kilo.

The box of corn flakes that cost you $3.54 in the grocery store gave only $0.11 to the farmer who grew the corn.

The beef rancher received $1.83 for the prime sirloin steak that cost you $14.04 in the store.

FIGURE 17-5 According to Statistics Canada, between 1997 and 2003, the price Canadian consumers paid for food increased by 13.8 percent. Now, consider the share that the farmers got. The average price received by farmers for their produce increased by only 2.1 percent during the same period. This means that the prices paid by consumers for food increased over six times more than the amount received by farmers.

Farm Size

The total number of farms in Canada has decreased, while the size of farms has increased. This does not mean the end of the family farm; it just means that the family farm is different from what it was in the past. Farmers are now responsible for providing food for more people than ever before. Larger farms allow farmers to produce that food in an economically and environmentally sustainable manner. Economic sustainability means that the farmer can make an income on the farm and compete in the global market. Environmental sustainability means that farmers' practices are such that they will not deplete the soil, pollute water, or cause other environmental damage. Larger farms can support practices such as crop rotation, integrated pest management, and other environmental farm practices.

The Changing Farm

Canada	Canadian Population × 100 000	Farm Population × 100 000	Total Number of Farms × 1000	Average Farm Size in Hectares
1931	104	33	729	91
1941	115	32	733	96
1951	140	29	623	113
1961	182	21	481	145
1971	215	16	366	188
1981	243	12	318	207
1991	272	9	280	242
1996	288	9	277	246
2001	311	3	247	273
2006	316	3	229	295

Global Markets

Our world has an increasingly global economy. Food is exported from and imported to Canada every day. If Canadian farmers are not competitive, then their products will not sell. However, many consumers and manufacturers are more concerned about the price of a product than its origin. Canadian farmers have to be sure that their products and the cost of production are reasonable in order to ensure a market for their goods. Traditional Canadian products are being replaced in Canadian shopping carts by imports from countries where labour is

FIGURE 17-6 Most people look at price and quality when buying produce. The country of origin is often overlooked. Do you buy Canadian?

much cheaper. For example, the biggest threat to Canadian apple producers is imported apple juice concentrates from China, as well as fresh apples from New Zealand, Africa, and Chile.

Farm Income and the Cost of Farming

Farm income is directly related to the cost of farming. Generally, the higher the **input** costs, or what it takes to produce the commodity, the lower the income. What inputs are needed depends on the type of farm. Some examples include

- Seed, fertilizer, and pest-control products
- Equipment, including tractors, harvesters, and tillage machines
- Storage equipment such as silos
- Animal housing and feed
- Greenhouses

Many farmers discover they need both an off-farm income and an on-farm income to keep their farms going. More farmers are working off-farm today than five years ago. Nearly half (48.4 percent) of all farm operators reported an off-farm job or business in the 2006 census, compared to 44.5 percent in 2001. As a result, their farm work has to be done around their other job. Often, the member of the farm family who can make the highest income works off-farm, while the others work on the farm.

FIGURE 17-7 The average cost of a new combine is about $250 000, the price of 10 mid-sized cars. Can you imagine having to spend that much money as a young farmer just starting out?

Land Competition

If you are growing a crop or providing pasture for an animal, land is a major cost of farming. As urban centres expand toward farmland, the price per hectare of land increases. A real estate or an industrial developer can pay more per hectare for land than a farmer can. This issue is being dealt with differently in various areas of the country. In Ontario, for example, the provincial government has established a greenbelt area around the Greater Toronto Area that restricts further development. This is one law that all provinces and territories need to consider as Canada continues to grow.

Changing Consumer Demands

FIGURE 17-8 Notice where the agricultural areas are located in Canada and where the major Canadian cities are on the map. Does this help you to understand the issue of land competition?

As times change, so do consumers. Farmers need to be able to keep pace with these changes. Historically, tobacco farmers in Ontario were well off. As times changed and society's tolerance of smoking decreased, so has the value of tobacco as a crop. Other changes have also made other crops more valuable. Asian vegetables such as bok choy and sprouts used to be hard to get at the grocery store. Now they are commonly seen and are grown in Canada to meet the demand of Canadians for Asian cuisine.

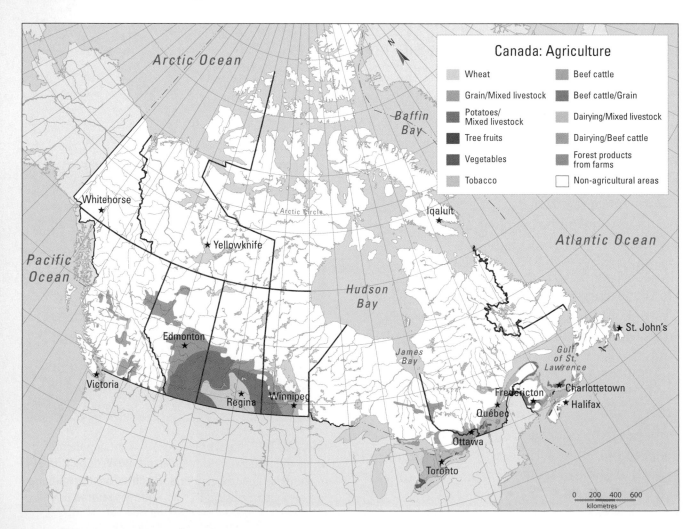

Health Concerns

As Canadians learn more about how food affects their health, farmers have to respond. When concerns about cholesterol became public in the 1960s, farmers and researchers looked for ways to reduce the amount of fat in meat animals. As a result, we have much leaner cuts of meat than in the past. A better understanding of the potential health benefits of Omega-3 fatty acids has led to a change in animal feed, and thus in more Omega-3 fatty-acid-rich foods. Homogenized milk used to be the most common type of milk purchased in Canada, but when concerns arose about its fat content, consumers started purchasing more low-fat milk products.

FIGURE 17-9 Do you know how probiotics can improve your health?

Emerging research and a greater understanding of nutrition and health has led to new products on grocery store shelves. **Probiotics** are a good example. Probiotics are beneficial bacterial cultures that, when consumed in the right amount, can lead to improved digestive health, a stronger immune system, and more regular bowel movements. Such improved, overall digestive health is a goal for many adults.

Science and Technology

Changes in science and technology have had a major impact on all of our lives in the past 50 years. They have also had a major impact on agriculture and how farms operate. These changes include research into such things as

- Animal welfare, behaviour, care, and nutrition
- Plant science
- Food science innovations such as the introduction of probiotics into food products
- Environmental farm practices
- Improved pest-management strategies
- The connections between animal health and human health
- Sustainable production systems
- Sustainable rural communities

Web connection

To find out more about leading-edge Canadian research into these and other issues, visit this Web site and follow the links.

www.mhrfoodforlife.ca

All these topics are currently under study at Canadian universities. Research has led to changes in how farmers manage their farms, for example

- Moving away from monoculture cropping to crop rotation
- The development of no-tillage technology to reduce disturbance of the soil

- Better animal housing based on an understanding of animal behaviour. For example, reducing the number of laying hens in a cage to reduce the impact of the pecking order
- Creating buffer zones along waterways to keep out grazing animals such as cattle and reduce the incidence of manure run-off
- Integrated pest-management strategies to reduce the use of chemical pesticide products

Who Will Be Able to Take Over the Farm?

The fact that the average age of the Canadian farmer was 52 in the 2006 census, up from 49 in the 2001 census, coupled with the fact that there are very few farmers under the age of 35, should concern Canadians. Attracting young farmers is difficult when the start up costs of farming are so high. This is further compounded by the fact that there are fewer, but larger more mechanized farms today than a century ago, which means that fewer farmers are needed. More and more children who were raised on farms are leaving them to work elsewhere, at least partially for these reasons.

Renewable Fuels from Agricultural Products

With the rising cost of fuel and the environmental impact of fuel sources such as oil, coal, wood, and nuclear power, more and more people are looking to renewable fuel sources. Two such sources are ethanol, made from corn, and diesel, made from soy beans. Increasing demand for these crops for fuel production could lead to higher prices for these commodities, raising the price of food and livestock feed products made with them. As well, farmers would be encouraged to grow these crops instead of others, thus decreasing the supply of food crops such as wheat and increasing the cost of those crops.

Another emerging renewable fuel source from agriculture is **biogas** (a gassy fuel produced by fermentation of organic matter). Methane is released from the decomposition of manure and other agricultural waste products. Harvesting this gas and using it to produce electricity is a solution that is gaining ground in the renewable-fuel field. When methane gas is harvested, its environmental impact is reduced, since the release of methane gas is a contributor to climate change.

Web connection

To find out more about renewable fuel sources from agricultural products, visit this Web site and follow the links.

www.mhrfoodforlife.ca

FIGURE 17-10 Did you know that technology now exists to create energy from the methane gases released when manure decomposes?

Stewardship, or managing the land in order to protect it for future generations, is an important part of farming. Pests on farms include much more than just the insects we tend to think of at first. Pests can also include rabbits that eat crops, mold that destroys crops, and birds that eat fruits, just to name a few. Integrated pest management (IPM) strategies are now being widely used in Canadian agriculture to reduce the need for chemical pesticides. By using IPM strategies, farmers in Ontario have reduced their use of chemical pesticides by over 50 percent since 1983.

IPM strategies involve a complex series of measures to control pests and disease in crops. Farmers monitor pests in their fields and orchards very closely, looking for both good and bad pests and levels of pests that could damage crops. When pest levels reach a point where they are a threat to the crop, called a *threshold*, farmers decide which pest-control measure they will use. Not all pest control involves the use of chemical pesticides. Examples of non-chemical pest-control methods include

- *Crop rotation*—Planting a different crop in a field each year to confuse pests
- *Physical barriers*—Fencing, or putting up mesh, to keep pests away from plants
- *Beneficial pests*—Introducing good pests that will destroy the non-beneficial pests
- *Secondary crop*—Planting a crop that will attract pests away from the main crop

Question

1. Food safety and stewardship are important issues in agriculture. How can IPM strategies help to ensure farmers can provide food that is safe for both humans and the environment?

1. Recyclable agricultural plastic is placed around plants to stop weed seeds from being deposited where they can grow close to the growing melons.

2. Weeds are allowed to grow in the rows between the plants as their root systems cannot get close enough to threaten the growing melons.

3. Every five rows, there is a row of wheat to attract the insects away from the melons.

4. The next season, corn will be planted in this field. The waste matter from the melon crop will act as fertilizer for the new corn crop. The root systems of the melon plants will protect the soil from erosion from winter run-off. Insects will come to feed on melons but will find corn instead.

FIGURE 17-11 This photograph shows a variety of IPM strategies in place in a melon crop.

FOOD SAFETY

We have already devoted an entire chapter to food safety, but it was in relation to food safety in the kitchen. In this chapter we will consider some of the strategies Canadian farmers use to ensure that the food they grow for us is safe to eat.

Careful Use of Pest-Control Products

Loss of a crop due to pests has always been a concern in agriculture. Finding ways to safely reduce the damage from pests is critical. Canadian farmers practise a variety of ways to control pests. IPM strategies, discussed above in the Thinking Critically feature on page 419, is one of the ways in which farmers try to ensure food safety while protecting crops from pests.

All pest-control products are subject to strict regulations by the Pest Management Regulatory Agency, a branch of Health Canada. All products in Canada must be assessed and approved for use, and must be reassessed for continued use on a scheduled basis. Foods are also monitored for pesticide residue by the Canadian Food Inspection Agency. In all provinces and territories, farmers are required to take special courses in order to get a license to use pesticides.

Biosecurity

Biosecurity means ensuring that barns and other areas that contain animals are free from disease, especially those caused by bacteria and viruses. When biosecurity practices are in place, animals are protected from diseases entering a barn or other enclosed area. Most people do not realize how many bacteria and viruses they can carry on their clothing, especially on their shoes, and that people most often cause the spread of a disease. That is why many farmers insist that you sanitize before going into a barn. When leaving the barn, the process is reversed. This sanitization ensures that viruses and bacteria do not pass from one farm to another. Prevention of illness is essential to food safety on a farm.

FIGURE 17-12 Do you know why these people are wearing protective clothing before entering the barn area?

Food-Safety Protocols

Food-safety protocols are part of a series of practices that farmers use to ensure that the food they produce is safe to eat. Protocols have been established by government agencies and commodity groups to ensure that safe food practices are followed. Each commodity is regulated by a specific set of protocols.

Hazard Analysis Critical Control Points (HACCP) were examined in Chapter 9: Food Safety, in relation to food safety in the kitchen. The same system is applied to farms in order to identify places where food safety could be compromised. This system is used on the farm, in vehicles that are transit to food-processing facilities, at mills where feed is developed, and in storage facilities. Safety measures are taken, records are kept, and independent auditors monitor the process.

Being able to trace the history of an animal is a very important food-safety measure. Bovine spongiform encephalopathy (mad-cow disease) outbreaks in Europe in the 1990s highlighted the need to know the history of a livestock animal. Canada has implemented an identification system for cattle. All cattle have individualized tags that identify each cow and are used to record the history of the animal. Information such as the farm the cow was born on and the food the cow has eaten is recorded and follows the cow. If there is a disease issue, any animal connected with the diseased animal can be traced through the tag system.

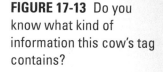

FIGURE 17-13 Do you know what kind of information this cow's tag contains?

STEWARDSHIP AND ENVIRONMENTAL FARM PRACTICES

Caring for the environment is important on farms since farmers live and depend on it for their livelihood. Establishing practices that protect the environment and ensure sustainability in agriculture are called environmental **stewardship**. Farmers have long considered themselves stewards of the earth. There are several practices farmers employ to safeguard the environmental and economic sustainability of their farms.

Waste Management

Improperly managed manure (animal waste) can contaminate both groundwater and waterways. **Nutrient-management plans** provide guidelines for safely managing all the nutrients on farms. This includes manure, fertilizer, and other nutrient sources that are critical to success. These plans help farmers benefit from the nutrients while protecting the environment. The following strategies are used in nutrient-management plans.

Nutrient-Management Plans

Strategy	Purpose
Soil and manure testing	To find out which nutrients are present and which nutrients need to be added to grow a target crop
Precise application of both manure and fertilizer spreaders, including using Global Positioning Satellite (GPS) technology	To control the amounts applied in specific areas of a field by using information from soil testing and crop type to tell the application equipment how much product is needed to grow the crop
Management of stored manure	To ensure that the manure does not leach into nearby water bodies or the water table
Location of new farm facilities	To ensure that they are placed a sufficient distance from waterways
Fencing and buffer zones	To keep grazing animals out of waterways and maintain an appropriate distance between waterways and land where fertilizers and pesticides are applied
Planning for emergencies	To know which procedures to follow in case of specific emergencies

FIGURE 17-14 Manure is stored in a concrete containment structure to prevent bacteria from leaching into the water table.

Providing Habitat for Wildlife

Most farms include areas that are unsuitable for crop production. This land is usually used as pasture or left fallow. Wildlife is very common in these areas and on woodlots, where trees block the wind to prevent soil erosion in the fields. Buffer zones around waterways also serve as habitats for wildlife.

Environmental Research

The agricultural sector is constantly researching the impact of agriculture on the environment and how to reduce that impact. Many modern practices are based on this research. Continued research into current practices and future trends will help people working in agriculture continue to lessen their impact. Emerging research, such as that involving biogas discussed earlier, is critical to our future.

Environmental Farm Plans

Every province in Canada supports its farmers in developing voluntary environmental farm plans. Some provinces supply funds through grants; others provide experts to assist farmers in developing their plans. Regardless of the support, governments and farmers know the importance of protecting the environment. Environmental farm plans help farmers stay aware of environmental concerns on their farms and make changes to reduce their impact. Farmers set goals and timelines for the achievement of their goals. This system of environmental farm plans is being adopted by other countries as their benefits become clear.

Web connection

To find out more about environmental farm plans, visit this Web site and follow the links.

www.mhrfoodforlife.ca

FIGURE 17-15 Have you seen this sign before?

Changing Tillage Practices

Many farmers are changing over to a tillage system that does not necessitate tilling the land to plant; instead, they inject the seed into the ground using a special piece of planting equipment called a no-tillage planter. Waste matter from the previous crop is left on the ground, and as it decomposes it provides nutrients for the next crop. The waste matter also protects the soil from erosion because it anchors the soil in place so that it cannot be washed or blown away. Another benefit of the no-tillage planting system is the reduction in fuel use because the farmer is not driving the tractor and plow over the field. Each time a farming process that requires fuel is eliminated, greenhouse gas emissions are reduced.

Literacy in Your Life

Before Reading

1. What do you know about organic food? What do you know about locally grown food? What foods do you eat that are grown locally?

During Reading

1. Why is Dungeness crab shipped all the way to China and then back to Canada?
2. The Vancouver area is described as the "cranberry capital of the world." What foods are grown in your area in large quantities? Is this food consumed in your community or is it processed in another place and then transported back to your grocery stores?

Language Extension

Locally means "pertaining to, characteristic of, or confined to a relatively small area, especially the area near home or work." It comes from the Latin root *locus*, which means "place."

FIGURE 17-16 Alisa Smith and James B. Mackinnon, the authors of *The 100-Mile Diet*, discover locally grown produce in a city supermarket.

Organic and Locally Grown Food

By Liz Metcalfe

So you've started to buy organic fruits and vegetables to support environmentally friendly farming practices. Is that the only thing you need to think about when choosing fresh produce? "You might also want to consider supporting local farmers," said James B. MacKinnon and Alisa Smith, the Vancouver-based authors of *The 100-Mile Diet: A Year of Local Eating.* "Eating locally grown produce not only strengthens the local economy, but also it may even be more environmentally friendly," they said.

Food Miles: Distance from Farm to Plate

The couple, who for a year ate only foods produced within a 160-kilometre (100-mile) radius from where they live, said they did it because of the growing gap between people and their food. "In Canada, even a turnip or an apple has typically travelled about 4000 kilometres from farm to plate," MacKinnon told an audience at the Living Green Show in Toronto at the end of April 2007. "That's the driving distance from Toronto to Whitehorse."

MacKinnon explained the absurdity of Dungeness crab being fished out of waters around Vancouver and Seattle, loaded onto cargo ships, and sent to China, where the meat is taken out of the shell and shipped back "so we can buy the Dungeness crab in Vancouver or Seattle. That's a 100-mile food product that travels about 8000 miles round-trip so that I can eat it," MacKinnon said. "That's possible only because the price of oil for the cargo ship is still low enough that it doesn't supersede the savings from the low wages paid to workers in China. We combine environmental harm with social injustice and the end result is cheap food."

Local Food Can Be Exotic Food

Renowned Canadian chef Jamie Kennedy, a supporter of using locally grown foods to explore and develop cuisines that define a region, and a founder of the Slow Food Toronto, told a rapt audience at the show that he prepared white bass from Lake Erie, and a strawberry sorbet from strawberries frozen in 2006, for Al Gore prior to Gore's appearance at the show.

"Think globally, act locally takes on a renewed resonance for me," said Kennedy. "A trickle-down effect can occur, but in this case it is the village-based economies that should occupy the top position. Recognizing the regional gastronomical uniqueness in a country like France took many generations to evolve," Kennedy said. "In Canada, we are just beginning. There are years of discovery ahead of us," he said. "We need to focus on what forms our own sense of [uniqueness]."

Why They Did It

Why eat locally? "It makes your life better," said MacKinnon, "although the beginning was a struggle because many diet staples aren't grown around Vancouver. Suddenly, we were eating borscht and more borscht for about six weeks," Smith said with a laugh. But by the end of the summer, they had found sources for most of the foods they needed and had learned how to can and freeze. That meant fewer shopping trips that winter.

"Now," she said, "we still eat about 85 percent locally. We just brought in a few things, like rice or olive oil, that we could never get in our region. This is really what we're trying for, that sense of balance."

"Your experiment can start small," Smith said. "You may decide that 'all the potatoes I eat this year will come from within a 100-mile radius. Or all my apples. Or maybe I'll just switch my morning juice from Florida orange juice to local berry juices.'"

"It was the best year of eating that either one of us has ever had," MacKinnon said. "When you're eating locally, you're eating food that has been harvested right at its peak of freshness and flavour and nutrition."

After Reading

1. The emphasis of the article is on locally produced food, yet the title is "Organic and Locally Grown Food." Can organics include locally produced foods?

2. What are some of the benefits of eating locally grown food?

Organic Agriculture

All unprocessed food is considered to be *natural* whether it is grown organically or conventionally, using pesticides. **Organic** food is produced by farmers who want to conserve soil and water, enhance beneficial biological interactions such as good pests and waste crop products used for fertilizer, and promote biodiversity without the use of synthetic fertilizers, pesticides, chemicals fed to animals, or genetically engineered materials.

Canada's organic agricultural sector has been growing steadily since the early 1980s. The sector's growth has increased significantly in the past few years and is expected to continue to grow.

In the 2006 census of agriculture, 6.8 percent of all farms reported that they were producing organic products. Three categories for organic food production were reported:

- *Organic, but not certified*—Operations that have not been through a formal certification process (whereby a third-party agent has visited the farm and charged a fee for certification). Some operations may define themselves as "organic, but not certified" because they have been following proper organic farming practices but have not been certified.
- *Transition*—Operations in the process of converting their farms to organic farming practices. Depending on the certifying body, this can take about three years.
- *Certified organic*—The procedure whereby an official certification body provides written assurance that products or production systems conform to specified requirements. Certification of products may be based on a range of inspection activities, including verification of management practices and auditing of quality assurance systems. Certified organic does not allow the use of synthetic pesticides, fertilizers, drugs, growth regulators, or processing substances or aids; materials and products produced from genetic engineering; equipment, packaging materials, or storage bins that contain synthetic materials.

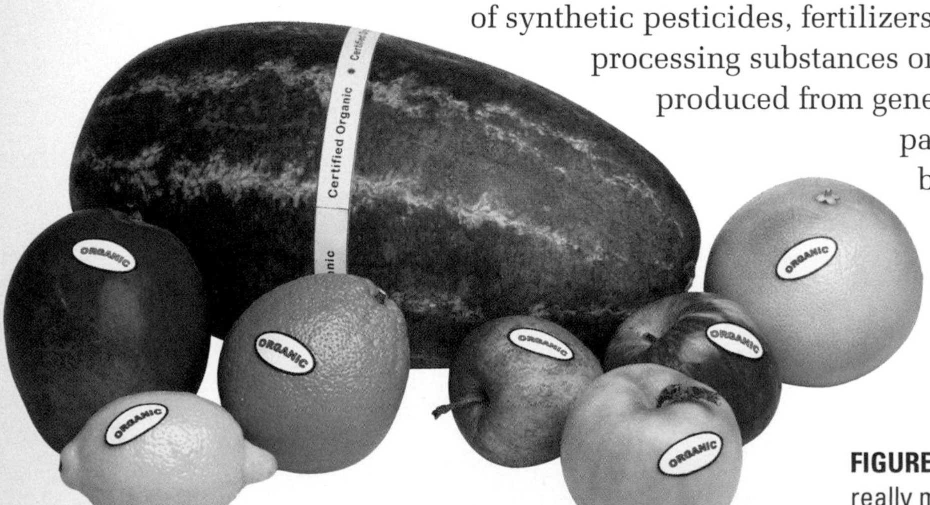

FIGURE 17-17 Do you know what organic really means? How can you be sure that you are getting what you think you are?

Farms Producing Organic Products by Certification Status in Canada, 2006

Certification Status	Number of Farms Reporting	Percentage of All Farms in Canada
Organic, but not certified	11 937	5.2
Transitional	640	0.3
Certified organic	3 555	1.5

FIGURE 17-18 Compare the percentages of farms that are certified to the percentage that are not. What does this mean for consumers?

Because consumers want attractive produce at an economical price, only small amounts of organic produce are available at grocery stores: 3 percent of fruits and 2 percent of vegetables sold in Canada. Due to higher production costs, organic produce costs more than conventionally grown produce.

Here are some quick facts about organic foods in Canada:

- Saskatchewan has the highest percentage of farms reporting organic production. Ontario has the second-highest percentage but is significantly behind Saskatchewan.
- Field crops are reported the most often as organic products.
- Fresh fruits and vegetables account for 25 percent of organic sales in supermarkets.
- Organic livestock production is the fastest-growing sector of organic agriculture in Canada.
- Canada exports a wide selection of organic products, from grains to packaged products.
- Organic wheat is Canada's biggest organic export.

Changes to the Regulation of Organic Products in Canada

New regulations in Canada will make it mandatory that all organic products be certified and meet the National Standard for Organic Agriculture. These regulations were put into place to protect Canadian consumers from deceptive and misleading labelling. Requirements were set out for organic products in interprovincial and international trade. This new regulatory program will build on existing standards and certification systems and will come into effect in December 2008. Part of these regulations will include an easily identifiable logo that will only be allowed for use on products that meet the new certification regulations. The Canadian Food Inspection Agency is responsible for this legislation and its implementation.

Web connection

To find out more about organic agriculture in Canada, go to this Web site and follow the links.

www.mhrfoodforlife.ca

GLOBAL INFLUENCES ON CANADIAN FOOD

As mentioned earlier, global markets put pressure on Canadian farmers to be competitive. In order to compete with the cheaper labour costs in countries like China, Canadians need to be efficient and cost effective in their production methods. The global marketplace also influences our food supply by providing a wider variety of foods. People now

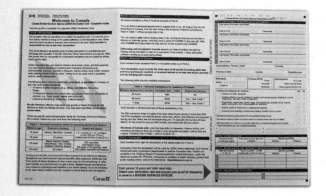

FIGURE 17-18 Have you ever wondered why Canada customs asks if you have been on a farm while you were out of the country?

Web connection

To find out how to calculate the number of kilometres your food travels to get to your table, go to this Web site and follow the links.

www.mhrfoodforlife.ca

want and are able to buy locally produced foods that used to be imported from all over the world.

In light of the globalization of food supplies, the spread of diseases from one country to another is a critical consideration in protecting the health of Canadians. It is important that everyone be careful, especially when travelling to and from other countries, not to bring diseases home to Canada's agricultural food system.

BUYING LOCALLY-PRODUCED FOODS

As you can see, there is much concern about the environmental cost of buying food from different countries and importing it into Canada. In the past 10 years there has been growing support of the local food movement. This movement wants to reduce the distance food travels to get to Canadians' plates and supports local farmers.

For example, for each Canadian who purchases 1 kilogram (2.2 pounds) of blueberries locally in August instead buying imported berries, we would save

- 1099 kilometres (682 miles) in transportation costs
- 253 grams (9 ounces) of greenhouse gas emissions

To learn more about buying locally, read the Literacy in Your Life feature on page 424 and the Healthy Living feature on page 429.

AQUACULTURE

Aquaculture is the science of farming fish, shellfish, and aquatic plants in fresh or salt water. Aquaculture products are grown in earthen ponds, freshwater lakes and bays, or in the open ocean. The fish are fed and cared for to ensure optimum health and product quality. Once the fish or shellfish reach an appropriate size, they are harvested, processed, and shipped to market.

Aquaculture involves both plants and fish. Currently, more fish and shellfish than plant crops are produced.

Aquaculture Crops

Type	Examples
Fish	Trout, salmon (fin fish)
Shellfish	Oysters, clams, shrimp
Plants	Watercress, water chestnuts

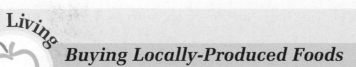
Buying Locally-Produced Foods

Years ago, most of the food on an average Canadian family's table was grown or raised within the community. Today, an entire grocery store chain can easily be filled with products that have travelled hundreds of kilometres before reaching the shelves. In the last 20 years, the import and export of food to and from North America has tripled.

Food represents more than one-quarter of goods being transported on Canadian roads and more than half of air freight, the most polluting form of transportation. Buying locally-produced foods minimizes the high costs of transportation and reduces the amount of fuel being used. A study by Food Share made a meal produced from a local farmers' market and calculated a total of **100 km** of food travel. The same meal made from imported foods required over **5360 km** of food travel.

Local produce is the **freshest** food you can buy. Fruits and vegetables can be picked just when they become ripe, which is when they taste the best and have the most nutrients. Foods that have to be transported long distances must be harvested long before they become ripe so that they don't bruise or spoil. Some of these foods are exposed to ethylene gas, a natural ripening agent, to make them ripen during transport or upon arrival at their destination. Genetic engineering can be used to reduce bruising and spoilage, and sometimes these traits take priority over flavour, texture, and vitamins. **Nutrients are also lost over time during storage and transportation.**

Buying local foods also supports other local small businesses, such as local abattoirs, processing plants, and small shops. Buying locally produced foods also means that farmers will receive the bulk of the money paid for the foods because these farmers often do their own processing, marketing, and/or selling directly to the consumer. This enables them to "cut out the middle person" since ordinarily, a large part of the money paid for a product would go to businesses that carry out these functions, such as food manufacturers and grocery stores that sell the products. **Many fine restaurants are now cooking foods obtained locally** and are being supported by clientele who believe this is the right choice.

A final concern about foods brought from abroad is that **other countries may have different pesticide regulations** and may have poor working conditions for labourers. Buying these products encourages these problems.

FIGURE 17-19 Some provincial governments have developed logos to help people recognize food produced by the province. Does your province have a logo?

Web connection

To find out more about aquaculture in Canada, go to this Web site and follow the links.

www.mhrfoodforlife.ca

Aquaculture is one of the fastest-growing food-production sectors in the world. In 2006, Canada's sector had record production and sales, up 24.7 percent from 2005. Every province and territory has fish farms although fish farming is predominant in coastal areas. Salmon is the largest crop, but shellfish are quickly catching up. Farmed fish can provide people with a steady, reliable supply of fish and seafood.

The federal Department of Fisheries and Oceans (DFO) is the main federal agency responsible for aquaculture in Canada. The DFO promotes and supports sustainable development of aquaculture. The following criteria must be met by people involved in aquaculture:

- Maintain the quality of life and the environment for present and future generations.
- Adopt an ecosystem approach and respect the interests and values of all resource users, and consider those interests and values in decision making.
- Identify, plan, develop, operate, harvest, process, and when necessary dispose of aquacultural products in the most efficient, competitive, and environmentally responsible manner, using best practices, which are practices that have been shown to be better.

The aquaculture sector has been the subject of a good deal of controversy. The criticism relates to concerns about the environmental impact of aquaculture operations, food safety, and contamination of existing wild stocks. Responding to these concerns is the responsibility of the DFO and the industry.

The DFO conducts research into aquaculture, including conservation, protection of fish species and their habitats, and the protection of marine ecosystems. A sustainable method of expanding aquaculture in Canada is the DFO's goal.

FIGURE 17-20 What do you know about aquaculture?

Mike Featherstone, Fisheries Biologist

Mike Featherstone remembers, "When I was growing up in Calgary, our family always watched *The Undersea World of Jacques Cousteau,* a television series that inspired me to learn scuba diving and to eventually focus on marine biology at university." Mike went to Simon Fraser University for a degree in science, where he was able to spend his first semester at the Bamfield Marine Sciences Centre in British Columbia. During his last semester of school, he began fishing and made it his career.

Now Mike is co-owner and president of Ocean Master Foods International. He operates three fishing vessels and their crews, and a fish-processing plant that employs a staff of 12. Ocean Master Foods harvests wild salmon, sablefish, and albacore tuna, and processes smoked and fresh fish for a wide community. Ocean Master Foods is committed to environmentally responsible fishing techniques that target strong stocks from a sustainable resource. On a typical day, Mike might check on the fishing fleet's location and activity, discuss current or expected problems, watch the weather forecasts, and work on financial and accounting projects.

Mike also works for the Pacific Urchin Harvesters Association (PUHA), a group of fishers and license holders involved in the sea-urchin fishery on the Pacific Coast. Red sea urchins are harvested for their roe (eggs) by divers who scoop the spiny creatures into large mesh bags. The roe is collected and then sent to Japan, where it must arrive in prime condition because it is served raw. Urchin harvesters must adhere to strict limitations on number and size of urchins to keep the population healthy and sustainable.

Mike was a participant in the Sea Urchin Summit held in Vancouver, British Columbia in March 2007. He is very concerned that the Pacific Coast Sea Urchin fishery is endangered because of the illegal, unregulated, and unreported Russian sea urchin fishery. This has devastated the local urchin fishery.

Mike also watches the Japanese market prices for sea urchins and coordinates urchin sales. He attends meetings on fishery issues such as species at risk, writes reports for the government, produces a newsletter for PUHA, and volunteers at Fish on Friday, a meals program operated for the less fortunate by the Salvation Army.

Mike loves his work and says, "Every day is a fresh challenge. I am proud that we try every day to produce quality products using best practices."

"I am proud that we try every day to produce quality products using best practices."

Connecting to the Community

In each Connecting to the Community activity you will find out more about your local community by completing one of two assignments. This section forms one part of your Connecting to the Community for Unit 5. For the activity, you will create one product from a choice of the following products.

A display case?

A PowerPoint presentation?

A poster?

A bulletin board display?

A script?

A brochure?

A game?

Chapter 17 Choices

1. Investigate and report on one of the agricultural commodities produced in your region. Make sure your investigation looks at
   - Food-safety practices applied during production
   - Environmental farming practices applied during production

OR

2. Create a product that will encourage people to buy locally. Include the following information:
   - The benefits of buying locally-produced food
   - Types of produce and the season(s) in which they are available locally
   - Fish or meats that are available locally
   - Recipes that include local foods
   - Places where people can buy local foods

Chapter 17 Summary

This chapter dealt with many aspects of agriculture in Canada. You learned about

- Putting agricultural history into perspective
- Current practices in Canadian agriculture
- Factors that affect the Canadian food supply
- Food safety in the agricultural sector
- Stewardship and environmental farm practices
- Organic agriculture
- Global influences on Canadian foods
- The importance of buying locally produced foods
- Aquaculture

Activities

1. Plan a meal for your family. Make a list of foods that would be on the menu. Go to this textbook's Web site and find the Lifecycles Project and the Food Mile Calculator. Calculate the savings you would gain by means of fewer kilometres travelled and a reduction in greenhouse gas emissions by buying the foods locally. Use the following chart to record your results.

Food	Kilometres Saved	Greenhouse Gas Emissions Saved

2. Write a report for your school newspaper on the practices farmers use to ensure food safety. Your report must be at least 250 words in length and discuss three different strategies.

3. Describe three ways that history has taught farmers how to improve farming methods.

4. Define aquaculture. Give some examples of products that are grown through aquaculture in general, and in your community, in particular.

5. The average age of farmers is increasing. What factors are keeping young people from farming? How can Canada help more young people get involved in farming?

Glossary

aquaculture the science of farming fish, shellfish, and aquatic plants in fresh or salt water

amino acids the chemical building blocks that make up proteins

antibodies proteins that help fight off harmful bacteria that may enter the body

antioxidants protect cells and the immune system from harmful chemicals in the air, certain foods, and tobacco smoke

baby formula a specially formulated liquid designed especially to meet the nutritional needs of infants

back bacon called Canadian bacon in the United States, is less fatty and has a milder flavour than side bacon

bakeware equipment used for cooking in the oven

bannock a flat, round, unleavened bread usually made from barley, rye, or oat flour; a staple in First Nations diets

basal metabolism the minimum amount of energy it takes to maintain life processes

"best before" date a label indicating the date before which the food product will still be good if kept unopened; must be on foods that have a durable life of 90 or fewer days

bigos a stew usually made with sauerkraut, meat, and additional ingredients such as mushrooms, sausage, apples, and tomatoes

bing Chinese flatbread similar to a tortilla or roti

biogas a gassy fuel produced by fermentation of organic matter

biosecurity ensuring barns and other areas that contain animals are free from disease

body image the mental image and the thoughts and feelings you have about your body

boeuf bourguignon beef stew containing burgundy wine

bond becoming emotionally attached, especially to a baby

borscht a type of soup from Ukraine; often contains beets

bran part of a grain that provides fibre, B vitamins, minerals, phytochemicals, and some protein

breastfeeding clinics organizations to help new mothers breastfeed their babies

budget a plan for managing your money so that you have enough to purchase the food you need

cache a place where food was safely stored away from predators or high temperatures

calories measurement of the energy provided by food

candling putting eggs on a conveyer belt and passing them over a strong light to determine the eggs' quality

canola a crop grown on the Prairies and harvested for its oil

carbohydrates the main source, and the most easily digested source, of energy

celiac disease a hereditary condition in which a person has an allergic reaction to gluten, a protein found in cereals such as oats, wheat, barley, and rye

chemical sensitivities adverse reactions to chemicals that naturally occur in, or are added to, foods

chlodnik a cold soup made from beets or fruit, and served on warm days

choclo barbecued Andean corn

cholesterol a fat-like substance present in all body cells and needed for many essential body processes

chutney spicy condiment usually made with fruit

circadian rhythm regular changes in mental and physical characteristics that occur in the course of a day

climate the average pattern or condition of the weather at a place over a period of years

colcannon mashed potatoes, turnips, and cabbage

comfort foods foods that make people feel good

commodity an agricultural product

convection oven an oven that uses a fan to circulate air around the space in the oven

cookware equipment that is used for cooking on the stovetop

coq au vin chicken stew containing white wine

cross-contamination results when bacteria are passed from one food source to another

culture the shared customs, traditions, and beliefs of a large group of people, such as a nation, a race, or a religious group

de pollo stewed chicken accompanied by rice and avocado slices

diabetes a disease that affects the ability of the pancreas to produce insulin

diet and health claims words and phrases describing a food in terms of health benefits (e.g., "… reduced risk of high blood pressure," "… reduced risk of osteoporosis); the wording is regulated by Health Canada

Dietary Reference Intakes (DRIs) comprehensive nutrient values that can be used to assess and plan diets for healthy populations

digestion the process of breaking down the food that you eat into nutrients that your body can use

double boiler two saucepans, one fitted inside and on top of the other, with boiling water in the bottom pan that gently cooks food in the top pan

Dutch oven heavy-gauge pot with a tight-fitting lid; can be used on top of the stove or in the oven

eating disorder extremely unhealthy eating pattern and behaviour related to eating, weight, and food in general

ectomorph a person who is lean, usually tall and thin, with long arms and legs and few curves

empty calories foods that are high in refined sugars and have no added nutrients

endomorph a person with an average to large frame, usually wide hips

endosperm part of the grain that consists mainly of carbohydrate and some protein

environmental farm plans help farmers stay aware of environmental concerns on their farms and make changes to reduce their impact; farmers set goals and timelines for the achievement of their goals

enzymes proteins produced in the body and found in some foods; promote certain biochemical reactions in the body

escargots snails

etiquette the conventional rules for conduct or behaviour in polite society

expressed milk milk pumped from the breast so it can be stored for later use

Fair Trade the payment of a fair price for a product, with a fair profit going to the producer; products also grown under environmentally friendly and humane conditions

fallow land not planted with a crop

family service at a meal, the table is set with plates and serving dishes are placed on the table so each person can take his or her own portion

farmers' markets specialize in locally-grown food, primarily vegetables and fruits

food additives substances added to food primarily to enhance flavour or to preserve freshness

food allergy food sensitivities caused by a reaction of the body's immune system to specific proteins in a food

food customs all the uses, practices, or conventions that regulate food habits

food guide a guide that helps people make food choices that will lead them to healthier lives

food habits the way people, as individuals, eat and cook foods on a regular basis

food insecurity not having access to enough food to eat

food intolerance a food sensitivity that does not involve the person's immune system

food patterns a reliable sample of traits, acts, tendencies or other observable characteristics related to food eaten by a person or group

food processing methods and techniques used to transform raw ingredients into food products for human consumption

food safety principles or practices that help prevent foodborne illness and keep food safe to eat

food secure with regard to country, having enough food to feed all people in that country

food sensitivity an adverse reaction to a food that other people can safely eat

food stylist a person who prepares food for advertisements, commercials, menus, and media events

food symbolism giving a food a particular meaning in a particular context

foodborne illness occurs when a person eats food that has been contaminated with a harmful micro-organism or pathogen

food-safety protocols a series of food practices that farmers use to ensure that the food they produce is safe to eat. Each commodity is regulated by a specific set of protocols established by government agencies and commodity groups

germ part of a grain that contains B vitamins, unsaturated fats, vitamins, minerals, and phytochemicals

gluten a protein complex formed when liquid is added to a flour mixture

glycogen in muscles, a form of sugar in which carbohydrates are stored

grading an assessment of food to help consumers be aware of the quality of a food product

halal in Islam, regulations surrounding food

haram in Islam, prohibited foods such as those containing pork or alcohol

hazard symbols appear on containers of household cleaning and kitchen products that are potentially dangerous because they are corrosive, explosive, flammable, and/or toxic.

Heimlich manoeuvre a safe procedure to help victims who are choking

histamine chemicals that the body produces during an allergic reaction. Effects can be felt in the respiratory system, gastrointestinal tract, skin, or cardiovascular system.

holubtsi cabbage rolls

hunger the physical sensation that tells your brain it is time to eat

hydroponics growing plants in water-based solutions with added chemicals and nutrients

immune system processes in the body that protect an individual from bacteria, viruses, and other harmful substances

immunoglobulin E (IgE) the antibodies created by an allergic person's immune system when the person is exposed to a food that he or she is allergic to

induction a non-contact method of heating that uses magnetic fields to transfer energy directly to the food being cooked

inflammatory bowel disease a condition in which the bowl is chronically inflamed

inputs costs the resources required to produce a commodity

integrated pest management a series of pest-control strategies that reduce the impact of pests on the environment

iron deficiency anemia a condition that results when a person does not get enough iron

jerky very thin slices of dried meat

kielbasa Polish word for sausage

kitchen literacy being able to read and interpret instructions in the kitchen

kitchen numeracy being able to understand and work with numbers in the kitchen

kolach a Ukrainian braided bread made for Easter

kosher in Judaism, describes a food that is permitted or "clean"

krupnik a soup made from barley and vegetables to which sour cream and dill are added for flavour

kuita a small, square pastry topped with poppy seeds, nuts, raisins, and honey; often served at Christmas in Poland

lacto-ovo vegetarians vegetarians who eat both eggs and dairy products

lactose intolerance an intolerance of dairy products

lacto-vegetarians vegetarians who include dairy products in their diet

leavening agent an ingredient or combination of ingredients that makes a mixture (e.g., bread dough) rise and become light and porous

lipoproteins the chemical groupings in which cholesterol circulates in the bloodstream

lomo salteado thin beef steak covered with onions and tomatoes

makowiec poppy seed cake

manomin wild rice

mansat a Bedouin dish made of rice and lamb

maple syrup a sweetener made by boiling the sap of the maple tree

marbling the fine white streaks of fat running through meat

market garden farm a farm with a store on site; consumers can harvest their own produce or buy freshly picked produce in the store

mesomorph a person with a muscular body, broad shoulders, narrow hips, and large bones

meushti Egyptian stuffed vegetables

micro-organisms various bacteria, yeasts, moulds, and other microscopic organisms

mish, a strong cheese made from skim milk

mole dark savory chocolate sauce

monoculture growing only one crop at a time on the same land year after year

Montréal smoked meat a type of cured smoked meat

no-tillage not plowing land so that waste matter from previous crops holds the soil in place and provides nutrients; seeds are injected into the soil through the waste matter

nutrient content claims words and phrases describing what a food provides or is missing (e.g., "source of fibre," "sodium free"); the wording is regulated by Health Canada

nutrient dense describes food with a high nutrient content and a lower energy content (calories)

nutrient management plans provide guidelines to safely manage all nutrients on farms, including manure, fertilizer, and other nutrient sources

nutrients found in food, these chemicals are required by your body for optimum health

nutrition facts table information mandatory on most packaged foods; designed to help consumers make healthier food choices

nutrition labelling regulations regarding nutrient-content claims and health claims on food

obesogenic culture a culture, as in Canada, in which there is constant pressure to eat too much

Oka cheese first made by Trappist monks in Québec in 1893; it is still made by them today

Omega-3 oil fish oil, rich in Omega-3 fatty acid believed to help lower blood cholesterol levels

organic food produced by farmers who want to conserve soil and water, enhance beneficial biological interactions such as good pests and waste crops used for fertilizer, and promote biodiversity without the use of synthetic fertilizers, pesticides, chemicals fed to animals, or genetically engineered materials

osteoporosis a condition in which bone density is reduced; the bones become too porous, making them weak and fragile

ovo-vegetarians vegetarians who include eggs in their diet

oxidation the exposure of food to oxygen

"packaged on" date a label indicating the date the food was packaged; must be on foods that have a durable life of 90 or fewer days

pathogens disease-causing agents, such as bacteria, parasites, or viruses

peer pressure the feeling that you have to do what your peers are doing

pemmican a mixture of dried meat and berries mixed with fat that was stored in a bison-skin bag and sealed with melted lard to prevent it from spoiling

perishable foods foods that will spoil

peristalsis a series of wave-like motions created by the expansion and contraction of the muscles of the esophagus; moves food through the digestive system

perogy small dumpling usually stuffed with cheese or potatoes

pesco-vegetarians vegetarians who exclude red meat and chicken but do eat fish and seafood

phytates compounds that interfere with the absorption of zinc

phytochemicals nutrients that come from chemicals in plants

plate service at a meal, the table is set without the plates; each plate is filled and then placed in front of each person

pluma moos a fruit soup made by Mennonites

polenta cornmeal mush that can be sliced and fried

poutine French fries with cheese curds and gravy

pressure cooker heavy-gauge pot with a lid that locks into place; creates a very high cooking temperature that cooks food quickly

probiotics beneficial cultures that, when consumed in the right amount, can lead to improved digestive health, a stronger immune system, and more regular bowel movements

proteins the nutrients that help the body grow, maintain, and repair cells and tissues

psychological needs needs that involve your mind and emotions

pulses edible seeds of crops such as peas, beans, and lentils

risk factor something that increases the chance that a particular condition will occur

root cellar an underground room for storing food, particularly fruit and vegetables

saturated fat fat from meat and dairy products; these unhealthy fats increase the level of LDL cholesterol in your blood and contribute to heart disease

seco de chivo goat stew served with a mound of rice

sedentary not active

self-confidence the assurance that you have in yourself and your powers and abilities

self-esteem the confidence or satisfaction you have in yourself

self-image the concept you have of yourself

serving pieces anything food is served from (e.g., platters, bowls, and cookware)

shourba egg yolks mixed with lemon juice and whisked into clear soup stock

soil erosion when soil is washed away by rain or runoff from melting snow

sourdough the oldest form of leavened bread; created by wild yeasts "souring" a flour-and-water mixture; this culture is saved and used for future batches

squab pigeon

status foods usually expensive foods that are often difficult to obtain

stewardship the use of practices that protect the environment and ensure sustainability in agriculture

subsistence agriculture practised by farmers who grow enough food only for themselves and their families

sushi Japanese food of seasoned rice with raw fish or vegetables

table setting tableware and serving pieces

tableware anything people use to eat their food with or from (e.g., cutlery, chopsticks, plates, bowls, glasses, cups, and linens such as placemats, napkins, and tablecloths)

tempura batter to coat fish or vegetables before deep-frying

time management knowing how long each step of your meal preparation will take and allowing sufficient time for each

tortilla Mexican flatbread

tortillas de maiz thin corn pancakes

tourtière a meat pie made from ground pork; it is unique to Québec cuisine

trans fat unhealthy fats created by the food-processing industry; trans fat not only raises LDL cholesterol but also lowers HDL cholesterol, which you want to have in a healthy body

unit pricing indicates how much a specified unit or amount of a product costs to aid in comparison of products

unsaturated fat small amounts of these fats are healthy and help to lower your risk of heart disease by reducing the level of LDL cholesterol in your blood; they include liquid vegetable oil, oil from seeds and nuts (except palm and coconut oil), and the fat found in fish oil

vegans vegetarians who exclude all animal products from their diet

vereniki cottage cheese dumplings

waribashi disposable wooden chopsticks

water displacement method method of measuring solid fat in which water is poured into a measuring cup, fat is added until the desired amount is reached, then the water is poured off

work plan accounting for all aspects of meal preparation, including preparation of equipment and ingredients, cooking, cleaning up, and serving

work schedule adding times of day to the work plan by determining meal service time and then working backward by subtracting the time required for each task; a work schedule tells you when each task should be performed

Index

Green vegetables
  beta carotene, 81
  biotin, 76
  folic acid, 75
  infants, 130
  iron, 80
  magnesium, 79
  vitamin B$_2$, 75
  vitamin E, 76
  vitamin K, 76
Greenhouse and technology, 33
Griddle, 265
Grill, 265
Grocer (CP), 311
Grocery stores, 312
  health inspections, 309
Grouse, 109
Growth spurts, 139
Guava, 100
  vitamin C, 76
Gullac, 42

Haggis, 47
Haida, 363
Halal, 36
Halibut, 363, 373
Ham, 109
  cooking temperatures, 216
Hamour, 391
Hamra, 391
Hand-operated rotary beater, 258
Hanukkah, 47
Haram, 36
Hard-boiled eggs dyed red, 42
Hardening of the arteries, 164
Hare, 109, 355
Harvest festivals, 48
Hazard Analysis Critical Control
    Points (HACCP), 227, 421
Hazard symbols, 239
Health Canada, 65, 111, 218, 305,
    324, 420
  food labelling, 313
Health Check symbol, 162
Health food stores, 310
Health inspections of grocery
    stores, 309
Healthy eating, 134–135
Healthy heart, tips for, 163
Heart and Stroke Foundation, 162
Heart attack, 164
Heart disease
  Canada's Food Guide, 93
  diet and health claims, 315, 316
  fats, 69
  food patterns, 33
Heart health
  factors affecting, 164
  lifestyle, and, 164

Heart healthy, 162
Heimlich manoeuvre, 245, 246, 247
Hemoglobin, 79
Herbs, remedies, as, 243
Herring, 109, 363, 373
High blood pressure, 164
  diet and health claims, 315, 316
High fructose corn syrup
    (HFCS), 114
High tea, 379
High-density lipoproteins, 70
Hinduism, 35, 36
Histamine, 175
Historical Perspectives
  breads, 287
  chopsticks, 395
  circadian rhythm, 140
  convenience foods, 343
  corsets, 185
  early Canadian diet, 8
  First Nations, 357
  general store, 304
  mushroom farming, 410
  pioneer, 304
  pioneer culture, 357
  refrigerators, 32
  remedies, 243
  West Coast Fish Canneries, 264
  wild berries, 357
Holubtsi, 372
Homemade cleaning products, 240
Homemade spray cleaner, 240
Homogenized milk, 417
Honey, 369
Honeydew melon, 100
Honeymoon, 50
Hot dog, 397
Huckleberries, 359, 363
Hudson Bay Company, 343
Hummus, 109
Hundred Mile Diet, 22, 424
Hunger, 11
  obesity, 11
  rural Canada, in, 10
Hydrogenated vegetable oils, 72
Hydrogenation, 71
Hydroponics, 33
Hypothalmus, 140

Iceberg lettuce, 100
Icebox, 32
Immune system, 128
  proteins, 68
Immunoglobulin E (IgE), 175
Impulse buying, 302–303
Incomplete proteins, 69, 159
Indoles, 81
Induction cooktops, 266
Industrialization, 31

Infants
  antibodies, 128
  banana, 130
  barley, 130
  bonding, 128
  bottle-feeding, 128, 129
  breastfeeding, 128, 129
  caring for, 128–131
  cheese, 130
  chicken, 130
  colicky, 128
  egg yolks, 130
  fish, 130
  foods, 130
  fruits, 130
  green vegetables, 130
  Heimlich manoeuvre, 247
  immune system, 128
  introduction of foods, 130
  meat, 130
  milk, 128, 130
  pasta, 130
  rice, 130
  sleep patterns, 131
  solid food, 129
  tofu, 130
  vegetables, 130
  vitamin D, 128
  whole-grain breads, 130
  yoghurt, 130
Inflammation, 116
Inflammatory bowel disease
    (IBD), 174
Ingredients. See individual
    ingredients
  food labelling, 312
  recipes, 279
  understanding, 280–282
Insulin, 87, 170
Integrated pest management, 412,
    417, 418, 419
  crop rotation, 419
  physical barriers, 419
  threshold, 419
Intestinal juice, 86
Inuit, 354–365
  Canada's Food Guide, 121–123
Iodine
  food sources of, 80
  salt, 80
  saltwater fish, 80
Iron, 78, 79, 156, 159
  athletes, 156
  deficiency of, 160
  dried fruits, 80
  egg yolks, 80
  fish, 80
  food sources of, 80
  for pregnant women, 153
  fruits, 80, 95

Photo Credits

2 Charles Gupton/Corbis; 4 Daniel Schürmann; 7 Tim Pannell/Royalty-Free/Corbis; 8 Canada's Official Rules, Health Canada, 1942. Reproduced with the permission of the Minister of Public Works and Government Services Canada, 2007.; 9 Tom & Dee Ann McCarthy/Corbis; 10 Farah Nosh/Getty Images; 11 Bill Ivy/Ivy Images; 12 With permission of Operation Sharing, card design by Innovative Graphics 1-519-533-0669; 13 Keith Beaty/Toronto Star; 14 Tom Grill/Royalty-Free/Corbis; 15 Radius Images/Alamy; 18 China Photos/Getty Images; 19 t Courtesy of Lesley Stowe, Lesley Stowe Fine Foods, Vancouver BC, Johnathan Cruz Photography, b Courtesy of Lesley Stowe, Lesley Stowe Fine Foods, Vancouver BC, Photograph by Maria DeCambra; 20 Michael Newman/Photo Edit; 21 l David Young-Wolff/Photo Edit, r Don Carstens/Brand X/Corbis; 25 Stockbyte/maXx Images; 27 Gunter Marx Photography/Corbis; 28 b Detail Nottingham/Alamy, t David Frazier/Corbis; 31 t Glenbow Archives/na-4334-23, b Courtesy of Farmers Feed Cities; 32 l H. Armstrong Roberts/Corbis, r DSGpro/istockphoto.com; 33 Stephen Chernin/Getty Images; 35 Michael Newman/Photo Edit; 37 Peter Flindell/istockphoto.com; 41 Yellow Dog Productions/The Image Bank/Getty Images; 43 Marsaili McGrath/Getty Images for KC Events; 44 Envision/Corbis; 45 Dick Hemingway; 46 John Miller/Robert Harding World Imagery/Corbis; 48 Jeff Speed/firstlight.com; 50 Clive Sawyer/Alamy; 51 Courtesy of Genève McNally, DreamGroup Productions Inc.; 52 Dynamic Graphics Group/Creatas/Alamy; 53 Courtesy of Jane Witte; 55 Rob Walls/Alamy; 58 Mitch Hrdlicka/Getty Images; 63 Dick Hemingway; 64 Stockbyte/Alamy; 66 Comstock/PunchStock; 67 Marco Cristofori/Corbis; 68 John Lund/Drew Kelly/

Blend Images/Getty Images; 69 Brian Hagiwara/Brand X/Corbis; 70 Roger Ressmeyer/Corbis; 71 John T. Fowler/Alamy; 72 Bill Ivy/Ivy Images; 73 PNC/The Image Bank/Getty Images; 74 Hulton Archive/Getty Images; 77 Andrew Rubtsov/Alamy; 78 Smith Collection/Iconica/Getty Images; 81 Mitch Hrdlicka/Getty Images; 82 Courtesy of Loreen Wales; 83 Jeremy Woodhouse/Blend Images/Getty Images; 91 4560266/istockphoto.com; 92 MAPS.com/Corbis; 093 l Canada's Food Guide, 1944. Reproduced with the permission of the Minister of Public Works and Government Services Canada, 2007., c Canada's Food Guide, 1961. Reproduced with the permission of the Minister of Public Works and Government Services Canada, 2007., r Canada's Food Guide, 1977. Reproduced with the permission of the Minister of Public Works and Government Services Canada, 2007.; 94 Eating Well with Canada's Food Guide, Health Canada, 2007. Reproduced with the permission of the Minister of Public Works and Government Services Canada, 2007.; 99 Courtesy of John Bishop; 100-101 Eating Well with Canada's Food Guide, Health Canada, 2007. Reproduced with the permission of the Minister of Public Works and Government Services Canada, 2007.; 102 CanWest News Service; 104-105 and 107 and 109 Eating Well with Canada's Food Guide, Health Canada, 2007. Reproduced with the permission of the Minister of Public Works and Government Services Canada, 2007.; 112 Bettmann/Corbis; 113 Bloomimage/Royalty-Free/Corbis; 114 Bill Ivy/Ivy Images; 115 Photofusion Picture Library/Alamy; 116 Al Harvey/The Slide Farm; 118 Jed Share and Kaoru/Corbis; 119 Amos Morgan/Getty Images; 120 Bill Ivy/Ivy Images; 121 l and 122 Eating Well with Canada's Food Guide for First Nations, Inuit and Métis, Health Canada, 2007. Reproduced with the permission of the Minister of Public Works and Government

Services Canada, 2007.; 123 Peter Arnold, Inc./Alamy; 127 Larry Dale Gordon/The Image Bank/Getty Images; 128 Plush Studios/maXx Images; 129 t Caroline Woodham/Photographer's Choice/Getty Images, b Gareth Brown/Corbis; 131 Jose Luis Pelaez, Inc/maXx Images; 132 Laura Eisenberg/istockphoto.com; 133 Michael Newman/Photo Edit; 135 Pixland/Royalty-Free/Corbis; 136 t Victor Last/Geographical Visual Aids, b Michael Newman/Photo Edit; 137 Stockbyte/Getty Images; 138 Jeff Greenberg/Photo Edit; 140 Blaine Harrington III/Corbis; 141 t D. Trask/Ivy Images, b Turbo/zefa/Corbis; 142 Dick Hemingway; 143 Photodisc/Getty Images; 144 Courtesy of Gordon Becker; 147 Maria Teijeiro/Digital Vision/Getty Images; 151 George S de Blonsky/Alamy; 152 Purestock/maXx Images; 154 Photodisc/Getty Images; 155 Darren Staples/Reuters/Corbis; 156 Kitt Cooper-Smith/Alamy; 157 t Brian Bahr/Getty Images, Courtesy of Hayley Wickenheiser, c Courtesy of Right to Play; 158 Kevin Sanchez/Cole Group/Getty Images; 160 Eising/Photodisc/Getty Images; 162 l and r Dick Hemingway; 165 White Packert/Photonica/Getty Images; 167 Nicholas Prior/Stone+/Getty Images; 169 Tom Grill/Corbis; 170 Bettmann/Corbis; 171 PhotoLink/Getty Images; 173 Geoff Manasse/Getty Images; 174 John A. Rizzo/Getty Images; 175 and 178 Dick Hemingway; 183 bananastock/firstlight.com; 184 The Bridgeman Art Library/Getty Images; 185 t Bettmann/Corbis, b Neal Preston/Corbis; 186 Jeff Greenberg/Photo Edit; 187 l Marcel Thomas/FilmMagic/Getty Images, r Dave M. Benett/Getty Images; 189 t Thomas Barwick/Riser/Getty Images, b Mark Savage/Corbis; 190 l Tom Wargacki/WireImage/Getty Images, c Evan Agostini/Getty Images, r John Shearer/WireImage/Getty Images; 192 Bill Ivy/Ivy Images; 193 Jerry Arcieri/Corbis; 196 t LEGO/Corbis, b Phototake/CP; 198 Klaus Tiedge/Blend Images/Getty Images; 199 Courtesy of Jennifer Eld; 202 Dex

Text Credits

16-17 "What's your eating personality?" Ylva Van Buuren, Canadian Living, http://www. canadianliving.com; **029** Canadian Geographic, http://www. canadiangeographic.ca; **44-45** "New Year a feast of symbols," http:// www.straight.com; **089** *Food For Today, First Canadian Edition*, Jane Witte et al., © 2004 McGraw-Hill Ryerson Limited; **95 and 97-98** *Eating Well with Canada's Food Guide: A Resource for Educators*, Health Canada, 2007. Reproduced with the permission of the Minister of Public Works and Government Services Canada, 2007.; **102-103** "Thriving on a Vegan Diet" by Michelle Magnan, *The Province*, Sunday, May 20, 2007, Live It! Section, Page: C19/FRONT, CanWest News Service; **108 and 110** *Eating Well with Canada's Food Guide: A Resource for Educators*, Health Canada, 2007. Reproduced with the permission of the Minister of Public Works and Government Services Canada, 2007.; **138-139** "22 Ways to Feel Good Inside," http://www. actnowbc.ca/EN/youth/22_ways_ to_feel_good_inside/, Adapted from "Feeling Good Inside and Out," www.goforyourlife.vic.gov. au; **141-143** "24 Ways to Turn Over a New Leaf," http://www. actnowbc.ca/EN/adults/24_ways_ to_turn_over_a_new_leaf/, Adapted from "Turning Over a New Leaf," www.goforyourlife.vic.gov.au; **145** "Healthy Eating, Healthy Aging," http://www.actnowbc. ca/EN/seniors/healthy_eating,_ healthy_aging/; **166-167** "How Sweet It Is!" http://www.bced. gov.bc.ca/health/sweetners.pdf; **210-211** Canadian Partnership for Consumer Food Safety Education,

http://www.canfightbac.org/ cpcfse/en/safety/safety_factsheets/ causes/; **216 and 221-223** Canadian Partnership for Consumer Food Safety Education, http://www. canfightbac.org/cpcfse/en/cookwell/ charts/; **227** QMI, http://www. qmi.com/registration/foodsafety/ haccp/; **240-241** "Pantry Cleaners: Recipes for Homemade Cleaning Products, Posted September 7, 2007 by Cynthia Townley Ewer, http:// organizedhome.com/pantry-recipes- homemade-cleaning-products; **246-247 text and images** Heimlich Institute, http://heimlichinstitute. org; **278-279** "Getting the most from our recipes," http://www. finecooking.org, The Taunton Press; **308-309** "10 Things Your Grocery Store Doesn't Want You to Know" by Sally Wadyka, http://health.msn. com/fitness/articlepage.aspx?cp- documentid=100165289; **313** *Table providing a list of some of the more common nutrient content claims and what they mean*, http://www. hc-sc.gc.ca/fn-an/label-etiquette/ index_e.html, November 26, 2002, Reproduced with the permission of the Minister of Public Works and Government Services Canada, 2007.; **315** *Nutrition Labelling Toolkit for Educators - What Do Nutrition Claims Mean?*, http://www.hc- sc.gc.ca/fn-an/label-etiquette/ index_e.html, November 26, 2002, Reproduced with the permission of the Minister of Public Works and Government Services Canada, 2007.; **319-321** *Food For Today*, First Canadian Edition, Jane Witte et al., © 2004 McGraw-Hill Ryerson Limited, Adapted from Canadian Produce Marketing Association (2003) and Department of Justice Canada (2002).; **323** Making the

Grade—Canadian Egg Marketing Agency. The extraordinary egg: Making the grade. (n.d.) Retrieved April 6, 2003 from http://www. canadaegg.ca/english/educat/ making-grade.html; **325** *Food For Today, First Canadian Edition*, Jane Witte et al., © 2004 McGraw-Hill Ryerson Limited, Source: Centre for Science in the Public Interest (n.d.).; **354** Cultural Division of First Nations Bands, http://www.ucalgary. ca/applied_history/tutor/imagefirst/ Culture.jpg, Copyright © 2000, The Applied History Research Group, University of Calgary, and Red Deer College; **359 and 361** Lovesick Lake Native Women's Association. (1985). *The Rural and Native Heritage Cookbook (vol. 1.)* Burleigh Falls, ON: Lovesick Lake Native Women's Association; **370-371** Mennonite Fellowship Meals by Derek Suderman; **402-403** Mennonite Historical Society of Canada,http:// www.mhsc.ca/mennos/cfood.html; **408 and 411-413** *The 'Real' Dirt on Farming: The People in Canadian Agriculture Answer Your Questions*, Ontario Farm Animal Council, www.ofac.org; *Update: the changing farm face* (2003) with permission of Ontario Agri-Food Education Inc.; **416** *Canadian Geography: A Sense of Place*, Wallace et al., © 2006 McGraw-Hill Ryerson Limited, Map Designer: Gary Birchall; **424-425** "Organic vs Locally Grown" by Liz Metcalfe, http://origin.liveearth. ca.msn.com/green/articles/ LiveEarthArticleGreen100MileDiet. aspx; **427** Farms producing organic products, by certification status, Canada, 2006, Source: Statistics Canada, 2006 Census of Agriculture.